The Sixties and the End of Modern America

David Steigerwald

The Ohio State University

The St. Martin's Series in
U.S. History

T0204787

ST. MARTIN'S PRESS, New York

For Susan

Editor: Louise H. Waller
Managing editor: Patricia Mansfield-Phelan
Project editor: Nicholas Webb
Production supervisor: Alan Fischer
Art director: Sheree Goodman
Photo research: Inge King
Cover photo: Marc Riboud/Magnum Photos

Library of Congress Catalog Card Number: 94-65218
Copyright © 1995 by St. Martin's Press, Inc.
All rights reserved. No part of this book may be reproduced, stored in a retrieval system,
or transmitted by any form or by any means, electronic, mechanical, photocopying,
recording, or otherwise, except as may be expressly permitted by the applicable copyright
statutes or in writing by the Publisher.
Manufactured in the United States of America.
9 8 7 6 5
f e d c b a

For information, write:
St. Martin's Press, Inc.
175 Fifth Avenue
New York, NY 10010

ISBN: 0-312-09007-2 (paperback)
      0-312-12303-5 (cloth)

Preface

The argument of *The Sixties and the End of Modern America* is that the sixties happened at the moment when modern U.S. society yielded to the postmodern age. The modern era, which we might date conveniently as beginning near the opening of the twentieth century, grew out of the nature of industrial capitalism. Mass production in heavy industry came to dominate business, and mass production in consumer goods created a companion culture. Mass-production industries fed on labor from great cities, which in turn became home to millions of immigrants. Whether from rural America or eastern Europe, new city dwellers settled into work within the industrial economy. In response to these changes, the administrative state emerged. Governmental power was used by liberals for social reform. In foreign policy it became possible for Americans to pursue their national interests and oppose colonialism at the same time. The United States became the first anti-imperialist Western nation.

Modernity guaranteed the ascendance of political liberalism in the United States. Big business discovered that the welfare state promoted stability; liberals learned that they could promote intellectual and cultural freedom and not interfere with capitalism. Thus, the consumer society could accommodate liberal freedom, provide the basis for a successful economy, and still turn culture into money.

What has come to be called postmodern society shares some of these conditions. But it is clear that many of the fundamental forces that propelled modernity petered out by the 1960s. Industrial technology provided business with the flexibility to move plants and automate work—in effect, to "deindustrialize." Urbanization evolved into suburbanization, and city cores began to deteriorate.

Modernist artists and intellectuals dismantled old ideas of politics, philosophy, and taste. Modernist culture, built on artistic innovation and inherently opposed to tradition, reached the point where all traditions were dissolved, leaving artists with nothing to renounce but art itself.

Other aspects of modernity persisted throughout the sixties—which is why it is often difficult to draw a distinct boundary between the modern and postmodern eras. The welfare state survived but came to symbolize the "establishment" and gave rise to challenges from both the right and the left. More important, the welfare state reached the limits of its effectiveness as an agent of reform. If the welfare state survived, it did so in a much changed form, tolerated as a necessary evil where it once was embraced as a means of improvement.

Modern group politics survived and continued to be a progressive tide in national life. A host of previously marginalized, even invisible groups, began to push their way into the political process and realize some power. Such groups included African Americans and women. Yet interest-group politics also reached the limits of its effectiveness. Minorities faced off against other organized counterforces and against one another.

The one real "winner" of the sixties was the consumer culture. This proved nimble enough to absorb profound challenges to values and taste, even to the point of marketing many of the challenges.

We still live in the sixties not because too many radicals are destroying the free market and national morals, nor because reactionaries are trying to reimpose Anglo-Saxon superiority and restore the nuclear family, but because we still live in the suburbanized, postindustrial, postmodern world ushered in by the sixties.

Although I have tried to write a general history of the period in order to provide a broad view of our society, I have the following political purpose in mind. Given the importance of the sixties to both the political left and the political right, it would seem that interpreting the decade as neither heavenly nor diabolical can help us to break the current social and political stalemate. Let me say what this book is not. My purpose has taken me away from the lighter side of the sixties. I haven't spent much time on rock and roll. The "flower children" who attracted so much attention at the time have drawn little consideration from me. Nor have I spent much time on the generation of Aquarius. I am not dismissing this part of American life as unimportant—whatever the decade of the sixties was or wasn't, it was a time of great fun, of deep sincerity and innocence, and of extraordinary release. I merely believe that the flamboyant aspects of the sixties were the consequences of historical forces rather than forces in and of themselves, and so I have not focused on them. If this strategy tends to make an exciting period rather bland, I can only hope that the soundness of the larger interpretation makes the method worthwhile.

A number of people have read bits and pieces and otherwise offered help. I thank Phil Brown, Warren Van Tine, Daniel Singal, Richard Polenberg, and Rochelle Gurstein for their effort. This book exists because of David Follmer. It was he who nudged me toward undertaking the project, though I wasn't convinced at the beginning how fruitful it would be. Now I'm glad he pushed.

David Steigerwald

Contents

Introduction

In his presidential inaugural address, John F. Kennedy began the era of the sixties by calling for his fellow citizens to subordinate their individual goals to the greater good of the nation. He believed they could speak with a single voice: "Let every nation know, whether it wishes us well or ill, that we shall pay any price, bear any burden, meet any hardship, support any friend, oppose any foe to assure the survival and the success of liberty." In 1974 Richard Nixon brought the age to an end when he resigned the presidency rather than face certain impeachment for crimes that resulted from cynicism, self-interest, and power seeking.

In the interval the United States underwent enormous change. As Kennedy was delivering his call for national sacrifice, white supremacy held firm in the South. African Americans in the South were all but disenfranchised; in some counties in Mississippi and Alabama no blacks had voted in the entire twentieth century. Those who questioned the system were often murdered. The nation's record of race relations elsewhere was not much better. Throughout U.S. society, male supremacy held. Women were denied basic equality in the workplace and were assumed to be domestic creatures. Those who cut an independent course had to own their own businesses, for corporations did not promote women, if by some strange chance they had women to promote. Those who worked in the professions were kept on the margins; women reporters, to cite one example, were forced to sit in the balcony during National Press Club luncheons and were routinely denied access to material male colleagues obtained for career-enhancing stories. Even the women's colleges imposed dress codes, limited their offerings in the sciences, and made home economics courses mandatory. In several states women could not sit on juries. In Massachusetts it was illegal for physicians to dispense information about contraception to their patients.

In cultural matters the censor and the moralist ruled. In New York divorce was granted only on grounds of adultery. Movies were screened, authors banned, and their books threatened. Privacy rights were routinely invaded. In particular, when sex and sexuality were at issue, the authorities were prudish at best and often repressive. The slightest hint of sexually suggestive material was enough to unnerve the cultural watchdogs. Universities exercised the right of *in loco parentis* and regulated the lives of their students, separating the sexes and imposing curfews.

As Nixon left office, these conservative elements of American life seemed not a decade distant but a world away. The nation's institutions, social mores, and habits of mind had been fundamentally challenged and transformed.

Nixon's resignation alone, however, has to give us pause before we celebrate the sixties as an age of human progress. For all of the vital changes that were achieved and the justice that was realized, many of the less appealing forces at work in 1960 were, if anything, more powerful in 1974. Americans in 1960 were the wealthiest people in history, but by 1974 the nation's wealth was spread no more effectively despite more than a decade of social reform. In the meantime the nation's cities sped along toward disintegration. An urban "underclass," made up mostly of ethnic and racial minorities, grew amidst a culture of violent despair. The so-called military-industrial complex, though questioned because of the Vietnam War, ground on as Cold War ideology in U.S. foreign policy persisted. The consumer capitalism that had brought the nation its unprecedented wealth was beginning to reveal a postindustrial future where decent, blue-collar jobs were eliminated or transferred abroad. Consumer culture not only survived the sixties but grew even stronger, thanks to the ballooning of the youth market. The alienation and meaninglessness of American life, against which earnest idealists of the early sixties rebelled, was soothed by the marketing of youth culture, based on its own clothes, music, drugs of choice, sexual values, and politics. In the end not much changed on these counts.

The United States in the sixties was not just living out the old dictum that for every motion there is an equal countermotion. Many of the developments that seemed entirely positive at the time turned out to produce opposite effects, unforeseen disasters, and paradoxical conclusions. Many of the very best ideas turned out to be not very good. The great liberal reforms of the day generated a lower- and middle-class backlash, principally because reforms were paid for by taxes on people who got nothing in return. Youthful radicals, who escaped the draft through college deferments, called attention to the disastrous war in Vietnam while also helping to create a resurgent patriotism among those whose sons and daughters had been sent to Southeast Asia. The liberation of culture from the censors freed artists but did little for art, which increasingly became the realm of investors and mass marketers. The sexual revolution of the "love generation" encouraged as much sexual violence and degradation as healthy freedom. The discrediting of the middle-class family brought women into a world of unfulfilling work and, by encouraging the breakup of families, tended to liberate men more than women, who were far more often saddled with sole responsibility for raising their children. There were only two unambiguous developments of the sixties, one very good, and one, in my mind, appalling: respectively, the civil rights revolution in the American South and the Vietnam War. Otherwise, there was plenty of intelligence and justice, foolishness and cruelty to go around.

The absence of clear winners or clear losers and the irresolvable nature of most public issues resulted in social and political stalemate, which is the foremost legacy of the period. U.S. progressives see the sixties as a moment of great change abruptly ended by war and right-wing backlash, the consequence of which was only a partial liberation of the nation. On the right, the decade is seen as the beginning of a national crisis in authority and morality, which in the end has hurt the poor more than anyone else by legitimizing antisocial behavior.

In a sense we have never left the sixties. The stalemate continues in our own day and is to be seen most powerfully in the enduring ideological split of the last twenty-five years between the self-proclaimed left and the self-anointed right. The sixties was the seed time of both, and indeed the period is at the heart of the respective interpretations of contemporary America.

CHAPTER 1

The End of Liberalism

 The rise and fall of the United States in the sixties was, more than anything else, the rise and fall of American liberalism, the resurgence of which was officially marked with the inauguration of John F. Kennedy in 1960. It was Kennedy who summoned the nation to unleash its idealism, and in so doing he sparked hopes for change and excited expectations that neither he nor his successors could meet. In countless ways, the idealism that liberals revived inspired attacks on liberalism itself.

The liberal rise and fall was so rapid that it is natural to look to dramatic events for explanations: to urban riots, to challenges from radical students, to the Tet offensive and the antiwar movement. Put in a much broader perspective, however, the liberal fate was bound up in a multigenerational saga, running back to the reform period of turn-of-the-century Progressives. Since then, liberals had been on the side of the "little guy"; they had been critics of the business mentality, though supporters of capitalism as a social system; they had used the government as the vehicle for reform and the mediator between interest groups; and they had marshaled the expertise of academics and intellectuals on behalf of their goals. In the 1930s Franklin D. Roosevelt institutionalized this reformist liberalism in the Democratic party when he brought together a coalition of working-class whites, African Americans, and other ethnic groups, liberal professionals, and intellectuals in the most dominant electoral majority in U.S. history.

The collapse of liberalism by 1968 represented the exhaustion of this modern liberalism. The Roosevelt coalition dissolved as an increasingly affluent economy brought industrial workers middle-class comfort, if not middle-class status, and workers, in turn, became "conservative." Because affluence was poorly distributed, racial tension overrode class solidarity. As liberals scurried to adjust, they fell into the trap of having to choose between supporting comfortable working-class and middle-class people, who made up the bulk of voters, or of helping impoverished minorities. In Lyndon Johnson's Great Society program of social reform, liberals sided with the poor minorities, to whom many of the reforms were directed, and jilted the working and middle classes, who were asked to pay for the reforms. With the Great Society, the liberals themselves reached an end point. When urban riots continued, class and racial divisions worsened, and political conflict increased, the liberals had no answers left.

The Liberal Reawakening

The liberal reawakening of the sixties began as a response to the failures of Adlai Stevenson, the Democratic presidential candidate in both the 1952 and 1956 elections. Stevenson was more a Democrat by birth than by conviction and was never tied to the labor–urban–ethnic coalition. As a candidate, he tried to skirt the party machinery by appealing to what he considered the electorate's nobler instincts: the commitment to a "common good" or a national spirit. Witty and sophisticated, Stevenson posed as the idealistic intellectual in public life, but that stance was ineffective against a war hero like Dwight Eisenhower.

Stevenson did not bring liberals back to the White House, but he did bring to public life issues that soon became fundamentally important to U.S. politics. Stevenson was a lonely critic of Eisenhower's dependence on nuclear weapons. He also shifted the discourse surrounding foreign policy so that it focused on the Third World, a vast and varied region that Eisenhower assumed could be browbeaten. Long-term success in the Third World, Stevenson argued, could not be achieved through Eisenhower's policies that propped up anticommunist regimes and initiated CIA-sponsored coups; it would demand that the United States live up to its democratic ideals and serve as an example for the postcolonial nations. On domestic issues, Stevenson had the audacity to insist that rampant materialism, seen so clearly in the desire for consumer goods, was destroying the nation's most cherished ideals, the ideals of public service.

Grace and style alone won Stevenson friends, if not voters, among them liberal intellectuals devoted to recapturing national government. Hoping to goad him into supporting what the liberal economist John Kenneth Galbraith called "the constituency and the policies that had brought the magnificent string of Democratic victories," the intellectuals brought Stevenson around to a 1956 platform that called for public housing, a raised minimum wage, a more pronounced commitment to civil rights and civil liberties, and social security increases.

It is not hard to see why Stevenson would yield to the intellectuals' advice. He was already borrowing more than just platform planks from them in the midfifties. His apprehensions about American materialism echoed an increasing liberal dissatisfaction over consumer society, suburbanization, and bureaucratic life that appeared in much of the social criticism of the period. In *The Lonely Crowd* (1950), for instance, David Riesman argued that Americans had become "other-directed" conformists, a population of middle-class people who measured their self-worth according to the opinions of others rather than personal or traditional moral goals. The other-directed person, Riesman pointed out, was most certainly not the pioneering individualist of the American past, an assessment echoed in other studies, such as William H. Whyte's similarly famous *The Organization Man* (1955). The upshot of liberal social criticism was that the United States was being plagued by its greatest successes. Americans enjoyed the wealthiest society in history, yet they were selling their collective soul, trading the nation's moral fiber for easy white-collar jobs that bought suburban homes and new cars. As Stevenson repeatedly insisted, abundance could not be an end in itself.

Works such as *The Lonely Crowd* were profound, substantive analyses of the American character in a bureaucratized setting, but in liberal hands they were turned primarily to tame critiques. To nag about conformity or to harp on the organization man's lack of drive was to concede that, on the whole, Americans were living well. They did not suffer from economic or political oppression; they no longer feared the horrors of epidemical disease (the dreaded polio virus having been whipped). Whereas the left-wing and liberal criticisms of the past had focused on capitalism's "inherent" inability to spread its benefits widely, anyone wishing to be a critic of American life in the late fifties had to begin by conceding that capitalism was working very well indeed. Accordingly, left-wing critics began to call attention to capitalism's cultural defects. Liberals, for their part, began to argue that the real problem was that Americans continued to think about both politics and economics in the useless old terms of individualism.

This was the common message found in the work of liberalism's most important advocate, Harvard economist John Kenneth Galbraith, who published two books during the decade that defined mainstream liberalism until 1968. In *American Capitalism: The Concept of Countervailing Power* (1952), he argued that American politics had achieved a nice equilibrium in which organized labor had grown strong enough to balance the power of corporations. With the federal government standing in as the referee, capital and labor now merely sparred, looking for compromises that would ensure stability. Galbraith's theory of countervailing power was the first expression of what soon became the theory of interest-group liberalism, which defended the role of interest groups in politics as agents of compromise and organized procedure.

Whereas *American Capitalism* defined liberal politics, Galbraith's *The Affluent Society* (1958) defined the liberal temper. In the guise of a discussion about general economic ideas, the book called on Americans to discard the past. According to the "conventional wisdom" to which business leaders and economists alike clung, economic success depended on the work ethic and on unflinching competition. The conventional wisdom was conceived in an "age of scarcity," Galbraith insisted, and its values were outdated, perhaps even destructive, in a society of unprecedented abundance and cooperative organization. Abundance made the competitive struggle unnecessary, and Americans needed to ease away from competition and address such problems as lagging public investment and the nature of work. There were not many other genuine problems. Poverty, for instance, remained: it was, Galbraith said, a "disgrace," though hardly a "massive affliction." Found only in "pockets" of the United States, poverty could be eliminated as a systemic problem through imaginative public policy, including public improvements on roads and bridges, low-income housing, and education. For the most part, Galbraith seemed to say, the nation's foremost problem was that all was right with the world, if only Americans could admit it.

Galbraith's work, compared to the radicalism that emerged soon after, was mundane—witty, interesting, but thoroughly safe and daring only by comparison to works by other Harvard professors. When he justified interest-group competition, he merely justified the status quo with a "concept." *The Affluent Society* endorsed the economic status quo as well. What Galbraith wanted, rather, was a change in spirit.

This call for a revival of the national spirit, which was so deeply indebted to Adlai Stevenson, was exactly what fired the liberal imagination. Poised on the brink of the sixties, liberals were beginning to feel that change was imminent. As Galbraith's steadfast liberal colleague, Arthur Schlesinger, Jr., wrote on the eve of John F. Kennedy's inauguration, "one feels that we are approaching such a moment now" when the nation was prepared to reaffirm its "vitality and identity." "The mood which has dominated the nation for a decade is beginning to seem thin and irrelevant; . . . it no longer interprets our desires and needs as a people; . . . new forces, new energies, new values are straining for expression and for release." Schlesinger outlined the liberal agenda: better education, improved medical care, civil rights, civil liberties, the "elevation of our popular culture," and an activist foreign policy. He and his colleagues could hardly be considered idle dreamers. Yet in the main the American failure was not one of program but of spirit, and the "challenge of the Sixties," in Schlesinger's opinion, was "the reorganization of American values," in order to beckon people out from crass materialism to some "national purpose."

The national purpose Schlesinger had in mind was twofold: fighting communism abroad and encouraging idealism at home. "The beginning of a new political epoch is like the breaking of a dam. . . . Thus the Sixties will probably be spirited, articulate, inventive, incoherent, turbulent, with energy shooting off wildly in all directions. Above all, there will be a sense of motion, of leadership, and of hope." A little more than eight years later, Schlesinger spoke in New York after Robert Kennedy's assassination, his exuberance replaced by deep personal grief after years of experiencing more turbulence and incoherence than inventiveness. Schlesinger had come to the conclusion that Americans were a "frightening people" evidently gripped by a "primal curse": "We are a violent people with a violent history, and the instinct for violence has seeped into the bloodstream of our national life." In 1960, however, everything was right with the world.

John F. Kennedy

The liberals correctly read the national temper in the late fifties. There were many signs that the nation was thirsting, if not for a resurgent idealism, then at least for something more interesting than Dwight Eisenhower and the reign of the bland. The consumer culture had left young people with a sense of emptiness, and they responded against the confines of middle-class existence by listening to rock-and-roll, reading *Catcher in the Rye* (1952), J. D. Salinger's story of alienated youth, or identifying with Hollywood's youthful self-exiles, James Dean and Marlon Brando. At the further reaches of cultural uneasiness, the beat poets, especially Allen Ginsberg, were making in-roads against conformity by plying forbidden themes of homosexuality, spiritual mysticism, and racial mixing. Unquestionably confined to a minority of youth, the emerging temper of nonconformity and alienation combined with the liberal resurgence in a developing mood that anticipated a great awakening.

What liberals needed after 1956 was a new standard-bearer. Stevenson's second defeat made him a liability. He was too elitist for the average voter, too much a member of the old Anglo-Protestant ruling class. By default, the field was left open for John F. Kennedy. An Irish-Catholic from an old Boston political family, Kennedy had his faults too. He was tarnished by old associations, a conservative bent, and a father widely known for his single-minded desire to drive his sons toward power. Joseph Kennedy, Sr., an assimilated Irishman who was nonetheless contemptuous of the Yankee elite, groomed his sons for politics and packed his daughters off to finishing schools. After the death of his eldest son, Joe, Jr., in World War II, the father turned his attention to John, a once-sickly, frivolous young man. Above all, John learned two things from his father: self-promotion and a contempt for weakness.

Although he spent nearly a decade in Congress before making his move for the 1960 Democratic presidential nomination, John Kennedy never identified with Democratic liberalism. When he embarked on his presidential bid, however, he reached out for the swelling liberal wave by appropriating Adlai Stevenson's themes. His move toward the nomination began with a 1957 speech on foreign policy in the Third World, where, he argued, Republicans had bungled relations through their uncreative, unquestioning commitment to the status quo. Rather than automatically opposing nationalist movements, Kennedy insisted that "the United States, itself a product of political revolution, must redouble its efforts to earn the respect and friendship of nationalist leaders."

Only Galbraith and a few others moved quickly to the Kennedy camp. Other liberals hoped the nomination would go either to Hubert Humphrey, who boasted strong records on civil rights and labor, or to Stevenson. Many were bothered by Kennedy's character or his uninspiring congressional voting record. Others continued to harbor anti-Catholic prejudices or were put off by his ties to the old Irish machine politics. Still others found his aggressive Cold War rhetoric inflammatory and dangerous and quite at odds with his calls for rethinking U.S. foreign policy.

If he lacked party loyalists, Kennedy had other strengths that his competitors soon envied: money, skill, and an aggressive band of close advisors. In the important May primary in West Virginia, he showed that he knew how to use all of his strengths. Although the state was thought to be so steeped in Protestant fundamentalism that Humphrey would whip him there, Kennedy played up his image and flooded the state with family and celebrity volunteers. When necessary, his campaign turned ruthless and set loose rumors about Humphrey's lack of service in World War II, a move that Humphrey never forgave. Kennedy's success in the primaries demonstrated that he was skilled enough both to overcome anti-Catholic prejudice and escape his inadequate congressional career.

As basic as his political skill was to his success, Kennedy had an image, more serious than mere sex appeal but not so profound as charisma, that allowed him to combine an innate conservatism with a subversive sense of the future. His aristocratic bearing and appeal to working-class ethnics combined with an image of youthful vigor and energy. "All at once you had something exciting," one young campaign worker recalled. "You had a young guy who had kids, and who liked to play football on his front lawn. . . . Everything they did showed that America was alive and active." Kennedy's obvious desire for conventional political power could not hide the hints that by his very nature he would threaten mainstream norms. As the novelist Norman Mailer wrote in one of the most famous descriptions of Kennedy, he would shake up the "spirit of the supermarket, that homogeneous extension of stainless surfaces and psychoanalyzed people, packaged commodities and ranch homes." Neither his ideas nor his methods were new. The novelty lay in Kennedy himself. "He had the deep orange-brown suntan of a ski instructor," Mailer gushed, "and when he smiled at the crowd his teeth were amazingly white and clearly visible at a distance of fifty yards." Watching Kennedy's arrival at the Los Angeles convention, Mailer had the sense that he had gotten trapped in a movie just at the scene when "the football hero, the campus king, arrives at the dean's home . . . to plead with the dean for his daughter's kiss and permission to put on the big musical that night."

Part of the Kennedy magic was the candidate's compatibility with television, which was only then coming into its own as an element in U.S. politics. Kennedy was unlike any previous politician in his instinctive embrace of the new medium or, rather, its embrace of him. It was not just his brilliant smile or "ski-instructor" looks that worked well on television. His vagueness, his malleability, the absence of sharp edges in his bearing—all made him the perfect suitor for what Marshall McLuhan, in one of the period's most singularly influential books, *Understanding Media* (1964), insisted was the "cool" medium of television. According to McLuhan, television was a "low-definition" medium and involved its viewers in a relationship with "depth": through listening, watching, and sensing, the viewer absorbed television. "The viewer is the screen," McLuhan wrote, and was therefore an intense participant in the exchange of the message. Kennedy offered evidence on this point. His self-deprecatory humor, the ease with which he bore imperfections such as his tendency to stutter "ums" and "ahs" as he spoke, and his "orange-brown suntan" fit McLuhan's description of television well.

The classic example of Kennedy's gift for television was his first debate, held in September, with the Republican candidate, Richard Nixon. Kennedy, like any good actor, rehearsed for the debate with experienced handlers who coached him in the art of general and evasive answers and who made certain that he dressed correctly. Nixon, on the other hand, prepared as if he were replaying his days on the college debate team. He arrived in Chicago only the night before the debate, and rather than rehearsing or relaxing, he isolated himself in his hotel room. He had only ten minutes of briefing and expected to rely on his stock of campaign addresses for his answers. He wore no theatrical makeup, and his light-gray suit blended into the background, so that, as journalist Theodore White put it, he "faded into a fuzzed outline." He "was tense, almost frightened, at turns glowering and, occasionally, haggard-looking to the point of sickness." Those who watched the proceedings on television overwhelmingly liked Kennedy; those who listened on radio rated the two men as equals.

Although the debate boosted Kennedy's self-confidence, increased the size of his crowds, and created momentum, he remained the underdog through most of the fall and was forced to hustle for support. Above all, he had to gain the support of the civil rights establishment. Neither he nor many other establishment liberals had gone out of their way to embrace the civil rights movement. The liberals genuinely disliked segregation, but they considered it an outdated custom peculiar to the South, and if that were true, then time and a few technical solutions would erase it. Kennedy implied as much himself when he casually confronted Harris Wofford, a campaign aide who specialized in civil rights. "In five minutes," he told Wofford, "tick off the ten things a President ought to do to clean up this goddamn civil rights mess." Wofford told him that "with one stroke of the pen" a president could eliminate discrimination in federal housing, and the "one-stroke-of-the-pen" comment became the candidate's position.

A single act of courtesy ultimately won over Martin Luther King, Jr., and other civil rights advocates. In mid-October, King had been arrested in Atlanta along with other protesters, but rather than being permitted to post bail, he received a sentence of six months at hard labor in a state prison. Wofford convinced Kennedy to call King's wife and voice his concerns. It was a potentially dangerous move that could have antagonized Southern Democrats, but it worked. Many in the civil rights movement, including Martin Luther King, Sr., switched their votes to Kennedy after the call. The elder King told reporters that he never thought that he would vote for a Catholic, but now he had to. Kennedy remarked to aides: "Imagine Martin Luther King having a bigot for a father. Well, we all have fathers, don't we?"

The phone call brought Kennedy an important constituency without losing the Democrats in the "Solid South." Even then, the election was the closest in modern American history. Kennedy won 49.7 percent of the popular vote, while Nixon won 49.6 percent. Questionable, probably fraudulent voting in Chicago, home of the Democratic machine of Richard Daley, helped Kennedy take Illinois's twenty-seven electoral votes. But he took New York and Texas as well. Many things went into the Kennedy victory, but then, he had promised many things. He had promised, in fact, to take the nation to a New Frontier.

The New Frontier

Like Kennedy himself, the new administration arrived in Washington energetic but without a clear direction. They were in agreement on what sort of character the New Frontier was to have. The New Frontiersmen valued manly clear-headedness and hated sentimentality and weakness. They sought an intelligent toughness and valued brains. Kennedy filled his administration with Ivy League Ph.D.'s, the "action intellectuals." Schlesinger wrote that the reception for presidential appointees seemed like a who's who of the intellectual elite "all united in a surge of hope and possibility"—and by a brash, arrogant self-confidence. When he first used the White House switchboard, speechwriter Richard Goodwin declared, "With a telephone like this we can change the world." The administration set up a "talent search," as Harris Wofford called it, in the hopes of finding public servants who fit the New Frontier type. Appointees could be many things, but they could not be "too ideological, too earnest, too emotional, and too talkative—and dull."

This mix of image and determination guaranteed that the New Frontier would not be glamor alone. If anything, the administration tried to be too substantive, too committed to programs even when they seemed doomed to failure, and too ready to formulate policy on the basis of ideas simply because they sounded new and innovative. The New Frontier's zeal for innovation and change ran against the commitment to realism, which recommended caution. They may have prided themselves on their pragmatic approach to government, but they were so certain they could "change the world" that they invited failure.

At its worst, the New Frontier introduced policies that were inherently flawed. In foreign affairs, for example, the administration relied on the ideas of Walt W. Rostow, a pioneer in "development theory" and a fancier of counterguerrilla military action. In his most important work, *The Stages of Economic Growth* (1960), Rostow argued that nations proceed in stages from subsistence agriculture to market agriculture to industrialization and, finally, to the production of consumer goods; as the standard of living gradually rises, a middle class emerges that demands political democracy. He argued that communist revolutionaries prey on societies on the brink of the "take-off stage," that point where nations leave poverty and reactionary politics behind. To counter that threat, Rostow called on the United States to aid Third World nations at the "take-off stage," which would not only satisfy the idealistic desire to help poor nations but would fight the Cold War as well.

Rostow's ideas fed most clearly into the administration's Latin America policy. One of the many international messes that Kennedy inherited was Cuba, where revolution had brought Fidel Castro to power in 1959. The Eisenhower administration considered Castro an immediate threat and trained an anti-Castro regiment in Guatemala, even as the prospects for counterrevolution grew remote. Upon leaving office in early 1961, Eisenhower pleaded with Kennedy to destroy Castro, and against the advice of some advisors, including Schlesinger, the young president gave the go-ahead in April for a counterrevolutionary invasion at the Bay of Pigs.

All the warnings he had received were borne out. The counterrevolutionaries fomented no general uprising, Castro was indeed well entrenched, and the United States, hoping to avoid the appearance of any involvement, was unwilling to use sufficient force to push the invasion through to success. Castro won an enormous propaganda victory, and Kennedy looked weak. Much to his credit, Kennedy took the blame for the Bay of Pigs fiasco.

To ensure that the fiasco would not be repeated, the administration launched the ambitious Alliance for Progress program, designed to support moderate leaders in Latin America against both the right and left. Kennedy offered $1 billion in aid and insisted that the program be cooperative, with the Latin Americans taking much of the initiative. The aid was designed to stabilize prices, expand productive capacities, and encourage private investment. The cooperating nations were also to commit themselves to education, democracy, and land reform. The whole idea was to fend off Castroism by relying on economic progress to undercut the region's entrenched aristocracy.

In practice, the Alliance failed almost across the board. Over the program's seven years, $4.8 billion was spent, not nearly enough to accomplish the ambitious goals Kennedy laid out in 1961. Determined to get fast results because of the perceived threat of leftist revolution, the administration forwarded money before any real planning had been done, and when the threat from Cuba subsided after the 1962 Cuban Missile Crisis, the will to engage in planning dried up. Similarly, as Castro became less and less important, the emphasis of the policies that were in place turned away from democracy and toward technical approaches to economic growth. Thus, instead of land reform, the Alliance supported commercial farming. As the leading students of the Alliance put it, the program failed because its "excessive idealism and overoptimism" were "slowly dissipated in encounters with harsh realities."

The program failed because Rostow's theories were flawed. His notion of economic development was based entirely on the experience of Western Europe and the United States, and he mistakenly saw the western experience as universal. Latin American reactionaries, moreover, proved far more adaptable than Rostow appreciated. Rostow assumed that U.S. and Western European investors wanted democracy to develop in the Third World, but in Latin America, northern corporations invariably preferred the stability of reactionary regimes to the flux of democracy.

In light of this infatuation with trendy ideas, it was a bit ironic that Kennedy's first success in foreign policy came in a classic power confrontation with Russia. In their first encounters, the Russian premier, Nikita Khrushchev, attempted to bully Kennedy, whom he considered inexperienced. The Bay of Pigs encouraged Khrushchev in his belligerence; accordingly, at the Vienna summit that summer, the Soviet premier embarrassed Kennedy with angry dismissals. For his part, after the Bay of Pigs Kennedy determined never to back down again and got his chance to prove his mettle soon enough. In October 1962, U.S. spy planes reported the construction of Soviet missile sites in Cuba, and Kennedy demanded that the Soviets dismantle them. Over a tense two weeks, administration insiders debated what to do, certain that they had to face up to Khrushchev and yet equally certain that they were drawing near nuclear war. Some advised air strikes, some a naval blockade, some diplomacy. Kennedy opted for the blockade, but he also raised the stakes by announcing the crisis on national television. There was the very real danger that he was locking himself into a course of action from which he could not back away, and there was also the chance that he would make diplomacy much more difficult. The world stepped to the brink, but Khrushchev backed down and agreed to pull the missiles out of Cuba in exchange for a U.S. promise not to invade the island. Having established his will, Kennedy began to lay plans for easing tensions with the Russians, though at the same time he continued to expand the U.S. nuclear arsenal and widen the possibility of military conflict by instituting greater military flexibility.

In domestic policy, the New Frontier was at its best when Kennedy proceeded cautiously and took care to balance experiments with mundane commitments to economic growth—in other words, when the rhetoric of change was subordinated to the rigors of responsible governance. Well before he made any concrete moves to address the demands for social reform, Kennedy took great pains to establish himself as a friend to the business community and as a proper manager of the economy. When he entered office, the economy still had not swung out of a slump that began in 1958. Unemployment hovered near 7 percent, and business, mired in that conventional wisdom, was wary of a Democratic administration.

Kennedy's own economic beliefs were rather like his political ideology: he was in favor of "growth," an economic doctrine that no one could oppose. When pressed for an elaboration of his views, he fell back on Galbraith. As he explained during a 1962 commencement address at Yale, the relationship between business and government, based as it was on outdated mutual hostility, "fails to reflect the true realities of contemporary American society." Instead of "some grand warfare of rival ideologies," economic policy needed to be conducted in a "sober, dispassionate, and careful" manner that sought "technical answers" to such problems as the national deficit, slow growth, and unemployment. What technical management meant in practice was shaped mostly by the competing pressures of business demands, political necessity, and the advice of his economic advisors, especially Walter Heller, a University of Minnesota economist who had joined Kennedy from the Humphrey camp after the election.

Although Kennedy was not certain how he was going to promote "growth," he was determined not to ruffle corporate feathers. His administration avoided aggressive antitrust action, an important decision in a business climate that was in the early stages of a wave of mergers and acquisitions, and it promoted free trade abroad. Kennedy promised to erase the budget deficit, a traditional business concern that Eisenhower's unprecedented $12 billion deficit in 1958 had heightened. Despite his efforts, Kennedy's relationship with corporate America was rocky until late 1962, when he yielded to Heller's persistent advice to spur growth with a massive tax cut. Theoretically, the cuts would return money to private hands and encourage both consumer spending and greater investment. Here was a policy that corporate America liked, even if it ran against conventional wisdom, and Kennedy committed himself to more than $10 billion in cuts.

Such policies appealed to corporate America but sat rather poorly with the liberals. The president, however, knew that the liberals had no place else to go and was more concerned with his right flank, especially the southern segregationists who continued to weigh down the Democratic party. At the same time, he worked to shore up old interest-group support and to develop new constituencies. Although his relations with organized labor were complicated, they were mostly good, especially with the United Auto Workers (UAW) and other large industrial unions. The president pushed through labor's pet legislation, an increase in the minimum wage from $1 to $1.25 an hour.

Kennedy also moved to foster the relationship between the Democratic party and two new constituencies, the civil rights movement and liberal women. True, the existing organizations in civil and women's rights had long been on good terms with the Democrats, but their natural constituencies were by no means locked into voting Democratic. More important, the older organizations did not represent what in the case of African Americans already had become a mass movement and, in the case of women, would grow into one by the end of the decade. Moving according to the working assumption that groups would organize and defend themselves if given a chance, Kennedy courted both constituencies with general statements and partial programs. Whatever his personal convictions about the issues involved—and he was certainly more sympathetic to the civil rights movement than to women's rights—he hoped that he would not have to declare, unequivocally, that these were just causes.

Kennedy and the Civil Rights Movement

In the case of the civil rights movement, justice was pursued quite outside the framework of conventional politics. As we have seen, neither Adlai Stevenson nor John F. Kennedy was particularly supportive of the movement. Organizations such as the National Association for the Advancement of Colored People (NAACP), as with the women's rights organizations, had been aligned with the Democratic party for some time. But the movement itself, with its roots in the South, was a whole new political entity when it emerged in the 1950s. Convinced that the South was backward, liberals could not imagine that the region could give birth to a revolution. They were stuck in a parochialism all their own, a "myopia," Arthur Schlesinger, Jr., once admitted; they were convinced that enlightened politics could only come from within the sophisticated Democratic coalition.

At the outset, the administration's political options did not favor active support for the movement. Unsure of his mandate and beholden to southerners, the president wanted to avoid upheaval. The practical options, as Kennedy saw them, were to placate the southerners and avoid large congressional battles while using executive power to provide help for the civil rights cause.

In practice, civil rights policy rested in the hands of the Justice Department and Robert Kennedy. As attorney general, the younger Kennedy was responsible for the appointment of a handful of segregationist judges to southern benches, who proceeded to obstruct rather than support civil rights advances. At the same time, the Justice Department was responsible for bringing suits against various communities for violations of voting registration law, school desegregation rulings, and a host of other federal commands. Kennedy surrounded himself with a small group of men, a few of them southerners, deeply committed to their work, personally courageous, and of unquestionable integrity, who performed the tedious legwork of documenting civil rights abuses. Meanwhile, the attorney general began to integrate his own department, where only 10 of 955 lawyers were black when he took office.

Whatever its legal or political virtues, the administration's legal approach to civil rights was slow and therefore well out of step with the accelerating movement. When activists launched the Freedom Rides in the spring of 1961, a multiorganizational effort to test the South's compliance with the federal ban on segregation in interstate travel, the Kennedys began to appreciate how difficult their balancing act was going to be. When the Freedom Riders were attacked by mobs in

Alabama, the administration faced the interwoven complexities of clashing political interests, commitments to constitutional justice, and obligations of federal power—not to mention heeding the instinct to do the right thing.

The drama within the administration's relationship to the civil rights movement played itself out through the conflict between Washington and the state authorities in Alabama and Mississippi. (For fuller details, see Chapter 2.) Robert Kennedy's determination to see the Freedom Riders come out of Alabama alive ran directly into the equally staunch determination of Alabama Governor John Patterson, a strong supporter of John Kennedy in 1960, to oppose any desegregation. Patterson faced dilemmas of his own: if he agreed to protect the Riders, white voters would throw him out of office; if he did not protect them, mob violence would erupt and the federal government would have to step in, which to defenders of southern glory amounted to the resumption of the Civil War. For his part Kennedy was obliged to uphold federal law against state obstructions and did not want the activists murdered. Yet he, too, worried about the political fallout of federal intervention in the South. And beyond the difficulties of domestic politics, Kennedy was increasingly worried about the international effects of the civil rights situation. The president was preparing for his Vienna summit with Khrushchev, and the ugly scenes from the South were ideal Soviet propaganda. "I think we should all keep in mind that the President is about to embark on a mission of great importance," Robert remarked as he pleaded for moderation on all sides.

When the riders came into Birmingham, they were beaten by a mob that had arranged with local authorities to have fifteen minutes of freedom to riot. As Patterson waffled over his course of action and as local authorities did their minimal duty, Robert Kennedy arranged for the riders to fly from Birmingham to New Orleans. Determined to keep the rides alive, young activists from Nashville drove into Birmingham with the intention of going on to Montgomery. This time, Patterson gave the attorney general his word that he would keep the peace, though at the same time he initiated legal action to stop the rides. Meanwhile, the Greyhound Bus Company could find no drivers brave enough to carry the riders. "I don't have but one life to give," the scheduled driver told his passengers. "And I don't intend to give it to CORE or the NAACP." Robert Kennedy lost his cool over this last-minute snag and berated the local Greyhound manager: "Well, surely somebody in the damn bus company can drive a bus. . . . I think . . . you had better be getting in touch with Mr. Greyhound or whoever Greyhound is."

When a driver was finally found, the ride proceeded to Montgomery. There Patterson reneged on his promise, arguing that he had no jurisdiction in Montgomery's city limits. Once at the bus depot, the riders were attacked again, this time even more viciously than in Birmingham. Several riders were severely beaten by a mob that turned on reporters, cab drivers, and anyone else who got in its way, including John Siegenthaler, the Justice Department official who had been negotiating with Patterson. Siegenthaler happened by the depot just as the riot broke out and drove into the crowd to help two fleeing riders. He was knocked to the ground and hospitalized with a concussion. His Justice colleague, John Doar, watched the riot in mounting horror from the Federal Building across the street and relayed a blow-by-blow account by phone back to Washington: "It's terrible! It's terrible! There's not a cop in sight." The only state official to distinguish himself was Floyd Mann, the state director of public safety, who took it upon himself, alone, to pull victims from the mob; visiting Siegenthaler in the hospital afterward, he broke down and wept.

The attorney general saw that he had been had and resolved to send in federal marshalls to protect what was left of the Freedom Rides. Patterson forced the decision on him, but so too did Martin Luther King, Jr., who announced his intention to fly to Montgomery from Atlanta in support of the riders. Having defaulted on his responsibility, Governor Patterson was free to denounce federal intervention as unwarranted and to pose as the wounded underdog.

Protected by the marshalls, King and the activists gathered with over a thousand supporters in Reverend Ralph Abernathy's First Baptist Church for a night of prayers, speeches, and strategy-making, only to face another mob siege. Through a tense night of sporadic violence, Patterson finally decided to declare martial law. After dispersing the mob and relieving the federal marshalls, however, the Alabama National Guard held the churchgoers captive. More tedious negotiations followed, during which federal officials had to deal with a Guard commander who insisted on sitting in a room full of Confederate flags. "I was treated like I might have been treated in Russia," the administration's representative, William Orrick, remarked. Patterson agreed to escort the riders to the state line, where they were handed over to Mississippi state officials. Once in the state capital, Jackson, they were arrested and jailed for violating state segregation statutes.

The Freedom Rides were exhausting to the administration, but they electrified the civil rights movement. It was not long before the battles were fought all over again, this time over the desegregation of the University of Mississippi, where a lone black man, James Meredith, attempted to register after winning a favorable federal court decision in 1962.

As the Rides did in Alabama, the Meredith case pitted the reluctant administration against a grandstanding governor. At first, Mississippi governor Ross Barnett denied Meredith entry into the University registrar's building. Barnett eventually yielded to Robert Kennedy's persistent pressure and agreed to permit the registration if the federal government staged a show of force at the Oxford campus, thus making it appear that he had to submit to superior federal firepower. To Barnett's dismay, Kennedy's idea of a show of force was less impressive than the show that the governor wanted. Barnett became even more discomforted when large gangs ominously began to arrive in Oxford, and he called the deal off. Unwilling to show any hint of compliance with federal orders, Barnett reiterated his strident defense of segregation in no less a citadel of southern life than the fifty-yard line during halftime of the Ole Miss–Kentucky football game on September 29.

Even President Kennedy's appeals failed to move Barnett—that is, until the administration threatened to reveal the ongoing negotiations on national television. Reacting to the one threat that would destroy him, Barnett suggested that the administration register Meredith at Oxford on Sunday night, September 30. Federal marshalls rapidly moved into Oxford, and along with grudging Mississippi state troopers, prepared to register Meredith on Monday. After Barnett announced that the defenders of the southern way of life had been "overpowered," a swelling mob began to attack the marshalls on campus. Events turned uglier when older, more dangerous rioters with guns replaced rock-throwing students, and the state troopers deserted. The president was forced to nationalize the Mississippi National Guard and send in regular army troops. James Meredith registered, but at the cost of another breakdown of order. A total of 160 federal marshalls were wounded, two people were killed, and over three hundred were injured in all.

However much they chafed at the restraints that bound them, both Kennedys believed they were at the limits of practical involvement. Short of massive military intervention, a "Second Reconstruction," the administration could only hope for gradual change. When he told *New York Times* writer Anthony Lewis that "I think these matters should be decided over a long range of history," Robert Kennedy was in effect pleading for the civil rights movement, as he put it after the Freedom Rides, to "cool off." Because the activists had no intention of cooling off, the administration's refusal to intervene essentially left the movement to a strategy of continued agitation. It also forced the movement to seek political change, as opposed to realizing purely legal victories.

If there was to be continued political agitation, the administration hoped it could be channeled in ways that were politically advantageous. With this in mind, the attorney general approached several civil rights organizations with a promise to arrange private funding for a voter education project. Registering voters would push activists on to the southern backroads and off the front pages. Having arranged funding, the attorney general expected to exercise some control over the movement. And, surely, any newly registered voters would vote for Democrats, at least in national elections. This is not to say that the administration was being cynical when it proposed the Voter Education Project (VEP). Rather, VEP was an admission that the federal government was powerless to do anything more than react to emergencies and otherwise hope that the South would obey federal law; accordingly, any further progress on civil rights had to come, as Burke Marshall, head of the Justice Department's civil rights division, plaintively wrote, through the "political process." As it turned out, VEP was anything but conventional politics. It was not the safe outlet Kennedy thought it would be. It became quite newsworthy, and the voters it registered went on to challenge, rather than work with, the Democratic party.

Martin Luther King, Jr., became the most conventional leader with whom the administration was compelled to work, which suggests that the movement remained quite out of the mainstream. King was a relentless activist, but he was willing to accept help and advice from wherever it came, including Washington. He was always respectful, even deferential, but always pressing nonetheless. When King hit the streets in Birmingham in 1963 and provoked the local authorities there into what seemed to be the worst spasm of official violence, he also provoked the president into an unequivocal stand in favor of major civil rights legislation. To maintain the pressure, King helped the old activists, A. Philip Randolph and his principal lieutenant, Bayard Rustin, organize a massive march on Washington in

August. To White House pleas that the march was ill timed, King replied that he had never engaged in any action that was not ill timed.

Forced to heed the pressure of the movement, the administration proposed the legislation that eventually passed as the 1964 Civil Rights Act. Passed after the Kennedy assassination, the act essentially outlawed any form of formal segregation, prohibited discrimination in hiring and other vital areas, and pledged to put federal power behind its enforcement. As important as the mid-decade legislation was, it nonetheless amounted to an incomplete and formalistic victory. When it became clear, as it quickly did, that civil rights legislation and legalistic approaches were incapable of dealing effectively with the plight of African Americans in the cities, when King himself began to take a populistic stand and call for a radical redistribution of economic power, liberals appeared rhetorically committed to civil rights but incapable of making good on much of their rhetoric.

The Women's Movement

Whereas the civil rights movement was in full swing when Kennedy assumed office, women were only experiencing the intensifying social changes that eventually create political movements. There was no women's movement as such in 1960—certainly not in anything like the form it soon took. Those organizations that dealt in women's issues were not powerful and had been single-mindedly focused on the not-very-popular Equal Rights Amendment (ERA), a measure that Kennedy had talked around, although it had been a "Democratic" issue for a long time.

In 1961 Kennedy agreed to establish a Commission on the Status of Women, which was as much a strategy for avoiding the ERA as it was a forum for women's issues. Only one "feminist," the lawyer and later co-founder of the National Organization for Women, Marguerite Rawalt, was placed on the task force, and other activists were stubbornly ignored. The commission's charge was obscure: it was to give attention to questions about the conditions of women, which were growing more important as women continued to move from the home to the workplace. Officially, the commission was to examine the "prejudices and outmoded customs [that] act as barriers to the full realization of women's basic rights." The commission's final report, issued in 1963, delayed consideration of the ERA in Congress and ultimately recommended against the amendment. Yet the commission marked a governmental watershed for the women's movement. It was the first comprehensive federal investigation into issues relating to women; it established the institutional precedent for permanent committees on women; and it legitimized governmental concerns for gender discrimination in employment and disparities in pay.

The commission was also politically important, although its effects were as ambiguous as its charter. Without question, Kennedy was interested in sustaining the support of liberal women, and mainstream liberals wanted to anticipate and absorb what many detected as an emerging cause. As Kennedy noted when he announced the establishment of the commission, women in 1960 represented one-third of the labor force, and it was quickly becoming acceptable for white, middle-class married women to work outside the home. The movement of women out of the home and into the workforce continued developments that had begun at least seventy-five years earlier. The process was irreversible, and it was just as inevitable that women would begin to assault the pervasive barriers to equality, which in 1960 were to be found in every aspect of American life. Several years before Betty Friedan published her pathbreaking broadside against the limits imposed on middle-class women, *The Feminine Mystique* (1963), Kennedy liberals moved to cover the political—though most surely not the cultural—lag that left women vulnerable to personal harassment and, more obviously, to forms of discrimination that were astonishingly overt, given the standards that the sixties ended with.

By attempting to placate ERA supporters with the Commission on the Status of Women, Kennedy provided a forum, even if inadvertently, for women to make their own case. This forum in turn enlivened activists and put them in touch with an expanding network of others interested in political organization. The commission opened the space in national life for women to begin organized action. In the summer of 1963, Kennedy signed the Equal Pay Act, which laid down a legal commitment to equal pay for equal work. It was followed by the prohibition on discriminatory hiring on the basis of sex in Title VII of the 1964 Civil Rights Act.

Kennedy's interest in cultivating the political favor of a distinct bloc of voters provided the accidental spark for organization. There was a great flaw in this political method, however: the inherent justice of the cause never had to be recognized or settled, and the results were confusing at best. The inclusion of a statute on gender discrimination in the Civil Rights Act, for instance, was the work of the conservative Virginia congressman, Howard Smith, who probably would not have been disappointed if his amendment derailed the entire bill. The "Ladies' Day in the House" brought snide laughter from the floor as incredulous representatives listened to Smith introduce his amendment on women. Behind this scene ran complicated crosscurrents. Smith told his House colleague Martha Griffiths that the amendment was a joke, but he had been a longtime and consistent supporter of the ERA and was probably sincere in offering the amendment. Moreover, Smith received support from conservative women constituents who insisted that white women be given the same protections as blacks. Northern liberals and women's pressure groups alike thus aligned with southerners whose politics were not exactly liberal and who were not very interested in establishing women's rights within a larger framework of the just society.

Precisely because Title VII was put through in so casual a way, women activists concluded that they would have to organize to advance their own cause and to hold the federal government to its new promises. Once founded in 1966, the National Organization of Women (NOW) fulfilled the interest-group logic of liberalism, for it sought to represent a group with clearly defined, singular interests aimed at equal rights in public life. But in turn the Democratic party forced NOW to narrow its focus to "women's issues," and mainstream ones at that, such as workplace regulation, reproductive rights, and child care, as if women were only interested in, or capable of speaking to, such issues.

Lyndon Johnson

Liberalism exhausted itself under Lyndon Johnson, who by conventional standards had stronger liberal credentials than John F. Kennedy. Johnson hailed from the hill country of central Texas, the son of a simple, idealistic farmer-politician and a well-educated gentlewoman who was always out of place in the isolated world of Johnson City. His formative world, depression-era Texas, could not have been farther from the wealthy, eastern world of John F. Kennedy. Johnson adopted his father's distrust of corporate wealth and political corruption, but took on his mother's dislike for the modest world the family inhabited. Johnson's father had been a failure, and Lyndon was determined not to follow in his footsteps even if he shared his father's ideals.

He began his quest for power in 1938, when he gained election to the House of Representatives. A populist Democrat, he quickly became loyal to Franklin Roosevelt and the New Deal. Through a lengthy process of self-promotion and party loyalty, Johnson worked his way to the Democratic leadership in the Senate by the 1950s where he gained a reputation as the foremost backroom politician of his day. He was a master of deals, manipulation, and brow-beating. He was infamously effective in one-on-one meetings, where he could apply the "Johnson treatment," a mix of bear hugs, finger-pointing, and back-slapping that instilled in many Washington figures a dread of meetings with him. Dwight Eisenhower, it is said, positioned aides on the corners of his desk to block Johnson's approach. Lawrence O'Brien, a Kennedy advisor, and later Democratic party national chairman, got the treatment when he first met Johnson at the 1960 convention. "He and I were introduced," O'Brien remembered, "and he took my hand and pulled me close, until we were standing nose-to-nose, and that, in terms of noses [O'Brien himself possessed a proud nose], was a summit conference." When unable to overwhelm physically, Johnson became a master puppeteer, wielding influence and controlling events indirectly and from a distance, so that his opponents often did not know what he had his hands in.

Like Kennedy, whose sexual escapades and shady associations ultimately tarnished his image, Johnson had an ugly side. In private, and sometimes even in public, Johnson mocked the very things he aspired to. He especially denounced the intellectuals, the hot shots, and assorted other enemies. Johnson also took childish delight in running afoul of Washington society. He punctuated his private language with obscenities. His escapades were plentiful and disturbing, from urinating on his grave site in order to shock accompanying reporters to revealing the scar from gallbladder surgery. Cartoonist David Levine depicted the scar in the shape of Vietnam in a brilliant cover page for the *New York Review of Books* in 1968. As the Vietnam War drained him, Johnson fell into deep periods of sullen paranoia that frightened even his closest aides. His perverse streak could turn downright nasty when he dealt with enemies. It was he and not Richard Nixon who first subjected antiwar protesters to government surveillance, and it was he who sanctioned the FBI's harassment of Martin Luther King, Jr., after the civil rights leader began to speak out against the Vietnam War. He reserved his deepest animosity, however, for Robert Kennedy, who was as brashly honest as Johnson was brazenly manipulative.

Yet Johnson was neither fool nor monster. The very drives that made him dangerous also made him gregarious and, after a fashion, warm and sincere. Whereas Kennedy's vices were controlled, refined, and secretive, Johnson's were so close to the surface that they spilled over into virtues. He was habitually on the telephone and would talk to anyone, a local party boss, reporters, or a foreign head of state. In his memoirs, Tip O'Neill, the Massachusetts congressman who felt compelled to break with Johnson over Vietnam, recalled an act of spontaneous personal decency, quite typical of Johnson. After hearing that several other Democrats were on their way to an O'Neill campaign fund-raiser, the president tagged along, without the Secret Service, to wish O'Neill good luck.

It was ironic that Johnson, given his lifelong and ultimately unsatisfied craving for adulation, followed John Kennedy. Johnson only dimly understood the Bostonian's appeal, and Kennedy's 1960 convention victory reinforced Johnson's insecurity. Everything about Kennedy aggravated Johnson. Kennedy was rich; Johnson was poor. Kennedy was sophisticated; Johnson was crude. Kennedy courted and won the respect of liberal intellectuals; the intellectuals considered Johnson a conniving hack. Kennedy effortlessly evoked popular affection; Johnson tried too hard to be loved, and the harder he tried, the more it bothered him that the "people" did not love him.

The two were joined when Kennedy, in a decision that every insider, including the Kennedys themselves, found peculiar, chose Johnson as his running mate in 1960. Kennedy's liberal friends were shocked, for to them Johnson was a con-man and, worse, a southerner. The bellwether liberal group, the Americans for Democratic Action, refused to endorse him; organized labor opposed Johnson; and above all, Robert Kennedy was very hostile to his brother's choice. Nor was there a compelling regional need to choose Johnson. As a southerner Johnson would be expected to balance the ticket regionally, but he was influential neither among the die-hards nor among the progressive forces for civil rights. At this point in his life, Johnson was more Washington than Texas.

The story behind the Johnson selection is almost amusing. After Kennedy won the nomination, his team considered the standard candidates—Hubert Humphrey, Missouri's Stuart Symington, Washington's Henry Jackson—and the only prominent figure they ruled out was Johnson. *Washington Post* publisher Philip Graham and Kennedy friend Joseph Alsop recommended, however, that Johnson also be offered the position. Evidently, Kennedy agreed that, out of courtesy, perhaps he should, and so he sent Robert to meet with Johnson to "sound him out." Johnson, apparently assuming that Kennedy was making a firm offer rather than a simple courtesy call, accepted the offer. The Kennedys were now stuck in a terrible bind. Robert met with Johnson again and tried to talk him into taking the party chairmanship. Johnson, perhaps faking, broke into tears: "I want to be vice president. And, if the president will have me, I'll join with him in making a fight for it." The only thing Robert Kennedy hated more than weakness was people in pain, and he relented: "Well, then that's fine. He [John Kennedy] wants you to be vice president if you want to be vice president." Putting the best spin on their confusion and searching for any rationale, the brothers agreed that Johnson as vice president would be less troublesome than Johnson as majority leader.

Once on board, Johnson was a team player, notwithstanding an occasional private comment about "that little shitass Bobby." Johnson worked hardest in those areas where the liberals presumed him weakest. When Kennedy needed someone to reassure the public over the developing situation in Vietnam, Johnson willingly accepted the challenge. On his visit to Vietnam in 1961, he threw himself fully into his role, riding rickshaws, shaking hands, and patting backs—he might as well have been in Austin. He came home with just the sort of recommendations for increased involvement that most of Kennedy's advisors were pressing on the president. Johnson also offered valuable advice on the Civil Rights Act when he urged a strategy of favor-granting to moderate Republicans, the very strategy that eventually ensured the act's passage.

The Great Society

In the aftermath of the assassination, Johnson was extraordinarily careful to let it be known that he intended to fulfill Kennedy's legacy. His caution made good political sense inasmuch as he did not have his own mandate. He also felt he needed to be more liberal than Kennedy had been. Shortly after the assassination he cornered Walter Heller and insisted: "Now, I want to say something about all this talk that I'm a conservative who is likely to go back to the Eisenhower ways. . . . It's not so, and I want you to tell your friends—Arthur Schlesinger, Galbraith, and other liberals. . . . To tell the truth, John F. Kennedy was a little too conservative to suit my taste."

To prove the point, he immediately set the administration, still comprised of Kennedy functionaries, to work on developing the antipoverty program that Kennedy had only been dabbling with. Mostly located in the Office of Juvenile Delinquency, an executive branch offshoot that had been established to deal with Eunice Kennedy's pet cause, the antipoverty program had been slowly developing experimental pilot programs designed to teach ghetto residents how to organize themselves for political action. Dubbed "community action," the program was built on the typical assumption that the solution to any problem was interest-group pressure. In this case, because no one really cared about the poor, the government was obliged to help them defend their interests against city hall, the local police, developers, and any other competing interest.

In this effort, as in all his policies, Johnson was driven by his ideals and his need for acclaim. In early 1964, the nation had begun to recover from the collective grief of the assassination, and the national mood had become decisively liberal. Johnson did not waste his moment. In his desire to do everything better, he enlarged the antipoverty program to a scope its advocates had never expected. When Kennedy liberals began to brief him on the antipoverty ideas, he exclaimed, "That's my kind of program. It will help people. I want you to move full speed

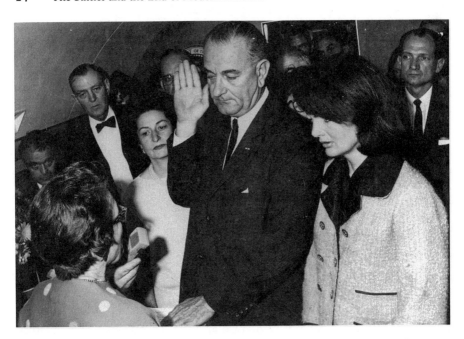

Lyndon B. Johnson is sworn in as president of the United States on November 22, 1963, as his wife, Lady Bird, and John Kennedy's widow, Jacqueline, look on.
[UPI/Bettmann Newsphotos]

ahead on it." The Kennedy men, still tentative about any sort of program, estimated that $30 million would do for starters. To their astonishment, they were told "to add another zero." Johnson's "War on Poverty" included job training, supplemental nutrition programs such as school lunches and food stamps, regional development in "pockets" of poverty, and community action. The War on Poverty paralleled an even broader effort at reform, the Great Society, which included programs for low-income housing, medical insurance for the poor and the elderly, and federal aid to education. All of these programs, Johnson assured skeptics, could be financed without tax increases. Quite the opposite: Johnson enacted the Kennedy tax cut in 1964.

As Allan Matusow shows in his study of sixties liberalism, the largest Great Society programs such as Medicaid-Medicare and aid to education worked in characteristically liberal fashion to put money directly into the hands of particular groups, sometimes without any clear specification of how it was to be spent and or how social justice was to be advanced. Health insurance was a good example. Instead of pushing for genuine national health care, which the American Medical Association had bitterly opposed since Harry Truman recommended it in 1948, Johnson settled for a program that provided health care to those who needed it the most: the elderly and the poor. At the same time, Medicare-Medicaid programs appeased the medical industry by leaving practical control of the program in the hands of doctors and hospitals. Without any system of federal control, health care practitioners had too few incentives to avoid unnecessary treatment or to restrain costs. Furthermore, the system delivered uneven care, because the impoverished Medicaid patients suffered from the same stigma as welfare recipients. Indeed, Medicare helped elderly patients by ensuring long-term health care, an important benefit in a society that increasingly put its elderly into nursing homes. But beyond that, the main effects of the Great Society health programs, as Matusow points out, were to enrich health care practitioners and fuel inflation that hurt both the poor and the working class.

Federal aid to education had something of the same history. The Elementary and Secondary Education Act of 1965 had been established on the premise that poverty was a cultural problem. As Francis Keppel, Johnson's education commissioner, explained, federal aid might "interrupt the cycle of poverty where we have a fighting chance." The monies provided by the bill were to be spent on eliminating disadvantages by providing for the purchase of new material and other resources in districts with many low-income students. The act set a precedent for federal funding of primary education, long considered a local matter in the United States. But it was passed only by appeasing local authorities and honoring the tradition of decentralization. Federal money was doled out directly to the local boards with very little federal supervision. Thus, the act sent money into southern school districts that were still resisting desegregation and into urban districts that spread the wealth to schools often without any regard for the incomes of students. If the aid ever improved the education of low-income students, it did so indirectly; if it ever broke "the cycle of poverty," it did so through sheer accident.

Still, with these programs Johnson could claim that he had brought benefits to "the people," and if a large part of "the people" happened to be doctors, lawyers, contractors, bankers, and sundry bureaucrats protecting their turf, so be it. The programs that brought aid directly to the poor were aimed principally at one constituency, urban blacks, and, as we will see later in greater detail, focused on political organization among them instead of providing hard-and-fast forms of economic improvement.

The political fallout from programs aimed directly at the black urban poor did great damage to the liberals. Johnson saw the Great Society as a monument to himself, and the result was too many programs hastily conceived and too quickly implemented to work well. Johnson had hoped the Great Society would pay political dividends, but it was so diffuse and uneven that it was often difficult to tell whose side the government was on—the forces of the status quo or the forces of change. The administration allowed itself to get stuck between the local machines that it wanted to help and the most aggressive voices claiming to represent the poor. Because he had no taste for institutional change or radicalism, Johnson might have been better served had federal programs been run through local political machines in the hopes that some aid might trickle down to the poor. At least that way someone would have been happy. Instead, the Great Society built up tremendous expectations, particularly in poor urban communities, that inevitably were dashed. Moreover, it ruined otherwise strong political ties between the urban political machines and the Democratic party.

All the same, the Great Society had its triumphs. School lunches and Head Start were successful in addressing their respective problems of malnutrition and educational deprivation, though neither was a cure-all. Head Start proved effective only as early intervention; its benefits were undermined once poor children moved into poor public schools. Other problems associated with poverty, such as infant mortality, also showed marked improvements through the sixties, especially among African Americans. Using the Johnson administration's definition of poverty, that is, anyone whose annual income was below $3,169 in 1964, one can argue that the Great Society led to dramatic improvements. By some estimates, the percentage of the population living under the poverty line dropped from 19 percent in 1964 to 11.6 percent in 1974, and according to other calculations, by 60 percent from 1960 to 1975. General prosperity may have been responsible for some of that improvement, though how much is a matter of debate. It is also true that the notion of a "poverty level" is arbitrary in that it assumes that anyone making a few dollars more than the mandated level is not poor. At least by his own measures, Johnson could claim substantial progress in his War on Poverty. Whatever else one says about the Great Society, it attempted to deal with the most intractable problems, and it is hardly a surprise that it did not achieve all it promised.

Because it addressed deeply embedded social ills, the Great Society could not provide quick and decisive evidence that it worked, and it therefore became easy for conservatives to condemn. Perhaps the Great Society's largest failure, in fact, was political rather than social or economic. In his attempt to bring benefits to everyone, Johnson missed one large group: the working poor and, generally, middle America—white, black, Chicano, urban, rural. The major programs like health care did not apply to them, and the inequitable tax system left them paying an unfair share of the burden for the increasingly expensive programs. Not the least irony here was that in attempting to go down in history as the most beloved reformer, Johnson actually lost the support of that group of Americans he best understood and most clearly identified with—working and middle-class whites.

Although the Vietnam War was equally important in destroying the New Deal coalition, the strains generated by the Great Society began to show as early as 1966, when the Republicans gained forty-seven seats in the House of Representatives and ran strong on the state level as well; many of the losers that year had been liberal supporters of the Great Society, and not coincidentally, Congress hedged on its commitments to social spending after the elections. By 1968 the electorate was in the midst of a full-scale backlash and ready to entertain demagogues like George Wallace and cynics like Richard Nixon. After 1968, increasingly shorn of its blue-collar constituents, the Democratic party looked more and more like an odd collection of interest groups, fringe organizations, and radicals. The most notable similarity it shared with the liberal wing of the party that came to power in 1960 was its elitism.

1968

In spite of the destructive political effects of Johnson's presidency, it was possible that a late-hour change of leadership armed with substantive changes in war policy could have salvaged the New Deal coalition. Indeed, given all the cynicism and absurdity at work in 1968, it is remarkable just how ready many Americans were to have their hopes salvaged.

The progressive forces within the Democratic party began speaking about, if not actually plotting, a palace coup as early as 1966. In the aftermath of the 1966 elections and with the spiraling intervention in Vietnam, antiwar Democrats, black activists, community organizers, student groups, and others began to consider raising an open challenge to Johnson, if necessary organizing a party of their own. About 2,000 representatives of this loose coalition met in Chicago over the Labor Day weekend of 1967 at the National Conference for New Politics (NCNP) to consider their options, among them the possibility of pushing Martin Luther King, Jr., into the presidential race.

The groups at the conference immediately fell to bitter fighting among themselves. The Black Caucus, infused with the spirit of black power that had supplanted King's nonviolent message, demanded the total acceptance of an outrageous thirteen-point program infused with anti-Semitism; perhaps its expectation was that the other delegates would reject the demands and thereby allow the Black Caucus to go its own way. Instead, in what one writer described as "an orgy of self-laceration and guilt," the white delegates voted to accept the thirteen points as a means of proving their goodwill. Sensing the possibility of taking the conference over, the Black Caucus then demanded control over all votes and conferences. Self-respecting white delegates left; others surrendered themselves to another day of brow-beating. In the end, the conferees voted down a proposed third party, but beyond that they had no funds, no alternatives, and no goodwill to help them proceed.

The McCarthy Candidacy

As the progressive organizations devolved into petty, self-destructive bickering, more viable challenges came from within the Democratic party. In the fall of 1967, some progressive Democrats, led by New York activist Allard Lowenstein, began to lobby prominent antiwar Democrats to mount an intraparty challenge to Johnson. The only candidate to present himself was Eugene McCarthy, a relative latecomer to the antiwar cause. McCarthy was an erudite poet-scholar, a one-time professor at a small college in Minnesota, and a Stevenson man. He was a bit of a snob, even in the snobbish Senate, which he once called "the last primitive society left on earth." Although his political origins were honestly progressive, his legislative record was no more than acceptable by progressive standards. He had become convinced that the war was unwise, that a negotiated peace was necessary, and that it was simply his historic duty to speak out. Otherwise, he was not sure that the United States was worth saving, and he thought that the reckless Johnson was an apt leader for a reckless nation.

Such was the state of affairs in late 1967 that eager New Politics liberals, especially young activists, fell in behind McCarthy. From the beginning, they sought an energetic idealist determined to bring down Johnson and stop the war; from the beginning, McCarthy envisioned his candidacy as nothing more than a quixotic quest. Basically a pessimist—and with so many people hoping for so much from him, his pessimism bordered on the cynical—McCarthy had neither the taste nor the desire for real campaigning. Hand-shaking bored him. Stump-speaking presented no challenge. Organizational necessities left him indifferent. At a moment when the fissures in the New Deal coalition had to be mended and the energy of the antiwar forces united, McCarthy was disinterested in both.

Events, rather than any effort of his own, propelled McCarthy from a lackluster dark horse into a political force. At the end of January, Vietcong and North Vietnamese forces combined in a massive surprise offensive, the so-called Tet offensive, in South Vietnam. Tet quickly turned out to be a gross military mistake for the Vietcong, but its political impact in the United States was dramatic. Since the administration had been trying to convince the public that the war was nearing a successful conclusion, Tet was a shocking event. Almost coincidental with Tet, McCarthy began campaigning in New Hampshire for the first presidential primary. McCarthy's aloof style conformed to the local Yankee reserve, and his campaign did surprisingly well. Celebrities, money, young people, other Democrats working on the sly—all followed by the media—joined the campaign. McCarthy electrified the nation by winning 42 percent of the vote; for a darkhorse running against a powerful incumbent, this constituted a victory. It was a strong enough indication of Johnson's vulnerability that it convinced the president's longtime arch-enemy, Robert Kennedy, to enter the race.

Johnson's people, while trying to downplay New Hampshire, were forced to read it as most pundits did: the vote was not for McCarthy but against Johnson. The president responded with a nationally televised address on March 31, ostensibly about Vietnam. Almost at the last minute, Johnson decided to add a conclusion to his speech that he had been mulling over for days. "I will not seek, and I will not accept," he told a stunned nation, "the nomination of my party for another term as your president."

Johnson's announcement was a surprise, even to those closest aides who knew that such an ending was possible. He explained that the painful decision was necessary in order to carry out his duties as commander in chief without interjecting partisan politics into the conduct of the war. He owed American servicemen and women as much, he believed. Moreover, the collapse of the Great Society had compromised his effectiveness as a domestic leader, so much so, he mused to his aides, that any other leader, even Richard Nixon, might have better legislative success in the future. But surely there was more to it, as there always was with Johnson. He had to have been unnerved by McCarthy's New Hampshire showing, not because it represented any true electoral threat (had he so desired, Johnson could easily have put together the effort to trounce the challenger) but because it was a public rebuke. Then, of course, there was now Robert Kennedy, whom Johnson hated, envied, and feared. For all his audacity, for all his ruthlessness, there was a squeamishness to Johnson, and ultimately he chose concession to the unpleasant possibility of running and losing, which would have been undeniable proof that the adulation he so badly craved did not exist.

It is possible that Johnson had a more insightful handle on the political equation than anyone else at the time. Both Robert Kennedy and Eugene McCarthy were formidable candidates, each in his own way. In spite of his many faults, McCarthy was heir to the Stevenson legacy, appealing to a lingering conservative idealism, a vague hope among elites both young and old that the United States could be more thoughtful, cultured, and refined.

Theirs was "a species of disinfected idealism," wrote Norman Mailer with typical contempt, "which gave the impression when among them of living in a lobotomized ward of Upper Utopia." The strength of McCarthy's stand on the war, taken at a moment when all other mainstream candidates were at most hedging on the issue, guaranteed him an assertive and vocal following, if not an immediately large one. Having been inconspicuous in national life before 1968, he had not made many enemies. McCarthy's candidacy was a lark, but then again, in 1968, anything was possible.

The Robert Kennedy Candidacy

Robert Kennedy, meanwhile, brought with him all of the Kennedy baggage, the good with the bad. He had made some very bitter enemies, particularly in the South, where his name was just below Martin Luther King's on the list of regional "heroes." To Kennedy's many detractors, his career had been a combination of self-advancement and personal vendetta—against unions, against the South, against Johnson. To Democratic regulars, Robert Kennedy was denouncing the Great Society's social failures, even though Johnson had done far more of substance for the poor than John Kennedy had. To the Democratic left, Robert Kennedy only broke with the administration over Vietnam after the emergence of a full-blown antiwar movement. When he announced his candidacy after McCarthy's New Hampshire showing, many influential observers thought Kennedy had gone too far. For in so doing, Kennedy threatened to undermine not Johnson but McCarthy, who had "survived on the lonely road [Kennedy] dared not walk himself," as the Stevenson liberal Murray Kempton wrote. "In one day, he managed to confirm the worst things his enemies ever said about him."

Kennedy had his friends, however, and a large capacity to inspire. Although he was a good deal less purposeful about it than his brother had been, he exploited the mass media. He had the looks, the bearing, the name, and the wit, all of which served his brother well, and while he was cool near the camera, he was also capable of much more public passion than his brother. Whatever his effectiveness before a mass audience, Kennedy revived old supporters and convinced many new ones that he was a new man, a quality that many in the New Politics assumed was a prerequisite for leadership among the young.

One could take this "new man" business to great lengths. According to the legend advanced by his supporters, John's death had transformed Robert. He became independent, laden with a profoundly tragic sense of life, which erased his priggishness and engendered a deep identification with life's underdogs. He was, as Jack Newfield of the *Village Voice* described him in an adoring book, the existential candidate who remade himself through experience. John Kennedy's assassination,

Newfield wrote, forced his brother to go through the searing identity crisis that most people go through during adolescence but that Robert Kennedy, wealthy and protected, had been spared. Robert Kennedy was on "the kids' " wavelength, for like them, he was infused with the idealistic commitment to changing society as he had changed himself; like young people, he sought "a newer world." Everything about him signaled identification with youth: the shaggy, untrimmed hair, the sloppy clothes, the loosened tie. Comprised of desperate hope, media hype, and genuine ideological affiliation, the Kennedy phenomenon of spring 1968 showed that people could forgive and forget in politics.

If Kennedy was the contemporary man, he was in many ways quite at odds with the temper of his times. He was the one devout Catholic among the Kennedy sons. In the midst of the sexual revolution, he was prudish. Of the Kennedy siblings, he was the most introspective, brooding, pessimistic, and volatile. In an age of demagoguery and political exhibitionism, he was shy. He was the most committed to family, the most dutiful son, and it took Robert Kennedy longer than his brothers to escape the shadow of his father. His childhood was gloomy as a result. Pushed hard to win—not just succeed—against the children of the WASP elite he confronted throughout prep school and, later, at Harvard, he may have felt that the family honor was on his shoulders. He knew his father's judgment was on the line. At a time when the traditional family was becoming an object of scorn among the enlightened, regarded as the slavery of the reactionary Catholic Church, Robert was the father of ten children. (His eleventh child was born several months after his death.) Paul Dever, a political colleague of both brothers, perhaps said it best when he described Jack Kennedy as "the first Irish Brahmin. Bobby is the last Irish Puritan."

Perhaps on the theory that opposites attract, Kennedy's nature appealed to many people who were seeking security and change at the same time. But Kennedy's brief moment in the limelight might also suggest that the goals of progressive America—racial justice, economic leveling, and a rational foreign policy uppermost among them—did not necessarily depend on a revolution in mind and morals. To be progressive did not require casting off traditional values. On this account, Kennedy shared much with Martin Luther King, Jr., another traditionalist in morals who was a far greater threat to the status quo. Indeed, these deep personal moorings, rather than experience, allowed Kennedy to become a leader of promise. As most observers saw, he was moved not by abstract theory but by personal involvement. The sight of a young child with her face badly bitten by rats did not move him to propose bureaucratic solutions, which might guarantee news coverage and legislative acclaim; instead, his answer was to organize an experimental housing project, with the cooperation of local foundations and Republicans alike, that gave residents control over the functions of their environment. This was not the working of the existentialist new man but the reaction of a patrician with deeply bred morals.

His campaign, in contrast to the image that he gained within the New Politics, was moderate in tone and tailored to his audience. He used his background as attorney general to emphasize his commitment to law and order. On

Vietnam, he called for negotiations leading to a coalition government in the South, which was a much less drastic proposal than the unilateral withdrawal that the antiwar movement was then demanding; and he was far less critical than McCarthy of the Cold War security state. On domestic issues he emphasized his commitment to civil rights and social reform, although he was vague on specifics. He spoke consistently about enfranchising the dispossessed, and he hardly left out any group—ghetto blacks, Hispanics, Indians, children, the other America. "I think there has to be a new kind of coalition to keep the Democratic Party going," he explained to Newfield. "We have to write off the unions and the South now, and replace them with Negroes, blue-collar whites, and the kids." "Poverty," he concluded, "is closer to the root of the problem than color," which in turn recommended a strategy that showed "the Negroes and the poor whites that they have common interests."

McCarthy and Kennedy battled through the primaries, together showing again and again how little voter support there was for the administration's candidate, Vice President Hubert Humphrey. When Kennedy edged McCarthy in the California primary, he won a major victory that potentially could have provided the momentum to move, as he said the night of the victory, "on to Chicago." A moment later he became another victim of political assassination in the United States in the sixties, the second Kennedy, the second idealist in three months. Kennedy's death took the breath out of liberal America.

Whether Kennedy could have taken the nomination and then gone on to the presidency, however, was problematic even with the California win. While he and McCarthy fought one another, Humphrey was stealthily picking up delegates where they really counted, not in primaries but in state caucuses. Humphrey was the candidate of the party regulars and was working his strong suit among insiders. Kennedy could have had the nomination only if he could have enticed a large defection from the Humphrey camp at Chicago. But what is beyond question is that Kennedy alone could have saved the Democrats from disaster. McCarthy's appeal was only to the antiwar liberals and did not even reach to the antiwar left; Humphrey appealed only to the traditional labor-establishment wing of the party. Only Kennedy, in search of that "new coalition" built on the old common bonds of economic grievance, stood the chance of maintaining any semblance of unity. No doubt he would have lost some support on both edges. But as his body lay in Manhattan's St. Patrick's Cathedral, the mourners who straggled in included Richard Daley, the intransigent Chicago mayor, and Tom Hayden, the longtime leader of the New Left, both Catholics, both weeping in private grief.

Chicago

Chicago thereafter was Humphrey's convention—or more accurately, Johnson's. McCarthy controlled some delegates but had no chance at the nomination; nor could he even demand his way on any of the planks, including the vital one on Vietnam. All he could do was be the gracious loser, but he did not do even that. Humphrey, for his part, was "boxed in," as he put it. He had spent a career as a loyal, liberal Democrat, but as vice president he was committed to toeing the party line as Lyndon Johnson set it down. On the all-important question of Vietnam, Humphrey was forced to regurgitate the message of war. On domestic issues, Humphrey was stuck with a gutted social agenda and reduced to a catalogue of liberal pieties. He was a candidate carrying Lyndon Johnson's failures without Lyndon Johnson's considerable political abilities. "He's a lousy candidate," Mayor Daley supposedly remarked. "If we're going to have another Lyndon Johnson, let's have the real thing."

Nearly every account of the Chicago convention alludes to the air of confrontation that clung to the city as the Democrats gathered to assault one another and as hippies, radicals, antiwar protesters, and street toughs gathered to do battle with Daley's police. What went on in the streets made for terrifying television; what went on in the convention was of far more lasting importance. Johnson expected to orchestrate the proceedings from afar, but while the great cowboy's hand was obviously in everything, the reality was that the party was too badly divided for Humphrey to canter smoothly through. On the one hand, labor, conservative civil rights groups, party regulars, and southerners aligned behind Humphrey; on the other, the antiwar forces, the intellectuals, the "young people," progressives committed to change for its own sake, and a smattering of Kennedy people aligned not so much behind McCarthy as against the Old Democrats.

Two issues, the plank on Vietnam and a credentials fight, marked the fault line. McCarthy expected to wield strong influence on Vietnam and had prepared a compromise plank, one quite agreeable to Humphrey, that promised an unconditional bombing halt. But Johnson balked at compromise and, much to Humphrey's dismay, had his forces ram through a platform that included a party-line defense of the war. That platform brought Humphrey the nomination, as regulars and conservative southerners pledged their delegations. But to many it seemed that Humphrey had finally sold his soul. To the advocates of the New Politics, Humphrey's nomination showed that the system was rigged, and they decided to fight over the process of delegate selection, not so much to win, but half out of spite and half out of a decision to call attention to the encrusted nature of the party. Vietnam was the symbolic issue, and both sides considered it the definitive plank. The credentials fight, however, drew from the radicals' challenge to southern delegations in 1964 and set the stage for the ultimate success of the New Politics in 1972, when the credentials procedure was reformed.

Whatever else it was, the Chicago convention, in purely party terms, was the pivotal point between the New Deal Democratic party and the New Politics Democracy. In the short term, Humphrey's victory coincided with the state of public opinion at large. New Politics liberals were not held highly in public esteem, and the Chicago disaster reinforced the public's fear that political radicalism and a breakdown in law and order were related. A mere 14 percent of poll respondents sympathized with convention demonstrators, while 66 percent supported Daley's use of police force against them. Yet Humphrey needed party unity, and even though many progressive voters, in the end, cast their ballots his way, he probably put off so many young people that he lost crucial votes.

Humphrey's convention difficulties, moreover, remained with him into the race itself. He began well behind Nixon in the polls—behind even George Wallace, the third-party spoiler, in some polls. Johnson continued to pull the strings, especially on Vietnam, preventing Humphrey from taking an independent stand. Indeed, Nixon, whom the press credited with having "a secret plan to end the war," was more the "dove" during the election than Humphrey.

In late October, after having kept Nixon abreast of movements in negotiations with the North Vietnamese, Johnson prepared to call a bombing halt and free up Humphrey to make last-minute appeals to the doves. Through a private emissary Nixon moved to convince South Vietnamese President Thieu to wait until after the American elections before going to the peace table, and then he broke his silence on Vietnam, claiming that he fully supported the bombing halt; he then accused Johnson of playing politics with the war. All he could do beyond that was ride out the pro-Humphrey surge that followed. "The bombing halt . . . undercut one of my most effective campaign issues," he wrote in his memoirs, "the inability of the Democratic leadership to win a permanent peace." The race ended much closer than it had appeared only a few weeks before, but Nixon still prevailed. As in 1960, it was extremely close, with Nixon taking 43.4 percent of the popular vote, Humphrey 42.7 percent, and Wallace 13.5 percent. Nixon won by only a half-million votes, 2 million fewer than he had in 1960 when he lost to John Kennedy.

The New Politics and Beyond

The New Deal coalition forged in 1932 finally dissolved in Humphrey's 1968 defeat. The party machines, organized labor, the white working class, and the southern conservatives broke apart or away from the party; the New Politics, comprised of constituencies that nursed grievances and therefore were energetic and outspoken—left-leaning civil rights advocates, mainstream women's organizations, the academic remnants of the university revolts, and by 1972 gay liberationists and environmentalists—stepped into the vacuum.

The groups that made up the New Deal coalition could never have united with the groups of the New Politics, so very different were they in goals and temperament. The southerners wanted no part of a politics that included unquestioning commitments to civil rights. Nor were working-class whites particularly eager to support such a coalition, for much of what the New Politics advocated came at their expense, from school busing to higher taxes for social programs. Organized labor rightly believed that the New Politics wanted to bring down the cigar-smoking labor bureaucrat and replace him with leaders like Cesar Chavez, the charismatic, Mexican-American leader of the United Farm Workers of America. Indeed, the clash between the New and the Old played itself out within the labor movement. Whereas labor reached the height of its political clout in the early sixties, after 1968 the movement was beset by internal insurgencies from young white workers who fought against the "alienation" of production-line work and black workers, particularly in the auto industry, who organized renegade groups to demand redress of racial grievances.

Women in the New Politics

The women's movement, meanwhile, presented perhaps the best chance for uniting the New Politics with some semblance of the moderate interest-group liberalism of the recent past, especially because by 1970 the civil rights movement had gone into steep decline. The women's movement had begun to establish momentum, and its foremost legislative goal, the passage of the Equal Rights Amendment, was not yet achieved. The movement continued to attract a wide variety of women, from old-fashioned housewives to political pros, abortion-rights activists, and radical lesbians. Yet the movement also faced internal problems that were similar to those that beset both the civil rights movement and the student left. The unity of the movement was fairly shallow and was maintained mostly by a skittish refusal among activists to criticize one another; in the late days of the sixties, that sort of decorum could not hold for long.

The first breaches in the movement appeared in August 1970. Betty Friedan, Kate Millett, Gloria Steinem, and other leading feminists, under the auspices of NOW, called a national women's strike as a prelude to putting together a broad-based forum of women, the National Women's Political Caucus. Friedan hoped that the Caucus might bring together "all political elements, from young and black and radical to white-haired Midwestern Republicans" and set the tone for an ERA drive. Friedan had in mind "a larger, broader political force than the constituency of the Old or New Left." But in fact the National Caucus effort offered an opportunity for competing groups of women to jockey for control: Friedan hoped to sustain an independent political voice for women; Steinem and New York congresswoman Bella Abzug sought to limit their coalition to New Politics groups in order to exert strong pressure in the 1972 Democratic convention; and radicals attempted to turn the Caucus into a referendum on sexual liberation. Friedan was stunned that any "calculating manipulation" would emerge among sisters. In much the same way that mainstream civil rights leaders rebuked radical black nationalists in mid-decade, so Friedan criticized the "female chauvinism" of radicals as "highly dangerous and diversionary." Bra-burning, wholesale renunciations of men, and strident lesbianism, she maintained, amounted to "navel-gazing and consciousness-raising that doesn't go anywhere."

The movement did manage to hang together on the ERA, which passed Congress in spring 1972. The amendment failed to gain passage in the states, however, in part because it faced a countermovement that included conservative women organized in Phyllis Schlafly's Eagle Forum. But ERA also exposed even more rifts among women, in this case along class lines. Indeed, ERA focused the class dimensions of women's issues because it would have led to the dismantling of long-standing protection for women in certain industries. The amendment's supporters argued that women did not need special legislation and that in any case equal rights was the more important achievement. But that brought little comfort to those women who enjoyed the benefits of protective legislation, and many union women spoke out against the amendment during the ERA congressional hearings. Partly in recognition of the class-based nature of feminism, movement leaders made consistent efforts to bridge class differences and connect the need to reform how work was done with issues of equal pay, sexual harassment and abuse, and domestic issues such as child care. NOW, after all, was linked with the United Auto Workers from the beginning—its original offices were in a union building—and the AFL-CIO eventually came around in support of the ERA.

Still, liberal women in the New Politics had the same difficulty relating to working-class women as their male counterparts had in relating to the proverbial beer-drinking line worker. If we can take as representative the sensibilities of Helen, a Boston maid whom the humanist scholars Robert and Jane Hollowell Coles interviewed, we can conclude that the gulf of class was bridged at some points and left gaping at others. Helen was a Catholic from working-class Somerville, a "loyal American" by her own assessment, and the mother of a son killed in the "necessary" war in Vietnam. Helen worked for a prominent Cambridge family steeped in New Politics liberalism and committed to all the right causes: women's liberation, racial justice, anticolonial movements in the Third World, antipoverty.

"The missus" worked in "public relations" and was "liberated," but at the cost of having Helen work longer and at more menial tasks than Helen had before in her earlier jobs. The missus was liberated, it seems, only by making impositions on another woman. "My husband thinks she's crazy, and so do I," Helen explained. "If I had money, I'd quit this job, and go home and stay home for a thousand years. . . . The missus . . . says women are in danger of 'stagnating.' Maybe in her dictionary I'm not a woman." Having drawn the class lines taut, Helen had to admit that there were moments of woman-to-woman sympathy. But those flashes of sympathy were quick and tentative, repeatedly snuffed out by the reappearance of the more pressing realities of class. In one incident, "the missus" broke down in tears after a distressing fight with her equally liberal husband, who was not "liberal" enough to work around the house. She leaned on Helen for sympathy, only to revert to form: "She asked me whether I'd work if I didn't need the money. I told her no, I wouldn't. She said I'd change my mind once I was at home all day, sitting and waiting for people to come back from school and work." "The missus" forgot that Helen did just that—except Helen waited for "the missus's" children instead of her own. The family would go on worrying about Africa, Latin America, and the right-wing fascists who opposed liberalism. Meanwhile, Helen was concerned with more immediate issues: "I think the missus is right: everyone should be equal. . . . [But] she doesn't want to be equal with me. . . . She's not going to 'liberate' [me] anymore than the men are going to 'liberate' their wives or their secretaries or the other women working in their companies."

The Election of 1972

Such tensions between class differences and the commonalities of gender—and of race—had hastened the collapse of the New Deal coalition. But, as George Mc-Govern's ill-fated 1972 presidential campaign showed, the same tensions made the

New Politics coalition inherently rickety. Like Eugene McCarthy, McGovern was an academic from the upper Midwest who emerged as a leading dove among congressional Democrats during the Johnson years. In contrast to McCarthy, however, McGovern ran a savvy campaign for the nomination. He never was the favorite among the Democrats. That position belonged to the moderate Edmund Muskie from Maine, and McGovern occupied the lower reaches of most polls along with Scoop Jackson, the hawk from Washington, and Humphrey. But Muskie proved an ineffective campaigner and was the victim of dirty tricks pulled by the Nixon campaign. Muskie's deeper problem was that a moderate campaign might have won the nomination in 1968 but not in 1972, after four more years of polarization within the party and the electorate at large. Indeed, the old Alabama demagogue, George Wallace, made substantial showings in the early Democratic primaries before being shot in Florida and forced from the race. This time around, the New Politics liberals, having learned the tricks of the delegate game, hustled their way toward the nomination by racking up successes in the party caucuses rather than the primaries. McGovern ought to have known what he was doing; he chaired the party commission that had reformed the selection process after the 1968 convention. By exploiting the rules they wrote, the McGovern forces built a commanding lead heading to the convention.

As a candidate, meanwhile, McGovern was a committed dove who ran with every intention of putting Vietnam at the forefront of the election. His dovish preoccupation, however, made it difficult to establish a domestic agenda. He campaigned as a populist, the candidate of the average American running against the corporate elite's man, Richard Nixon. Hoping to cultivate a broad following, he promised a guaranteed subsidy to every family and tried to keep his attention on the widespread sense of "alienation," the one thing that seemed vague enough to gloss over the vast divisions between potential Democratic voters. That sense of disillusionment accounted for Wallace's strong showing, McGovern believed. Thus, while the other Democrats eagerly lambasted Wallace, McGovern avoided attacking the demagogue in hopes of attracting a traditionally Democratic blue-collar constituency.

McGovern was no Robert Kennedy, however, and his support came almost entirely from the New Politics. Anticipating such a possibility, his campaign staff aimed to solidify a coalition of youth (especially now that 18 year olds were preparing to vote for the first time), minority groups, women, and the various antiwar constituencies. McGovern campaign manager Gary Hart described it as a "movement already in progress, . . . an insurgency campaign outside the regular structure" of the party, and it was that with a vengeance.

When they gathered at the convention in Miami Beach, the McGovern forces were prepared to oust the New Deal coalition once and for all. None of the Iowa delegates was a farmer; the New York delegation had nine gay liberationists but only three labor representatives. In revenge for 1968, the New Politics liberals dumped Richard Daley's Illinois delegation in a bitter fight and replaced it with a delegation, led by Jesse Jackson, that ignored Chicago's potent white ethnic voters. As Chicago's favorite populist wit, Mike Royko wrote, "anybody who would reform

Chicago's Democratic Party by dropping the white ethnic would probably begin a diet by shooting himself in the stomach." McGovern and his staff nonetheless congratulated themselves, as Gary Hart claimed, for having "vindicated the faith . . . in the ability of the people, citizens, individuals, to govern their own political affairs"—a "triumph of political reform."

"The people" bore no relation to the majority of Americans. Reality sank in once the campaign began, and it became clear to everyone but McGovern that "the people" were not so interested in voting for him. McGovern's appeal to alienation did not prevent many in organized labor from jumping to Nixon, and Nixon hardly needed to play the themes that he had been practicing since 1968 in order to collar ethnic, working-class votes. Law and order and opposition to forced busing were themes, to be sure, but Nixon was able to sound them in moderate tones, especially with Wallace out of the race. The result was a historic shellacking for the Democrats, with McGovern taking only Massachusetts and the District of Columbia, thus leaving control of the Democratic party in the hands of New Politics liberals and the majority of the electorate either in the Republican party or, more commonly, among the swelling ranks of independent voters. The New Politics liberals, meanwhile, emerged from 1972 not the least humbled. Instead, they remained well organized, highly motivated, and powerful enough to carve out a significant place in national political life. They also were inherently incapable of constituting an electoral majority; as a consequence, they were doomed to the role of a cantankerous opposition.

CHAPTER 2

The Civil Rights Movement

 In the course of fifteen years, the southern civil rights movement profoundly altered a large region of the nation, reshaped United States history, mobilized the country's most oppressed group, forced the nation to reckon with racism, its original sin, and exposed the great gap between national myth and promise on the one hand and reality on the other. Composed of common people organized in institutions of their own creation, it was a populist revolution that, by any historical comparison, scored enormous victories at a minimal cost in violence. As such, the civil rights movement transcended its historical place, but it also was the quintessential sixties movement. It demonstrated the heights to which ideals could move people. When the movement's idealism waned, so too did the nation's.

The New South and the Origins
of the Civil Rights Revolution

The system of race subordination in the South was at its heart a form of labor oppression, whereby rural planters controlled black labor by promoting a dual strategy of legal repression and social supremacy. Though obviously not limited to rural areas, segregation was the dominant characteristic of the South's rural, agricultural condition. When the South began to urbanize, the foundations of race subordination began to crack. Modernity came to the South only incompletely throughout the first half of the twentieth century, although cities grew and industries were established. Beginning with World War I, moreover, African Americans began to move north in search of factory work, thus inaugurating the "great migration" so important to the history of the sixties.

But the modern age lasted only several decades for the South, from the 1940s to the age of deindustrialization. During World War II, the South was permanently wrenched from its social torpor. Its men, both white and black, saw a wider world, and black men especially did not want to go back to the farm. Defense industries and military bases located in the South brought a strong federal presence. Defense work was stable, thanks to the Cold War, the pay and benefits were good, and as a result of pressure from civil rights leaders, governed by federal antidiscrimination laws. Mass-production industries eager to escape northern unions also moved south.

As the southern economy modernized, the region attracted national chain stores, white-collar industries such as insurance, and consumer industries, such as Coca-Cola in Atlanta. Finally, in the 1940s cotton growers perfected the mechanical cotton picker. Because it eliminated the demand for intensive, unskilled labor in the cotton fields, this was perhaps the most important development for the southern social system.

The mechanization of cotton production essentially eliminated the reason for segregation. In its aftermath the rural South was depopulated: nearly 3 million blacks moved north between 1940 and 1960, and hundreds of thousands more moved into southern cities in one of the largest peacetime population migrations in history. The anonymity of the cities, even under formal segregation, gave blacks the room they needed to develop institutions and communities of their own. Work at mass-production factories provided a measure of economic independence that was impossible in the rural South or the small towns. Economic independence, in turn, created the opportunities to demand political rights. The influx of national capital into southern cities threatened the local power of race supremacy because national business did not have a stake in the southern way of life. Corporations may not have wanted to shake the system, but their interests lay in having as many customers and potential workers as possible—white or black. Similarly, white-collar professionals who either moved south or were natives had no deep stake in an antiquated social system, one that was quite ugly, often unstable, and, as southerners began to discover, unnecessary to maintaining race and class privilege. White southerners discovered that they could do what white northerners did: move to the suburbs.

As these changes filtered through southern society, new interpretations of constitutional law contributed more decisively to change. Legislation prohibiting discrimination in federal hiring, the prohibition on race-restrictive covenants in real estate, the desegregation of the armed forces, and other rulings in the 1940s were all important and set precedents for further federal legislation and court rulings. Then, in 1954, after years of litigation by the National Association for the Advancement of Colored People (NAACP), the Supreme Court struck down the long-standing separate-but-equal doctrine in the landmark *Brown v. Board of Education*, which declared segregation in public schools unconstitutional and which applied to all other forms of public segregation as well.

Industrialization, urbanization, and legal developments created the general social conditions out of which the civil rights movement grew. But the movement arose far more immediately within African-American communities that were themselves products of segregation. The paradox of the South's system of race subordination was that blacks had to construct their own institutions and maintain their own culture through which they built a qualified autonomy. Without question, African-American communities were materially inferior to the dominant white society; but under the dominating power of whites, blacks taught their own children, maintained their own churches, and even, in cities like Atlanta, had their own banks and department stores. Southern blacks, meanwhile, comprised the most substantial and distinct subculture in the United States, encompassing a mix of rural, southern, and African folkways that could hardly have been more different from the emerging mass culture. Although mass culture was penetrating their community through television, movies, and contact with relatives who had gone north, black southerners were less corrupted by the homogenizing power of cultural blandness than any other group of people, and their isolation was a strength.

We would miss the dynamics at work if we were to regard the foot soldiers of the civil rights revolution as terrorized and dehumanized people who finally had enough. It would be better to understand them as having defied forces that attempted to grind them down. They were the Selma school teachers, who ignited the 1965 local marches for voter registration; or they were the countless versions of Rosa Parks, the genteel Montgomery seamstress who began the bus boycott of 1955; or they were the hundreds of citizens of Greensboro who raised their children with the determined self-respect they needed to sit in at the Woolworth's lunch counter in 1961; or they were the cab drivers, factory workers, domestic servants, and janitors who lived in communities that were dependent but autonomous and that provided the cultural foundations necessary for people to make a revolution. Beginning in 1955, these were the common folk who destroyed white supremacy, revived American liberalism, and inspired the world.

In December 1955, one of those common folk, Rosa Parks, a local seamstress and secretary of Montgomery's NAACP branch, refused to move to the back of the bus as the law insisted and was arrested. Parks's arrest brought the segregated public transit system into the courts where it could be challenged on the basis of the recent Supreme Court rulings. Not content to leave the matter to the courts, Montgomery's black community rose up in a massive, largely spontaneous, bus boycott. Blacks made up the overwhelming majority of riders, and the boycott won overwhelming support in their community, so that day after day Montgomery buses rolled empty while people walked to and from work. Local authorities prodded, harassed, threatened, and defied the boycotters but were defeated after a fight of more than a year, when the Supreme Court ruled Montgomery's segregated public transportation unconstitutional.

The Montgomery bus boycott marked the beginning of a powerful grassroots movement. It was the first time an entire community had rallied against segregation and the first time the national media paid much attention to racial strife in the South. Centered around the churches, the boycott had a large following around an institutional core and found a natural leadership in the local ministers. It also marked the emergence of a charismatic young preacher, Martin Luther King, Jr., as a civil rights spokesman and leader of the movement's main organization, the Southern Christian Leadership Conference (SCLC).

A mere twenty-six years old and fresh out of Boston University graduate school, Martin Luther King, Jr., was fated to lead the movement, for he embodied the dual nature of the community that he served. Born and raised in Atlanta, he never suffered the harshest treatment that segregation had to offer. Rather, he grew up in one of the nation's largest and strongest African-American communities, in the home of one of the city's most prominent black ministers. Nurtured through the black schools, he dreamed of becoming a philosopher, although his father pushed him toward the ministry. As part of a compromise, he went north to Crozier Seminary in eastern Pennsylvania and then on to graduate school at Boston University. He was still thinking about a university career when his father convinced him to take the pulpit of Dexter Avenue Baptist in Montgomery. By going to Montgomery, he returned to his roots with a Ph.D. from an illustrious program at a major northern university steeped in the major theological doctrines of his day and well schooled in Western philosophy. In this way, he personified the aspirations of his community for equality and achievement. At the same time, he was a southern Baptist preacher, and no amount of fancified education could take him out of that cultural background. So his father knew best. The younger King blended the spirit of the preacher with the thoughtful, reasoned analysis of the scholar, but he was temperamentally unsuited for a scholarly career. He was a preacher by nature, like it or not.

Yet in the years from 1955 to 1960, the bus boycott seemed to be a single victory, almost an aberration. White southerners mounted their own organized effort in defense of segregation. Known as "massive resistance," the segregationist reaction was an outright defiance of federal law. School districts shut down rather than comply with *Brown*, and public facilities were closed down rather than be desegregated. Local and regional elites banded together in White Citizens Councils, dedicated to the organized political defense of segregation; and politicians responded by falling over one another in defense of "states' rights" and the "southern way of life." Some politicians, like Alabama's George Wallace, discovered that moderation on the race issue cost them at the polls in the mid-1950s. Thus Wallace, for one, vowed never to be "outniggered."

Massive resistance set up a confrontation between the federal government and the southern states, and the clash came in Little Rock, Arkansas, in 1957. Never really a bastion of segregation, Little Rock slowly had set about to comply with federal court orders to desegregate city schools. During the process, massive resistance swept into the city, and plans were manipulated to ensure desegregation's failure by centering on Central High, a large inner-city school already burdened with a combustible mixture of white students. Responding to public outcries, Governor Orval Faubus, who was up for reelection, called out the National Guard to prevent black students from attending Central and in so doing registered a direct denial of federal power. Only such a constitutional provocation could have forced a reluctant President Eisenhower to enter the civil rights fray. In Little Rock he had no choice but to act, and he did so with a decisive show of force, using 1,000 troops of the 101st Airborne to protect Central High's new black students.

Martin Luther King, Jr., and the First Wave of Revolution

The intervention in Little Rock was a lone exception rather than the rule during the late fifties, and the five years that followed the Montgomery bus boycott saw little tangible progress in civil rights. School desegregation moved with all deliberate slowness; by 1960 only 6 percent of southern schools had begun to desegregate, and only 1 percent of black children in the South went to integrated schools. The 1957 Civil Rights Act included a measure ensuring that violators be tried before local juries—a measure John Kennedy supported—which amounted in practice to a guarantee that white southerners could violate the law without fear of conviction. Massive resistance heightened the southern political commitment to segregation and widened the assault on the Constitution, as when Alabama banned the NAACP. As a result, organizational problems plagued the movement. SCLC leaders were learning how to be administrators on the job. Ella Baker, the administrative head of SCLC, had difficulty earning the respect of male preachers who were both egotists and chauvinists. Years of legal harassment had drained the SCLC and NAACP so badly that the movement could not afford a voting registration drive that organizers planned after the 1957 civil rights bill passed. Competition between organizations prevented complete unity. Almost as if to punctuate these troubles, a deranged woman stabbed King while he was signing copies of his book, *Stride Toward Freedom*, in New York in September 1958.

By 1960 the presidential campaign preoccupied the leadership of SCLC and NAACP. The African-American vote was by no means automatically Democratic in these years, and the movement's leaders wisely played the parties against each other, though neither party had much to offer. Before the famous phone call to Coretta King, John F. Kennedy seemed as much a foe as a friend, and whatever the nominee's inclinations, the Democrats still were the party of the Southern Bourbons. On the other side, the Republicans had advanced civil rights legislation in 1956, 1957, and again in 1960, but their too-obvious motive was to split the Democrats rather than advance the cause. Richard Nixon, the Republican candidate, had a relatively respectable record on civil rights but, like Kennedy, tried to appeal to civil rights leaders without alienating southerners.

Nonviolent Social Protest

Because mainstream politicians could not be expected to effect change, the movement had to force the issue. Yet in 1960 it was not clear what might spark public protest. Part of the problem lay in the nature of King's methods of protest. He employed nonviolent confrontation, a form of social protest drawn from Henry David Thoreau, the nineteenth-century American writer, and most effectively employed by Mahatma Ghandi, the twentieth-century leader of the independence movement in India. In theory, nonviolent confrontation allowed a weak group to confront much greater power and therefore recommended itself as a tactic in the South where the movement stood to lose in any violent clash with white authorities. Most important, however, the tactic also brought the movement sympathy. Especially in a news-drenched society, the sight of peaceful protesters confronting armed policemen or thugs, accepting blows without retaliating, was a powerful way to gain attention, and nothing worked better to solidify political coalitions or create pressure on Washington. There was also an element of hope in King's view of nonviolence. By provoking violence from the opponent, literally by suffering physi-

**Civil rights leader and charismatic preacher Martin Luther King, Jr., symbol-
ized the hopes and dreams of many communities for equality and justice.**
[Leonard Freed/Magnum Photos]

cal attacks, King believed that protesters could soften the enemy's heart by appealing to his instinct for justice.

Nonviolent activism was important in other ways. In a society where a mere
glance at a white woman or the simple act of registering to vote could bring a
beating or death, personal survival depended on considerable self-discipline. Southern blacks traditionally had to learn the fine line between developing personal
dignity, on the one hand, and becoming "uppity," on the other. For some, especially
older people, the result was a haunting, pervasive, nagging fear. Nonviolent activism employed this culturally mandated self-discipline to cross the line of sanctioned
behavior. In recalling their participation in the heady events of the movement,
many participants remembered shedding the burdens of fear, so that the act of
protesting was itself liberating. Nonviolence, finally, was intensely moral. Not only
did it hold great appeal for the fervently Christian African-American communities,
but also its moral integrity transcended the regional or race-specific culture and tied
the movement to a wider Christian tradition. King himself rarely spoke of nonviolence in terms of its provincial appeal or of the movement's goals in terms of
African-American rights. He spoke of a universal morality, appealed to a general
sense of human justice, and envisioned a "beloved community" that knew no
barriers between people. King's movement was not about particular rights; its goal
was the moral redemption of the United States.

For all its strength, nonviolent activism did have its faults, too. For one thing, not everyone involved or interested in the movement accepted the reasoning behind nonviolence. The tactic demanded mass mobilization, a slow, inexact form of protest. People typically sacrificed only for specific reasons at specific times. If King and the SCLC hoped to allow people to organize on their own, they would also have to wait for events to drive people to activism, and the movement lived and died as local issues came and went. In moments of inactivity, the movement produced little or no energy and therefore no mass mobilization.

The Sit-Ins

At the very moment when the movement appeared to be in a swoon, people were organizing quietly and persistently at the local level. Sporadic protests, only loosely affiliated with the national movement, continued to erupt through these otherwise dark years in many southern communities. It was just one local protest, grown out of the strength of a tightly knit community, that reignited the entire movement. In February 1960 a handful of black students from North Carolina A&T staged a sit-in protest at the lunch counter of the Greensboro, North Carolina, Woolworth's store. Denied service, they launched a campaign that by the end of the week had some 1,600 students spreading the protests to other downtown stores. City authorities predictably tried to preserve the status quo, and it took six months of protest—and a one-third drop in profits at the targeted stores—before they agreed to desegregated counters. The Greensboro protests were not so spontaneous as they appeared. The students who initiated and led the sit-ins had been raised within a community that had a long tradition of resistance to segregation and many institutions that encouraged self-determination—a strong NAACP branch, local black colleges, and influential churches.

Although the sit-ins grew out of the institutional heritage of local resistance to degradation, they sparked similar sit-ins across the upper South and the seaboard states. By the end of 1961, an estimated 70,000 people participated in over 100 nonviolent protests from Florida to Virginia, from Maryland to Arkansas. They met sporadic but frequent violence from police, the Ku Klux Klan, and other thugs, and aroused consistent opposition from local politicians and business leaders. In Nashville, they were assaulted by gangs; in Orangeburg, South Carolina, they tasted tear gas; in Jacksonville, they were pistol-whipped. Yet they succeeded in their most important efforts, especially in a difficult campaign in Atlanta, the capital of the "New South." The movement was desperately in need of a tonic, and the sit-ins provided it.

The larger power of the sit-ins, meanwhile, lay in their youthful character. In a nation increasingly preoccupied with the behavior of youth, the protesters offered a twist on the popular image of young rebels: they certainly were rebels, but theirs was a true rebellion, aimed not at upsetting the older generation but at transforming the United States. Their goal was redemption, not destruction. Even conservative institutions such as the *Richmond News Leader* complimented "the colored students, in coats, white shirts, ties" who stood their ground to the "white boys [who had] come to heckle, a ragtail rabble, slack jawed, black-jacketed, grinning fit to kill." Many young people were attracted to the movement for the same reason that had attracted a serious, soft-spoken math teacher from Harlem, Bob Moses: "They were kids my own age, and I knew this had something to do with my life."

As Moses sensed, this generation of young African Americans shared a set of unique experiences. As high school students, they awaited the integration that was supposed to accompany the *Brown* decision; they never saw it. At the same time, they watched the emergence of African independence movements; in 1960 alone, twelve new nation-states emerged in Africa. The point was not lost on them. Like their white cohorts, these young African Americans were attending college in greater numbers than ever before, thereby giving testimony to both the aspirations of and improvements in their communities. They had been inspired by Martin Luther King and, initially at least, were devoted to him. The heightened expectations of a generation spurred many to join the movement and delivered the one quality that had been missing since the Montgomery boycott, impatience. As King said throughout his life, nonviolence was not the same as passive acceptance or even patient negotiating. By design, it was intended to be confrontational and, if necessary, to provoke violence from the opposition. It had to be impatient, and that quality the students had in abundance.

The Student Non-Violent Coordinating Committee

The mainstream organizations needed the students and were quick to help them. James Farmer, head of the Congress for Racial Equality (CORE), instructed protesters in nonviolent methods, and King was arrested with the Atlanta protesters, thus setting the stage for the Kennedy phone call at the end of the presidential campaign. King's SCLC encouraged the students to convene their own organization, the Student Non-Violent Coordinating Committee (SNCC), in April 1960 and offered them the talented guidance of Ella Baker, the determined, one-time administrative head of SCLC. Dedicated at the outset to nonviolence, SNCC was an example of King's desire to see others develop their own institutions, and he welcomed the students to the center of the historical stage. "What is fresh, what is new in your fight," he told them, "is the fact that it was initiated, led, and sustained by students. You now take your honored places in the world-wide struggle for freedom."

King christened the most energetic but also the most controversial organization within the movement. SNCC brought students into a group that was so thoroughly democratic that it hardly could be called an organization. Its "spiritual father," James Lawson, warned the students against any kind of hierarchy, even to avoid elections, and to allow leadership to pass from volunteer to volunteer. Although the students built some structure, SNCC mostly thrived on shared ideals and, eventually, on an intimacy bred of danger and crisis. SNCC students also insisted on their independence from the mainstream groups. As much as they owed King, the students increasingly saw him as the sort of "hero" who undermined true democracy. The students stepped to the working motto: "Go where the spirit say go. Do what the spirit say do."

The Freedom Rides

The first great episode of activism after the sit-ins began in the spring of 1961, when Farmer of CORE, in cooperation with SNCC's contingent at Nashville's Fisk University, laid plans to tackle segregation in interstate travel by taking buses into the Deep South. Earlier in the year, the U.S. Supreme Court had applied previous rulings against segregated travel to bus and train terminals, as well as airports, but there had been little compliance. Farmer, a hulking man involved with some of the earliest Ghandians in the United States, had recently been appointed to head CORE. He was itching, he said, "to embrace these masses of willing revolutionaries" and lead them into the heart of the black belt. "Our intention," Farmer recalled, "was to provoke the southern authorities into arresting us and thereby prod the Justice Department into enforcing the law of the land."

On May 4, an interracial group of thirteen riders—seven blacks, six whites—embarked from Washington, with the group split between a Greyhound bus and a Trailways. As they moved through the seaboard states, shifting seats as they went, disembarking at various stops, and ignoring the "colored only" and "whites only" signs in the terminals, they encountered little more than nasty looks and a pushing match, broken up by police, in South Carolina. In Atlanta, they dined with Dr. King, who praised them and sent them on their way, at the same time warning an accompanying reporter for *Jet* magazine that "you will never make it through Alabama."

King was nearly correct. The riders ran into serious trouble in Anniston, Alabama, just across the state line. A mob met the Greyhound at the terminal, and the driver could not back out before someone slashed several tires. Not long out of Anniston, the tires lost air, and the bus pulled over. When it did, the pursuing mob firebombed the bus. The riders pushed their way off behind a frantic state agent who was riding undercover. Outside, the mob fell upon them until state troopers arrived to drag the riders back to an Anniston hospital. All that was left was the burning hulk of the bus, ably captured in a wire-service photograph and sent worldwide. When the Trailways bus pulled into Anniston, well behind the Greyhound, a handful of local toughs boarded and assaulted the riders, including Walter Bergman, a 61-year-old retired University of Michigan professor, whom they beat unconscious. Once the beatings stopped, the driver, who had stood by with local police during the assaults, sped on to Birmingham.

Alabama's largest city, Birmingham, was also its most racist and perhaps the nation's most racist. In anticipation of the Freedom Riders, the police agreed to allow the Ku Klux Klan fifteen minutes of uninterrupted violence. The "deal" was an open secret in town. The Trailways riders discovered it when they disembarked into a mob of Klansmen and others. Completely unrestrained, the mob attacked the riders with fists, pipes, and heavy key rings. Walter Bergman was attacked again. The attackers spilled outside, where they assaulted another rider as well as several reporters. Having used up their time, the Klan yielded to police. The riders, left to fend for themselves, straggled to the home or church of Fred Shuttlesworth, the town's leading activist. Battle-weary, they debated whether to go on to Montgomery. They had made headlines the day before, and the international publicity, as we have seen, caught the attention of Attorney General Robert Kennedy, setting off the sparring between the federal and state governments. Their scars, fears, and weariness got the best of them, and they accepted Kennedy's offer to fly to New Orleans.

Just as the battered group gathered at the airport, the Nashville students, prodded by the relentless Diane Nash, one of the leaders of the Fisk contingent, decided to send another group to Birmingham. "If they stop us with violence, the movement is dead," Nash told Shuttlesworth. The students kept the pressure on both federal and Alabama authorities by pressing toward Montgomery, but they remained caught between the varying political needs of each. In Montgomery, they disembarked and began a press conference with the many reporters who joined them, only to discover that the terminal was deserted. Suddenly, a mob slithered from various hiding places and began a vicious riot. "People came out of nowhere," John Lewis recalled, "men, women, children, with baseball bats, clubs, chains—and there was no police official around." They tried to stay together; some were tossed and some jumped over a retaining wall to a parking lot below. The mob, estimated at over 1,000, chased some into nearby taxis. One rider had his leg broken, and another had his clothes set on fire. John Lewis and James Zwerg, the lone white male, were caught near the loading platform and set upon. Lewis was knocked unconscious when someone hit him with a crate; a state official then served him a court injunction for violating segregation laws. Zwerg was beaten brutally, his face bloodied, his teeth knocked in. Montgomery police, having seen fit to arrive, refused to call an ambulance for him.

In the face of such a breakdown of order, brought on by Governor Patterson's duplicity, President Kennedy had no choice but to send in federal marshalls. The next set of arrangements, which took the riders from Montgomery to Jackson, Mississippi, was considerably more secure. All the parties involved understood that the riders would be escorted to Jackson, where they would be arrested for violating state law. At least, it was understood, they would be protected. Once arrested in Mississippi, the riders were shifted between three different jails, including the Parchman penitentiary; they were routinely denied cigarettes, often beaten, and at one point lost their mattresses; some were tortured with electric cattle prods or had their handcuffed arms wrenched up over their heads.

The Freedom Rides were high drama that capitalized on the sit-in spirit and increased the momentum of the movement. Like the sit-ins, the rides inspired a wave of imitations, and within a year the entire South was traversed by groups testing terminals and succeeding. CORE's initial plan, as Farmer rather grandly stated it, was to "fill the jails of Mississippi" in order to make "segregationist practices so expensive and inconvenient as to become unfeasible." Throughout the summer, over 1,000 riders traveled through the South; more than 300 were arrested in Mississippi alone. They didn't fill the jails—"Southern cities and states have almost unlimited jail facilities," Farmer quipped—but they burdened municipalities, especially in Jackson. They also pressured the White House, for many riders were not just radical black students or representatives of white fringe groups. Rather, they were prominent northern liberals and well-known representatives of mainstream institutions from across the country. By summer's end, the attorney general coaxed the Interstate Commerce Commission into ruling that interstate carriers must not only obey Supreme Court edicts but must also post signs that promised services without regard to race.

The most important development for the future of the movement was the degree to which the rides strengthened the students. Whereas the sit-ins created youthful idealists, the Freedom Rides produced battle-scarred veterans who had tasted southern brutality at its worst. Particularly those who had engaged in both the sit-ins and the rides had every right to see themselves as leading activists. The riders, even more than the sit-in leaders, gained immediate prestige within the movement, and many of them, John Lewis, James Bevel, Diane Nash, and Stokely Carmichael to name the most obvious, became important leaders among students. In the process they grew more critical of the established movement, even to the point of self-righteousness. Having put their lives on the line, they began to expect everyone else to do so and were quick to accuse others of cowardice. The students were deeply disappointed, for example, when King refused to join them in the ride out of Montgomery. They were even contemptuous of James Farmer, the CORE leader, who did join them, but who appeared to be more committed to building his organization's image than to serving the cause itself.

The Rise of SNCC

Robert Kennedy came to SNCC, CORE, and SCLC with his plans for the Voter Education Project (VEP) in order to forestall just the sort of intensified activism that Freedom Ride veterans intended to maintain. Whatever the administration's motives, there was good cause to take Kennedy up on the VEP offer. First, it was a way to firm up the administration's relationship to the movement, which conceivably would entail greater federal protection. Moreover, as White House aide Harris Wofford pointed out, the administration promised money for projects that the movement had wanted to run since the midfifties. There was no reason for the organizations to refuse the money, especially if, as they believed, the federal government was willing to help.

To SNCC, however, VEP was a troubling proposition. They were attuned to the cynical side of Kennedy's motives and understood that he wanted the movement toned down. Some direct-action advocates rejected voter registration on the grounds that it was too tame. Against that argument, James Forman and others insisted that voter registration was the most aggressive form of activism. What sounded like a boring process of filling out registration forms was in fact deadly business. In small southern communities where everyone knew everyone else, it was easy to keep an eye on strangers or on locals who might put strangers up or, worse, get the idea that they were allowed to vote. Both the volunteer and the potential registrant put themselves in serious danger. At the very least, a sharecropper might reasonably expect to be evicted for registering, while a volunteer might reasonably expect to tangle with a plantation owner who feels, as one volunteer put it, "that he has the prerogative to shoot us on sight when we are in the house of one of his negroes." To Forman, a somewhat older Chicagoan who was SNCC director in 1961, VEP would be a strategic confrontation with "the wrath of southern racists" and strike against the fear that held the bulk of the black population in check.

The manner by which SNCC went about running VEP affirmed Forman's view. They considered themselves guerrillas whose job was to move into a community, learn its particular needs, and teach people how to stand up for themselves. To fit into the communities they served demanded sensitivity to local customs and conditions. Knowing that good guerrillas always identify with the people, they adopted the traditional dress of sharecroppers, bib overalls and t-shirts. Theoretically, when SNCC members moved on, they would leave behind viable, self-governing organizations of people who could work for their own interests in their own way.

The Albany Movement

Given their broad purpose, there was nothing to keep VEP workers from organizing and participating in other forms of direct action. In southwest Georgia, for instance, Charles Sherrod, Cordell Reagon, and a few others settled into a registration campaign in the counties around Albany, counties, as one SNCC member put it, so rural that there was not "even a hint of a town." The SNCC group dabbled in some direct action in those rural counties but directed their main activities to organizing in Albany, a sizable town with a complex, stratified black community. In November 1961 Sherrod and Reagon led a group of teenagers into Albany's bus station to test the new ICC ruling against discrimination. The youngsters meekly retreated before the police, but word spread that the children had stood up to the sheriff. The incident ignited a citywide movement that, though bound up initially with voter registration, put direct action to work for more than a year.

Albany became the widest single protest since the Montgomery bus boycott, eventually including King and SCLC. Unlike Montgomery, however, the Albany protest was a failure. Albany's police chief, Laurie Prichett, appeared to be the stereotypical, hulking, cigar-smoking sheriff. But by studying the mistakes of other cities, he concluded that he could frustrate nonviolent protest. He would arrest protesters but charge them for promoting civil disorder rather than for violating segregation laws, and above all, his officers would exercise maximum restraint. Prichett arrested plenty of people: 267 in one day alone. Since the town jail had room for only 30, the chief arranged to fill up the county jail, the county work farm, and the jails in the surrounding counties, threatening to put demonstrators in "jails all over Georgia." Albany's black community sent its people en masse; black maids went to jail under assumed names so they would not be fired; some participants went to jail several times; and those who did not supported them with food and visits.

Albany became a war of attrition, which favored the town authorities. People had jobs to keep and lives to lead, and the longer the city commission refused to negotiate anything, the more the energy dissipated. In an attempt to keep the spirit alive, Albany leaders appealed to King, who in mid-December participated in his first direct-action march, accepted his first arrest for engaging in a nonviolent demonstration, and had his first chance to turn down bail.

King's presence brought a flood of national media attention, but Prichett was prepared to ride that out as well. By keeping his men in check, the police chief prevented the sort of blood-spilling that kept the media swimming like sharks around a protest, and without sustained media attention there was no pressure on the Kennedys to intervene. Moreover, the town's leading citizen, James Gray, headed the state Democratic party and was a Kennedy friend. He was also a regional media mogul, and he wined and dined the visiting press corps, which obligingly reported on the "restraint" of the city fathers. Under pressure from Gray, the city authorities agreed to release most of the protesters, especially King, without bond, provided that King leave town and the marches stop. They did not give in to any substantive demands.

King left jail having accepted a compromise, and for that he was criticized. In July, he had the opportunity to redeem himself when he and Ralph Abernathy were convicted on the Albany charges. Both men went to jail, but the city's leaders, with the encouragement of Robert Kennedy, secretly paid the Abernathy–King fines. Determined not to be undone, King planned to march and be jailed again, but a federal judge, one of Kennedy's segregationist appointees, ordered him to avoid marching. King wanted to ignore the injunction, but Kennedy personally pressured him, arguing that denying a federal injunction struck against all of the good work that the federal courts were doing. When King relented, the march took place without him, and the marchers were arrested. In the process, the wife of one of the movement leaders was beaten in nearby Mitchell County while delivering food to some of the arrested marchers. The beating set off a riot, and Prichett seemed much more in command than did King. After the federal injunction was lifted by a higher court, King did march, was arrested, and won a promise that there would be no further arrests for violating segregation. What seemed like a hard-won victory was quickly turned into a large defeat, for the city, rather than accepting desegregation, simply shut down all of those public facilities that were objects of protests—the parks, the tennis courts, the library among them.

The Albany movement was a personal failure for King because he had put his own prestige on the line. Criticism came from all sides. The NAACP, worried about its slipping influence, not only refused to support the protests but actively worked to sabotage them. Segregationists claimed that King, the outsider, did not have the support of the local black community, and as painful as that was, it was partly true. The locals were split among themselves, and, as King's aide Andrew Young put it, some people believed that simply the "spontaneous appearance of Martin Luther King could bring change." King and his colleagues concluded that they were wrong to rush in as a favor to the local movement because in so doing they had risked their credibility.

To SNCC members, Albany had different results. For the community itself, the action was successful. "We showed the world," Charles Sherrod boasted. A more circumspect Donald Harris, taking a longer view, claimed that the protests destroyed the pervasive fear in the black community. "The black community can and does, as a community and as individuals, respect themselves more." Yet SNCC members considered Albany a personal failure for Martin Luther King. Some SNCC members thought he was too religious, too otherworldly to play hardball politics. To others, King was too caught up in his national image and was too materialistic—the man wore silk pajamas in the city jail after all. During Albany, some activists began to scorn him as "de lawd," a harsh tag that at once conveyed their contempt for King's view of himself and their resentment of his inherent prestige. They shot these stinging barbs in a face-to-face meeting in which King listened, agonizing, almost in tears. It is hard to think of any other leader of similar stature, in any other time or place, who would have put up with their criticism. And King did because at bottom he shared the SNCC view that people should run their own movement. Nevertheless, Albany pointed up the different missions that SNCC and SCLC had developed. SCLC had become a national organization whose success was measured by its power in national politics. For SNCC, the measure of success was at the grass roots. Albany, in any case, was a parting of the ways, with King and SCLC moving toward a more unified, coherent national strategy and SNCC toward greater radicalism.

Birmingham

For his part, King was well aware of the consequences of his failure in Albany, and he reasoned that he needed a dramatic victory elsewhere. Figuring rightly that the city fathers of Birmingham would be unable to copy Prichett's model of official restraint, SCLC targeted that notorious town for a confrontation. Since World War II an estimated fifty bombings had given the city its nickname, "Bombingham"; one of its klaverns was reputedly the most violent Klan group. Yet the New South was arriving even there, and the city's moderates were trying to edge Bull Connor, still chief of police, out of power. Where the moderates were wealthy and united, Connor's only appeal was to racism. The city's economy was increasingly obliged to northern capital, especially the steel industry. Most important, Birmingham's black community had been battling segregation since the midfifties and was led by Reverend Fred Shuttlesworth, whose flamboyance matched his loyalty to King. Shuttlesworth's people had desegregated the buses and the terminals only to reach an impasse, and they needed King as much as King needed Birmingham. "Birmingham is where it's at, gentlemen," Shuttlesworth told SCLC. "As Birmingham goes, so goes the nation."

SCLC opted for gradual escalation, first boycotting several downtown stores and then organizing ever larger street demonstrations. Unlike anything SCLC had done, the Birmingham plan was developed in minute detail. King was edgy anyway when, on April 2, 1963, he entered a city preoccupied with the mayoral election between a reform candidate and Connor. King's campaign was nearly undone from the beginning, when the moderate candidate, Albert Boutwell, beat Connor. Many black leaders wanted to give the new mayor a chance. "We didn't anticipate the need for Martin King at that time," one black business leader laconically recalled. King met a startling apathy, and SCLC, despite its tedious planning, could not recruit enough people willing to go to jail. And it was running out of bail money for those who had. Fearing that a disaster in Birmingham would destroy him, King marched against a court injunction and on April 13 was hustled into the Birmingham jail.

The national press was overwhelmingly critical of King's protests, and so too were local white clergymen, who accused him of inciting "hatred and violence." King responded to his critics in his famous jeremiad, "Letter from Birmingham Jail." Written in the margins of newspapers smuggled out of jail, King's essay became the defining document of the movement. Alternately conciliatory and unyielding, he took aim at the charge that the Birmingham protests were "unwise and untimely," a charge, he wrote, that he had heard many times before. "We know through painful experience that freedom is never voluntarily given by the oppressor. . . . But when you have seen vicious mobs lynch your mothers and fathers at will and drown your sisters and brothers at whim; when you have seen hate-filled policemen kick and even kill your black brothers and sisters; when you see the vast majority of your twenty million Negro brothers smothering in an airtight cage of poverty; . . . then you will understand why we find it difficult to wait."

Eloquent though it was, the "Letter from Birmingham Jail" aroused neither the media nor the Kennedy administration. When he bailed out several days later, King faced difficult decisions. Many people had gone to jail, but the authorities had been restrained, and it looked as if SCLC could not recruit enough people to make the protests work. James Bevel, a self-described "chicken-eating, liquor-drinking, woman-chasing Baptist preacher," offered what seemed the last best idea. Bevel had been running successful workshops for students from college down to elementary schools, and he argued that the young people should be used in marches. There was opposition among the protest leaders, but in the absence of alternatives, King bought Bevel's idea. On May 2, Bevel's troops, including children as young as 6 years old, walked into police lines and into jail, singing as they went. Nearly 1,000 marched that day, and some 600 went to jail. The next day, perhaps 1,000 more walked out of the Sixteenth Street Baptist Church. This time the authorities attacked with high-powered fire hoses capable of ripping the bark off trees at 100 feet and of rolling a person backward down a street. Angry onlookers heaved objects at firemen, while the marchers attempted to move in the opposite direction. They were headed off by snarling German shepherds leashed to equally menacing policemen. When the dogs plunged into the crowd, they created the dramatic and troubling pictures that came to symbolize Birmingham.

Now a renowned episode in the history of the movement, the "children's march" generated an outpouring of reaction, not all of which was favorable. On the one hand, the story played powerfully over the national news, especially on television, which revealed to national audiences the vicious attacks against the children.

On the other hand, King faced serious criticism for exposing children to such dangers. Robert Kennedy warned against this "dangerous business," and Birmingham authorities, with obvious hypocrisy, denounced the children's marches as exploitative. From the other extreme, Malcolm X, spokesman of the Nation of Islam and the leading voice for black separatism, scorned King's strategy: "Real men don't put their children on the firing line."

For King, none of these arguments mattered. The parents of the children, far from raising objections to the marches, were themselves streaming into the churches for mass meetings. King's career and his movement were at stake, and the children's marches proved, to use a Shuttlesworth term, a "spectacularism." After years of organizational difficulties, many political compromises, and a great deal of personal anguish, King found nourishment in the unity and energy that the children generated. For once, little that happened in the larger world mattered. King's movement touched the nation more powerfully than when, as in Albany, he had been most determined to affect the nation's mood. President Kennedy explained the next morning that the pictures of the dog attacks "made him sick," and he dispatched Burke Marshall to Birmingham to mediate negotiations. This time, King negotiated from strength. SCLC aimed its demands—an immediate end to segregation and to discrimination in hiring—at the business elite, the town's much-ballyhooed reformers. The boycotts were hurting business, and the new image of Birmingham as a progressive city was at risk. Marshall's arrival itself indicated that the White House was feeling the pressure. Movement leaders raised the pressure by flooding the downtown business districts with thousands of marchers, frightening off white shoppers and increasing the boycott's effectiveness.

On May 7, the two sides settled an agreement that ended segregation in Birmingham. SCLC conceded only the demand for immediate action. The plan to end segregation would proceed according to a timetable that worked first in store restrooms and moved through lunch counters and schools. There would also be safeguards against discrimination in hiring and a biracial mediation committee. The stickiest point concerned the disposition of those children still in jail. King wanted all charges dropped, a demand that the business leaders could not meet directly. At this point, the Kennedy administration entered and took responsibility for collecting the children's bail.

Unwilling to stand by the agreement that others had made, meanwhile, Bull Connor and Alabama Governor George Wallace conspired to destroy the accord: By unleashing their forces, they hoped to incite violence in the black community or force the federal government into an intervention that would embarrass the business leaders. Night riders bombed the home of King's brother, A. D. King, and the black-owned Gaston Hotel, which had served as movement headquarters. The bombings set off riots in the black neighborhoods. In the chaotic aftermath of the hotel bombing, Wallace's state troopers charged bystanders and rioters alike, ruthlessly beating anyone who could not escape. Worried that the tenuous agreement would collapse, President Kennedy, after receiving assurances from both King and the Birmingham business leaders that they stood by the accord, appeared on national television to announce, finally, his unequivocal support for civil rights. "Are we to say to the world," he asked, "that this is the land of the free, except for Negroes, that we have no second-class citizens, except Negroes, that we have no class or caste system, no ghettos, no master race, except with respect to Negroes?"

The death-knell of segregation having been sounded, the South erupted. Through the summer, nearly 200 communities engaged in nonviolent protests. Well aware that they no longer held the upper hand, embattled white supremacists lost whatever sense of restraint had bound them. SNCC volunteers in Mississippi began to feel the effect of Birmingham through increased violence aimed at voter registration drives. Medgar Evers, the head of the Mississippi NAACP, was assassinated in his front yard in June. In Danville, Virginia, authorities attacked protesters even more ruthlessly than in Birmingham, hospitalizing forty-eight of them. In the most appalling act of all, four young girls at worship were murdered when Birmingham's Sixteenth Avenue Baptist Church, the spiritual heart of the local movement, was bombed at the end of the summer.

The March on Washington

Called a failure the year before, King was hailed as a modern-day Moses in a national outpouring of support. Money flowed from Hollywood and New York; in Chicago, a gospel-blues benefit for SCLC netted $40,000 in one night. Though always hopeful that Kennedy would embrace the cause, King remained skeptical of Kennedy and therefore decided to maintain pressure with a national march on Washington.

As the moment for the march approached, official Washington braced for what many of the city's occupants were sure would be a huge race riot. Simply the thought of 100,000 blacks in one place unnerved many—only because so many of the town's power elite never noticed that hundreds of thousands of African Americans already lived in Washington. The city banned liquor sales. Local hospitals prepared, and 4,000 troops stationed in the area were put on the ready. Washington's ball club, the Senators, canceled two home games, and few fans complained. Conservative congressmen wrung their hands over the onrushing hordes, whom they believed were communist-led.

The march succeeded beyond the organizers' hopes. At least 250,000 marchers converged on the city and gathered at the Lincoln Memorial. It was an almost mystical event. The huge interracial throng listened to folk singers Joan Baez and Bob Dylan, wept to Mahalia Jackson, and heard a host of speeches—all in celebration of the moment. In the end, all were treated to Martin Luther King, Jr.'s finest moment, his "I Have a Dream" speech, which in terms of eloquence and power is arguably the finest American speech since the Gettysburg Address (and not much longer). King's sermon ended with the ad lib flourishes that made it famous: "Free at last! Free at last! Thank God, almighty, we are free at last!" King was at his best, placing civil rights not in the narrow context of region or race but in the most universal Christian tradition. His appeal to a general sense of justice might not have changed the hearts of racists, but it moved reasonable Americans. Even

President Kennedy, watching the proceedings on television, turned to his aides and remarked of King, "He's damn good."

As SCLC strategists hoped, the march produced enough momentum to push through the Civil Rights Act (1964) and the Voting Rights Act (1965). Both bills were passed, of course, after the Kennedy assassination. President Johnson used his legislative finesse to drive the bills through, in part by promising federal money for the home district of Senate Minority Leader Everett Dirkson (R–Ill.). The Civil Rights Act banned segregation in public accommodations, permitted the government to withhold funds to segregated public programs, outlawed discrimination in hiring, and promised financial help to communities undertaking the desegregation process. The Voting Rights Act came slightly later and after another series of protests, this time in Selma, Alabama, were put down with official violence and vigilante murders. The Voting Rights Act allowed the federal government to supervise voter registration in the South, increased federal power to bring suit against communities, and led to a stunning reenfranchisement. From 1964 to 1968, black registration in Mississippi rose from 6.7 to 59.4 percent and in Alabama from 23 to 53 percent; in the South generally, three out of five eligible African Americans registered.

Even as the march was producing the long-awaited fruits of legal justice, there were signs of serious problems within the movement, which in retrospect were hints of the immediate future. Some activists whined because there was not enough room at the speaker's podium for everyone. Malcolm X, in Washington to meet with SNCC activists, denounced the proceedings as "the farce on Washington." Bob Moses, as usual ignoring high-profile events, spent the day picketing at the Justice Department. CORE's James Farmer protested the march by remaining in a Louisiana jail. SNCC President John Lewis was forced to rewrite a tough but honest speech. Lewis intended to call for a new "Sherman's March to the sea" with a "scorched earth" policy of direct action. He settled on a tamer assertion that the movement would not stop until "the revolution of 1776 is complete," though he kept his criticism of national politics. "The party of Kennedy is also the party of Eastland," he insisted. "The party of [Jacob] Javits is also the party of Goldwater. Where is *our* party?"

Seen more broadly, the breach within the movement was most marked in the contrast between King's national strategy and SNCC's continuing efforts in VEP. Together, the march and the subsequent national legislation provided liberal America with the conscience-soothing impression that racism, being just a southern thing, had been vanquished. Meanwhile, SNCC was meeting its destiny in Mississippi, where the voting drives were coming ever nearer to a barely controlled race war.

Mississippi and Freedom Summer

In 1962 Bob Moses had brought a small registration effort to Mississippi because it was, as the Ole Miss historian James Silver put it in his thoughtful 1963 book of the same name, a "closed society." Moses determined to attack the state's infamous voting registration process. An aspiring voter had to "interpret" two sections of the state constitution to the satisfaction of the registrar. A throwback to the old literacy tests designed to discriminate against poor folks of both races, the registration process, because it left the judgment to the discretion of local officials, had become a weapon against black voting. Moses settled in Greenwood, the seat of the Delta county of LeFlore. LeFlore was hard core, "a really tough place," according to John Doar of the Justice Department. Its population was 64 percent black, only 9 percent of whom were registered to vote (though it might be said that LeFlore was not the worst in Mississippi; in at least two other Mississippi counties, no African Americans were registered). Poverty was the rule. On average, a black child completed only 4.3 years of school, and the median family income was $595 per year.

Several weeks after establishing a Greenwood office, three SNCC workers barely escaped a mob by sneaking out of the building's roof. Moses, who had been working in a nearby county, returned to the looted office; tired and seeing nothing to be done, he went to sleep on the office couch, much to the amazement of the other workers. "I just didn't understand what kind of guy this Bob Moses is," one colleague remarked, "that could walk into a place where a lynch mob had just left and make up a bed and prepare to go to sleep." In February 1963 Moses escaped death when night riders fired thirteen 45-calibre bullets into a car he was riding in. The driver was hit twice, once in the back of the head, but survived.

Undaunted, SNCC brought practically its entire Mississippi staff into the county. That spring, Greenwood citizens undertook a massive registration effort, which made national news and brought into town, among others, the comedian Dick Gregory, who delighted locals with his audaciousness. Authorities responded with arrests and beatings in jail. By summertime, sixty-two of SNCC's sixty-seven Mississippi staff members were in jail, forty-five doing hard labor at the LeFlore County work farm. Widespread publicity brought federal attention, but only enough to cut a deal with the local authorities whereby the government would drop pending civil rights suits if the local protesters were released.

Here in Greenwood the federal dilemma, which left the administration to hope that civil rights would be resolved through the political process, became all too apparent and endangered the lives of everyone involved in the registration drive. SNCC volunteers evidently assumed that there would be some federal protection, but according to Harris Wofford, no one in the administration believed that the federal government had the power to protect volunteers, especially in remote areas. There might have been miscommunication, but if Wofford is right, the administration's encouragement of VEP seems all the more cynical. Surely Kennedy's people knew that violence would accompany any serious registration drive.

Moses recognized that the federal dilemma left SNCC in a completely untenable position. In a thoughtful analysis of Greenwood, he concluded that the related burdens of poverty and race presented staggering problems. SNCC was asking whites in the Delta to permit blacks to vote "in an area where they are educationally inferior but yet outnumber the white people." Moses doubted that the nation would "push this down the throats of white people in the Delta, and it will have to be pushed down their throats because they are determined not to have it done."

There was no alternative but to figure out how to pressure the Justice Department to do what most whites in most places would not want. The question was, how?

The answer was "Freedom Summer." SNCC would recruit white students from around the nation, but mostly from elite universities, to spend summer 1964 registering voters in Mississippi. Like Kennedy, they would appeal to youthful idealism and count on the desire of the nation's brightest young people to join in the most inspiring movement of their time. It was a controversial decision. For complex reasons, many of the native Mississippians in SNCC opposed the idea, partly out of a sense of inferiority to wealthy, Ivy League whites, partly because they feared outsiders would undermine their local organizations. Moses saw the project ideally as producing "an island of integration in a sea of separation," but he supported it mostly for lack of other plans. James Forman, again attending to the psychic side of revolution, argued that the plan would break down lingering fears of whites. Above all other reasons and regardless of what else happened, where white students went, federal protection was bound to follow. "It was just that gross," remarked one SNCC activist.

To carry off what Forman knew was a "tricky proposition," SNCC brought white volunteers to Oxford, Ohio, in June 1964 for two week-long training sessions. Those who came conformed to the character type that SNCC wanted. The volunteers were generally from well-to-do backgrounds, and more than half of the applicants came from the nation's top schools. In their first contact with the white students, SNCC members were aloof, hoping to impress their charges with the deadly seriousness of the moment. To the white volunteers, the SNCC activists were glamorous, underground guerrillas. They were a politicized version of the stereotypical black: bad, arrogant, and way outside the mainstream. Before the week was out, those initial impressions and lingering stereotypes were mostly put aside.

Once in Mississippi they depended on one another; therefore, strong personal relationships between the new volunteers and SNCC activists were a tactical necessity. Mississippi was a deadly place; as organizers expected, white supremacists were determined to resist the 700 "invaders." Over the summer, there were sixty-seven bombings or arson fires directed against the movement, 1,000 arrests, eighty beatings, and eight people critically wounded or killed. The most notorious act of violence occurred in Neshoba County, where Michael Schwerner, a veteran activist, James Chaney, a local black man, and Andrew Goodman, a summer volunteer from New York, turned up missing in June. Widespread publicity drove President Johnson to order the otherwise indifferent FBI, which did not even have a field office in the state, to launch an aggressive investigation. When search teams combed the area, they turned up a number of bodies. Two mutilated corpses were dragged from the Mississippi, prompting one volunteer to observe that "things are really much better for rabbits here. There is a closed season on rabbits. . . . Negroes are killed all year round." Eventually, the three bodies were found buried in an earthen dam. The FBI charged a group of Klansmen with the crime, including a Neshoba County deputy sheriff, but could not convict them of murder.

In the midst of violence, Freedom Summer yielded gains. A total of 17,000

African Americans made the dangerous trip to their county courthouse, though only 1,600 were successfully registered. SNCC brought between 3,000 and 3,500 mostly rural, poorly educated Mississippians into "Freedom Schools," exposing them simultaneously to the four "Rs": reading, 'riting, 'rithmetic, and radicalism. There were moments of great interracial harmony, and Freedom Summer, to some degree, met Moses's ideal of an "integrated sea." Forman was probably correct: the appearance of white volunteers did help break down the remaining psychological barriers to black self-development. Many locals recalled with pride sharing a meal or their home with the bright young whites. As Fannie Lou Hamer concluded, during Freedom Summer "people learned white folks are human." The sight of young black volunteers, many of whom were also well educated and articulate, was even more inspiring to locals. Many locals called SNCC activists "Freedom Riders." One woman recalled watching Bob Moses, "a little bitty fella," stand up to the local sheriff. "From that day on, I said, 'Well, I can stand myself.' " Amzie Moore, the NAACP veteran who originally worked with Moses, insisted that SNCC was "the only thing in the twentieth century that gave courage and determination to blacks in the South."

Yet these victories exacted costs from all of the participants. Having lived through the summer on the strength of great idealism, they were all the more deflated when that idealism disappeared.

For local Mississippians, this deflation ran its course when they attempted to organize their own political party, the Mississippi Freedom Democratic party (MFDP). Excited by the developments of the summer, they seized Bob Moses's plan to run primaries, hold a state convention, and proceed to Atlantic City, New Jersey, where they would try to replace the regular segregationist party at the Democratic Convention. In a sign of growing political awareness, over 80,000 Mississippians voted in the MFDP elections. Once in Atlantic City in August 1964, they hooked up with liberal supporters and earned a hearing before the credentials committee. Fannie Lou Hamer, a sharecropper-turned-activist who embodied SNCC's vision of a grassroots leader, gave dramatic testimony of beatings and denials of constitutional rights, including her own eviction from the plantation on which she had lived for eighteen years. Her televised speech was interrupted when President Johnson, wishing to avoid any controversy at "his" convention, quickly asked the networks for special time. The administration then went to work behind the scenes, pressuring MFDP supporters until a compromise was worked out. The regular Democrats stayed, but the MFDP was given two at-large delegates and a promise that the party would seat no future delegation that practiced discrimination.

As things go in party politics, the deal was not bad, considering that the MFDP had been born only several weeks before. But the high idealism of the newly politicized Mississippians had raised hopes well beyond compromises. The bitter fact was that simply organizing and demanding did not bring power.

The summer's effects on SNCC itself were equally disheartening. Several years in Mississippi convinced many in the group that nonviolence was no longer a useful tactic; in Mississippi the tactic neither shamed racists into accepting the beloved community nor provoked federal intervention. SNCC activists, furthermore, developed great admiration for how the rural folks protected themselves. People such as Hartman Turnbow, who at Moses's prodding became the first black in the twentieth century to register to vote in Holmes County, were often well armed. "This nonviolent stuff ain't no good," he once remarked. "It'll getcha killed." Other activists were surprised to discover that Fannie Lou Hamer was less than committed to nonviolence. One recalled that after looking at the bullet holes fired inside Hamer's home, he saw that "there was a loaded rifle in each corner of the room. As I went through the house, I saw a loaded rifle in each corner of every room." Throughout the summer, many SNCC activists were regularly packing weapons—"armed self-defense" they called it—and Forman posted an armed guard around SNCC headquarters in Greenwood.

Of course, the difference between nonviolence and self-defense was subtle. King himself had never been opposed to self-defense. But the acceptance of armed self-defense was another step away from King and another indication of how SNCC's form of activism—its isolation, its reliance on the people of the countryside—had forged a uniquely searing experience. Isolated in Mississippi against an overwhelmingly powerful force, always having seen themselves as guerrillas, SNCC members increasingly identified themselves not with King or the United States but with the armed anticolonial movements of the Third World.

Freedom Summer also created racial tensions between black members and white volunteers. Some tension grew out of the very reason why the white volunteers had been recruited: they drew publicity. The media flooded the state only because the volunteers had come, though it was unfair of SNCC members to criticize volunteers for this attention, given that they had anticipated the media's response in the first place. The white volunteers, meanwhile, often were inadvertently condescending. Activists on their campuses, involved in student governments and editors of their college papers, they were adept at the organizational side of politics—writing press releases, shifting money around, and answering telephones—and gravitated to these sorts of jobs. Such jobs were as close to leadership roles as one could have in SNCC, and they were the ones most coveted by locals for whom such activity was a completely new challenge. At times, the overly eager and articulate white students intimidated those whose education was greatly inferior. Some SNCC members, no doubt harried and tense, questioned the motives of white volunteers whose larger lives were not really caught up in Mississippi; others simply found these volunteers clumsy and unreliable.

Racial tensions also grew out of the sexual encounters among Freedom Summer workers. The project was an explosive mix in this regard. The white volunteers were at an age when they would naturally seek personal liberation from stifling parental expectations or northern cultural norms. Young blacks, many of whom were poor, southern, and engaged in tearing down racial barriers, were tossed together with volunteers who personified the sort of life they could never have. The intoxicating mix of danger and radicalism encouraged relationships and sexual experimentation, as did the intense affection within the SNCC community. In this atmosphere, sexual relationships spun out of a dizzying mix of personal and cultural motives that crossed class and race lines at the same time. It appears that black men and white women were most frequently matched precisely because such relationships broke the most serious taboos for both. For black men, here was an opportunity to assert a long-denied manhood; some white women were so taken with the men's sexual frankness, Mary King wrote in her thoughtful autobiography, "that a few of them fluttered like butterflies from one tryst to another." Some white women succumbed to black men simply out of guilt—an unhealthy situation for both partners—and black women came to resent the relationships between white women and black men.

The slide away from nonviolence and the incipient racial tensions should be seen as part of a larger historical pattern. Both developments specifically rejected the overriding principles of the civil rights movement. After Freedom Summer, SNCC increasingly cut its ties with mainstream liberal groups. Within the organization, racial tensions boiled over into an open debate in 1965 on the disposition of whites within the organization, which ended with the decision to separate the activities of white and black activists. By this time, however, there were fewer than two dozen whites in SNCC, while older members like John Lewis and Bob Moses drifted out of the movement in disillusionment.

From Civil Rights to Black Power

For King and the established movement, ten years of hard-won victories had left a bittersweet taste. Having won a revolution against segregation at a minimal cost of blood, King had to admit that African Americans continued to occupy a subordinate position in national life. As his colleague Bayard Rustin put it in his succinct analysis of the movement's future, the "decline of Jim Crow has also seen the rise of *de facto* segregation in our most fundamental socioeconomic institutions." The legal strategies used to conquer segregation would not work against a market-based social system—mostly northern, mostly industrial, mostly urban—that worked against African Americans who were starting out at the bottom. Indeed, the obstacles now were "of far greater magnitude," Rustin wrote, "than the legal barriers [the movement] was attacking before: automation, urban decay, *de facto* school segregation." Moving against these deep problems required that the movement shift its attention from equal rights to "achieving the fact of *equality*." Rustin recommended a well-organized political strategy based on a liberal political coalition that worked toward an expansion of public-sector participation in the economy, not unlike that contemplated in the Great Society.

The Meaning of Black Power

Nearly everyone knew that the movement was at a crossroads, but there was by no means a consensus that Rustin's was the proper direction. If anything, SNCC, having been radicalized during Freedom Summer, scorned coalition politics and sped toward "black power." Formally, black power was the slogan around which Stokely Carmichael, executive director after John Lewis, attempted to keep SNCC together.

Carmichael used the slogan during the "Meredith March" of 1966, when SCLC and SNCC came to Mississippi to march in honor of James Meredith, who had been gunned down at the beginning of a one-man march through Alabama. In a short time, Carmichael's slogan became the nationwide symbol of black militancy.

The exact meaning of black power was never very clear. Before 1967, when he tried to elucidate his ideas in *Black Power*, Carmichael suggested that the slogan was only a call for economic self-determination, not unlike the strategies that had lifted the United States' other historic ethnic groups. At other times, however, he saw matters in purely political terms, with black power, for example, marshaling voting strength to elect black representatives. At other times, he implied that it paralleled Malcolm X's program of racial separation. At yet other times it was a fuzzy call for cultural awareness. In short, it was up to the listener or the speaker to define.

Whatever its definition, black power clearly marked the end of SNCC. The expulsion of whites, the burnout from Freedom Summer, the adoption of armed self-defense—all lent themselves to increasing militancy. More important, the drain of Freedom Summer led to a transfer of power to a new group of activists. James Forman excepted, none of the new members had much association with the original movement. Carmichael, it is true, had been a Freedom Rider, but he was a loose cannon. The newcomers were more likely to be northerners, or in Carmichael's case, Caribbean, and more likely urban than rural. Above all, they had never been loyal to King. Instead, they were more likely to embrace Malcolm X as their guiding prophet; rather than southern Christianity, their influences were more likely to come from the increasing vogue of Third World radicalism, their heroes infamous guerrilla fighters like Che Guevara and Ho Chi Minh.

Black power was based on a culture gap as well as a generational gap within the movement and demonstrated the shifting scene of racial issues from southern common folk to urban young people. King knew that he had to counter the power of the new message. He acknowledged that black power contained a "psychological call to manhood" that was a powerful antidote to the "indelible imprint of inferiority"; the radical assertion of race pride was beneficial. The real issue, however, was how best to gain strength beyond mere self-esteem, and here King categorically rejected the notion that blacks could develop economic or political power by going it alone. King's reasoning was similar to his rejection of violence: the numbers just were not there; the black community was not large enough to build economic independence through isolation. By focusing on racial independence, black power ignored the hard economic facts of automation and job loss. "However much we pool our resources and 'buy black,' this cannot create the multiplicity of new jobs and provide the number of low-cost houses that will lift the Negro out of the economic depression caused by centuries of economic deprivation." Carmichael was wrong to equate black power with the strategies of earlier immigrant groups. "No one has ever heard the Jew publicly chant a slogan of Jewish power," King reasoned, "but they have power. Through group unity, determination and creative endeavor, they have gained it." Rather than giving in to mere rhetoric, earlier groups stuck together but then worked within the system. Economic and political logic left blacks no realistic choice but to continue with coalition politics under the liberal umbrella.

Even as he tried to give black power its due, King miscalculated the extent to which it indicated an important shift in African-American politics. Black power was far less a program for change than a diffuse reaction to events and conditions in the inner cities, which began to erupt with unnerving regularity beginning with Harlem's 1964 riots. The cities, not the South or even a national movement, became the locus of political energy, and working-class and underclass people became the constituency. King's movement was held together by the tightly woven culture and traditions of southern communities, but black power developed among people who lacked the cohesive, stable, and independent communities that nurtured the southern revolution. Committed advocates of black power believed that they could bring political coherence to their constituency only through dramatic and basic appeals. In their hands, the rhetoric was more than just a reaffirmation of manhood, as King believed; actually, it offered a means for holding together communities beset by dislocation, frequent uprooting, apathy, and irrational rage.

The Black Panthers

At least at its most radical, as in the hands of the Black Panthers, black power was such a means. Whereas cultural nationalists proceeded to make black power a vehicle to self-esteem and private profit, the Black Panthers employed it purely in its political form as a means of organizing the otherwise unorganizable people of the ghettos—"the young lumpenproletarian cats," as Panther leader Bobby Seale called their members. Armed self-defense was their rallying cry, and their stated purpose was to hold the police accountable for actions in their community. The Panthers were the baddest of the bad. They were denounced in the media, which exaggerated their inclination to violence, harassed by every branch of law enforcement from local police to the FBI, used as scapegoats by politicians, driven into exile, and murdered. To FBI director J. Edgar Hoover, the Panthers were "the most active and dangerous black extremist group in the United States," which, coming from someone who thought Martin Luther King was a communist, was quite a statement. But the Panthers had purpose. From 1967 to the early 1970s, they gathered over 4,000 members in thirty-three cities, circulated a weekly paper to over 100,000 readers, established free-breakfast programs, set up medical clinics, and organized political education classes for their communities. Although the Panthers were viewed with general dismay by a majority of African Americans nationally, and although the attention they received was far out of proportion to their numbers or accomplishments, the Panthers were the only grassroots, working-class radical movement to emerge out of the riot-torn cities.

The party was primarily the creation of Bobby Seale and Huey P. Newton, two "brothers off the block" who began to pick up the radical temper of the day while attending classes at a small community college in Oakland. Newton in many ways was like the Muslim leader Malcolm X: self-taught, charismatic, uncompromising, and blessed with a certain instinctive genius. The party he and Seale began to build served something of the same function as the Black Muslims: it brought discipline and purpose to inner-city people, many of whom had come north in the Great

Migration only to slide into the abyss of ghetto life. When Newton began to organize "police patrols" to follow Oakland police in the neighborhood, the Panthers thought they were putting into action Malcolm's dictum that blacks should defend themselves "by any means necessary."

In 1967 Newton was arrested for shooting an Oakland police officer and thereafter had to direct the party from jail. During his three-year incarceration, he became a local folk hero, and the party flourished as the "free Huey campaign" attracted new members, sympathizers, and donations. A host of new leaders emerged—Seale, David Hilliard, and Bunchy Carter in Los Angeles, and Fred Hampton in Chicago. The most prominent was Eldridge Cleaver, who became a *cause célèbre* of leftist intellectuals when *Ramparts* magazine published a series of letters, later collected in *Soul on Ice* (1967), that he had written to his lawyer while serving time for rape. When Cleaver joined the Panthers, he brought his fame, his book royalties, his contacts with the white left, and his rage with him.

Although their reputation as violently antiwhite terrified the mainstream, the Panthers' coalition politics and opposition to black racism made them unique among the many black power organizations that sprang up in the late sixties. They drew their program from distilled Marxism, mostly from the Algerian revolutionary Franz Fanon, whose book on Third World revolution, *Wretched of the Earth*, was translated into English in 1965 and immediately became influential. The white left embraced Fanon's contention that political violence provided a therapeutic liberation for the oppressed and therefore could be an end in itself. But Newton adopted *Wretched* as his theoretical guide because, unlike Karl Marx, Fanon believed the most downtrodden, the lumpenproletariat, could be organized for revolution. Otherwise, the Panthers were self-taught Marxists who believed that the class struggle was universal and transcended race and ethnic boundaries. That being so, they allied with anyone willing "to move against the power structure."

Their willingness to engage in coalitions with other radical groups made good sense after 1967 when the New Left was strong. The same reasoning that led Rustin to seek a liberal coalition worked for them. The Panthers recognized that they could not pull off a genuine revolution alone, and they were serious enough not to content themselves with black power rhetoric. On this score they had more in common with Rustin and King than with other advocates of black power, most of whom embraced fantasies of race separation or committed themselves to cultural nationalism. The Panthers' ten-point program was simple and direct: it included jobs, housing, education, and an end to police brutality. They disdained black nationalism on the theoretical grounds that it was racist; on the practical level, they concluded that the cultural nationalists were more interested in making money selling dashikis than in real revolution.

Dealing in coalition politics, however, was not completely beneficial. In too many cases, white radicals romanticized the Panthers as violent guerrillas—the flip side of the mass media image. Whereas white radicals, middle-class kids mostly, merely spoke about "offing pigs," the Panthers, legend had it, were really doing it. The Panthers shared some of the blame here; their rhetoric was inflammatory. They made the dehumanization of authorities popular through the Panther paper, where they were the first sixties radicals to employ the term *pig* regularly. Maybe their language was appropriate to their embattled communities, but it did not translate well. Meanwhile, they became the fashion, "radical chic," as the writer Tom Wolfe put it in his sardonic description of the fund-raising party the composer Leonard Bernstein and his wife threw for the New York Panthers. For those who can afford them, fashions come and go. And once the white left committed itself to the antiwar movement and went off on its spree of self-destruction, the Panthers were forgotten. Asked to speak at a 1969 rally in Oakland, David Hilliard found that the once-receptive white students had no interest in the Panthers. "They'll come for the Vietnamese," he lamented, "but not for us."

If ultimately the Panthers accomplished precious little, their failures are in part explained by the active government repression that was thrown at them. They were constantly harassed; all of the leaders spent time in jail in the late sixties, save Cleaver, who escaped into exile in Cuba and Algeria. All of their branches were infiltrated by government agents who acted as provocateurs and tried to push the party into violent confrontations, petty thievery, and drug use. In December 1969, Chicago police, acting with the aid of an infiltrator and in alliance with the FBI, raided a Panthers' apartment and killed local leader Fred Hampton while he lay in bed. The killing momentarily sparked outrage from mainstream groups that otherwise shunned the Panthers, but it left the members themselves shell-shocked.

There was a more compelling reason, however, for their ultimate failure. Just as Johnson's Great Society failed in part because it targeted the people at the bottom of the social heap, so the Panthers failed by trying to stage a revolution with people mired in self-degradation through alcohol, drugs, and crime. They were a spontaneously built radical organization of "young lumpenproletarian cats" trying to organize others like them. As a tactical matter, they had their work cut out for them. As if provocateurs weren't trouble enough, they were constantly dealing with members—jackanapes, Cleaver called them—who breached discipline by robbing stores, getting high, or shooting at police. Poor people who recruited poor people, the Panthers had no independent economic base from which to work, no chance to build bridges with white working-class organizations, and no way to sustain themselves indefinitely. It speaks to the beauty of the sixties that the lumpenproletariat cats would politicize their bleak conditions at all. But in the end Huey Newton was wrong about the lumpenproletariat: they do not make revolutionaries, particularly when the conditions in which they live get worse and destroy any hope for change.

"A Radical Redistribution of Economic Power"

The failure of the lumpenproletariat brings us full circle to Martin Luther King, Jr. Comparing King's successful southern revolution to the Panthers' aborted northern revolution is a lesson in revolutionary theory that reminds us that stable communities are important to sustaining political movements and that people who have a stake in society are more willing to sacrifice than those who are dispossessed.

King might have done well to study the Panthers' faulty Marxism. For in response to the rise of black power, the urban crisis, and the waning of his influence, he moved to the left and launched an effort to retool his nonviolent movement in the cause of economic revolution. Willing neither to shift to black nationalism nor to settle into the NAACP mainstream, King gradually discovered that he had but one option: to head a movement of poor folks, organized along lines of class rather than race.

The SCLC's Move North

In 1965 King made his move to transform SCLC into an urban movement, choosing to launch his new efforts in Chicago. The city had a well-organized black leadership and a huge black population, and was the foremost example of de facto segregation. Most black Chicagoans lived in rigidly demarcated ghettos that contained some of the United States' worst slums. City schools were thoroughly segregated, not by law, but because they were neighborhood-based, and black schools were notoriously underfunded.

In early 1966 King took a modest apartment on the west side, in a neighborhood that had been thoroughly destabilized by the classic process of urban decay: an influx of poor, rural migrants into old neighborhoods generated white flight out of the area and left it to the disintegrative effects of poverty, crime, and drugs. It was an appropriate place to begin a campaign vaguely conceived to address ghetto life. On the advice of James Bevel, who preceded him into Chicago, King grandly announced that his goal was to "end slums," presumably by dealing with education, housing, and unemployment all at once. For more than two months, King managed only to induce a tenant revolt in one building, where he used rent money to fix what an absentee landlord had neglected. The locals and Bevel began quarreling, with the locals wanting to keep the focus on schools. King was going off in several directions at once. In July, he called a mass meeting at Soldier Field, but only 30,000 of an expected 100,000 showed. Just as disheartening, two days later a large riot erupted, and while King and his aides ran frantically through the west side streets pleading for calm, gang members and other youths yelling "black power" broke store windows and fought police.

Desperate, King decided to focus on one issue, discrimination in housing. He planned marches through white neighborhoods to call attention to Chicago's common practice of race covenants. Both the sharper focus and the marches temporarily rekindled the spirit of the southern movement. Supporters flooded Chicago, the cameras watched, and the marchers met white mobs that were larger and, by some accounts, uglier than any they had met in the South. When King threatened to march in Cicero, a working-class suburb infamous for its racism, city authorities quickly agreed to a plan for ensuring the enforcement of open-housing laws and fair treatment in the lending process.

If anything, King's victory seemed to call attention to the problems with his new strategy. In Richard Daley, he faced an adversary who was much different from Bull Connor, certainly one who, at least before August 1968, was difficult to depict as a racist. Daley's machine, after all, had always included blacks; in fact,

Daley owed his last election to south side votes. He had commandeered a hefty portion of Great Society money, much of which was to be spent, one way or another, in the black community. The problem with the Daley machine was not that it was overtly racist but that it was perfectly adapted for compromise, which allowed it to absorb the complaints about housing and file them away as another bureaucratic item.

The deal that King and Daley cut, moreover, did help some black Chicagoans, mostly those who could afford to move out of the slums. Because it did nothing to alleviate the misery of Chicago's poor, King's compromise seemed more like a face-saving gesture than a victory. When he left town, he left only a small operation, taken over by a young Jesse Jackson. King took with him the last attempt at an interracial movement for equality, leaving Chicago's black community, and implicitly the black community nationwide, in the hands of machine politicians or black power advocates.

There were just too many clashing groups, too many cross-cutting interests at work in the North, and the moral issues, no matter how vigorously asserted, were not so clear. King could focus on the moral necessity of integration in the North, but it did not carry the weight it did in the segregated South. If he continued to focus on integration as the northern strategy, he risked losing support from everyone but liberal elites, people whose support he welcomed but whose comfortable suburban existence made their commitment to racial justice hypocritical. Northern whites were not the least ashamed of their snarling opposition to King; many of them were ethnic minorities too who had managed to carve out a piece of the American dream and were not about to give it up. What was immoral racism in the South was community control in the North, something that black power advocates were demanding for their communities.

The Riverside Speech

Then there was the war in Vietnam, which by 1967 was clearly destroying the Great Society. Against the advice of mainstream colleagues, King decided that he had to speak out against the war. After several tentative criticisms, he came out full square against the war in April in a speech at Manhattan's Riverside Church. He was uncompromising. The war was profoundly wrong, he said. Bad enough that the billions spent destroying straw huts in Indochina could best be used at home, but the war was directed against the very people it was purporting to liberate. Was it a coincidence that U.S. military might was being flung at nonwhite Asians often by nonwhite soldiers whose own communities needed liberation? The United States' own 1964 Nobel Peace Prize winner had to conclude that "the greatest purveyor of violence in the world today" was the United States. One-time colleagues, mainstream associates, and even friends immediately and roundly denounced King. An angry President Johnson encouraged more FBI surveillance. The press claimed that King had gone into opposition and had relinquished his role as a constructive leader in race relations. Whatever the assessment, it was clear that King no longer saw much value in a coalition with liberals.

The Poor People's Campaign

The Riverside speech was a sign of King's growing estrangement from the mainstream, an indication that his movement to the political left was not just an expedient effort to address the challenge of black power. And he kept moving in that direction. Prodded by a young activist, Marion Wright, who had been continuing work with poor folks in the South and who was responsible for coaxing Robert Kennedy to visit Mississippi before his death, King and the SCLC decided to organize a poor people's march on Washington. It would be just another march perhaps, but it signaled a fundamental shift in SCLC movement strategy and a clear decision on King's part. The likely thinking behind the poor people's campaign was that the post–civil rights crisis among African Americans was one of class rather than race. If that were so, then the solution obviously had to focus on economics. Nothing more clearly illustrated how far King's thinking had shifted: in announcing the plans for the poor people's march, he went far beyond a mainstream call for another New Deal, make-work, government jobs program and called for "a radical redistribution of economic power."

It was during the planning for this march, in April 1968, that King went to Memphis to protest on behalf of striking sanitation workers. Many of his aides thought he should not go; there was too much to do elsewhere, they thought. But to King it made little sense to talk about supporting poor people and then refuse to go and lend a voice to the cause of Memphis garbagemen. So he went. On April 3, the people of Memphis called him to a church meeting. He wanted to stay in his hotel, for it was terribly stormy—the beginning of tornado season—but he went anyway. His speech was oddly melancholy, revealing a man who was obviously very tired. His speech would have moved any Christian, however. It was inspired prophecy. A true believer would doubt that King himself was speaking, for the source was more sublime.

> I've been to the mountaintop. Like anybody I would like to live a long life. Longevity has its place. But I'm not concerned with that now. I just want to do God's will. And he's allowed me to go up to the mountaintop. . . . And I've seen the Promised Land. And I may not get there with you. But I want you to know tonight that we as a people will get to the Promised Land. So I'm happy tonight. I'm not worried about anything. I'm not fearing any man. Mine eyes have seen the glory of the coming of the Lord!

The next afternoon he was murdered. News of King's assassination touched off the worst single spasm of urban violence in a decade of widespread rioting. Over a hundred cities suffered some rioting, with the most destructive eruptions in Washington, D.C., where ten people died, and federal troops were called out to protect the Capitol itself.

In King's absence, SCLC had to go on with the march, which now took on the aura of a long dirge. In spite of SCLC efforts, the campaign was poorly organized. Once they got to Washington, which by May 1968 had seen one too many marches and protests and was in no mood for another no matter what the point, the marchers stopped near the Lincoln Memorial and built a group of plywood shacks that they dubbed Resurrection City. While organizers tried to feed marchers, offer medical care, and make speeches, they also found themselves wondering, once encamped, what to do next. They had not really bothered to think that they would be stymied. But coming into the midst of a grudging indifference, they found themselves with no one to talk to, no one who would attack them, and no clear hook issue around which they might organize a set of demands. Then it began to rain—and rain and rain. Tensions rose as expectations dropped.

In the midst of the protest, Robert Kennedy's casket was driven by the Lincoln Memorial on its way to the Capitol. As the entourage went by, the clouds broke and a shining moon appeared. A children's choir began a plaintive rendition of the "Battle Hymn of the Republic"; the throng, powerfully moved, joined in. But the moment signaled death, not life; defeat, not victory.

CHAPTER 3

The Vietnam War
and U.S. Foreign Policy

 "American leaders were not evil men," the left-wing historian William Appleman Williams wrote in his most famous work, *The Tragedy of American Diplomacy* (1959). The policy that they pursued against weaker nations "was not the result of malice, indifference, or ruthless and predatory exploitation. They did not conceive and excuse some dreadful conspiracy. Nor were they treacherous hypocrites. They believed deeply in the ideals they proclaimed." U.S. foreign policy had been built on "imperial anti-colonialism," Williams argued, and in so doing he depicted exactly how the United States would blunder into the Vietnam War.

Beginning with World War I, U.S. foreign policy was guided by dual assumptions, first, that the nation's international interests could flourish best in a liberal world and, second, that the United States could serve itself and the cause of international justice at the same time. Before World War II, this set of assumptions led to policies that pushed free trade, disarmament, and moralistic rhetoric in more or less equal proportions. Emerging out of World War II with unprecedented power, challenged only by the Soviet Union, U.S. policymakers revised these Wilsonian assumptions and acted as though the failure of democracy anywhere constituted a threat to the United States' vital interests. The Cold War twist on the traditional policy, dubbed the containment policy, was more aggressive and more interventionist than the original policy had been because it defined the United States' vital interests as global in scope and because it assumed the nation had the power to extend itself globally.

This expansive understanding of vital interests and national obligations led U.S. policymakers from the Truman administration in the late 1940s to the liberal administrations of the sixties into Vietnam. Vietnam became the place where liberal assumptions failed, where U.S. illusions about international democracy and Western benevolence were exposed, and where a century of steadily expanding American power was halted. The Vietnam War marked the end of an era in world affairs. The war showed that there were limits that even as great a power as the United States had to recognize and that the bipolar, Cold War world was in fact multiform. Richard Nixon, the illiberal sixties president and the beneficiary of liberalism's undoing, learned this lesson, and much to his dismay and only after inflicting terrific destruction against his enemy, concluded that he had to bring the war to an end.

Vietnam and Containment

Since the late 1800s, Vietnam had been a French colony, an exotic part of the French Empire little developed except for the exploitation of rubber resources. When the Japanese conquered the small colony in 1941 in a drive to wrest control of rubber and oil resources, they permitted the French to remain as administrators. The only force resisting the invaders emerged in remote areas of the North, not far from the Chinese border, under the command of Ho Chi Minh, a communist activist who founded both the Vietnamese Communist party and the Vietminh, an umbrella group of Vietnamese nationalists. In the latter days of World War II, the Americans, interested in aiding any anti-Japanese force, offered aid to Vietminh guerrillas and established political contacts with Ho Chi Minh.

These early contacts were consistent with the United States' traditional opposition to colonialism, and at that point in time, when the United States and the Soviet Union were still official allies, Ho Chi Minh's communist affiliations were of no great concern. It was simple for President Franklin Roosevelt to follow an anti-imperialist policy toward wartime Vietnam: in the larger scheme of things, Vietnam was of no strategic importance, and he disliked the French anyway. By all indications, Roosevelt expected to put the region under the control of the United Nations and to wean it toward self-determination.

The onset of the Cold War, however, altered U.S. priorities in Southeast Asia. By 1947 the primary objective of U.S. policy was to stop the spread of communism, which according to the containment theory was linked to the Soviets regardless of when or where communist movements emerged. For Vietnam, the shift in priorities led the Truman administration to retract the minimal political contacts with Ho Chi Minh and gradually shift U.S. support behind the reestablishment of French control. In 1947, when civil war broke out between the Vietminh and the French, the U.S. decision to support French colonial restoration automatically became a commitment to support a war for that restoration. The costs for that commitment grew quickly. With the United States giving $133 million in military aid in 1950 and $50 million in technical and economic assistance from 1950 to 1952, it was paying one-third of the French war costs.

When Dwight Eisenhower assumed the presidency in 1952, he inherited Truman's Vietnam policy, the main principles of which he supported. The fateful decisions he made on his own were entirely in line with containment. Throughout the early fifties, U.S. policy was to trade military help for promises of political reform, but the French had learned that by threatening to leave Vietnam to the communists they could extort increasing aid from the United States. Despite massive U.S. help, the Vietminh defeated the French during the famous battle of Dien Bien Phu in the spring of 1954, during which the administration briefly considered but ultimately rejected intervening on behalf of besieged French forces. Eisenhower and Secretary of State John Foster Dulles were wary of military commitments in Asia, but, more important, they believed that the French had bungled the whole business of restoration. Exactly when they reached the conclusion is unclear, but in mid-1954 when the Vietminh, the French, the Soviets, the British, and the Chinese met in Geneva to reach agreements on Southeast Asia, Eisenhower and Dulles decided that it would be best for the United States to go its own way in Vietnam. U.S. policy in Vietnam thereafter was intended to promote an independent, democratic society. But what U.S. policymakers had in mind was an anticommunist bastion formed in the United States' image.

Ngo Dinh Diem

Eisenhower attempted to foster a Western outpost in Vietnam by throwing U.S. support behind a single leader, Ngo Dinh Diem. The French had chosen Diem to act as a transitional premier, but the man had a number of the qualities Washington was looking for: he was a nationalist who had opposed French colonial rule; he was Western-oriented and had lived in the United States for several years; and he was unquestionably anticommunist.

What the administration did not see, and what became the core of the American tragedy in Vietnam, was that every quality that recommended Diem to the United States made him a poor candidate for leading a stable, independent South Vietnam. As a Catholic, he represented a small minority of approximately 10 percent of the population. He was a northerner, and the long-standing animosities between those in the South and those in the North made him an outcast in the new nation that he was supposed to rule. He was a nationalist, but he was not widely known among the majority of Vietnamese and he was far less popular than Ho Chi Minh. His anticommunism, though fierce and uncompromising, was indiscriminate: Diem believed that all Vietminh were communists and that all competitors for power were Vietminh. All of these vices might have been overcome were Diem a good politician, willing to rub elbows with the masses, compromise with foes, and construct political coalitions. But he was unwilling to engage in any of those tasks and could never build the mass base of support necessary to sap the popular strength of Ho Chi Minh.

Some U.S. advisors saw these problems immediately. The very first State Department and CIA assessments of Diem warned against his monklike behavior. J. Lawton Collins, the general in charge of the mission in Vietnam in 1955, found Diem inscrutable, weak, and indecisive. But Dulles had committed himself, and he believed his faith was substantiated after Diem routed several groups of paramilitary opponents in 1956.

Only an optimist—or someone who did not think Vietnam was very important—could have been inspired by the overall situation. The North faced enormous difficulties in building an economy, but it contained over half of Vietnam's 25 million people and was well led and well armed. The South, on the other hand, was largely agricultural, much of its population was isolated in remote and primitive villages, and even with Diem's successes, it had no institutionalized political processes.

The Americans focused on economic and military development, while Diem concerned himself with political consolidation. The administration launched a massive aid program that poured in $1 billion in economic and military assistance from 1955 to 1961. Diem moved to centralize power with institutional changes and violent repression. He expanded the governmental bureaucracy, strengthened the executive powers, established a national assembly, and watched his brother, Ngo Dinh Nhu, create a national political party. These institutional strategies coincided with a ruthless anticommunist campaign launched in 1957 against the estimated 10,000 to 15,000 Vietminh who remained in the South after Geneva. Excess marked the campaign: the regime shut down opposition newspapers, arrested some 65,000 political opponents, and killed some 2,000 others.

Taken together, the plan for economic development and Diem's political reforms, superficially successful, laid the basis not for a stable South Vietnam but for the Second Indochina War. Over 80 percent of the economic aid came in the form of export–import credits, which did little to modernize the Vietnamese economy. More than one-third of the imports were consumer goods, which went to city dwellers, bureaucrats, and the black market. The vast majority of Vietnamese, who lived in the countryside, gained nothing but trouble from their nation's relationship with the United States. The one program that potentially could encourage economic development on a mass scale was land reform. At U.S. insistence, the regime developed a program to settle abandoned lands in the Mekong Delta and the Central Highlands, reduce ground rents, and limit landholdings to 247 hectares. But Diem never quite grasped the purpose of land reform. Instead of giving land to tenants, he often restored it to landlords. Much of the best land, particularly the productive rubber plantations, was defined as untouchable, only 20 percent of the cultivated rice land was made available, and the program was begun too late to bolster Diem's political popularity.

In contrast to the economic program, Diem's efforts at political consolidation were quite successful; nonetheless, they contributed to his undoing. Diem refused to delegate authority, involving himself in everything from military affairs to supervising visas to installing air conditioning in the national library. Worse, Diem was part of a family package, and much of his effort at political centralization brought power into the hands of a tight circle of relatives. Of all the family members, the most important was his brother, Nhu, who headed the domestic police force and the Can Lao political party. Nhu's wife, Madame Nhu, held no official post but best symbolized this strange collection of characters. A sharp and ruthless intriguer, she was the real backbone of the regime. The U.S. journalist David Halberstam described her well as "an Ian Fleming character come to life: the antigoddess, the beautiful but diabolic sex-dictatress who masterminds some secret apparatus that James Bond is out to destroy." Unlike both Diem and Nhu, she enjoyed the public display of power. "She was the only one of the family who walked the way a dictator should walk," Halberstam went on, "with flair and obvious enjoyment, trailed by a line of attendants."

The national assembly, meanwhile, was primarily a gathering of pro-Diem or pro-Nhu representatives, with no true opposition. It existed only to endorse programs that the government initiated. Government representatives in the countryside were appointed by the Ngos, who used them to replace local elders and to undercut traditional structures of village governance. To many in the countryside, these were the same abuses that the French inflicted. One peasant explained to the American writer James Trullinger that "the happiest day in my whole life" was when Diem's forces ousted the French from his village. "But then we saw that the government of Mr. Diem was sometimes very cruel and sometimes just like the French." In fact, Diem was more disruptive than the French because he was more anxious to consolidate power. Moreover, by assaulting the traditional political structures, he reignited the guerrilla movement in the countryside that had been reduced to as few as 1,700 by the end of 1957.

It was a crucial point, which many communists recalled as "the dark years." Not only was Diem's anticommunist crusade tremendously successful, but also the regime in the North was split over whether to support a renewed insurgency in the South. The southern guerrillas believed that their hand was forced, resumed arms, and created the Vietcong movement. The Communist party in the North gradually approved the resumption of arms, partly because the southerners had forced its hand and partly because Diem's unpopularity made the South ripe for infiltration and subversion. Although Ho Chi Minh's objective was to overthrow Diem and reunite Vietnam under communist rule, he was anxious to control the southern movement; Ho feared that too much violence would provoke U.S. intervention, which would raise the cost of reunification dramatically. He hoped to win, but at a minimal cost. To achieve that tricky balance, he oversaw the organization of a new umbrella movement, the National Liberation Front, in December 1960. Given these developments, William Duicker's description of the Vietcong stands as the most reasonable: it was a "genuine revolt based in the South," though it was "organized and directed from the North," at least after 1959.

Vietnam and the New Frontier

If John F. Kennedy were to make any "new departures" in Third World policy in 1961, Vietnam was a good place to start, for a host of new conditions offered him the chance to change directions. As the communists began to reintroduce growing numbers of southerners into the conflict, it was increasingly clear that Diem's Army of the Republic of Vietnam (ARVN) was unable to match the guerrillas. At the same time, however, tensions between the Soviets and Red China created diplomatic possibilities and set the context in which a reasonable public relations campaign could have eased lingering Cold War tensions in domestic politics.

At the outset of his presidency, Kennedy was completely undecided about

Vietnam. In summer 1961, as the crisis in Vietnam swelled up around him and after the series of difficult episodes with the Soviets—the contentious summit meeting with Khrushchev, the resumption of Soviet atomic testing, and a growing crisis in Berlin—Kennedy began to see Vietnam as the place where he had to stand firm. U.S. policy in Vietnam became caught up in Kennedy's personal diplomatic sparring with the Russian premier. "That son of a bitch won't pay any attention to words," he said of Khrushchev.

Policy Options

By fall 1962, administration thinking had boiled down to two very different sets of recommendations. The so-called Taylor–Rostow report issued dire news from South Vietnam and recommended a significant increase in U.S. aid, including advanced weapons and a task force of some 6,000 to 8,000 advisors and support troops, with future increases anticipated. The report claimed that South Vietnam was salvageable, but the problem was one of confidence: Diem doubted that the Americans really wanted to save him, while the Americans doubted Diem wanted to be saved. U.S. intervention would arrest that mutual pessimism. Very different recommendations came from the Democratic elder statesman Chester Bowles, who called for the neutralization of Vietnam. Such a plan would appeal to the Soviets, who wanted to limit Chinese influence, and to the Chinese, who wanted the Americans out of the area; it would permit the Americans to avoid a thankless commitment, and, at the same time, it would put Ho Chi Minh in a position where he would bear the blame for further violence in Vietnam. Administration members hailed the Bowles report as "praiseworthy" but brushed it aside. Arthur Schlesinger, Jr., described it as "an imaginative proposal, but it seemed rather too early or too late."

Kennedy adopted the Taylor–Rostow recommendations, although he added the qualification that the aid would be offered as part of a long-term plan that included military and political reforms. To Kennedy's shock, Diem sharply criticized the Americans for demanding reform and made it known that he did not want U.S. troops in Vietnam. After agonizing over the policy in the first place, Kennedy was forced to decide whether to back out or to continue in Vietnam on Diem's terms. He chose the second course. "Diem is Diem, and he's the best we've got," he muttered.

Why, in spite of Diem's clear liabilities, did Kennedy decide to back him with a dramatic increase in aid? The Kennedy liberals had decided that U.S. "prestige" was at stake in Vietnam. They had decided that the United States' prestige would be inalterably damaged if it did not make good on its commitment to Diem: friends would lose confidence, and enemies would think they could move with impunity. As Walt Rostow insisted in a 1962 national security paper, a loss in Vietnam would "generate defeatism among governments and peoples in the non-Communist world, or give rise to frustrations at home." If the Americans faltered in their commitment to Vietnam, Secretary of State Dean Rusk claimed in 1965, "the communist world would draw conclusions that would lead to our ruin and almost certainly to a catastrophic war." In effect, whereas Eisenhower supported Diem in order to avoid U.S. military involvement in Vietnam, the Kennedy administration, spurred on by its obsession with "prestige," decided that saving Diem necessitated that involvement. To put it as plainly as the tortured logic allows, the U.S. commitment had become the reason for deeper U.S. commitment.

This feeble thinking grew out of the evolution of U.S. policy itself since World War II. On the one hand, Kennedy wanted to encourage the legitimate aspirations of the Third World, but on the other, he was stuck in Cold War anticommunism. These two conflicting impulses blended together in a policy based more on fuzzy notions of political psychology than on hard-and-fast national interests. U.S. policymakers refused to develop a hierarchy or a sense of priorities in foreign policy; they assumed that the nation's vital security was tied up not just in Western Europe but also in lowly, isolated Vietnam. As Kennedy himself fretted, "I don't know where the non-essential areas are." Kennedy liberals regularly defined vital interests in psychological terms, as matters of "prestige," "credibility," and "confidence." Surely these are elements of international relations, but the fiasco in Vietnam illuminated the danger of using such ideas to define national interests and to formulate extensive political and military commitments in a chase after securing them, since it is impossible to know when confidence has been secured or prestige restored. In the long run, this incalculable goal enticed both Kennedy and Johnson into constant increases in the U.S. commitment.

Circular reasoning tied U.S. prestige to the unreliable, increasingly remote Diem. The Americans believed that they could make up in sheer will what Diem lacked in competence. They had the best minds, the best weapons, the most money. When searching for policies, Kennedy turned to Robert McNamara, his secretary of defense, a Berkeley graduate, Ford's chief executive officer at the age of 44, and a creative, well-respected corporate manager whose specialty lay in his innovative use of computer analysis. Or he could turn to McGeorge Bundy, a Boston Brahmin who came from a dean's position at Harvard to head Kennedy's National Security Council. And there was Rostow, always ready to put his pet theories into play and for whom Vietnam became a game of blending counterinsurgency operations in an ever-widening war. In addition, McNamara brought to the Pentagon a cadre of experts who helped him bring computerized management into the Defense Department's conduct of Vietnam policy in the hopes of fighting a "rational" war—that is, one designed to achieve the desired results at the lowest costs.

The Strategic Hamlet Program

Through 1962, the policy worked. Once Taylor–Rostow aid found its way to the Mekong Delta, the ARVN earned some field victories and gained confidence. Vietcong casualty rates increased. The new American weapons, especially the gun-carrying helicopters, discouraged the guerrillas. U.S. advisors, whose numbers rose to over 9,000 by the end of the year, took active roles in ground battles, flying helicopters, and offering strategic advice. The new "strategic hamlet" program, under which whole villages were moved into fortified towns, created a sense of political improvement in the government.

All of these improvements were temporary. The casualty rates evened out as the Vietcong made adjustments to the new military situation. The advanced weaponry did not bring any major Vietcong defeat; rather, it forced the insurgents to be quicker on their feet. "You have to land right on top of them," one American officer explained, "or they disappear." The guerrillas quickly discovered that when ARVN troops landed, they did not stay long. For the most part, ARVN forces would sweep through a village and sweep back out, leaving the Vietcong to return at night to work their organizational and propaganda strategies. U.S. advisors often found that villagers played along with this tug-of-war, warming up to the ARVN but protecting the Vietcong at the same time. "It's always one hundred VC," one advisor told journalist David Halberstam, "and they always went thataway." Despite military reverses, the Vietcong made startling political gains. By late 1962, they had organized an estimated 300,000 members and could rely on more than 1 million sympathizers.

The strategic hamlet program also failed. Based on Rostowian ideas about controlling the sentiments of the people, the hamlet program was perhaps the worst thing the regime could have done if gaining popular support was its goal. The lives of rural Vietnamese revolved around their villages, which contained not only their extended families but also their traditions, their ancestral burial grounds, and the very essence of their world. To uproot them left them physically and spiritually homeless. Based on the faulty view that the Vietcong was separate from the villagers themselves, the Americans wrongly assumed that the hamlets could be protected from "infiltration." Worst of all, the administration and the Diem regime had two completely different sets of goals. To the Americans, the hamlet program was essential for cutting into Vietcong political strength; Diem and his brother, Nhu, who actually administered the program, saw it as a means of securing loyalty. Instead of working out from secured areas, as the Americans wanted, Nhu established hamlets in the regions of loyal administrators. Working "in the absence of a coordinated pacification effort . . . and with only perfunctory attention to defense and socio-economic administrative improvements," as one administration study put it, Nhu implanted hamlets in only six of the forty-one provinces in South Vietnam by fall 1962. The strategically important Delta had been ignored completely, "probably for political reasons."

The End of the Diem Regime

The failure of the hamlet program created bad blood between civilian officials in Washington and the Diem regime. For their part, Diem and Nhu began to see the U.S. effort as more trouble than it was worth. They obviously needed U.S. military aid to fight the Vietcong but increasingly saw the constant demands for reform as threats to their power. One way out of their dilemma was to negotiate with Ho Chi Minh, and in spring 1963 the brothers secretly offered to have the Americans withdraw in exchange for a peaceful settlement of the war. Ho offered to recognize a coalition government in the South headed by Diem, promised not to act toward speedy reunification, and agreed not to permit either Russian or Chinese troops in the North. For Diem, such an agreement would take care of his two biggest problems: the Vietcong and the Americans.

We cannot know what would have come of these negotiations because the most dramatic single event since Geneva interrupted them in early May. The "Buddhist revolt" began as an isolated incident in Hue, when government troops shot into a crowd of protesters. When the government blamed the violence on the Vietcong, further protests erupted among the Buddhists, who saw themselves as the true moral voice of the people. The protests climaxed when one elder monk committed suicide by lighting himself afire in the middle of a Saigon intersection. The powerful moment, caught by a wire-service photographer, shocked Western opinion, encouraged other self-immolations, and impelled wider protests in southern cities. Madame Nhu made matters worse when she callously referred to the protests as "barbecues." In late August, under U.S. pressure, Diem promised Ambassador Frederick Nolting that the government would leave the protesters alone. Then, surely with Diem's knowledge, Nhu's special police forces launched a series of raids against the Buddhists, vandalizing temples, arresting more than 1,400, and finally exhausting U.S. goodwill. As Kennedy aide Roger Hilsman wrote, the raids, undertaken in direct contrast to Diem's promise to the faithful Nolting, "violated our deepest sense of decency," and worse, were carried out with "disdainful arrogance, contemptuously confident that we would swallow this just as we had swallowed so much in the past."

This time the administration did not have to swallow, for in response to the collapsing situation, a group of dissident generals sounded out the administration to see if it would support a coup. The overtures were received in Washington on Saturday morning, August 24, a hot summer weekend when most of official Washington habitually leaves town, but particularly this weekend, with the city bracing for Martin Luther King's march on Washington. A mere handful of advisors, including Hilsman, George Ball, and Averill Harriman, took it upon themselves to reverse eight years of U.S. policy. Given the outrages of the regime, they cabled back to Vietnam, the United States "would have to face the possibility that the regime could not be preserved." That simple statement amounted to U.S. approval of a coup. Kennedy subsequently did nothing to alter the decision. The new ambassador, Henry Cabot Lodge, Jr., was instructed to distance the U.S. mission from Diem, even after the August plot failed to materialize. Apparently, Kennedy had reached conclusions about Diem that were similar to the conclusions Diem had reached about the Americans: that he was more trouble than he was worth. Even with this resigned decision, U.S. policy drifted for the next two months, as the administration awaited developments among the Vietnamese themselves. On November 1, the dissident generals summoned the courage to carry through their plot, seized key government installations, and assassinated Diem and Nhu.

The administration denied any complicity in the coup, but that was the truth only in the strictest sense. True, the Americans did not lead or aid the attempt, but they did make it clear that they would support any subsequent government, and the

CIA had kept constant contact with the plotters. When Diem sought Ambassador Lodge's help, he was told he might take refuge in the embassy if he did so without his brother. Loyal to the end, Diem refused, and it cost him his life, which at that point the United States no longer cared to save. The administration did not carry through the coup, but it did nothing to discourage it, and in promising to support a change in government, Washington probably offered the dissidents the most important support of all.

Less than a month later, Kennedy himself was assassinated, and thus his policy in Vietnam raises more questions than it had a chance to answer. Many of Kennedy's closest associates subsequently claimed that he was on the verge of reversing policy in Vietnam. It is true that in summer 1963 he dabbled with a plan to withdraw U.S. advisors, which included some modest diplomatic overtures to the communists. But the bulk of the evidence suggests a different conclusion. What dabbling Kennedy did toward a withdrawal was mostly an indication that Vietnam, despite all the American effort, remained a secondary concern. More important, the support of the anti-Diem coup did not indicate any willingness to cut the U.S. commitment. If anything, the coup renewed hope, despite much contrary evidence, that the generals would bring positive change. Accepting the coup was therefore a sign of continued commitment to Vietnam, if not to Diem. Ultimately, Kennedy attempted to muddle through a difficult situation, hoping for success. He continued to think that the U.S. effort might succeed short of a military commitment that would raise the stakes. In the end, therefore, his policy appears to have been not unlike that of Ho Chi Minh, who similarly hoped to win by avoiding a large-scale conflict.

Johnson and the Americanization of the War

One way to gauge Kennedy's probable intentions is to look at the policy of his successor, Lyndon Johnson. Johnson inherited not only the distressing situation in Vietnam, but also most of Kennedy's foreign policy team. Secretary of State Rusk remained, as did Secretary of Defense McNamara, National Security Advisor McGeorge Bundy, and Walter Rostow. These men were the primary shapers of policy under Kennedy, and they did not alter that policy under their new boss. Even more than in domestic policy, Johnson needed the Kennedy men. His strength lay in domestic politics, and it made sense to keep experienced advisors.

Yet the price for that continuity was that Johnson could not respond to new opportunities for rethinking U.S. policy. The Sino-Soviet relationship continued to disintegrate, and the Soviets seemed interested in improved relations with the United States. French President Charles de Gaulle began pushing a plan for a neutralized Vietnam that gave the United States the opportunity to save face. Diem was dead, which meant that U.S. policy since 1955 had failed. Nonetheless, Johnson stubbornly clung to the old policy. If anything, Johnson and his advisors took the assumptions of the Kennedy years and exaggerated them. Instead of seeing the breakdown of Sino-Soviet relations as an opportunity, they decided that the communist powers, the Chinese in particular, would probably be even more expansionist as the independent outbreak of Third World revolution invited more meddling. U.S. policy in their hands no longer was a means to contain a single threat from the Kremlin but an anchor against disorder and revolution everywhere.

Johnson's own insecurities led him to fear anything short of success in Vietnam. In his famous explanation to biographer Doris Kearns, Johnson complained that Vietnam was destined to destroy his historic mission as a reformer:

> I knew from the start that I was bound to be crucified either way I moved. If I left the woman I really loved—the Great Society—in order to get involved with that bitch of a war on the other side of the world, then I would lose everything at home. All my programs. All my hopes to feed the hungry and shelter the homeless. All my dreams to provide education and health care to the browns and the blacks and the lame and the poor.

Failure in Vietnam, he feared, would generate "an endless national debate . . . that would shatter my presidency, kill my administration, and damage our democracy." Evidently, Johnson equated his presidency with democracy, but that begged the question: who, then, was the enemy? First, he told Kearns, there were the conservatives, who "never wanted to help the poor or the Negroes in the first place." Then there was Robert Kennedy, "leading the fight against me, telling everyone that I had betrayed John Kennedy's commitment to South Vietnam." Only after this list of domestic enemies did Johnson include, in a final, apocalyptic flourish, that once they saw him so weakened, the Soviets and the Chinese "would move in a flash."

This summary came from a man who was deeply embittered and essentially in self-exile on his Texas ranch after 1968, but it is fair to say that Johnson measured Vietnam in the context of domestic politics. U.S. policy in Vietnam had no merits of its own to recommend it. The Americans had searched for political stability there, but Diem had eliminated his opposition so efficiently that no organized force was left to replace him. The generals had no taste for administering the country. The hamlet program lay in shambles, and when Diem was ousted, his network of regional and village officials collapsed. The North Vietnamese introduced their own troops into the conflict for the first time in an attempt to deepen the chaos in the South and thereby keep the Americans from military intervention. In what the historian George Herring calls a "colossal miscalculation," Hanoi, presuming that common sense would prevail in Washington, gambled that it quickly could raise the stakes so high that the Americans would withdraw.

Hanoi's escalation instead gave rise to the notion that U.S. policy should focus on the North instead of the South. The Americans proceeded to employ military pressure in order to force Hanoi to suspend its aid to the Vietcong. Such a strategy would allow the United States to play to its strength, military might, and at the same time escape the troublesome obligation to bring a reformist government to Saigon. If the United States fought off the North, Johnson figured, the South would have time to reorder its domestic affairs.

The Gulf of Tonkin Resolution

By summer 1964, the administration was looking for an excuse to use military force directly against the North. On August 1, North Vietnamese patrol boats engaged the U.S. destroyer, *Maddox*, while it was involved in electronic espionage in the Gulf of Tonkin off the North Vietnamese coast, and the administration decided to retaliate against any similar confrontations. The *Maddox* and another U.S. vessel returned on August 4 and reported that their radar had picked up enemy fire. The ships were operating in heavy seas, however, and their equipment was unreliable. No concrete evidence exists that the ships were attacked, but no matter. The administration used the incident as a pretext for retaliatory air strikes against North Vietnamese ships.

In order to show Hanoi a united front, Johnson sent Congress a joint resolution that permitted him to take "all necessary measures to repel any armed attacks against the forces of the United States and to prevent further aggression." An astonishingly few members questioned the resolution, considering how open-ended it was and that it practically surrendered Congress's constitutional power to declare war. It passed unanimously in the House and 98 to 2 in the Senate, with only Oregon's Wayne Morse and Alaska's Ernest Gruening dissenting. J. William Fulbright, who later became the most important congressional opponent of the war, led the floor fight for the resolution. Most members of Congress either supported Johnson's actions or were ignorant of the situation in Vietnam. In supporting the president and rushing to the colors, Congress conceded one of its most vital constitutional checks on foreign policy and greatly reduced its power to influence administration decisions.

Rolling Thunder

Through the fall, the administration decided to pursue a sustained bombing campaign that would proceed through "gradual escalation." In early February, Johnson launched operation Rolling Thunder, supposedly in response to a Vietcong attack on the American air base at Pleiku in which nine Americans had been killed. As with the Gulf of Tonkin, Johnson misled the public concerning the real nature of the bombings. From the outset, Rolling Thunder was much more than a policy of retaliation. McGeorge Bundy, who was in Vietnam at the time of the Pleiku attack, called for a "generalized pattern of reprisal" through which the United States would match "the level of outrages in the South" without bothering about the details of specific incidents or worrying about choosing corresponding targets. He went on to counsel moderation: "We must keep it clear at every stage both to Hanoi and to the world, that our reprisals will be reduced or stopped when outrages in the South are reduced or stopped." But Bundy's argument was for a policy of continuous, gradually increasing bombing.

Within two months Bundy was justifying "the present slowly ascending tempo of Rolling Thunder operations" as "wholly consistent with existing policy"—and indeed it was. The purpose of the bombing was twofold: to demonstrate the United

States' resolve "both to Hanoi and to the world" and to boost the morale of the southern regime. Bundy disavowed any intention to destroy or conquer North Vietnam, much in the spirit of William Appleman Williams's historic U.S. policymaker. The need for continuous bombing, he insisted, was primarily political: it was "the improvement of the situation in *South* Vietnam." If that were the goal, then the administration could offer bombing halts as concessions in the hopes of starting negotiations, and the president began to dangle unilateral halts from his very first major addresses on the war. Johnson sincerely claimed that "we want nothing for ourselves," as he told his audience at Johns Hopkins University in April 1965. In that famous address, the president promised unconditional negotiations and spoke of bringing a New Deal-style development project to Southeast Asia that would use the "vast Mekong River" to "provide food and water and power" and "enrich the hopes and existence of more than a hundred million people." Although the Hopkins address was meant for domestic consumption, it is also true that Johnson's hopes were moderate. That is, he sought nothing more than a stable regime in South Vietnam and, all things considered, did not want to destroy the North. This moderation was shallow, however, for it advanced as its one uncompromising goal something that was objectively unachievable—a U.S.-approved government in the South capable of providing stability and independence. Bundy himself was not the least bit certain that the bombing campaign would succeed; the odds, he estimated, ranged somewhere between 25 and 75 percent.

Bundy's pessimism was well founded. Instead of gaining a confident stability, South Vietnam endured a succession of indifferent, corrupt, and inefficient military leaders, and the administration quickly found itself considering further involvement. By summer Secretary McNamara conceded that the bombing campaign was no longer lifting morale, but rather than calling Rolling Thunder a failure, the administration decided that further escalation was necessary. McNamara argued that the program must be continued because, like a drug addict in constant need of the fix, the southern regime would collapse without it. Despite the "failure of the situation to improve," to abandon "the program would have a distinct depressing effect on the morale in South Vietnam." Escalation was the only answer the administration was willing to consider, and by midsummer that answer included ground forces. U.S. ground forces had already been introduced to guard air bases and then were followed in summer by some 50,000 more. The fateful decision to introduce U.S. ground troops effectively Americanized the war, and in dispatching them, Lyndon Johnson passed the one line of restraint that every president since Truman had recognized. Yet the political situation in Saigon grew worse. The Buddhists refused to participate in any new government, students launched scattered anti-American riots, and the generals refused to assume political responsibility.

Although administration officials believed that a military solution was possible, only the most fervent optimists—Rostow, some military men, and perhaps a few others—thought it would be merely a matter of military might. From the outset of its assumption of the war, the administration set certain boundaries and war aims. Moving within the parameters of the Cold War and the nuclear age, U.S. policymakers ruled out an invasion of North Vietnam for fear that it would bring the

Chinese into the war and lead at least to another Korea-like stalemate and possibly an even more dramatic superpower confrontation. The administration was willing to abide by Cold War restraints, first, because its war aim was not to defeat the North directly but to build political stability in the South. This was not a timid strategy but one that recognized that the war was a civil war and not an invasion from the North. Second, the administration believed that it could achieve its war aims most successfully by working within the Cold War boundaries. The United States never invaded North Vietnam but, within the boundaries thus set, waged a brutal and aggressive war built on the assumption that U.S. military superiority would compel the communists to give up the fight short of total destruction. No one questioned U.S. military superiority—least of all the communists, who knew best of all how ferocious the United States was—and indeed the Vietcong were almost completely destroyed. Washington was never quite able to grasp the notion that ultimately this superiority never mattered. The Vietnamese proved more tenacious and more willing to endure extensive destruction than U.S. policymakers expected, and beyond that, the issue still came down to whether a stable, pro-Western regime could be implanted in the South. The issue, in the end, was political and not military.

The War on the Ground

In a number of ways, the very conduct of the war made political stability impossible. The ground war brought U.S. and ARVN troops into regular conflict with villagers, did little to build public loyalty to the Saigon regime, increased the hostility between ARVN and U.S. troops, eventually resulted in growing casualty rates that alarmed the American public, and only made the southern regime more dependent on the United States.

Westmoreland's Strategy

The U.S. ground war began in late 1965 when General William Westmoreland, the head of American forces in Vietnam, supplied with almost 200,000 troops by the end of 1965, moved beyond the passive strategy of protecting air bases to a strategy of attrition. This strategy was designed to sap the will of the enemy by killing enough troops over a long period of time. Westmoreland settled on a three-part plan: "search-and-destroy" missions against the Vietcong, the securing of urban areas, and a general "pacification" program. Westmoreland's offensive strategy was neither truly conventional nor guerrilla warfare. Unlike conventional tactics, it relied on relatively small, mobile light-infantry units. Although Westmoreland tended to concentrate troops toward the North, he did not want to use them to hold territory. As a result, more than a few soldiers were led to wonder, along with Harold "Light Bulb" Bryant, a GI from East St. Louis, why they "would fight for a hill all day, spend two days or two nights there, and then abandon the hill." On the other hand, U.S. units were usually much larger than Vietcong guerrilla units; they also were mechanized, which made them far less mobile than the guerrillas and the light infantry of the North Vietnamese.

To some extent, search-and-destroy worked as Westmoreland envisioned. Under his command, U.S. casualty rates were low, for the guerrillas avoided prolonged and direct confrontations. In those instances where direct clashes erupted, superior U.S. power inflicted heavy losses. In fall 1965, U.S. troops of the 1st Cavalry, inexperienced and fighting on strange terrain, killed 3,000 North Vietnamese regulars in their first major engagement during a two-week battle in the Ia Drang Valley while suffering 300 dead. Although any commander would take a ten-to-one ratio, the battle of the Ia Drang showed that U.S. units were slow and dependent upon air power. The North Vietnamese were wary of meeting Americans head-on, which left U.S. troops to the frustrating task of chasing them while taking a casualty here, another there. Westmoreland's ground strategy, then, generally worked as it was designed, but it also left U.S. troops fighting on the enemy's terms without decisively countering his mobility.

Search-and-destroy also brought Americans into regular contact with rural villages, where they had to deal with the war in its basic complexity. Some villages were secure and loyal to the southern regime; some harbored and abetted Vietcong (VC) guerrillas; others were thoroughly VC; and still others were caught in the cross fire and wavered back and forth depending on what forces happened to be in their midst. In the heat of fighting, U.S. soldiers did not distinguish the political affiliations of villages and as a consequence destroyed civilian homes and killed the innocent and pragmatic along with active enemies. Often tense and tired, reminded constantly that old women and young children could be as deadly as an armed man, GIs could cross the line of proper conduct and kill noncombatants. The most notorious atrocity, the murder of more than 200 civilians, including women and children, at the village of My Lai in spring 1968, which resulted in a national uproar during the trial of the unit commander, William Calley in 1971, was ample evidence that Vietnamese civilian life had become cheap. Indeed, the most troubling aspect of My Lai was that few GIs considered it remarkable.

The Air War

It is impossible to know how many civilians were killed by ground forces, and it was also easy to exaggerate, given the publicity surrounding My Lai. Any focus on murders in the jungle, furthermore, distracted attention from the more important source of destruction and civilian deaths, the air war, which almost certainly resulted in hundreds of thousands of civilian deaths in North and South Vietnam, Cambodia, and Laos. It became quickly apparent that Rolling Thunder had no discernible military effect—movement to the south steadily increased along with the U.S. commitment—nor did it bolster the southern regime. Yet after a brief bombing halt at the end of 1965, the administration met failure with redoubled effort, expanding the list of approved targets to include transportation facilities and supply depots and increasing the assault against infiltration routes. In the North, U.S. pilots regularly attacked around the Hanoi–Haiphong area, striking at all known military targets, as well as industrial centers, bridges, and roads. In the South, they attacked around civilian areas with permission from the government and set up "free-fire zones," Vietcong strongholds where they needed no authorization to unleash their loads.

As U.S. officials liked to point out, the air war was carefully conducted and avoided outright destruction of civilian targets. But the extent of American bombing was unprecedented: the United States dropped more tons of bombs during the Vietnam War than had been dropped in the history of warfare. Much of the aerial assault, especially against the North, came from huge B-52s that flew high-altitude sorties from Guam. Capable of carrying up to twenty-seven tons of bombs, the B-52s would "carpet bomb" their targets. They could leave an area pockmarked and looking like the moon, where huge craters often filled up with water to become small lakes. One guerrilla leader described the B-52 raids as the most humbling experience, worse even than the torture he received at the hands of the South Vietnamese police. The carpet-bombing technique provided a few seconds of terrifying warning; as the bombs came closer and closer, it was common to lose control of one's bladder. Once a group of Russian advisors was visiting the jungle camp where Truong Nhu Tang, a leader of the National Liberation Front, was staying when it was visited by B-52s, and the group had a knowing laugh when the Russians appeared after the raid with their pants urine-soaked.

As with the search-and-destroy missions, of course, American bombers did not attack civilian targets regularly, but there was no way of engaging in such a huge bombing operation without inflicting collateral damage. In the North, by the Defense Department's own estimate in 1966, "collateral damage" included 1,000 civilian casualties a week, and CIA estimates ran more than double that figure. Civilian casualties may have run as high as 300,000 annually by 1968. General Westmoreland once told reporter Neil Sheehan that these casualties concerned him, "but it does deprive the enemy of the population, doesn't it?" The "rules of engagement" that allegedly hamstrung U.S. flyers were routinely flouted, as the war was taken into Laos, Cambodia, and against civilians as well. Like soldiers in the heat of combat, U.S. pilots were not as picky about where they bombed as official justifications claimed.

U.S. Technology

The heavy reliance on air power was the centerpiece of the assumption that technological superiority would prevail against a primitive enemy. Along with B-52s, chemical weapons, and napalm, U.S. troops used all manner of ingenious devices, from the best in mobile armor and helicopters that were central to the conduct of the war to exotic weapons better suited to James Bond. The Army, for example, tried to use radio-powered fleas to light on guerrillas and emit signals that would permit the enemy to be followed into the jungle. Unfortunately, it proved impossible to find fleas that knew the difference between a guerrilla and other warm bodies. Schemes ranged from the silly to the absurd: Secretary McNamara once seriously considered the possibility of setting up a laser boundary around South Vietnam.

The enemy responded with a strategy that was as primitive as U.S. technology was advanced. He dug into the earth, deeply, extensively, and systematically, and carved out an astonishing network of tunnels that ran from the outskirts of Saigon to the Cambodian border. The guerrillas, their families, whole villages, and regular northern units lived, sometimes months at a time, in tunnels that included living areas, hospitals, ammunition factories, headquarters, and stages for theater and music. Running hundreds of miles in all, the tunnels laced the ground underneath the strategically vital areas to the north and northwest of Saigon and allowed the Vietcong to launch attacks and escape again. Once the Americans discovered the extent of the system, they employed specially chosen men—"tunnel rats," loners with wild streaks—to drop in and destroy the tunnels, often engaging in hand-to-hand combat as they did. True to form, the Americans also developed gadgets to detect movement underground or to warn of sudden movement above. In early 1967, the Americans attempted to destroy the tunnel network once and for all. A week of B-52 bombings was followed by an infusion of 30,000 troops, who were followed by earth-moving equipment that ground up what was left of the so-called Iron Triangle, a densely forested region just north of Saigon. Undaunted, the Vietcong rebuilt the tunnels in time for the Tet offensive in January 1968.

Relying on technology played to U.S. strength and limited U.S. casualties, but it had restrictive effects of its own. It produced a varied arrogance that gained expression in the cockiness of officers, the complacence of troops, and sheer wastefulness. The well-stocked Americans provided the Vietcong with much of the material later used to kill them; everything from dud bombs to empty beer cans were put to use in booby traps and ammunition. It was a method of war that certainly contributed to the surreal character of the Vietnam experience. U.S. troops often went from air-conditioned night clubs one night to steamy, dangerous jungles the next day. U.S. pilots kept bankers' hours, bombing in such regular and predictable intervals that the rhythms of Hanoi revolved around American raids.

The U.S. Combatants and REMFs

Although these strange circumstances did not hamper the military effort, they did produce a cumulative sense that Vietnam was unreal. GIs were the first to admit that it was possible to be in Vietnam without actually being in Vietnam. Depending on how one measures particular duties, between 75 and 90 percent of Americans stationed in Vietnam were not assigned combat duties. The vast majority were support troops: warehousemen, paper shufflers, mechanics, bartenders, and nurses, among others. Although some GIs moved from support duties to combat roles, the majority were either one or the other, either fighting "in country," the "real Vietnam," or working in the rear as "REMFs" (which, in the vulgar language of the war, stood for Rear Echelon Mother Fuckers). The contrast between sitting at an air-conditioned desk job in Da Nang or Saigon and trudging through jungles near the Cambodian border predictably caused tension between Americans. "I didn't believe Nha Trang was part of Vietnam," one soldier explained of a base his infantry unit had been brought to. "They had barracks, hot water, had mess halls with three hot meals and air conditioning. Nha Trang was like a beach, a resort." Trained to kill and determined to play the part, this soldier and his buddies stood out in Nha Trang as if they belonged to another place or time. "They reacted like we was some kind of animals, like we these guys from the boonies."

The tension between infantry soldiers and REMFs was not solely a matter of temporary duty but was entwined with the inequalities of U.S. society. Sometimes nothing more than the luck of the draw would distinguish between the two. Whereas caprice works on individual levels, the general fate of GIs was dictated by educational level, age, and, indirectly, class status and race. Because the military channeled personnel according to acquired skills and education and because enlistees with both could bargain their way to safer jobs, those with little beyond high school educations were far more likely to serve in combat roles, while others with postsecondary education were more likely to take assignments in the rear. Younger men were disadvantaged in this process. Consequently, the average age of Americans in Vietnam was barely over 19, in contrast to the 26-year-old average of World War II soldiers. Class differences in U.S. society shaped educational and work opportunity, which in effect meant that military assignments also worked against working-class men. Up to 80 percent of Americans in Vietnam were from working-class backgrounds, with the remainder made up of patriotic enlistees, cadet officers from the military academies, and assorted luckless emigrés from the American middle class. Because the American class structure was also racially skewed, African-American men served disproportionately in combat roles, even though they were drafted roughly in proportion to their numbers in the general population. Indeed, the standardized tests given to enlistees probably discriminated against them. In the first two years of the ground war, 23 percent of combat deaths were black soldiers, against the slightly more than 11 percent of African Americans in the domestic population. The message was not lost on Richard Ford III when he walked into the Nha Trang resort and found that "almost everybody is white."

The military took steps to hide or minimize class-skewed casualty rates. One means of glossing over the problem was to turn over units quickly, thereby minimizing the chances of any individual dying. Americans were put into Vietnam on a thirteen-month rotation, meaning in practice that a GI would be "in country" about ten or eleven months. This was good public relations, perhaps, but rapid rotation was incompatible with military efficiency. Common sense warned GIs to keep their heads down when all they needed to do was stay alive for a year. Worse, units were not rotated together; they barely had time to gain jungle experience and form the mutual dependence necessary in a combat unit before they were broken up by departures and arrivals. The last thing a GI who had a week or two left in his hitch wanted was to go out next to a new arrival, but it was common. In response to complaints from his civil rights constituency, President Johnson took steps after 1967 to lessen the proportion of African-American casualties, but racial tensions only mounted, as troops responded to the deteriorating racial situation at home. By most accounts, race made no difference in combat units, where the demands of survival muted animosities, In the rear, however, GIs segregated themselves and played out the conflicts of home. Class conflict was never as obvious as race conflict, but it lurked underneath the combat soldier–REMF split and infused the tense relationship between draftees and officers, particularly in country. Not until Richard Nixon entered office was the draft reformed to eliminate class bias, but by then, when U.S. troops were pulling out, the lottery reforms were too late.

The most unrelenting source of frustration for the Americans remained the South Vietnamese elite. After more than two years of watching coalitions shift and generals come and go, Johnson backed Nguyen Cao Ky as prime minister, an unstable air force officer whom one administration official described as "absolutely the bottom of the barrel." No sooner had Ky taken the helm with American blessings than he was faced with a crisis at home, as the Buddhists took to the streets again, joined by a wide variety of protesters. The cities themselves, which had long been the areas most firmly under government control, became almost unmanageable, partly because an estimated 4 million refugees from the countryside began to flood into them. The constantly enlarged U.S. presence increased urban instability because the influx of American goods flooded the black market and provided larger incentives for corruption.

Tet

It was remarkable that, despite this environment, the Ky regime managed to survive. In 1967 Ky and his running mate, Nguyen Van Thieu, were officially elected under a new constitution, which allowed Johnson to claim that political progress was being made. Strictly speaking, Johnson was correct but only when the Ky–Thieu regime was measured against the vacuum of power that had existed since Diem. There was little question that the huge U.S. presence alone held up the regime. To convince an increasingly troubled American public that both military and political progress was genuine, Johnson launched a public relations campaign, highlighted by a return visit from Westmoreland in late 1967. Westmoreland assured Congress that the war could be won in as soon as two years if the national resolve remained. The administration readily handed out to its congressional friends optimistic reports from other military sources and encouraged them to visit Vietnam for themselves.

This optimism belied increasing divisions within. Robert McNamara resigned; his resignation was effective upon selection of his replacement. Although the Joint Chiefs of Staff (JCS) and Rostow argued that Johnson should resist all pressure to change policy, still others maintained that the U.S. commitment could be rearranged in order to reduce casualties and ease public concerns. Johnson was contemplating this last, middle course of action when on January 30, 1968, the Vietcong launched a well-coordinated surprise attack on government-held cities, hoping that the many refugees and urban dissidents would join in spontaneous rebellion. The Tet offensive, launched during the New Year's holiday, brought the Vietcong into most major areas, including the U.S. embassy in Saigon. In the imperial city of Hue, the battle grew particularly bloody and in three weeks claimed 500 American and ARVN lives, perhaps 5,000 communists, and as many civilians, several thousand of whom were

In February 1968 a captured Vietcong guerrilla officer is shot by South Viet-namese national police chief Brigadier General Nguyen Ngoc Loan.
[*AP/Wide World Photos*]

assassinated by the Vietcong. Elsewhere the Vietcong were quickly turned back in a resounding military defeat. Vietcong losses ran about 32,000 against only slightly more than 3,000 combined ARVN and American deaths.

The Tet offensive, like the war itself, was more important in its political than its military aspects. The guerrilla movement was irreparably damaged, and once again the "body counts" tallied about ten to one in the Americans' favor. The thorough destruction of the Vietcong forced Hanoi to assume the largest share of fighting thereafter. The ARVN fought relatively well, but the offensive forced the government to pull troops back into the cities and therefore away from pacified areas, thus undermining much of the progress that had been made in late 1967. Whatever the outcome, the breadth of the offensive undercut popular confidence in ARVN protection. In the United States, the offensive refuted the administration's public relations campaign and snuffed the proverbial light at the end of the tunnel. Tet jolted many people who previously were bewildered by events in Vietnam and convinced them that the war was pointless, if not endless.

Johnson first reacted with stiffened resolve, and sensing the president's mood, JCS Chairman Earle Wheeler suggested to Westmoreland that the time was right to put in a new and ambitious troop request. Wheeler had his own agenda. Worried that Vietnam was weakening U.S. strength in Western Europe and Japan, he sought to use a new request from Westmoreland as leverage for a general troop increase, even for arguing again that the reserves be mobilized. Never one to turn down largess, Westmoreland was happy to have more men sent his way, and he assured Wheeler that more troops "would turn the tide to the point where the enemy might see the light." Wheeler coaxed the figure of 206,000 new troops from Westmoreland and forwarded the request to the White House without explaining that they were not all to go to Vietnam. At the same time, many military higher-ups, Wheeler included, spoke of the need to expand the war against a staggered enemy.

Wheeler's plan backfired, for in the beleaguered atmosphere of the White House, the request was taken at face value. Johnson handed the matter over to McNamara's successor as secretary of defense, Clark Clifford, an old Washington hand, trusted LBJ confidant, and self-professed hawk. New on the job and bewildered himself, Clifford decided that it was time for a full-scale review of U.S. policy. Civilian officials in the Pentagon, many of whom had growing doubts about the war, conducted the review and argued that Westmoreland's request would force Congress to cut domestic spending 20 to 30 percent and foreign aid by half. Hanoi would match any U.S. manpower increase, and therefore no clear end to the war was in sight. Clifford was shocked. He was even more appalled by the inability of the Joint Chiefs to offer any reassurance. Were the new troops enough to affect the war in a reasonable amount of time? If not, how long would the war take? How many more troops would be needed? To all of these basic questions, the answers were vague and dissatisfying. Clifford came away from his study convinced that the request could not be granted.

Johnson himself probably agreed with Clifford. Instead of seeing the Tet military victory as a reason for expansion, he came to see it, as George Herring has pointed out, as a sign that the South Vietnamese were ready to resume a larger share of the war and as an opportunity to open negotiations from a position of strength. The military situation had improved, but domestic opposition to the war had increased as well. Congress reacted bitterly against the Westmoreland troop request, and Johnson's own standing seemed damaged when he barely won the New Hampshire primary. Taking some moves to limit the conflict would soothe growing public criticism, and he began to consider a bombing halt. Johnson outlined essentially these positions in his nationally televised speech on March 31, 1968 and then added in closing his dramatic announcement that he would neither seek nor accept the Democratic nomination of 1968.

Johnson's decision not to seek reelection was not an admission of failure in Vietnam. In fact, very little changed in U.S. policy after March 31. The negotiations that began in May went nowhere; both sides continued to follow the policy of negotiating while fighting. Although some cosmetic changes were made in U.S. tactics—Westmoreland was replaced by Creighton Abrams, who put more emphasis on pacification than on search-and-destroy—the administration stepped up its bombing and launched an aggressive antiguerrilla campaign, the Phoenix program.

Tet did not end the war in any formal sense, but it showed that the qualitative end had been reached. That is, the war was doomed to be a stalemate, and the offensive bore out as much. It was impossible for the North Vietnamese to realize an outright military victory against the United States, and as long as U.S. troops were there, some semblance of an anticommunist regime would remain in the South. Yet there was no way that the United States could conjure up a southern government that would be popular, stable, democratic, and truly representative.

The communists undertook the offensive, in fact, in an attempt to break the stalemate. Negotiations of a sort had been ongoing since 1965. Neither side could afford to incur international disrepute by avoiding negotiations, yet neither was serious about ending the conflict at the table. Because the administration refused to recognize the National Liberation Front (NLF), its only negotiating adversary was North Vietnam, whose fundamental premise was that the U.S. intervention was illegitimate and that unilateral U.S. cessation of hostilities was necessary before negotiations could begin. At the table, they insisted on absolute self-determination for the South beginning with a coalition government that included the NLF. Johnson's position was just as uncompromising. He demanded a complete cease-fire, the mutual withdrawal of U.S. and North Vietnamese troops from the South, and the establishment of a southern government that did not include the NLF. The administration considered the NLF a communist front, even though its leadership and much of its urban constituency were noncommunist nationalists and included many of the country's professional and business elites.

The enduring tragedy of Vietnam lay in Washington's refusal to see that the North Vietnamese interests were not identical to those of their southern comrades, that however close the two were, however dependent the NLF was on the North, the two were not the same. The North Vietnamese were willing to carry through Ho Chi Minh's prophetic claim that he would lose ten people to every one American but in the end would still prevail, and they were willing to do so because national reunification was their ultimate goal. For the southerners in the NLF, many of whom were noncommunists, the ultimate goal was a coalition government that would give them the room to rise to power; they envisioned, in other words, an independent South Vietnam rather than one subsumed by northern communists, a goal that was quite close to what Washington said it wanted. The NLF's principal quarrel was with the puppet regime. For the North Vietnamese, the Americans were the principal enemy, and they therefore had less incentive to compromise with the United States.

The Americanization of the war threw out of balance the fine distinctions between the NLF and the North. For the more the Americans weighed in, the more the North committed itself and the more the communists dominated the NLF. The more they did so, the more the only noncommunists capable of creating a demo-cratic, popular, and independent government in the South were swept aside.

Nixon, Realpolitik, and the End of the War

Richard Nixon's election to the presidency in 1968 marked the beginning of the end for the U.S. presence in Vietnam. It was a fitting end too: tragically long in coming and wastefully violent. Although Nixon sold himself as the candidate of moderation in 1968, he was a dedicated anticommunist with a hellish love of military might. Nixon's contradictory impulses led to a relentless military pounding of North Vietnam intended to bring them to the peace table. Nixon, the self-professed defender of the "silent majority," the average citizen, approached Vietnam in a way that reflected what many Americans had come to feel: that we either should fight to win or get out. Nixon did both.

Not that Nixon was following the crowd. Instead, he worked according to an understanding of international relations, strengthened by a growing relationship with a Harvard political science professor, Henry Kissinger, that was basically new as the guiding idea behind U.S. foreign policy. *Realpolitik*, the notion that stability was assured through a carefully maintained balance of power, became the guiding scheme of Nixonian diplomacy. No one liked admitting it less than Nixon, but the world had changed to the point where Americans could not have their way everywhere around the globe. The Russians were close to parity in military strength; the Chinese were an undeniable power in their region of the world; and U.S. policymakers could serve the national interests best by admitting as much and making do within this more complicated world. Adopting that doctrine led Nixon to seek working relationships with Russia and China, "détente" it was called, not in order to become friends but merely to ensure U.S. power in a relatively stable world.

To both Nixon and Kissinger, Vietnam had become an obstacle to, rather than an integral part of, American security, because it drained U.S. resources and weakened the nation in relation to Russia and China. Had it been realistically possible to win the Vietnam War, they would have spared no effort at doing so. As it was, they entered Washington determined to accomplish two ends: to bring the United States out of Vietnam through "peace with honor," and to take whatever other steps were necessary to ensure the strength of the South Vietnamese. The two men probably disagreed about which of these was most important. Kissinger, who cared less about domestic politics, worried about the drain of the war on U.S. resources, or at least he was more willing to accept U.S. withdrawal. Nixon, on the other hand, persisted in the conviction that the South Vietnamese could sustain themselves, and thus the two had different definitions of what a "peace with honor" was.

Vietnamization and the Invasion of Cambodia

The new administration set out to end the war through diplomacy and threats of violence. Nixon counted on his reputation as an anticommunist and believed that Hanoi would enter serious talks simply because of threats, most of which he made good on. In 1969 and 1970 he secretly bombed Cambodia, and toward the end of 1969 he nearly set out on a once-and-for-all campaign until his advisors convinced him to postpone it. Meanwhile, he launched the policy of Vietnamization, through which U.S. troops were gradually withdrawn, leaving the ground war to the South Vietnamese. A renewed pacification effort, this time accompanied by some genuine land reform and based on strengthened village security forces, secured perhaps 85 to 90 percent of the southern countryside. The Phoenix program was stepped up, and some 20,000 suspected Vietcong were assassinated.

Vietnamization checked domestic unrest, and successful pacification promised some relief to the Ky–Thieu regime. Then Nixon made a costly blunder. In March 1970 Prince Norodom Sihanouk, the popular ruler of Cambodia, fell in a military coup. Although the administration probably did not engineer the coup, it clearly welcomed it. Sihanouk had long played a delicate balancing game in his attempt to keep Cambodia neutral in the war; he maintained relations with the United States and permitted the Vietcong to use parts of eastern Cambodia as a staging area. The U.S. military had been eager to press into Cambodia, especially to find the infamous COSVN, the nerve center of the communist military effort in the South. Nixon saw the coup as an opportunity to buy time for the Thieu regime and demonstrate his toughness.

The invasion of eastern Cambodia scattered COSVN and disrupted NLF military efforts, but only temporarily. Because COSVN was nothing more than a group of people instead of a large, immobile command center, NLF officials simply moved deeper into Cambodia and then returned when the Americans withdrew. When Nixon announced the invasion on April 30, he kicked off an unprecedented wave of campus protests, including the tragic confrontations between students and police at Kent State and Jackson State. To the communists, through the invasion Nixon, as one NLF official who fled along with COSVN put it, had "traded a few immediate and short-term military gains for the unpredictable consequences of intruding into an already volatile Cambodia and for severe, long-term political debits at home."

The Cambodian invasion partially undermined the gains made the year before. The invasion set off a chain of events that led to a tragic civil war in Cambodia. Hanoi, more impressed with Nixon's domestic opposition than with his threats, began to stall in the ongoing secret talks. Having provoked widespread protests, Nixon moved again to quell discontent and accelerated troop withdrawals. Meanwhile, Vietnamization began to show its weaknesses. Pacification had been modestly successful, but it spread the ARVN thin. American morale reached its lowest point, with soldiers caught between war and withdrawal. Racial tension worsened; "fragging" incidents, in which troops killed or wounded their unit officers, peaked; and drug use skyrocketed.

Kissinger and the Peace Accords

Kissinger decided to produce some headway by revising U.S. demands. In May, he outlined a new position that called for a U.S. withdrawal in exchange for all prisoners of war; meanwhile, northern units would remain below the 17th parallel, and Thieu would stay in power. In some ways, Kissinger was recognizing military realities, since it would have been difficult to root the enemy out. Furthermore, these proposals included a promise from Hanoi to reach a political settlement before a cease-fire. For the Americans, it offered an avenue out of Vietnam through an agreement that might be sold as "honorable."

For Thieu, however, the proposal prescribed disaster. A cease-fire in place that left northern troops in the South obliged him to win a military victory. To him,

Kissinger's proposals smacked of faithless betrayal. South Vietnamese opposition forced Kissinger to rely all the more on secret negotiations with Le Duc Tho, the North Vietnamese diplomat, which allowed him to work without interference but had a price as well. Tho proved Kissinger's equal as a negotiator, and the politically skillful North Vietnamese exploited the differences between public diplomacy, in which they were the essence of sweet reason, and private negotiations, where they were stubborn and duplicitous. Kissinger's new proposals provoked a flurry of encouraging diplomacy, but the talks broke down over the issue of whether the Thieu regime should be left in place.

The stagnant situation remained until March 1972, when Hanoi launched another massive offensive. The communists knew that the United States could not help the ARVN, for only 95,000 American personnel remained in Vietnam, and only a tiny portion of those were combat troops. The "Easter Offensive" was designed to test the success of Vietnamization and to improve Hanoi's bargaining position. The North hoped to increase the territory under its control and, if the ARVN performed badly, the U.S. negotiating position would be weakened. The purpose of the offensive, then, partly showed that Hanoi was seriously considering a return to negotiations. Like Tet, the offensive failed: the ARVN held its ground and suffered 25,000 casualties to 100,000 communist losses.

The offensive once again provoked Nixon's violent disposition. Though faced with the possibility that the Russians would cancel an approaching, historic summit meeting, Nixon approved a massive bombing campaign, mined Haiphong harbor, and blockaded the North Vietnamese coast. In moving so aggressively, he forced both the Chinese and Russians to decide whether their support for the Vietnamese was worth the disruption of détente. Both decided it was not. While maintaining ties with Hanoi and publicly condemning the U.S. response, neither permitted the bombings to destroy the emerging relationship with the United States, and both privately insisted that Hanoi begin serious negotiations.

Once they resumed discussion in fall 1972, Le Duc Tho and Kissinger devoted themselves to finding an agreement, which was reached after Kissinger agreed that a tripartite commission would oversee elections in the South sixty days after the cease-fire. Kissinger sacrificed Thieu in the frantic process of negotiations. Hanoi, worried that Nixon would renege on the agreement if he won reelection, insisted on a November deadline. But Thieu, understandably shocked by the agreement that Kissinger brought him, insisted on 129 textual changes and rejected the commission scheme and the cease-fire in place.

Thieu's opposition and, as it turned out, Nixon's uneasiness about the agreements threatened Kissinger's handiwork just as he announced "peace is at hand." Le Duc Tho and Kissinger therefore resumed several weeks of bickering and adjustment until, in mid-December, the talks died again. Again in response, Nixon unleashed a terrifying air assault on the Hanoi–Haiphong area that outpaced any single round of attacks during the entire war. The Christmas bombings, so inappropriately timed, set off outrage both nationally and internationally, but the two sides resumed bargaining and, on January 8, 1973, concluded an agreement that was hardly different from the one that had been on the table in October.

The peace accords were, as Kissinger put it, intended to provide a "decent interval" between the U.S. withdrawal and a communist victory. No doubt such was Kissinger's position. It was also one shared by the Vietnamese, both South and North, who resumed fighting before the year was out. Nixon, who tried to sell the agreement to Thieu by promising renewed U.S. support if Hanoi breached the accords, convinced himself that the accords were workable. Whether or not he could have made them so is a moot point, since he became ensnared in the Watergate scandal and resigned his office before the North Vietnamese launched their final offensive. Nixon's successor, Gerald Ford, had neither the will nor the support to save the South. The U.S.-backed government went down to defeat, ending the United States' longest war.

CHAPTER 4

The Social History of the War

 In the annals of military history, the U.S. war in Vietnam will stand as one of those embarrassments that great powers suffer occasionally and that pose momentary difficulties but no serious weakening. Millions of Vietnamese died in their extraordinary fight for independence, but the roughly 60,000 dead and missing Americans comprise a casualty list that is not very impressive in terms of modern warfare. We need to dwell on this perspective for a moment in order to comprehend the complex ways in which Americans experienced the Vietnam War. One of the alleged benefits of fighting the high-tech war was that it was supposed to minimize disruption at home. For many Americans, the war was distant, the sort of thing that happened to a relative, a neighbor, or a member of one's church; somewhat in the manner with which people regard a strange disease, natural disaster, or violent crime, the majority of Americans were not directly touched by Vietnam. Apathy and indifference was the rule before 1968, and only slightly less so thereafter.

Yet Vietnam, even more than civil rights, was the defining event of the sixties, for it reflected and pronounced the wider social currents in all their ambiguity. It was a liberal war fought in an age of high liberal expectations, and yet to its critics it signaled the persistence of imperialism, racism, and arrogance among leaders who were otherwise enlightened people. It combined the rational efficiency of bureaucracy, technology, and intellect, yet put it to use in a war that was rationally indefensible. Opposing what was supposed to be a war fought for democracy in South Vietnam brought harassment and jail. The war exposed great moral ambiguity, not only of national purpose but of individual purpose as well. Many activists were convinced of the immorality of U.S. policy; undoubtedly, however, a few opposed the war, and many more avoided the draft because they did not want to interrupt their comfortable lives at home. Who was to say that college students who shirked their duty were more moral than the men who fought in Vietnam? The moral question was irresolvable, and when it became the center of the debate, Vietnam became a matter of the heart rather than of the head.

Limited War and the Media

Lyndon Johnson attempted to fight the Vietnam War with as little disruption to domestic life as possible, only to create the single most divisive issue in American life since the Civil War. Johnson heeded a number of different motives in hoping to isolate the war from American life, but the intention to fight quietly fit into both the military and political interests of the administration. The president was genuinely concerned that a broadened effort in Southeast Asia would undermine the Great Society. The commitment to a limited war, which underlay the strategy of gradual escalation, also recommended against beating the war drums at home. The war planners believed that democracies were poor at fighting limited wars because people had to be whipped up into a frenzy just to get them to make the necessary sacrifices, and once whipped up they got out of control. The war planners worried that public enthusiasm would pressure the administration to go beyond its limits, which would narrow diplomatic options and conceivably invite a wider war with China that all feared. All things considered, the president no doubt saw the prudence in McGeorge Bundy's recommendation, offered along with his lengthy defense of Rolling Thunder in February 1965, "that we should execute our reprisal policy with as low a level of public noise as possible."

The Adversarial Relationship of Government and Media

As a means of setting the domestic tone of the war, this strategy proved as tricky as the military equation. Obviously, the public had to be told something about the conduct of war. From the very beginning, the administration faced the delicate business of telling the public as little as possible.

Here was the source of what became known as the "credibility gap"—the gap between what sources outside the administration were saying about Vietnam and what the government itself was willing to admit. It was also the source of conflict between the government and the national media. The conduct of limited war at home gave rise to two important developments that have remained part of Vietnam's lasting legacy: a growing public cynicism about the integrity of government, and an antagonistic relationship, often exaggerated but nonetheless still evident, between the media and the government.

In the undeclared war that Vietnam was, extensive government censorship of the media was not legally possible. The American media and the military had to live with one another on the basis of informal, voluntary press guidelines, which prohibited the press from reporting only those facts that had direct military value, such as troop movements. Unable to control exactly what journalists said, the military was guarded, prone to prevarication, and poised for confrontations with reporters. At the same time, the media had become free to meddle in ways that certainly had not been possible in the past. Although the number of accredited journalists in Vietnam was no larger than it had been in World War II, the media was far larger as an industry and more omnipresent as a force in public life, thanks especially to the growth of television. Legitimized as a profession through university instruction, both print and electronic journalism encouraged an aura of critical detachment and objectivity among their practitioners. The media had the power, the opportunity, the legal freedom, and the temperament to involve itself in Vietnam in an unprecedented way.

The relationship that developed between the media and officialdom was a complex one. Reporters were not the antagonists that they were often made out to be and that some occasionally pride themselves on having been. When he went to Vietnam in 1961, for example, *New York Times* reporter David Halberstam became part of a press corps that included some hustling, independently minded reporters but that was by and large quiescent. Most reporters were content to take their information from government sources. At that early stage, the most newsworthy item was the introduction of U.S. aid and advisors under Taylor–Rostow, and most reporters, like the U.S. personnel they were there to report on, expected the tide of the war to turn. Complacency was predictable under these circumstances.

Halberstam, Neil Sheehan, and a handful of other reporters were more energetic than most. "What obsessed them was *the story*," Halberstam later explained, and they were willing to widen their angle to include lower-level officers, Vietnamese civilians, and trips into the jungle. Halberstam's wanderings resulted in his skeptical reports back to the states and a book, *The Making of a Quagmire* (1964), which was highly critical of both the Diem regime and the conduct of the war.

Halberstam's book set something of a precedent by which the media stood as the government's adversary. But the degree to which even the energetic reporters were adversaries, as well as the extent of official resentment against the media, has been exaggerated. Halberstam himself exaggerated when he claimed that the struggle between official news and "the reporting of a small handful of newsmen" became "a major foreign policy struggle." Like practically all other reporters, Halberstam was steeped in U.S. Cold War thinking. For all his criticism, he saw the conflict in official terms as an invasion from the North, and he accepted as an article of faith that "Vietnam had become vital to our national interests." He concluded *Quagmire* by reiterating what U.S. officials were telling themselves: that none of the options seemed very good, but that withdrawal was no·option at all, for it would betray the Vietnamese people, damage U.S. prestige, and "intensify" communist pressure elsewhere.

Johnson's Handling of the Media

It is no surprise, therefore, that Lyndon Johnson found the public relations side of the conflict easygoing at first. The Gulf of Tonkin incident raised no more suspicion among the American media than it did congressional opposition. No one badgered Johnson or asked penetrating questions during the August 4 press conference at which he announced the incident and the retaliatory air strikes. Instead, all substantial press coverage merely reported the incident as the administration had described it: as an unprovoked attack on a U.S. vessel in neutral waters.

Although the uncritical acceptance of the government's version demonstrated the potential success of fighting the quiet war, the administration understood that the media's willingness to accept its version of the facts was limited. A successful public relations strategy had to be planned. One part of the strategy that emerged through 1965 was to keep the media off balance by stressing peaceful intentions while upping the military ante. The Hopkins speech, for example, included nothing that was dramatically new, but the administration wanted the emphasis on Johnson's "unconditional talks" to be interpreted as a serious new direction. Similarly, the bombing halt in May was adopted mostly for public relations reasons. When the administration began the large-scale introduction of troops that summer, it did so with as little publicity as possible.

The administration also exerted back-channel influence on journalists, sometimes through attempted seduction, other times through pressure and cajoling. Johnson was particularly keen to gain the support of Walter Lippmann, the dean of American journalists. He awarded Lippmann the Medal of Freedom, he wined and dined him, and he pretended to listen to his advice. At other times, the administration denied privileges to critical reporters and leaked information to favorites. But in so doing, the administration only angered independently minded journalists. The more Johnson tried to direct the news, the more suspicious the media became.

Johnson's relations with the media, in any case, turned on events in Vietnam. The introduction of ground troops altered those relations for obvious reasons. It meant that the administration was committing to a wider war, and public interest in Vietnam increased as Americans began to die regularly. Several scholars have shown, however, that the commitment of ground forces was not an unqualified danger to the administration. Before late 1967, the typical war story detailed the adventures or misadventures of American soldiers; similarly, stories about the air war focused on the pilots' skill with their high-tech weaponry. The enemy remained faceless, nameless, and for the most part evil; indeed, U.S. reporting was dominated by stereotypes about both Asians and guerrilla fighters.

Television and Print Coverage of the War

Much of this on-the-spot reporting was from television journalists. Vietnam was the first "living-room war," the first to be broadcast into homes on a regular basis, but its effects are not clear. Like their print colleagues, television journalists preferred to think of themselves as "objective" rather than biased one way or another, and accordingly, their coverage of the war was shaped more by the nature of the medium than by the messenger. With its fundamental time limitations, television was rarely able to show more than a glimpse of the war at any one time. Perhaps 20 percent of television reports from Vietnam dealt with battles; the remaining reports covered official pronouncements, the political situation in the South, or the personal interest stories for which television has such a strong penchant. Even the coverage of men in battle was usually tame. Most battle sequences showed GIs stalking through the jungle or firing their weapons at an unseen enemy; only about one-third of the battle stories showed casualties, which may have been graphic but were probably not enough to turn the national stomach. Who can say that battle scenes appalled viewers in any significant numbers? They were as likely to evoke the response that "war is hell," especially from men who had fought in World War II or Korea, or to leave viewers benumbed and apathetic.

To be sure, critical reporting emanated from both mainstream print and television journalists. In August 1965, for instance, CBS's Morley Safer happened on a group of Marines who, having just concluded an extended fight with guerrillas, were in the process of destroying the village of Cam Ne. Safer's piece showed several soldiers setting fire to thatched roofs with their Zippo lighters. The network, rightly expecting serious political consequences, hesitated but aired the piece with a balanced narrative: "There is little doubt that American firepower can win a military victory here. But to a Vietnamese peasant . . . it will take more than presidential promises to convince him that we are on his side." Safer's piece was dramatic and critical—the narration made no attempt to explain the incident away—and caused the expected political fallout. Johnson called CBS News president and personal friend, Frank Stanton, and complained that CBS was "fucking me." Later critics claimed that Safer staged the episode. But one GI who participated (and who, incidentally, almost killed a group of women and children huddling in one of the huts) recalled: "That's just the way we did it. . . . That's why people bought Zippos."

The bulk of criticism coming from mainstream print journalism issued from the *New York Times*, whose coverage of the war was by no means completely hostile. In late 1966, after the North Vietnamese claimed that U.S. bombers had destroyed civilian neighborhoods in Hanoi, *Times* reporter Harrison Salisbury arranged a trip to the city, ostensibly to view bomb damage. Having seen at firsthand some of the carnage of World War II, Salisbury was not impressed by the damage he saw and concluded that it resulted from bombs that had missed military objectives. He nonetheless speculated that U.S. pilots were being asked to perform impossible tasks in flying into densely populated areas. Because civilian casualties were inevitable, the air campaign raised the political and moral stakes. Salisbury wondered whether, "in their deep commitment to the theory of air power," the president and his military advisors "might not have overlooked some basic considerations of national welfare and American interest."

Press coverage of the war grew more skeptical toward the end of 1967, when many journalists, both in Washington and Vietnam, concluded that there was a "credibility gap." The term itself originated in Vietnam, where the daily military press briefings had come to be known as the "Five O'Clock Follies." Johnson's frequent exaggerations and desire to keep the press guessing made reporters skeptics, if not cynics.

The credibility gap reached its widest during Tet. Coverage of Tet was controversial mostly because the news media swung from covering the optimistic assurances of military and administration officials to the dramatic stories such as the invasion of the U.S. embassy—a terrific swing indeed but one that merely followed events. Initial reports were cast in dire terms, but these first reports came from a press corps that was as surprised as everyone else. There were dramatic events to cover, and reporters who had been languishing in boredom for months were not going to miss the embassy invasion, ignore the chaos in Saigon, or turn back from the siege at Hue. Coverage of the embassy invasion was live and exhaustive. Television cameras rolled into Hue with U.S. troops and remained beside them during the long battle for that city. On February 2, NBC showed the chief of South Vietnam's national police pull an alleged Vietcong commando into the middle of a

Saigon street and shoot him point blank in the temple. The suspect collapsed, blood squirting as if from a small fountain.

From the administration's point of view, the media was fixing on these disturbing events and ignoring the larger picture of military victory. Within weeks, however, the media gathered itself and began reporting on the military consequences with fair accuracy. Peter Braestrup and Don Oberdorfer contend that the damage to public opinion already was done, particularly by coverage of General Loan's street justice. But as Braestrup also has noted, there is no strong evidence that the Tet coverage adversely influenced public opinion. Public confidence in the war effort diminished after Tet, but this decline was part of a trend that had been in motion since 1966.

Indeed, ultimately the media's disillusionment with the Vietnam War paralleled the similar decline in confidence among both administration insiders and the public at large. For all of their professional objectivity, they could not immunize themselves against the criticisms that were being leveled at the war by establishment critics, whose views commanded serious attention. Both the newspapers and television covered the Senate Foreign Relations hearings, which under the control of committee chair J. William Fulbright did much to legitimize dissent against the war. Salisbury might be dismissed as, in William S. White's words, a renegade filled with "intolerable self-willed dissent," but could Fulbright or Walter Lippmann? Through 1967, more and more insiders began to entertain doubts about the war and were willing to leak word of dissent within the administration to the press, thereby introducing even more doubts into public discussion and certainly raising further doubts among journalists about whether the administration itself believed in the war. As the fighting worsened and more Americans died, the public, without prodding from either the press or the antiwar movement, began to doubt that the war was worth it. As one journalist explained, the growing skepticism of the media was in effect a response to the market. "Whenever your natural constituency changes, then naturally you will too."

Lyndon Johnson's quiet war became so loud it forced him from office. Troubled as his relations with the press were, they were not to blame for his political demise. Indeed, Richard Nixon turned his press relations, which were worse than Johnson's, into political advantage. By 1968 the press had gained the reputation—only partly deserved—as biased, adversarial, and elitist. Media coverage of the war moderated and reverted to its pre-Tet form—concentrating on GIs, reporting on southern politics. Nixon, in contrast, waged a campaign of outright hostility against the press, thoroughly out of proportion to the degree of opposition coming from the media—or from the dwindling antiwar movement for that matter.

Establishment Critics and the Failure of Reason

The administration was forced to battle over public opinion because it could not control all of the information flooding into general circulation. But the war was never a matter of public relations, a struggle over that amorphous thing called public opinion. Diem would have fallen regardless of what Americans thought of him; the Vietcong would have continued to trudge through the jungles indifferent to the nightly news in the United States. The crisis in Vietnam was, first and foremost, the result of the flaws inherent in U.S. Cold War strategic thinking, and no amount of media manipulation or poll watching could alter that.

The first important critics of the war called attention to these basic flaws, and in so doing from the very outset they ensured that the war would not go unopposed, even if their criticism cannot be said to have stopped it. As early as 1963 and 1964, a handful of establishment critics set up an indisputably powerful—indeed irrefutable—critique of U.S. policy. J. William Fulbright, Walter Lippmann, George Ball, George Kennan, and Hans Morgenthau were never part of the antiwar movement, the expressive activism of which ran directly against their conservative temperaments. They were establishment types to the bone, each a charter member of the policy-making elite. Ball had been a Stevenson Democrat taken into the Kennedy administration as an assistant secretary of state. Kennan and Morgenthau were the dominant U.S. theorists of international relations. Fulbright was a Rhodes Scholar, an Arkansas senator, a leading candidate for secretary of state under Kennedy, and chairman of the Senate Foreign Relations Committee. Lippmann was the dean of American journalists and the most experienced observer of international affairs in the United States. These were not people inclined to march in Washington peace parades or burn draft cards.

The establishment critics offered varied perspectives of the perils of U.S. policy. Ball was the closest to the policy-making process and was skeptical of the Vietnam commitment from the early days of 1961. When Kennedy committed himself to the initial Taylor–Rostow involvement, Ball warned him that "within five years we'll have three hundred thousand men in the paddies and jungles and never find them again." His grasp of the future was firmer than Kennedy's, who told Ball: "George, you're just crazier than hell." Like many Kennedy men, Ball remained to work for Johnson, where he found himself gradually pushed out of influence because of his opposition to the bombing campaigns. Rolling Thunder would be futile, he argued, because all the suppositions underlying it were flawed. It would not destroy the will of the North Vietnamese, it would not improve the morale of the South, and it would not alter the political problem that was at the heart of the crisis in South Vietnam. Rolling Thunder would necessitate ground troops, make it tempting to increase the scale of U.S. involvement, force the consideration of using nuclear arms, and threaten the Chinese. McGeorge Bundy dismissed Ball's arguments out of hand. "My hunch is you will want to listen to George Ball," Bundy advised Johnson, "and then reject his proposal."

Ball's criticism of the methods of war were offered as an insider and were accordingly more narrow than the objections that the others raised. To Lippmann, Kennan, and Morgenthau, the issue was not how the war was being waged but why. As theorists and seasoned observers, they saw Vietnam in terms of the balance of power and long-term national interests. Vietnam, they maintained, was too distant to defend practically and was not strategically important in any case. That lowly nation contained no vital resources, and only the most enormous leap of fantasy could see it as economically important. As Lippmann forth-rightly put it: "A primary vital interest is one in which the security and well-being of a nation are involved. Our security and well-being are not involved in Southeast Asia or Korea and never have been." Southeast Asia was, however, well within the natural and historic sphere of the Chinese to whom it was both militarily and economically important. War in Vietnam therefore threatened to bring on a major conflict that would certainly endanger the delicate balance of power for no good end.

To the administration's claims that it was fighting not for selfish national interests but for democracy and the well-being of the people of South Vietnam, these critics responded that the United States had no business serving as the world's policeman. The "prestige" argument did not fly with them: it was simplistic to believe that failure in Vietnam would unleash communist uprisings throughout the Third World. Moreover, there was a great deal less dishonor in behaving like a great power and admitting a mistake than in pursuing a deeply flawed policy.

Some presidential aides thought that the best part of political wisdom lay in granting hearings to critics like Lippmann and Fulbright, as Johnson confidant Harry McPherson recalled, while ignoring "the extremist demonstrators, except to say that he could appreciate their concern." Johnson took this advice at first, but primarily because he was confident that he could convince the establishment critics to see things his way.

The Moderates' Opposition to the War

In the uncertain days of 1965, many concerned citizens misread this self-confidence as tolerance and assumed that the administration was interested in conducting a civil debate on Vietnam. Hopeful that reasoned debate might influence the course of events, the fledgling antiwar movement started out on a moderate strategy designed to emphasize concern rather than opposition. The moderates continued to believe that Johnson was sincere when he called for a policy of restraint in the 1964 election and assumed that the president's political antennae would be receptive to the advice of supporters. These were still the days when the administration's reform-ist promises had not been tarnished. Moderate opponents of the war, disturbed though they were by the increasingly evident flaws in policy, nevertheless wanted to avoid demands for immediate withdrawal, were careful to include criticisms of the communists in their writings and speeches, and sought to focus their energies on holding Johnson to his publicly stated commitment to a negotiated settlement.

The effort at relatively civil argument was best seen in the teach-in move-ment. In March, a small group of University of Michigan faculty members pro-posed to lead an informal, nighttime study session and wound up with a gathering of several thousand students and faculty. Other universities followed Michigan's example, and soon the teach-in movement was commanding even Johnson's atten-tion. Hoping to counter the criticism and still confident of winning over the intellectuals, the administration brought a group of eighty-five professors to Wash-ington meetings supposedly to hear their criticisms. Meanwhile, the administration sent forth a "truth team" of advocates to several midwestern universities to participate in teach-ins. The State Department set the terms of defense with the publication of *Aggression from the North*, in which it marshalled supposedly secret documents to prove the war was a straightforward communist invasion much as Korean had been.

This game of point–counterpoint culminated with two events: a national teach-in in mid-May and a televised debate between McGeorge Bundy and Hans Morgenthau in June. Over a hundred colleges and perhaps 100,000 people were connected by telephone for the teach-in. Organizers had hoped to recruit "a large, representative group of scholars" who might engage in "responsible debate," but because McGeorge Bundy agreed to participate, the teach-in informally was billed as a direct confrontation between the administration and its critics. Bundy, the administration's smoothest and most academic spokesman, dropped out literally at the last minute; Johnson was angry that he had agreed in the first place and rearranged his schedule for him. Probably because he was able to control the format, Bundy did debate Morgenthau on national television the following month. The two sparred over whether the war in Vietnam was the sensible way to contain China, with Morgenthau relying on the professorial instinct to mull over complexities and Bundy stating matters in terms of stark choices, war or humiliation. When Morgenthau attempted to find some middle ground, Bundy attacked him for undue pessimism and ended his presentation by ridiculing Morgenthau's scholarship. Reasoned debate thus turned into a personal attack.

Toward Confrontational Debate

It was only a matter of time before the season of civil debate degenerated into insults and moralizing. The administration's idea of debate was to try public relations and, if that failed, to compel agreement. Given the determination to fight the war even though precious few sound reasons could be offered for doing so, serious discussion of the war was bound to turn into name-calling and emotionalism. The teach-ins themselves, while largely organized in good faith, were denounced as one-sided and irrational by the administration, sometimes in terms that were themselves inflammatory and insulting. Secretary of State Dean Rusk was referring to the teach-in organizers when he sneered in late April at "the gullibility of educated men and the stubborn disregard of plain facts by men who are supposed to be helping our young to learn—especially to learn how to think." At the same time, the administration's so-called truth team also met with what its chairman called "emotional outbursts" and moralistic hypocrisy in several of its stops, especially at the University of Wisconsin. Some in the antiwar movement were ready to meet insult with insult and to lambast the war planners as, in the words of one speaker at the national teach-in, "men of unparalleled arrogance, stupidity, and incompetence."

The establishment critics felt this chilling atmosphere as much as anyone. Their reasoned conclusions brought them grief in the form of rebukes and bitter responses from the administration. Lippmann became not only *persona non grata* at the White House but also the butt of graceless personal attacks. Ball was edged away from the policy making until he was essentially without a voice. For his troubles in the debate with Bundy, Morgenthau received a rash of anti-Semitic, xenophobic hate mail and an Internal Revenue Service tax audit that he was always convinced had been politically motivated.

J. William Fulbright's situation was perhaps the most illuminating, for he had guided the Gulf of Tonkin Resolution through the Senate because, so he has claimed, he trusted the administration to act in good faith and with prudence. When Johnson showed none of those statesmanlike virtues, Fulbright began to voice misgivings; he, too, found himself pushed out of the way. Certain that he no longer could exercise influence within the White House, he launched a series of hearings through his Senate Foreign Relations Committee in 1966 and 1967 that became the focus of respectable opposition to the war. The Fulbright hearings were an embarrassment to the administration, for the renegade chairman regularly heard testimony from informed critics and exposed, through the appearances of the administration's own people, just how ill conceived the war was.

Insult was a venomous ingredient that the administration injected into the debate after 1965, and it had predictably poisonous results. Questioning the patriotism of people who had extended criticism in good faith only raised questions about the administration's own integrity and, worse, about the moral climate that the war in Vietnam was creating. Even the establishment critics began to see the war less as a momentary mistake than as a serious flaw. George Ball concluded that the war was proof of the old aphorism about power corrupting. "Men with minds trained to be critical within the four walls of their own disciplines to accept no proposition without adequate proof . . . all too frequently subordinated objectivity to the exhilaration of working those levers and watching things happen." Lippmann was far harsher: "Johnson's America is a bastard empire which relies on superior force to achieve its purposes, and is no longer an example of the wisdom and humanity of a free society." Fulbright summed up his dismay in *The Arrogance of Power* (1967), where he chastised policymakers for assuming that the United States should play the role of the world policeman. Humbling though it was, Fulbright decided, the war showed that there were limits even to the power of the mighty United States. Thomas Powers has written that "once insult became a weapon in the argument over the war, there could be no middle ground." The increasingly moralistic tone of moderate criticism showed as much. This political point of no return, as Powers has argued, left critics of the war no choice but to hit the streets in protest in the hopes of putting pressure on the administration. From 1965 the war was no longer a matter for debate but a matter for confrontation, which in turn strengthened the hand of radicals who not only were eager to force confrontations but also were determined to use the antiwar movement as a basis for a broader radicalism. For the administration, this development was not undesirable, since the more the antiwar movement was associated with the radical fringe, the easier it was to condemn and the less likely it was to win public sympathy. But the broader effect of this development was to make the war at home irreconcilable and to coarsen public life to such an extent that the wild events of 1968 became possible.

The Antiwar Movement

It is difficult to speak of the opponents of the war as a united "movement." They were a widely varied group of citizens, gathered together in numerous groups and often at odds with one another over strategy and analysis. There was no single leader and no group dominated—only one person, the longtime pacifist radical, A. J. Muste, had general credibility. Those who flocked into or associated with one or several of the organizations were just as varied and hailed from all ranks and areas of American life: clergy, teachers, suburban housewives, students, union members, country folk. It is true that the antiwar movement overlapped with political radicalism, but it is equally true that sixties radicalism and the movement were distinct, in spite of the best efforts of the media and the government to depict them as one and the same. By 1967 the stereotypical "peacenik" was a drug-using hippie with no respect for authority or country; in fact, the antiwar movement was a cross section of the nation. For the sake of discussing with some coherence an entity that was not necessarily coherent, however, we might distinguish five branches of the antiwar movement, each of which had its own analysis of the war.

Composition of the Movement and Origins

First, there were the moderates, who included mainstream antinuclear activists from the National Committee for a Sane Nuclear Policy (SANE) with Social Democrats of various types. To the moderates, Vietnam was an aberration best dealt with through respectful, even deferential criticism. Unlike most others within the movement, moderates never demanded a unilateral U.S. withdrawal and habitually balanced criticism of the United States with demands against the North Vietnamese.

Second there were traditional pacifists, whose roots lay in the honorable tradition of the twentieth-century American peace movement, where Protestant reformism mingled with radical humanism. Opposed to war on basic principle, the pacifists sought to build on links between the civil rights movement, left-wing labor groups, and other traditional progressives, although by 1965 they believed the war had become the paramount issue in American life. By that point as well, most pacifists agreed with A. J. Muste's conclusion that moderation was no longer possible and that the war exposed a national corruption so deep that nonviolent revolution was necessary.

A third branch, the principal organization of campus radicals and the most aggressive group of organizers, the Students for a Democratic Society (SDS), shared much with the pacifists, particularly the conclusion that the establishment was beyond redemption. They were not necessarily committed to nonviolence, however, were harsher and often more sanctimonious in their criticism, and based their fundamental views not on Christian principles but on contemporary ideas about personal alienation and the technocratic society.

Fourth, on the movement's fringe, holdovers from the Old Left were joined with younger fringe radicals organized in what *Village Voice* writer Jack Newfield termed the "Hereditary Left," self-avowed communists given to a dogmatism and factionalism more in keeping with the 1930s than the 1960s. Never influential within the movement, they saw the war in simple terms as imperialistic genocide and advocated what they thought was the party line of Soviet or Chinese foreign policy.

By 1967 a fifth wing, the hippies, emerged mostly from SDS ranks, reflecting the growing influence of cultural radicalism within the American left. To the hippies, the war represented the predictable violence of the straight establishment. The solution was simple: everyone had to lighten up and have fun, as Abbie Hoffman recommended in his primer, *Revolution for the Hell of It* (1969).

Notwithstanding this variety, the origins of the antiwar movement lay in the persistence of pacifists, who though scattered after World War II and cast in disrepute during the McCarthy Red Scare, reorganized in the late fifties in an antinuclear movement. When the political climate began to change, so pacifists began to assert themselves. Kennedy was no friend of pacifism, but he inadvertently helped the cause; the Bay of Pigs, Berlin, and the Cuban Missile Crisis heightened anxiety and created a growing popular constituency for the peace movement. In the unnerving atmosphere of nuclear crisis, otherwise quiet people were compelled to act as Dagmar Wilson did in 1961. An illustrator of children's books, Wilson combined with several of her suburban Washington friends to organize Women Strike for Peace, a movement built on the essentialist belief that it was "woman's work to make the whole world a home" and that women were therefore obliged to work for peace. The papal encyclical, *Pacem in Terris*, Pope John XXIII's call for world peace, and the February 1962 student campaign that brought several thousand college activists to lobby in Washington added legitimacy to peace activism.

Initially a blend of pacifists and disarmament activists, the fledgling peace movement developed a critique of Cold War thinking by 1963. U.S. policy, they believed, had assumed a momentum of its own and was spinning out of the control of misguided leaders who had set it in motion but who were no longer able or willing to arrest it. The Cold War had become sheer madness, played for stakes far out of proportion to what was necessary in the normal game of diplomacy. Only a society enmeshed in a false sense of technological security, only a people who had become morally numbed by the combination of superficial affluence and personal meaninglessness, would permit such a game to be played in their name. The duty of those who remained sane was to recover moral sensibility and restore a sense of proper proportion to national policies.

Like their civil rights comrades who were compelled to confront police dogs, peace activists were called to bear individual witness against militarism. Individual action was as varied as the activists themselves and included everything from prayer vigils to street confrontations to the most dramatic form of protest, self-immolation. Eight Americans burned themselves to death in protest against the war, beginning in November 1965 when a Baltimore activist and Quaker, Norman Morrison, driven to despair after reading an account of a U.S. bombing of Vietnamese civilians, walked to the front of the Pentagon and doused himself with kerosene. Several days later, another pacifist, Roger LaPorte, attended a draft-card burning in New York City and reportedly was so shocked to hear counterprotesters calling on antiwar activists to "burn yourselves, not your cards!" that he proceeded to do just that, choosing the United Nations plaza as his pyre.

Organized Resistance

For the movement as a whole, the two favored means of protest by 1965 were draft resistance and protest marches. Draft resistance came in several forms—refusing induction, picketing or disrupting draft boards or induction centers, or, for some, fleeing into exile. Resistance was a form of radical individual opposition to the war, for unlike participation in a march or signing a circular letter, refusing military induction was a direct confrontation between a young man and his government. Resistance was laden with ethical and political meaning: to resist the draft was to reject the standard understanding of patriotic duty, even of masculinity, and carried with it both a willingness to endure the ridicule and hatred of fellow citizens and an obligation to redefine patriotism.

The most common act of draft resistance was draft-card burning, which was often done in groups during organized protests. The first "burners" defended their actions on the grounds of the post–Holocaust Nuremberg Laws, which held individuals responsible for participating in the crimes of their government. Convinced that the war was indeed criminal, the burners maintained that they were obliged by accepted global ethics and international law to refuse the draft. Theirs were unprecedented acts, but few of the first burners were prosecuted. One who was, Tom Cornell, a Catholic antinuclear activist, burned his first card in 1960 and eventually burned ten, by his estimate—"I think I have the record," he later speculated. In response to the first collective burnings, Congress, angered by the "filthy, sleazy beatnik gang . . . thumb[ing] their noses at their own government," as some members called the protesters, increased the penalty for draft-card destruction and stepped up prosecutions. The first burner to be convicted, David Miller, refused to accept a suspended sentence and was given two and a half years in prison. By 1968 the average sentence for draft evasion had risen to 37 months, up from 21 in 1965, while the number of prosecutions peaked in 1972 at 4,906.

The prospect of serving time for resistance gave pause to some. Even student radicals in SDS were reluctant to advocate outright resistance at first, preferring instead to call for some form of alternative service, ideally through domestic work in ghettos. But on balance the hesitancy with which most activists approached open resistance to selective service came from their understanding of how grave the act was, and, if anything, there was considerably more courage than cowardice among draft resisters.

Organized, collective resistance escalated with the radicalization of the movement, so that by the end of 1966 SDS and other groups began rallying around the antidraft slogans, "Hell no, we won't go!" and "Not with my life you don't!" Antidraft groups popped up on eastern campuses and in New York and Boston; in early 1967, a group engineered a mass card burning in Central Park. West Coast activists convened an organization, simply called the Resistance, based on the principle that even accepting deferments was a form of criminal compliance with the system. The Resistance organized a mass card turn-in that fall. More than a thousand cards were turned in during ceremonies in eighteen cities, after which SANE leaders Dr. Benjamin Spock, the famous baby doctor, and William Sloane Coffin, Yale University chaplain, along with three companions, submitted them to the Justice Department. Justice officials refused to accept the cards, but Coffin, Spock, and the others were charged with and eventually found guilty of conspiracy to disrupt selective service. Meanwhile, the Catholic priest Philip Berrigan and a group of friends broke into a Baltimore customshouse, poured blood over draft files, and accepted arrest, an act that Berrigan, his brother Daniel, and seven others repeated several months later, this time using homemade napalm to burn files.

Organized resistance reached its high point in the mid-October 1967 Stop-the-Draft Week. In the Bay area, Berkeley's militant students, community groups, and the Resistance aimed to shut down the large induction center in Oakland. When the nonviolent tactics of the pacifists failed, militants took over and conducted a huge street demonstration of perhaps 10,000 people, some of whom came prepared to fight. The march to the induction center turned into a running battle with Oakland police. Moving from block to block, throwing up street barricades when they could, and falling back when police approached, the crowd fought what activists quickly glamorized as a successful guerrilla action. Although the Oakland induction center was never shut down, the hand of the militants was strengthened, for the Oakland battle inspired the dreams of activists nationwide.

If Stop-the-Draft Week was the organizational zenith of draft resistance, it also tended to eclipse the core of such resistance, individual acts of noncompliance. Draft resistance had escalated to match the war, so that draft-card burning became lost in the acceleration of protest—paradoxically, at a time when individual resistance in all forms was peaking. By 1970 resistance reached such lengths that some states struggled just to muster their selective service quotas; from September 1969 to March 1970, over half of the men called in California refused to show up, and the state had to call 18,000 in order to meet its 7,800-man quota. There are no firm numbers on how many men refused to register nationally, but there were at least several hundred thousand and perhaps as many as 2 million. For tens of thousands of those who lost deferments, exile, usually in Canada but occasionally in Europe, became their fate.

Dissension and Divisions within the Movement

Besides draft resistance, the antiwar movement was committed to regular demonstrations, the organization of which often generated competition between groups. The first significant antiwar march, which brought more than 20,000 people to Washington at Easter in 1965, was portentous in this regard. SDS was the principal planner and decided to include the left fringe groups, the procommunist DuBois clubs, the Harvard radical group the May 2nd Movement, and others, along with more moderate and traditional pacifist groups. SDS's decision to include the far left angered moderates, led by civil rights leader Bayard Rustin, who held hopes of maintaining a liberal coalition. Veteran activists, who remembered both the debilitating factionalism of the radical left in the 1930s and the Red Scare of the 1950s, were also edgy about SDS's policy. Some pacifists argued that the fringe groups be excluded on the grounds that they were advocates of violent revolution and therefore not pacifists.

SDS leaders and some pacifists, especially David McReynolds and Dave Dellinger, editor of the pacifist journal *Liberation*, countered by arguing that excluding the far left would interject the exhausted politics of the past. "The mood of the students," Dave Dellinger wrote in SDS's defense, "tends to be a little scornful of both the Communists and the anti-Communists. There is a heritage of ideological rigidity that they don't want to get bogged down in." A policy of exclusion would discredit the movement and imply that there was reason to worry about communists in the movement. To let the moderates win and dictate participation in the march would be a sellout because the moderates continued to foster the illusion that a "coalition with the Marines," as the radical historian Staughton Lynd derisively called the moderate strategy, would end the war. Finally, two of the movement's most prestigious figures, A. J. Muste and the old Socialist Norman Thomas, weighed in and arranged a compromise between SDS and the moderates that permitted radical participation. The march came off with much greater participation than anyone had dared hope and greatly enhanced SDS's prestige.

Still, the jury-rigged nature of the movement was evident. Veterans like Muste were less impressed with the success of the Easter march than by the divisions it exposed. Rather than gloating, Muste maintained, "It is obviously time for very serious discussion of philosophy, program and strategy in the peace movement." Muste's concern over debilitating divisions was raised not just by the march, but by the appearance of problems elsewhere. On the West Coast, the Vietnam Day Committee, an antiwar organization that not only mixed ideological variations but threw cultural radicals into the brew as well, stirred up controversy when it ran a teach-in that was so one-sided that one participant denounced it as so much "pure crap." Even as it was realizing its first great success—indeed because of that success—SDS was thrown into a crisis of purpose that produced a historic split in the group between the founders of the organization and a group of relative newcomers. Although it had embarked on an independent strategy, SANE suffered a similar fate when the membership heatedly debated whether to mingle with the left. The debate was so intense that Dr. Spock resigned in the midst of it.

The best the movement could manage was to paste together successive umbrella organizations. Beginning with the National Coordinating Committee to End the War in Vietnam in late 1965, followed by several reincarnations under the banner of the Mobilization to End the War (MOBE), antiwar activists consistently organized large, even historic demonstrations, but more often than not the coordination was minimal, the leadership loose, and the activists at cross purposes.

The March on the Pentagon

The Pentagon march of October 1967 was ample testimony here. Inspired by the apparent success of the Oakland demonstration's "mobile tactics," the National Coordinating Committee embraced the concept of moving "from protest to resistance." The committee invited hippie leader and Oakland organizer Jerry Rubin to take the movement into "the business of wholesale disruption and widespread resistance and dislocation of the American society," in Rubin's words. The huge throng of over 100,000 that descended on Washington included all sides of the movement. The event was to run for several days, with a series of celebrity speeches and a march to the Mall, all capped off with a march across the Potomac to the Pentagon. This rough schedule seemed almost the extent of organization, however; there was no central leadership and people appeared, as Norman Mailer put it in his famous description of the march, *Armies of the Night* (1968), "unaffiliated or disaffiliated." The march was deprived of its symbolic leader, A. J. Muste, who had died the previous February. Exact plans were "hard to concretize," Dave Dellinger later explained, other than to say it would be a mix of "Ghandi and guerrilla," a synthesis of the new radicalism and the old pacifism.

What happened became a centerpiece of movement mythology. On Saturday afternoon, October 21, the demonstrators sat through the usual speeches by the political and cultural stars at the Lincoln Memorial. Then some 50,000 laid siege to the Pentagon, where they indulged in the most fantastic of scenes. The marchers made their way along a prescribed route to the north parking lot of the complex. They came face to face with a line of military MPs. Everyone went about the business of disruption after their own fashion. "There was no leadership," one protester said, "that was what was so beautiful." SDSers handed bullhorns around to anyone who wanted to make a speech. The celebrities led their own contingents in another round of spontaneous oratory mixed with impromptu press conferences. The hippies settled in for an attempt to levitate the building through group meditation. A small group broke through the police line and found its way into the Pentagon, where they were roughly rounded up. Protesters sang to the troops, called for them to "join us!," and stuck flowers in gun barrels. According to movement mythology, "two, possibly three MPs defected or attempted to defect." "We had come to the Pentagon to confront the war makers," one participant wrote, "only to discover that many armed men in uniform are just like us." Mailer thought "the air was violent, yet full of amusement." Another activist thought "it most resembled . . . a football game when spectators rush the goal posts." Utopia had met Hell and for a moment prevailed.

People came and went as the day turned into a chilly autumn night. Several thousand intended to camp out. Evidently bored with the vigil, the news media packed up and went home. Then the real action began. Regular paratroopers, backed by federal marshalls, moved toward the crowd, which attempted to hold its line by nonviolent tactics of locking arms and sitting down. The regulars went easy on the demonstrators, embarrassed perhaps by being used against nonviolent fellow citizens. The marshalls were an altogether different class, and they made a serious assault, dragging protesters out of their lines and beating them with billy clubs. They reportedly singled women out for particular abuse, reckoning that male protesters would attempt to rescue them and make themselves vulnerable to added beating. Through the "massacre," as Mailer called it, a Vietnam veteran named Gary Rader grabbed a bullhorn and appealed in military cadence to the troops; over the attempts of a nearby

A Vietnam protester resists military policemen during the October 1967 march on the Pentagon in Washington, D.C.
[Leonard Freed/Magnum Photos]

officer to drown him out, Rader conducted a swift teach-in about Vietnam. The arrests continued until only a hundred or so were left to see the dawn.

Activists proclaimed the Siege of the Pentagon an unqualified success. They alleged that the establishment's brutality had been exposed, that a heartfelt sympathy between the movement and the troops had been established, and that the diversity of genius embodied in the movement's variety had been successfully focused without compromising anyone's principles or belittling anyone's fears. The establishment was somewhat less enthusiastic. The president and his family had driven around the remnants of the protest on Sunday to see "what a hippie looked like" but otherwise tried to ignore the event. Congressional conservatives denounced the whole business as a communist plot, a line of reasoning that Johnson may have privately encouraged. The general impression of the march, fostered by the national media, was that the counterculture had arrived in its most obnoxious manner, and from that point on public sympathy for the movement consistently decreased.

Assessing the Antiwar Movement

If it is hard to square the euphoric assessments of the activists with the all-too-obvious breach between the movement and the majority of Americans, it is too easy to sum up the sense of accomplishment, the wonderstruck descriptions of union between protesters and soldiers, and the giddy appraisals of revolutionary potential as sheer romanticizing. There were, in fact, substantive reasons for optimism of a sort. The war had been dragging on for more than two years, no end was in sight, and even the original hawks were admitting its futility. Bundy had left the administration soon after the teach-in movement, and the more dramatic resignation of Secretary of Defense McNamara, who watched the Pentagon siege out of his office window, was soon in the offing. Johnson himself was growing more and more reclusive, trapped in the belly of his own White House war machine. A wave of urban disturbances culminated in the great Detroit riot that summer and, when added to the emergence of black power, had created the impression that African Americans were on the brink of outright civil war. The counterculture had established itself earlier through a series of love-ins that caught the attention of the nation, much to the consternation of pious radicals and parents alike. Revolution was not entirely out of the question.

But then again, of course, it was. No coup against the U.S. establishment was in the cards. A revolution required the participation or sympathetic acquiescence of a majority, and the movement could count on neither. So why the optimism? The answer lies in the internal dynamics of the turn in strategy and temperament. The days of protest focused the movement on the main issue, the war. In contrast, the strategy of resistance contained within it an imperious quality that overwhelmed the issue, so that for many the act of resistance became an end in itself. The "mobile tactics" of the Oakland riots and the thorough decentralization of the Pentagon siege inspired optimism mostly because, as ends in themselves, they were entirely successful—activists did toy with police and they did entice soldiers. "Our presence, our civil disobedience, *was* the message," George Dennison wrote of the Pentagon march. It was easy to be optimistic if action itself was the end of activism.

It went unsaid, furthermore, that the shift to resistance paralleled President Johnson's steely determination to ride the war out. The increasing stridency of the movement matched the administration's increased efforts to mislead the public and harass its opponents. The antiwar movement became an unwitting accomplice to the coarsening of public life. Tied to the conduct of the establishment, the antiwar movement was a captive of policy, and when Richard Nixon began to deescalate, the movement began to diminish. Indeed, the movement never got the measure of Nixon, who mollified the public by withdrawing troops, sustained the bombing, and scorned protesters all at once.

The antiwar movement was a qualified failure. Certainly, it was much less successful than its symbolic counterpart, the civil rights movement. There is no tangible evidence that the administration felt direct pressure from the movement, and it is painfully obvious that no policy was reconsidered. Nor can the movement claim to have had more than a modest effect on U.S. electoral politics, which, if anything, tilted rightward beginning with the 1966 off-year elections. Johnson paid for the war with his political life, but his debtors were not the activists; he was a good enough politician to count on the media and the radicals themselves to discredit the movement in the eyes of the public. He was right on this score. The movement never gained public sympathy after 1967 when it in effect conceded the struggle over its public image.

Marginalized in the larger scheme of national politics, the peace movement floundered after 1968. Nixon's promises to win "peace with honor," the policy of Vietnamization that reduced U.S. casualties after 1969, the revision of the draft, and federal harassment of activists took the steam from the movement, though by no means was it destroyed. As Charles DeBenedetti, the foremost student of the peace movement, has concluded, "in this war no victory was decisive, at home or abroad." Some of the largest demonstrations took place in response to the persisting war. In April 1969, one hundred thousand or more marched again in Washington; the next spring, in response to the invasion of Cambodia, over 1 million college students struck all across the nation. The campus revolts brought outbreaks of violence, especially from authorities. During melees associated with the protests, Ohio National Guardsmen killed four students at Kent State University; guardsmen killed two at Jackson State in Mississippi while storming a dormitory. Through 1970, draft resistance turned into something like guerrilla war as fringe groups began bombing federal facilities and selective-service offices, at times egged on by FBI infiltrators and informants. A self-anointed band of radicals at the University of Wisconsin capped off a series of bombings by blowing up the university's Army Mathematics Research Center, killing an innocent young physicist. In April 1971 a peace coalition organized the largest of all marches, which brought perhaps half a million to Washington. Several weeks later, another, more radical group descended on Washington with the intention of shutting down the city by sitting in streets and government buildings, but they were routed by police, much to President Nixon's satisfaction.

Radical pacifists like Dave Dellinger not only regretted the violence of antiwar activists on principle but also knew it was self-defeating. The size of the Nixon-era demonstrations belied the poor organization of the movement as a whole. No new converts were being made. Indeed, the political lines solidified after 1968. The liberal center, the very existence of which had prevented the war from becoming an "us–versus–them" issue, had dissolved, and the war had become "us–versus–them." So the Nixon administration believed; so the radicals believed. What progress opponents of the war made came through the most mundane of channels, congressional action, and could not honestly be connected to the antiwar movement. SANE, along with a few other persisting moderates, mounted lobbying campaigns in support of several bills designed to overturn the Gulf of Tonkin Resolution, restore congressional control over war making, and force Nixon to set a specific date for total U.S. withdrawal.

Still, there is little question that the movement kept the issues of Vietnam in the public's mind, even if the public did not want to recognize them. Activists prevented the government from waging war without proper checks—though one might well compare Vietnam to Korea and argue that the government might have withdrawn from Vietnam anyway. The successes of the movement, as George Herring concludes, were "limited and subtle." "Perhaps most important," he writes, "the disturbances and divisions set off by the antiwar movement caused fatigue and anxiety among the policymakers and the public, and thus eventually encouraged efforts to find a way out."

The War and the Silent Majority

Although it is an extraordinarily complex matter to judge, public opinion about Vietnam nonetheless can be summed up simply: Americans were ambivalent. They agreed that communism had to be stopped, but they doubted that it could be halted in Vietnam. They believed that the war was a terrible waste of lives, but the lives they worried about were American, not Vietnamese. They approved of every aggressive U.S. initiative, from Rolling Thunder to the Christmas bombings of 1972, but only insofar as those initiatives promised to end the conflict. There was an ebb and flow to public opinion; poll respondents typically fell in behind specific presidential actions but stayed in the ranks only if that action worked. Because no U.S. initiative worked, public opinion gradually slid away from each of the presidents. Most Americans opposed the war by 1968, but most despised antiwar protesters as well. The result was a bundle of conflicting attitudes probably summed up by a man whose son was killed in Vietnam: "I think we ought to win that war or pull out. . . . I hate those peace demonstrators. . . . The sooner we get the hell out of there the better."

Evidence of widespread doubts about U.S. policy existed even before the war on the ground began, although Johnson initially believed differently. He had his way with the nation in the aftermath of the assassination, and it was during the honeymoon of 1964 that Johnson pushed through the Gulf of Tonkin Resolution. That apparently decisive action not only came with the near unanimity of the Congress but with 85 percent support in opinion polls as well. His landslide victory against Goldwater in 1964 reinforced his assumption that the public would support a widened effort. But the initial approval of the Gulf of Tonkin episode did not translate into consistent support, and there is good evidence that the war planners recognized as much. They did not fear a surge in public opposition, but they were concerned that the public's patience was short and that the "limited war" might generate great frustration if it became inconclusive, as in Korea. Johnson, his aide Harry McPherson has written, was caught in a bind: "He was trying to summon up just enough martial spirit and determination in the people to sustain a limited war, but not so much as to unleash the hounds of passion that would force him to widen it." Public frustration did not take long to show itself either; by the time the administration had committed itself to escalation in February 1965, Harris polls showed that 35 percent wanted U.S. withdrawal and 75 percent supported a negotiated settlement.

Because Johnson did not intend to negotiate seriously, public opinion would hold only as long as there was significant military or political progress. There was, of course, precious little of either. According to pollster Lou Harris, Johnson enjoyed a bare plurality of support (46 percent to 42 percent) for the last time in July 1966, and from that point until the political disaster of the Tet offensive nearly two years later, his support declined.

Johnson was never able to win public opinion to his side, but neither was the antiwar movement. Middle America never liked the hippie radicals who allegedly dominated the movement. But more important, the movement was populated by middle- and upper-class whites; those who fought the war were overwhelmingly working class.

The Draft System and Class Bias

The class divisions between those who fought and those who stayed home were a function of a draft system that was the creature of bureaucratic accumulation. It was essentially the same universal draft that had been in place since the Korean War, but because it had been used mostly in peacetime, the system was run unevenly by local draft boards composed, as Selective Service Commander Lewis Hershey liked to think, of "little bands of neighbors" sitting in judgment of their communities' young men. Over the years it was in operation, the system had created an expanding number of ways to avoid the draft. Deferments were easy to come by. The most common, and the one that did most to highlight the class discrepancies in the system, was the college deferment, by which a young man in good standing with any institution of higher education could put off service. There were many other deferments. Anyone working with a company engaged in defense-related work could obtain a deferment, even if the particular individual was himself not engaged in defense work. Theoretically, even a janitor at Dow Chemical, which did a great deal of the chemical-weapons work, could avoid the draft. Eldest sons, husbands, and fathers could obtain deferments—and not a few hasty marriages were the result. Medical excuses were honored, so men starved themselves, shot themselves, in countless ways partially maimed themselves; some managed to find friendly or sympathetic doctors to provide sufficiently poor diagnoses. Some claimed homosexuality, others madness, and others failed IQ tests. Because draft decisions were made locally, what qualified a man for a deferment in Tupelo may have differed from what qualified him in Toledo. Peace Corps service merited a deferment in New York but not in other states. Mortuary training earned a deferment in Illinois but not elsewhere. Some local boards were generous in granting conscientious objector status; other boards rarely gave them. And beyond deferments were the many service-oriented methods of staying out of Vietnam: the National Guard, the Coast Guard, even enlistment, which gave a man at least some measure of control over his military assignments—all were means of avoiding the war.

The draft was so porous that David Surrey's description of it as "a very manipulatable system" has the ring of understatement. The system was easily manipulated, a quality that was more likely to generate public cynicism than patriotism. There was no reason why men should disrupt their lives when they did not have to. One University of Michigan student told an interviewer that "if I lost a couple of years, it would mean $16,000 to me. I know I sound selfish, but, by God, I paid $10,000 to get this education." Nor were college students alone in looking out for number one. As a Delaware defense worker said, "I'm making good money and having a ball every weekend. Why the hell should I want to go?" Clearly enough, the demise of patriotism that was so often the cause of establishment hand-wringing was not exclusive to student radicals. As Lawrence Baskir and William Strauss write in their systematic study of the draft, "avoiding Vietnam became a generation-wide preoccupation." In all, 8,769,000 were given permanent deferments.

This "very manipulatable system" begs a glib description of its functioning: one had to be poor, dumb, crazy, unlucky, or some mixture of each to wind up in Vietnam. Johnson did not plan out a policy of using only working-class draftees, and he was genuinely proud of those people who went. Nevertheless, the draft worked, again as Baskir and Strauss put it, as an instrument of Darwinist social policy, preying overwhelmingly on working-class 18- and 19-year-olds, who were smart enough to get through high school but who were not, could not, or did not want to attend college. In practice, the generous deferment system worked in favor of young men of means. Beyond the college and graduate school deferments, which were the most clearly class-biased mechanisms, those who earned deferments were those who knew how to obtain the right information and how to put it to use. David Surrey notes, for instance, how medical excuses varied by race and class: for between $1,000 and $2,000, a man in Los Angeles could pay for orthodontal braces and get a deferment; in 1968 whites received twice as many medical deferments as did blacks. The reserves were also a haven for middle- and upper-class men. Even the exiled community reflected class privilege. Draft dodgers were far more likely to have been middle-class men whose deferments, especially college deferments, had expired; deserters, who had been unable to keep out of the service, were typically working class.

Those Who Served

The system engendered cynicism over time, but it did not necessarily function without the approval, support, or acquiescence of those who went. Many who were drafted or who enlisted willingly went to do their duty as they saw it. Over and over, men who served in Vietnam explained that they were moved to fight not only by their desire to defend the country against communism but also by John Kennedy's call to national service. It was part of the ambiguity of "bearing any burden" that the same spirit that moved people to enter the Peace Corps or go to Mississippi moved others to fight in Vietnam. Others had less noble reasons, such as the vet who told Mark Baker that "I wasn't a patriot. I didn't join for the country. . . . I wanted to kill the bad guy." Philip Caputo, whose *A Rumor of War* (1977) was one of the first cultural coming-to-terms with the war, joined the Marines "partly because I got swept up in the patriotic tide of the Kennedy era but mostly because I was sick of the safe, suburban existence I had known most of my life." Just as the fervor of Kennedy idealism drove people in very different directions, so, too, did the boredom of affluence evidently push young people to mind-altering drugs and to military service. While radicals at home fantasized about guerrilla warfare and hung Che Guevara posters in their dorm rooms, these soldiers got to experience it. Other men treated the service as if it were an appendage of the humdrum life and merely went along with the system. "The one clear decision I made about me and the war," another vet recalled, "was that . . . I was not going to defraud the system in order to beat the system." Or there was the imprudent medical student who was expelled from Johns Hopkins for stealing the arm of a cadaver and leaving it with a tollbooth attendant on the Baltimore Beltway: "A week later, I had my draft notice. They turned me right into the board."

Enlistees or draftees, patriots or hapless, the men who fought in Vietnam came from the middle and lower ranks of U.S. society. Class differences within the system were inevitably borne out in casualty rates. The prowar journalist Joseph Alsop figured in 1968 that only three graduates of Ivy League colleges had been killed in Vietnam. Although Harvard remained all but unscathed, the working-class neighborhood of South Boston—Irish-Catholic and staunchly patriotic—lost twenty-five young men. With a population of 34,000, that toll gave South Boston the highest casualty rate of any community in the nation. No wonder, then, that the neighborhood built the first memorial to Vietnam veterans.

Economic disparities explain why African Americans died well out of proportion to their numbers in Vietnam, even after the military, in response to criticism from civil rights groups, took steps to reduce their combat role. The Army had been held out as a valuable vehicle for job training, and the Defense Department even revised its qualifications in special programs for men who hailed from specially designated "poverty areas." Over 40 percent of those inducted under these programs were black men. Draft boards rarely included black members, but enlistment officers prowled inner-city neighborhoods, selling the military as the one place in U.S. society where everyone was equal. As a means of social mobility, the military left something to be desired, since many of those brought in under these programs were given combat roles. What skills they acquired were of dubious value. Philip Caputo begins *A Rumor of War* with the observation that three years of enlistment left him "more prepared for death than I was for life." Another vet recalled that "when they put me in Vietnam, they got a damn zero to start with." "In country" he acquired one skill: "Killin' goddamn gooks."

A powerful sense of class grievance also infused the way the average American understood the war. Working-class parents sent their sons away because establishment liberals had called them to defend the nation. But that same establishment did not call its own children, who all too often responded by joining antiwar protests. "I've got one son, my youngest, in Vietnam," a woman explained to Brendan and Patricia Sexton. "He couldn't get out of it by going to college. . . . We can't understand how all those rich kids—the kids with the beads from the fancy suburbs—how they get off when my son has to go over there and maybe get his head shot off." It was possible to wonder whether the government tolerated the protests precisely because "these privileged kids" were the ones "carrying Viet Cong flags around, saying they want the enemy to win," another parent mused. "If *my* son was doing that, instead of kids whose papas have a lot of pull, he'd be locked up damn fast." The cause of the antiwar movement was probably damaged far more by the gap between the protesters and the people fighting the war than by its hippie image, even if the two are difficult to separate. "People needed to hear it from the guy who fought it," complained one antiwar veteran when he spoke of the character of much of the movement, "not [from] those assholes at Yale whose biggest decision was getting Daddy's Mercedes."

Especially at a time when establishment liberals seemed determined to start programs for everyone but them, working-class Americans were bound to be bewildered, if not terribly disillusioned, by the war. They had good reason to believe that they were being made saps, forced to fight a war that the establishment did not want to win in a conventional manner, the purpose of which was elusive to say the least and at which the children of affluence could safely turn up their noses. Little wonder that working-class respondents to opinion polls vented both doubts about the war and resentment against the antiwar movement. "I'm against this war," one woman whose son was killed in Vietnam explained with simple eloquence, "the way a mother is, whose sons are in the army, who has lost a son fighting in it. The world hears those demonstrators making their noise. The world doesn't hear me."

The War and the American Character

The war at home was a swirling mix of tensions. As such, it reflected the growing divisions in U.S. society—and did much to establish the stalemate that has sustained and rigidified those divisions—more starkly than did the period's other major developments. The war forced Americans to reconsider the most fundamental assumptions about the nature of their society: about its moral purpose, its strength or weakness of character, its historic role, its masculine attributes, the legitimacy of its political system. These were issues too complex and too open to interpretation to result in any clear national agreements, and the longest and most destructive legacy of the war in the United States is that it generated irreconcilable conflicts among fellow citizens.

Americans traditionally had clung to the idea that all their wars were righteous causes, which was why the nation always won its wars. They did not like to think that they fought for straightforward national interest or, worse, that they were not the good guys. The U.S. mythology of war was shaped around those beliefs and in turn fed the willingness of many young men to go to Vietnam. Again and again, Vietnam vets recalled that the glamorization of war in U.S. culture underlay their expectations. They saw themselves as cowboys going to fight the "injuns"; indeed, John Wayne, the hero on the white horse, pops up frequently in veterans' accounts of the war. Popular culture reinforced the virtues of patriotic duty and masculine valor. "Ever since the American Revolution my family had people in all the different wars," explained David Ross, an Army medic who served in Vietnam from 1965 to 1967, "and that was always the thing—when your country needs you, you go. You don't ask a lot of questions, because the country's always right." Absorbing military virtues was a part of growing up for many boys in the fifties and sixties, and parents who themselves had gone through a "good war," World War II, expected their sons to go to Vietnam as part of their coming of age. One soldier put his situation a bit more tersely than Ross: "If my folks had to send their little poodle, they would have cried more tears over that than over me. But I'm supposed to go, because I'm a man."

Although U.S. culture was in the throes of historic changes in temperament, the popular depictions of war continued to stress the traditional view of martial America. Hollywood managed this feat primarily by ignoring Vietnam altogether. The film industry poured forth its usual fare of World War II films, where good was good and bad was bad and everyone knew the difference. While U.S. soldiers were engaged in a war of dubious value, their Hollywood counterparts fought in block-busters. *The Guns of Navarrone, The Dirty Dozen, Midway, Bridge over the River Kwai,* and countless other lower budget, less impressive productions reminded viewers that the United States was both winner and good guy. Hollywood's response to Tet was more gung-ho than President Johnson's. Whereas LBJ decided against running for reelection, Hollywood released George C. Scott in *Patton,* which domi-nated the year's Academy Awards with its portrayal of a real blood-and-guts soldier who was stymied not by the German Army but by the direct orders of his own, politically driven superiors. It was Richard Nixon's favorite film; he is said to have watched it dozens of times. The only Hollywood effort to address the Vietnam War was John Wayne's *The Green Beret;* its theme song became a hit. The movie itself was so clearly Wayne's attempt to excuse the war that it had nothing to do with reality. Television mirrored the film industry. The networks' version of war came in World War II dramas such as *Twelve O'Clock High* or *Combat* or was the stuff of comedy as in *McHale's Navy* and, somewhat later, *Gomer Pyle.*

It was all the more peculiar to have these standard renditions of the war experience repeated when American soldiers were fighting a guerrilla war in jungles and rice paddies. The gap between the two made it difficult for those at home to understand the Vietnam experience and just as hard for vets to digest what they went through. Not many commentators at home could appreciate the surrealistic character of Vietnam; not many conveyed the wide range of experience.

Needless to say, the war itself had an unsettling effect on the nation's military myths. One of the dominant motifs of those myths, which goes back to the nineteenth-century frontier, was that the American soldier, like the cowboy, was an instinctive loner, an exile from civilization, and that his pioneer spirit was very much part of the justness of his cause. This was precisely *Patton's* reassuring mes-sage. It was not easy, however, to find that motif in a war where B-52s flying at 50,000 feet routinely dropped bombs on rural villages; war by military and political bureaucrats was hard to square with tradition. American GIs tried to keep the myth alive themselves by referring to the enemy as "injuns" and speaking of being "in country." But to be whisked in and out of a firefight by helicopter was not to disassociate oneself from technology. John Wayne's *The Green Berets* attempted to keep alive the frontier hero, but in part it was that quality that made the film so hard to swallow. The actual policy that created the special forces like the Green Berets took more of its spirit from James Bond than from James Fenimore Cooper. If anyone deserved to be seen as the lonely pioneer in this war it was the Vietcong.

The greatest challenge of all was the war's assault on the myth of U.S. benefi-cence. Many Americans went to Vietnam expecting to give out candy to the children, to be welcomed and loved the way the Americans who liberated Western Europe in World War II were. They had to believe, along with the Catholic Chaplain Reinard Beaver, that "greater love hath no man when he lay down his life for a stranger. . . . That is what the United States is doing in Vietnam." One reason why the hawks were so devoted to the illusion that the Vietnamese wanted them there was that to admit otherwise was to call into question the selflessness of the United States. Many Americans in country initially behaved according to traditional form, only to be disabused of this particular myth when they discovered that "the Vietnamese people" were often the enemy. Reports of atrocities were simply incomprehensible to many Americans at home, who were certain that Americans were congenitally incapable of such acts. The common defense against charges of atrocities—that U.S. troops were driven to kill civilians because there was no way to tell a civilian from a noncombatant—might have been true enough as a condition of the war but was itself evidence that Americans were unwanted and hence was no defense at all. It was not unusual for Americans at home to look for any indication of beneficence. "Is there nothing we did over there that you have the fairness to acknowledge?" a distraught mother queried the journalist Gloria Emerson. What of the orphanages, schools, and medical supplies? There had to be something.

The effects of the war on U.S. culture in the sixties are hard to draw, largely because cultural forms simply do not respond to immediate circumstances. In retrospect, it is clear that the Vietnam experience paralleled, and in some ways therefore reinforced, some of the major cultural themes of the sixties. The adrenaline rush of combat was the ultimate experience in an age in which people were seeking intensified experience. Whereas people at home grew increasingly restive over the stiflingly bureaucratic nature of life at the end of the modern age and began to see that the rationalized society was quite possibly insane, GIs in Vietnam could claim that they had lived through the utmost madness. They were living Joseph Heller's *Catch-22* (1955). The value of Michael Herr's overpraised *Dispatches* (1968) lay not in his hip prose or stabs at eroticism—imitating Mailer is no path to profundity—but in the less self-conscious description of war's insanity.

The real cultural impact of the war, in any case, was not felt until the 1980s, when the triumph of Ronald Reagan and American conservatism provided a congenial environment for a flowering of books and films directly related to Vietnam. Even then the results ran the gamut from the trite (Reagan's touting of the war as a "noble cause") to the dangerous (*Rambo*) to the respectable (Oliver Stone's *Platoon*) to the near-profound (Philip Caputo's *A Rumor of War*, perhaps, Tim O'Brien's *Going after Cacciato*, and some of the journalistic assessments of the conflict), a reminder that the war ushered in political and cultural stalemate at home.

CHAPTER 5

The Reddish Decade

 The revival of liberalism brought with it a revival of the American left. That the two should rise and fall together was not unique to the sixties. A surge of radicalism accompanied every spurt of liberal reform in the twentieth century. If anything, the so-called New Left of the sixties was more closely tied to liberalism than previous leftist movements had been, no matter how hostile the radicals claimed they were to liberals. The New Left certainly was tied to the fortunes of mainstream liberalism, for the New Left rose and fell with the Democratic party, into which it blended as the prospects for revolution, never bright to begin with, faded after 1968.

The Not-So-Old Left
and the Not-So-New

When the radicals of the sixties proclaimed themselves the New Left, they did so in order to distance themselves from the radicals of the previous generation. To the new generation, the so-called Old Left, composed of radicals who had come of age during the 1930s, was wedded to tired beliefs and mired in old battles; the Old Left was trade unions, Social Democrats, Jewish intellectuals, and Marxism. The New Left, in contrast, pictured itself as free of dogma—of all ideology for that matter—committed to the vital causes of the present, and determined to reinvent radicalism through experience.

But the New Left, at least at its inception, was not so free of the past as its members thought, nor was the Old Left so old. The New Left prided itself on its originality, but U.S. radicalism in the twentieth century had always been "new" in the sense that radicals were typically undogmatic, defended civil liberties, and were wary of extending state power into private lives, even when they called for something akin to socialism. Since the Progressive era and World War I, U.S. radicals had blended reformism, Freud, and pacifism with democratic urges far more often and with greater conviction than they had embraced revolutionary Marxism. Indeed, as veterans of the political battles of the 1930s, when Stalinists tried to impose the party line on all left-wing organizations, the generation that made up the Old Left developed an abiding hatred of communism, one as deep, if not deeper, than that of Cold War liberals. The Old Left was not very dogmatic as radicals go.

Theoretically, an aversion to dogma should have led to flexibility, but by the 1950s, Old Left radicals were entangled in a serious predicament. Their political roots ran back to working-class movements that grew out of harsh conditions, and their ideas were born in a day when capitalism did not distribute its fruits fairly or widely. Little in their experience had helped them recast radicalism into a critique of the affluent society; as a consequence, it was not always easy to distinguish them from Schlesinger–Galbraith liberals. "Most of us no longer thought of ourselves as Marxists," Irving Howe wrote of his colleagues at the journal *Dissent*—the essential Old Left forum. "We became gradually convinced that any expectation of putting together a new socialist system, as proud in its coherence as Marxism had once been, was not only premature, but a fantasy better to abandon." Before he committed himself to working within the Democratic party, Michael Harrington had to lose his "bookish, ineffective, impractical Marxism," which was sophisticated "in inverse ratio to any possibility of changing the world." It was only out of sheer cussedness that Howe and his colleagues continued to speak of themselves as socialists. "If nothing else," he wrote in anticipation of one of the New Left's major themes, upholding the socialist banner "helps suggest that we do not wish to be accepted as members of the Establishment."

For young people groping for radical ideals, the Old Left was not much help. They had to turn from the Howes and the Harringtons and listen instead to renegade intellectuals such as C. Wright Mills and Paul Goodman. Both thinkers were of the Old Left generation, but both were quirky. Goodman hovered around the Beat poets, though he never was one; Mills was a complete outsider, a Texan among the New York crowd at Columbia, a hipster motorcyclist among academic professionals, "an educated cowboy of the Left," in Irving Howe's estimation.

For aspiring young radicals, the virtue Goodman and Mills shared was that they attacked capitalist society not on economic grounds but on the basis that, by its greatest success, it had created a culture that deprived both work and community of any satisfying meaning and warred against beauty. In their own ways, both men argued that the United States' wealth had destroyed the moral basis of a good society; they looked beneath affluence and uncovered moral and cultural sterility. To some extent, even their work paralleled the liberal criticisms of Eisenhower's America and its suburban, corporate culture. But where liberals might wring their hands over the lack of public spirit or the emptiness of mass culture, the radicals insisted that these ills were directly traceable to capitalism's bureaucratic organization of work, its destruction of organic communities, its irrational use of technology, its corruption of reason into mere rationalism, and its trivialization of basic pleasure into consumer wants. Later, when the New Left spoke of the need for communities "robustly concerned with the common good," it evoked Mills, who taught that only by thoroughly overhauling the economic and political system could those traditions be recaptured.

Mills spoke with particular strength to a contemporary crisis of meaning in which individuals had become so unhinged from the rich associations of public life that living itself seemed a waste of time. So, too, did one of the other main sources of New Left inspiration, the European existentialist writers Jean Paul Sartre and Albert Camus, who were imported from France thanks to Howe and *Dissent*. Sartre and Camus, however, brought with them a rationale for action that was not clearly part of Mills and Goodman's perspective. The existentialists rejected liberalism's boasts about universal improvement and its faith in unfolding reason and disputed any comprehensive claims that humanity served some preordained purpose, whether "God's plan," Marx's deterministic class war, or liberal progress. The individual was responsible for acting well or humanely in the here-and-now and was capable of altering immediate circumstances. Working from Sartre and Camus, the New Radicals believed that modest individual acts of opposition to the prevailing order could challenge authority. One could be radical without being yoked to theory, obliged to party line, or, for that matter, even certain of the outcome. "The path of taking action without certainty of the effects," New Left leader Tom Hayden wrote of the existentialist influence, "represented a confidence that the individual mattered in history, that nothing was entirely determined, that action created an evidence of its own." One could be committed to nothing more formal than "to change the way we, as individuals, actually live and deal with other people," as Hayden's colleague Richard Flacks put it. Existential radicals "strive at every occasion to enhance the ability of people to affect their environment, to be centers of initiative, to be self-expressive, to be free."

By design, the New Left had "no sure formulas, no closed theories." It embraced both Mills and Camus because those thinkers insisted on the simple and direct application of ethics. Mills told them what was wrong, whereas Camus focused on why it was their obligation to tackle the problems. That was as close as the first New Radicals came to developing any system of their own. Beyond these obvious influences, there were a hundred others working on young idealists in the late fifties. If they read Mills once in college, it was after having read *Mad* magazine in high school. If they lived under the specter of the Bomb, they learned to worry about it, along with the rest of the nation, only after Sputnik. If they gained inspiration from Camus, it came along with having heard Kennedy's Inaugural Address. This was the beauty of the New Left: its sensitivity to experience, its simple conception of democracy, and its openness to intellectual originality.

Port Huron: The First Incarnation of the New Left

The New Left was made up of young people who entered college just as the spirit of the civil rights movement rejuvenated the hopes of the liberal-left. They came to campuses that still had dress codes and curfews, that monitored the gatherings of men and women—when they admitted women at all—and that were racially exclusive and often ethnically homogeneous. Some came from households that had realized the American dream and went to schools such as Michigan and Harvard, schools that would not have accepted their parents a generation earlier. Others, Bob Ross, Steve Max, Sharon Jeffrey, Mickey and Richard Flacks, were "red-diaper babies" whose parents had been Communist party members, active trade unionists, or socialists. They had been weaned on political activism; some had been precariously cradled in homes held together in fear of political witch-hunts.

College Protest Organizations

The New Left was born among northern college students, but its birth was precipitated by events in the South. Just as the Greensboro sit-ins in 1960 propelled young African Americans like Bob Moses into the civil rights movement, so they galvanized the inchoate activism of northern radicals. At Harvard, students who had been dabbling in the revived peace movement were encouraged by the sit-ins and organized Tocsin, a mixed bag of reformers, red-diaper babies, pacifists, and skeptics—Harvard's one student organization committed to public protest. Students at Berkeley organized an activist group, and so did students at Oberlin, Swarthmore, and the University of Chicago. At the University of Michigan (UM) in Ann Arbor, the sit-ins touched off sympathy boycotts against the local Kresge and Woolworth stores. The UM protesters became easy pickings for a tiny cadre of radicals, led by Sharon Jeffrey, daughter of United Auto Workers (UAW) organizers, and Al Haber, a local radical who had been trying to put together a chapter of the socialist Student League for Industrial Democracy (SLID). Haber was determined to rekindle student radicalism, the growing potential for which he discerned in subtle signs of creeping idealism. The time was ripe, he felt, but the only organizations that reached beyond their respective campuses were flawed. The National Student Association (NSA) was broad-based and included many sincere people, but it was a CIA front. Despite its enormous prestige, SNCC could not have gone national without losing its cohesiveness as an organization. All in all, then, Haber thought SLID was the best vehicle for organization, in part because its history of radicalism went back to the pre–World War I years and at various times included among its members Jack London, Upton Sinclair, and John Dewey.

In June 1960, the parent organization, the League for Industrial Democracy (LID), decided to reorganize SLID as the Students for a Democratic Society (SDS) and appointed Haber as intercampus organizer. The inauspicious birth of SDS, which soon became the heart of the New Left, was witnessed by no more than a few dozen students from schools scattered across the country. Even with Haber's enthusiasm and the utter lack of alternatives, SDS gained only 250 or so new members in the first two years—hardly a bounty.

Haber was doubly burdened: not only was he starting a new organization from the bottom up, but he was also obligated to the parent organization. He knew from the start that the elders would not welcome his aggressive plans for SDS, and he spent most of 1961 pleading and feigning anticommunism. At one point he resigned, only to be rehired because LID itself lacked any alternative routes into the awakening student movement. No national convention was convened in 1961. Actually, SDS consisted of Haber in the New York office—where he slept under the mimeograph machine—and Tom Hayden, an aspiring journalist who had graduated from Michigan to take SDS's other paid position, "field secretary."

As Haber and his few colleagues prepared for a 1962 convention at a UAW camp at Port Huron, Michigan, the division between the generations erupted. LID was worried about Haber's ambitions, in part because direct political action threatened its tax-exempt status as an educational organization. A far bigger threat was an ideological one. When Haber spoke of his plans to structure SDS chapters on a wide-open and informal basis that resembled university seminars, LID officials immediately interpreted this ambition as childish naivete and insufficiently anticommunist.

SDS versus LID

The division widened into open conflict at Port Huron. Hayden, the group's leading intellectual, prepared a statement of principles—filled with "existential humanism"—that openly challenged the Old Left. Hayden criticized organized labor for selling out its principles. More important, he suggested that the United States was partly to blame for the Cold War, and he raised the possibility that the Soviet Union, rather than being "*inherently* expansionist . . . and bent on taking over the world," was actually "a defensive and paranoid status quo power." Getting away from the stodgy politics of their predecessors, the students wanted to devote their energies to building "participatory democracy."

The LID elders had no problem with participatory democracy, but Michael Harrington, LID's representative at Port Huron, denounced the rest of the draft. It was much too vague in its views on communism, he charged, and its hostility toward liberalism rendered it useless as a vehicle for coalition building. A night-long, beer-soaked, old-fashioned leftist debate ended inconclusively when Harrington had to return to New York. It was the sort of engagement that Harrington loved most of all—beer and polemics—but it horrified the students, few of whom understood the complicated history behind LID's anticommunism. As Hayden recalled, it "was too much for my innocent midwestern mind to fathom."

Relations between SDS and LID were badly damaged at Port Huron. LID's board of directors set up an inquisition, with Harrington serving as chief prosecutor, that grilled Hayden and Haber with anticommunist litmus tests. The board held up funds, changed the lock on the office door, and threatened to disown the group. SDS leaders discussed cutting ties with LID but finally decided on reconciliation. At the board's demand, the students rewrote their statement of principles with Harrington's criticisms in mind. At the same time, Norman Thomas, the patriarch of American socialism, counseled Harrington and LID to be patient with SDS.

Yet the damage was done. Todd Gitlin remembered the affair as akin to "the blind and rageful blunders of petty proprietors fearful of losing their franchise to the new boys and girls on the block—which guaranteed exactly that outcome." Harrington later wrote that he had been stupid and conceded that "we of the Fifties were simply too weak to serve as a point of departure for the New Left of the Sixties." Meanwhile, Haber, Jeffrey, and Hayden recognized that the break between the generations presented the chance to launch an independent student movement.

"There couldn't be a more perfect setup," Hayden concluded. "We were giving birth to some new force in American politics. And Michael, purely by virtue of being older and having other attachments, was being an obstacle in the delivery room."

The Port Huron Statement

That "new force" was given its most systematic definition in the Port Huron statement, which became the founding document of the New Left. Hayden put to paper the unique outlook of the young radicals, captured in its famous opening line: "We are people of this generation, bred in at least modest comfort, housed now in universities, looking uncomfortably to the world we inherit." The young were a minority, but one seething with urgency, because the prospect of nuclear apocalypse meant that "we may be the last generation in the experiment with living." There were no ready alternatives, for "the liberal and socialist preachments of the past" had little to say to this generation.

Intent on avoiding a manifesto filled with "platitudes," Hayden and his colleagues built the statement around their analysis of the nation and the world at large. At home, they found a crisis in values, where political cynicism and dogmatic sloganeering had "replaced the idealistic thinking of old" and destroyed any sense of alternatives. Americans were lost in a glaze of apathy, going through the motions of living in exchange for the crumbs of affluence. Students floated through universities that had become "cumbersome" bureaucracies rather than "initiator[s] of new modes and molders of attitudes." The two national political parties were depressingly similar, and the Democrats were deeply corrupted by the presence of the Southern Democrats. Voters shuffled mechanically to the polls to cast ballots for politicians over whom they exercised no true control; and many Americans, namely, the southern blacks and the poor, did not even have the privilege of being thus insulted. The economy was run by corporate "remote control" in pursuit of stockholder profits taken off the backs of workers who could find no meaning in their work. The guardians of the economy were unwilling to employ technology aimed at providing affluence to all or liberating people from "drudgery." Organized labor, driven by "vestigial commitments, self-interestedness, [and] unradicalism," bought into the system and renounced old principles.

In international affairs, the students charged that the United States had become obsessed with nuclear weapons and superpower conflict and ignored the important revolution of expectations in the colonial world. U.S. policy toward the Third World had only two narrow goals: to protect foreign investment and to stem communism. The first goal led to hypocritical support of procapitalist regimes and opposition against socialist governments. "Unreasoning anti-communism," bad enough at home, bore little relation to the facts of the international system when it was clear that the Soviet Union had become conservative, was not expansionistic, and "has failed, in every sense, to achieve its stated intention of leading a worldwide movement for human emancipation." If anything, U.S. foreign policy had "been more effective in deterring the growth of democracy than communism" and had tarnished the allure of democracy in the process.

The Port Huron statement was respectably thorough and moderately leftist. Hayden considered it a "living document"; it would provide flexibility and be open to change and interpretation. It was also a product of the moment. The statement demonstrated how indebted the first generation of the New Left was, not necessarily to the Old Left, but to the intellectual and political environment of the late fifties. Like their liberal-left elders, Hayden and his colleagues eschewed ideological systems and considered the citizenry's alienation a predictable product of the bureaucratized, impersonal age. Like their elders, they found themselves struggling to confront the social problems of affluence rather than scarcity. Even their most original contribution to U.S. radicalism, the commitment to participatory democracy, drew heavily from the experimental, radical democratic theory of John Dewey.

Inasmuch as the statement had been formulated in the spring of 1962, however, it was not only realistic but in some ways also prescient. Months before the Cuban Missile Crisis, they were watching Kennedy's nuclear trigger finger. The critique of U.S. policy in the Third World predated the massive commitment to Vietnam and stands as a farsighted warning against the danger of war. The students advanced their general line of argument against Cold War policy at a time when only a handful of scholars and intellectuals, the journalist I. F. Stone and the historian William Appleman Williams among them, dared to suggest that the United States shared blame with the Soviets. This was a line that neither the Galbraiths nor the Harringtons had the courage to take in 1962. The statement also called for a massive antipoverty program well before administration liberals committed themselves to just such an effort. The document was not without its daring.

Nor did it lack originality. Even where they drew clearly from their elders, the students added twists. The New Left argued that alienation and apathy could be overcome. Apathy could be reversed through experiments in decentralization, for example, which might encourage a reversion of work back to a craft basis so that workers could "make whole, not partial, products," or the breakup of the cities into "smaller communities," thereby reconnecting the individual to the civic order. "Participatory democracy," the essence of Port Huron's original message and the clarion call of the early New Left, was not just a vague ideal that meant different things to different people (though it had this effect, to be sure). Rather, it was meant as an antidote to the ills of bureaucratized society. Personal fulfillment was to be realized through civic participation.

By focusing on alienation rather than on class domination as the fundamental problem underlying all other problems, the authors freed themselves from the dogma of the Old Left and set themselves to look elsewhere besides workers and trade unions for the source of radical renewal. The "labor metaphysic," as the New Left began to call the long-held faith in an insurgent working class, was a product of the age of scarcity that ignored how conservative workers had become. Port Huron looked to the civil rights and peace movements as better models of radical politics and, most important of all, to students as the vanguard of a New Left.

Here indeed was an original claim—that students were ideally situated to lead. According to the Port Huron authors, their unique generational perspective suited them to lead, and although the vast majority of their fellow students were as apathetic as many of their fellow citizens, it was clear that student activism was quickening. Any New Left movement that was to be formed had to fulfill certain requirements: it needed "real intellectual skills," it had to be distributed broadly across the country, it must have the ability to recruit young people, socialists, and liberals into one movement, it had to generate controversy, and it was obliged to simplify the complexities of modern life so that issues could be "felt close up by every human being." The university was the ideal location, probably the only place, where all of these prerequisites could be established. Student radicalism could not "complete a movement of ordinary people making demands for a better life." But the authors left little doubt that students would be the vanguard of a new radicalism.

To suggest that students themselves should lead the way toward change was an obvious bit of self-justification that contained problematic claims. Port Huron was essentially a primer for the radicalization of middle-class youth, which was not in and of itself a drawback. There is no reason why middle-class people cannot become radicals, but the character and consequences of their radicalism depend very much on what their grievances are and how they seek redress. There was such a strong self-referential undertow to Port Huron that the radicalism of the New Left was at least in part designed to overcome not the arms race or racism but the discomfort of the students themselves. From the first, New Left politics was in danger of becoming mere therapy. If therapy led middle-class radicals to work for worthy ends through self-sacrifice—in antipoverty programs, in antiwar protests, for example—all to the good. But the focus of radicalism could shift from civil rights or antiwar issues to the university, which was neither the seat of oppression nor a likely spot from which to ignite revolution in the rest of society. In the long run, the deepest flaw in the New Left was that, given its suppositions, it could encourage mere rebelliousness masquerading as radicalism, a phony radicalism that saw politics as a vehicle for exhibitionism and self-assertion rather than change.

The Port Huron group's sincerity submerged this potential source of corruption. To them, participatory democracy was something to be lived as if it were the golden rule. The Port Huron meeting itself symbolized goodwill and serious activism, and was a long-lasting inspiration for the participants. Something special happened there, and the students sensed it. The trouble was in sustaining the spirit.

One means of doing so was to embody participatory democracy in the organization itself. Here the young radicals demonstrated how much they were influenced by SNCC; they, too, wanted to mesh relentless commitment with a disdain for organization, to fight for democracy and prove that a group could be democratic. SDS meetings were based on Haber's "seminar model" and resembled rambling discussions more than business meetings; anyone could have a say and pretty much for as long as one wished. Officers were elected annually, but the leadership was changed every year, and it never meant much to be "president." Like SNCC, SDS was an anti-organization, a group of people dedicated to common goals without leaders or hierarchy. The drive toward self-effacement served, according to Hayden, as "the perfect organizational formula for the suppression of middle-class ambition."

Sustaining the original spirit depended on the value of the group's ends, and the Port Huron statement never made clear how participatory democracy was to be achieved on a national basis. SDS had to decide whether students alone could make a revolution or whether they could act only as catalysts for other groups, and if the latter was the case, what groups. The first generation of the New Left inclined toward the latter view: students, however unique, could serve only as catalysts, they thought. But the harder question concerned where that activism was to be directed, since, as they declared at Port Huron, SDSers knew that radicalism meant little when confined to the university.

ERAP

Accordingly, in 1963, many SDSers began to show some interest in grass-roots organizing in northern cities. Sharon Jeffrey was already working in a Philadelphia slum for the National Student Movement and was pushing her colleagues to make a concerted effort among the urban poor. Hayden expressed the tilt of thinking when he worried that SDS might be "inevitably assigned to a vague educational role" and hoped that the organization might apply SNCC's political methods to the North. In August 1963 Hayden secured a grant from the UAW to launch the Economic Research and Action Project (ERAP), which became the basis for SDS's attempt to ignite the energies of the poor. The timing was fortuitous. Just as SDS committed itself to urban activism, President Johnson announced his intention to fight the War on Poverty. The students, again ahead of the game, presumed that they constituted the leftward front of the war, and so they planned moves into nine cities, most notably Chicago, Newark, and Cleveland.

ERAP was as emblematic of the early New Left as the campus uprisings were of the late movement. To begin with, ERAP was the product of the ideological evolution that Port Huron inaugurated. It was to be, as Hayden called it in an essay written jointly with Carl Wittman, an activist from Swarthmore, "an interracial movement of the poor." Hayden and Wittman predicted that the civil rights movement would have to move north. There it would progress best by working on economic grievances and aligning with poor whites who, it was hoped, would be organized by ERAP. While conceding that both the race-based nature of the civil rights movement and the "counterrevolutionary" racism of poor whites presented obvious difficulties, they argued that it was possible to focus on economic demands that would benefit both groups. Beyond that, ERAP's more important purpose, the authors claimed, lay not in the "immediate value of students to the Negro and economic movements" but in what the students themselves would learn through the effort; ERAP was a lesson in "improving the quality of our work and making opportunities for radical life vocations."

As New Left writing went, this was pretty dull stuff—"a cumbersome document," Hayden called it. Nonetheless, it demonstrated the determination to evolve toward a certain kind of realistic radicalism. The "interracial movement of the poor" implied that students could not be revolutionary on their own but could be agitators. Moreover, the essay contained a hard-headed economic analysis. Hayden and Wittman expected factory automation to swell the ranks of the unemployed as technology replaced workers; consequently, affluence was assumed to be partial and temporary. The newly unemployed had the makings of a class-conscious movement, providing they were organized and radicalized. This analysis was much to the liking of the Old Left; indeed, Bayard Rustin, Harrington, and A. Philip Randolph were making the very same arguments. ERAP was a reversion to the labor metaphysic, except that it threw in participatory democracy as the organizing method and ultimate end.

Ultimately, ERAP was supposed to help the poor help themselves by conquering their own alienation; it was also a means for students to do the same. ERAP was pure existential radicalism. As Todd Gitlin wrote, showing the poor how to organize "signals the congealing of individualized concerns into organized expression. The very process of massing into a movement contributes to a sense of personal power and thereby makes possible further steps." It was not long into the program that organizers in different cities began to formulate their own variations on the theme, partly in response to the white poor's marked reluctance to let themselves be taught how to help themselves. In Chicago, the Jobs or Income Now (JOIN) project followed the Hayden line and organized unemployed residents of the mostly Appalachian uptown neighborhood. The Cleveland project, finding it impossible to gather the unemployed, began to organize around neighborhood issues such as rents, police protection, and eventually welfare rights. Time and again, ERAP volunteers found that their constituency was quite willing to stand up and make demands for specific changes on specific issues that meant something directly to them; but that was a far cry from being revolutionary. Meetings were supposed to be forums for debate, discussion, and the reconnection of the individual to the community; but too often poor folks just came to complain. Participatory democracy worked: people were moved by those things that most directly affected their lives, and engaging in the collective did ease the sense of alienation. It just did not quite work the way Port Huron had envisioned. The Clevelanders' acronym GROIN, which stood for Garbage Removal or Income Now, seemed an apt metaphor for these difficulties.

For the students themselves, ERAP showed that participatory democracy was a draining experience. The volunteers lived together under spartan conditions in urban communes. Privacy and intimacy largely had to be bypassed, and much of the time was spent in grueling discussions of strategy aimed at producing collective agreements without resorting to voting. For Sharon Jeffrey and Paul Potter, ERAP was an effort to live the "authentic life," unshackled from the restraints of middle-class life.

It was grueling just the same, and although some volunteers hung on in their respective cities for years, ERAP evaporated rather quickly, doomed by 1965 to obscurity among the New Radicals for a number of reasons. There were objective problems that probably could not have been altered very much. The mass of unemployed workers who had theoretically been expected to join forces failed to materialize, and those who did, Paul Potter has written, "were an extremely disparate group of people." ERAP also had to contend with harassment from local officials and intimidation from landlords. The poor whites who were the objects of

ERAP efforts were often from Appalachia and held fiercely to their mountaineering tradition of stoical independence; for them, poverty was not something to organize against but a humbling fact of life. Soon, the projects became so independent that they took on a life of their own that defied centralized coordination, which, among other things, meant that the projects depended on the commitment of the volunteers themselves. As in SNCC, the participants' intense idealism was bound to burn out sooner or later.

ERAP was also only one of several possible directions for the New Left, and it is unlikely that it could have carried an entire movement along with it. The most fundamental problem with the projects always came back to the issue of purpose. If the New Radicals were there to help the poor, they would have been well advised not to expect too much to begin with. But if they were there to live "authentically," then ERAP was insincere, unnecessary, or temporary. Paul Potter illustrated the psychic dynamics best when he claimed that the major shortcoming in Hayden's plans for an interracial movement was that ERAP "was not *our* analysis. . . . Virtually no one in SDS knew anything about automation. Second, we knew even less about poverty." Potter had spent two and a half years in Cleveland, he came to believe, because he did not think his middle-class grievances were legitimate and his "gut feelings" urged him to seek out people whose grievances were real. ERAP was based on what students by the midsixties were denouncing as the "politics of guilt." Driven by their "guilt-ridden liberal identities," Potter and his colleagues sought out that "funny class" called the poor and, in giving themselves over to the same old economic radicalism, wound up "with a slightly different portion of the same well-chewed piece of gristle so many American radicals had gnawed and choked on before."

Potter went to Cleveland in search of authenticity, then, only to conclude that he had done so for phony reasons. The students should have spent their energies, he concluded, exploring their own ideas and motivations. Again and again, Potter contrasted ERAP doctrine to what he thought was necessary: an "ideology" of their own that held on to the vague, open-ended thinking of Port Huron. For Potter, the problem with ERAP was its attempt to bring something like closure to New Left thinking, or at least a concrete direction that he considered incompatible with discovering their place in time. But by rejecting an ideology that presumably set a firm sense of purpose and a strong direction, his pleas amounted to a call for collective self-analysis, which seems even less fruitful than guilt as a basis for radicalism.

From Protest to Resistance

When ERAP closed shop in 1965, SDS was beginning to accumulate members. One of Potter's main claims was that a more flexible doctrine would have allowed SDS to accommodate these new recruits and allow them to join in the collective search for a generation's purpose. If the purpose of radicalism was to discover the sources of student discontent and act accordingly, then it followed that the universities were as good a setting for revolution as the urban ghettos—indeed, better ones.

ERAP's failure sent the New Left, as Potter wished, back to Port Huron by return-ing the mantle of revolutionary vanguard to the students.

Berkeley

There had been many signs—protests here and there, more and more campus organizations, a burgeoning sense that things weren't as they should be—that the United States' college students were indeed moving toward opposition. In Septem-ber 1964, at the close of Freedom Summer, students at the University of California at Berkeley organized mass protests against university prohibitions on campus politi-cal activity. Since the 1930s, the university had banned most public forms of activism in an effort to squelch campus communists. Over the years, students took their politics to Telegraph Avenue at the edge of campus. As the pace of activism picked up, authorities looked with increasing concern to the sidewalk politicking. After deciding that the sidewalk area where students had been gathering belonged to the university, the administration banned political activity there as well. The ban awaited students who returned from summer break, some of whom had spent their summer working with SNCC in Mississippi. On one occasion when some activists defied the ban, the police attempted to arrest one of the leaders. A crowd surrounded the police car, held it hostage during an impromptu, day-and-a-half sit-in, and forced the administration to rescind the new regulations.

The administration assumed that offering concessions and keeping matters quiet would end the protests; instead, the students used the issue to launch the Free Speech Movement (FSM), led by a strange collection of leaders that included Bettina Aptheker, the daughter of the prominent communist scholar, Herbert Aptheker, one Young Republican, and Mario Savio, who, like Hayden, had a conservative and unpolitical Catholic upbringing. When the administration went back on its compro-mises and tried to discipline the students, the FSM took over the main administration building, marking the first time students had ever used direct-action tactics against their own university. The occupation of Sproul Hall also turned into the first mass arrest of students at their university; indeed the 773 students whom the state police hauled to jail represented the largest mass arrest in California history.

FSM's appearance at Berkeley, though spontaneous, was not accidental. Leftist students had been organizing there for years and had inaugurated the sixties in the Bay area with a May 1960 demonstration at San Francisco City Hall that the police had violently dispersed. Along with Greenwich Village, Berkeley had become the nation's postbohemian center. Popularized first as a mecca of the Beats, it was in the process of becoming the home of hippie living, psychedelic drugs, and acid rock. Looming against the counterculture, the university stood out as a symbol of "the establishment." In the infamous description of President Clark Kerr, Berkeley was the "multiversity," the centerpiece that connected research and learning to the United States' corporations, military, and governmental institutions.

Partly because of their early connection to the counterculture, Berkeley's stu-dent radicals were less like the original SDS members and more akin to the second generation of the New Left. Their backgrounds were similar to the Port Huron group—red-diaper babies, many of them Jewish. But the Berkeley radicals aimed their attention at the university itself and stood the Port Huron statement on its head: instead of using the university as a base from which students would move into the community, the Berkeley activists sought revolutionary change within the institution. As Mario Savio, the FSM's charismatic leader, argued during the Sproul Hall sit-in, Berkeley was pretty much the same as Mississippi and the FSM pretty much the same as the civil rights movement. "The same rights are at stake in both places," insisted Savio, "the right to participate as citizens in democratic society and to struggle against the same enemy."

Beyond free speech and a generalized clamor for a more responsive, humane institution, student activists at Berkeley never set their sights on unified goals, and they spent the whole of the sixties launching protests that were often aggressive in inverse proportion to the depth of the issue at stake. Even free speech became an exaggerated issue. At first a simple matter of civil rights, the movement devolved into demands for absolute freedom of expression. Within a year, the FSM became known, by opponents and advocates alike, as the filthy-speech movement.

The difference between the early and the later New Left can be seen, moreover, by comparing Hayden and Mario Savio. Hayden was, or wanted to be, the Bob Moses of the student movement, a self-effacing leader by force of example and intellect. Savio, in contrast, gave every indication of reveling in celebrity. His strength was magnetism, which Hayden lacked. Where Hayden was potent behind a typewriter, Savio was at best a second-rate mind, even by loose New Left standards, but he grew in front of a crowd. In place of Hayden's thoughtful idealizing and often obtuse theories, Savio offered exaggerated rhetoric based on the vague discontents of the day. His most famous speech, offered as a war whoop at Sproul Hall, shows as much: "There is a time when the operation of the machine becomes so odious, makes you so sick at heart, that you can't take part; . . . and you've got to put your bodies upon the gears and upon the wheels, upon the levers, upon all the apparatus and you've got to make it stop. And you've got to indicate to the people who run it . . . that unless you're free, the machines will be prevented from working at all."

There was little sense of perspective here. Savio was free to return home and follow in his father's footsteps as a machinist or, for that matter, to attend a less "oppressive" institution. His impending fate at Berkeley—dismissal—was not exactly a march to prison. But Savio caught the mood of fellow students in a way that Hayden's "interracial movement of the poor" never could. Savio told them they were not free, which meant in turn that they had to fight, then and there, for themselves. The shift from radical outreach to university rebellion, inaugurated at Berkeley, appealed to a much larger chunk of a generation that was ripe for rebelliousness if not radicalism.

Impetus to Rebellion: The Vietnam War

The question remains: why did people like Savio and the students for whom he spoke believe they were not free? Kirkpatrick Sale, SDS's first historian, has laid out the reasons as clearly as anyone could. The students rebelled, he writes, because the institutional fabric of the nation was unraveling, and the resulting crisis of authority was made infinitely worse by the idiocies of those in charge, especially those engaged in fighting the Vietnam War. In a society inviting rebellion against authority, this particular generation of students was uniquely suited to oblige. There were more people under the age of 25 than ever before. Many of them had grown up with parents who only recently had achieved middle-class status and who had responded by giving their children all the benefits of affluence. More young people were entering college at a moment when both the technological demands of the economy and the Great Society were increasing the size and importance of universities, and these trends continued throughout the period. Whereas 3,789,000 students began the decade in college, 7,852,000 were enrolled at decade's end, giving the United States more college students than farmers, construction workers, miners, or transportation workers. Students were a force, and a new one, in the United States.

The issue that ignited the student movement, the Vietnam War, was also the one that marked the divide between the Port Huron group and the university rebels who followed them. SDS was hardly known on campuses until it led the Easter peace march in 1965. The success of that protest enhanced the organization's reputation enormously and established it as the principal voice of activist students. Unlike ERAP, the war was an ideal instrument for forging the students into a movement. The issue allowed a certain independence because it relieved the New Left of having to follow SNCC or pursue the dreams of an interracial movement. Moreover, the war touched them as it did no other group. Students and other members of their age group were being asked to fight, and even with easy deferments the war was behind a great many personal decisions and narrowed many options. As an organizational strategy, focusing on the war was fruitful and almost certainly accounts for SDS's swelling ranks, which reached over 100,000 by 1969, with countless other sympathizers. Finally, the commitment to the war coincided with a changing of the guard, as the Port Huron veterans burned out in ERAP, moved on (as Dick Flacks did) to more or less regular lives, or moved aside, as good democrats, for new blood.

One such newcomer, Carl Ogelsby, was influential in turning SDS toward the war issue. Already over 30, married, a father of three, and holding down a real job as a technical writer for a defense contractor in Ann Arbor when he entered the movement, Ogelsby was an odd sort for SDS. A romantic at heart, he had begun to question his own work and by early 1965 found himself writing press releases in preparation for the Easter march. From the beginning of his relationship with SDS, he was concerned with foreign policy. Although he did not clash with the "old guard" veterans of Port Huron as many of the newcomers did, he played a crucial role in turning attention away from ERAP when many of the old guard could not quite bring themselves to let go.

The war suited the new guard much better than it did the old. The new guard was much larger and therefore less cohesive and in need of a general issue around which to rally. As Todd Gitlin describes them, the new members of SDS were midwestern and southwestern, rarely Jewish, more likely to come from working-class backgrounds, and not particularly intellectual—Ogelsby notwithstanding. They brought with them a sixties version of "prairie" independence; like traditional midwesterners they were skeptical of authority when they were in a good mood but more often were outright contemptuous of it. Their parents had voiced their own distrust of the eastern establishment by voting for Barry Goldwater in 1964, which meant that the members of the New Left were the alienated children of the alienated followers of the New Right. Indeed, this was a strange political phenomenon rich in irony. Their parents believed that eastern liberals were bent on destroying U.S. institutions, which they taught their children to respect. As children often do, they repaid their patriotic parents by opposing the war. The Texan Jeff Shero explained the difference between the old guard and the new in just this way: "If you were a New York student and became a member of SDS, it was essentially joining a political organization, which was a common experience. In Texas to join SDS meant breaking with your family, it meant being cut off. . . . If you were from Texas, in SDS, . . . it meant, 'You Goddamn Communist.' " The new guard, hailing from that provincial wasteland somewhere west of the Hudson and east of San Francisco Bay, had no experience with left politics, no taste for a coalition with the labor-socialist forces, and wouldn't know a Stalinist from a Trotskyist from a Manhattan gallery owner.

Initially, antiwar sentiment was attractive to the new guard because it demanded little intellectual rigor; it was opposition from the gut. In 1965 student activists did not see Vietnam as an imperialist war. Instead, they saw the Vietnamese as alienated existentialists, and they opposed the war on the grounds that an ethical person was obliged, as New Left journalist Jack Newfield wrote, to "say no to the machine and the officers giving the orders to kill."

In the process of building opposition to the war, however, the New Left sharpened its attacks on U.S. society in general and began to single out the liberal as the oppressor. Paul Potter began to lay down this line of reasoning at the Easter march. SDS president at the time, Potter delivered the principal address, which took as its theme the hypocrisy of the United States' policy in Vietnam. Port Huron was the point of departure behind his charges against the administration's "saccharine, self-righteous moralism," its deceit, and its violence. But he added an important twist. The war managers, he explained, were not "particularly evil men"; they personally would never "throw napalm on the back of a ten-year-old child." But their decisions, reached at and supposedly sterilized by great distance, had the same effect. "What kind of system is it that allows 'good' men to make those kinds of decisions?" Potter asked. "We must name that system. We must name it, describe it, analyze it, understand it, and change it." Potter never named the system himself. He merely implied that Bundy, Rusk, McNamara, and the others had to be stopped, no matter how decent they happened to be.

The other turn in Potter's speech was toward a straightforward denunciation of the system, which was, of course, capitalism, even though he avoided the term. Ogelsby picked up this direction during the next major march in November 1965. The war managers "are not moral monsters." Quite the contrary; "they are all liberals." The Vietnam War was "fundamentally liberal," from its origins to the present.

The task at hand was to name the sort of liberalism at work, for it certainly bore no resemblance to the nation's revolutionary tradition. Ogelsby chose the name that was to stick: the system was "corporate liberalism," he said, a system that molded together the capitalist search for profit, anticommunism, and imperialism—a combination of "richness and righteousness." Just as Ogelsby gave Potter's system a name, so he drew out the implications. So powerful was the system, so good were liberals at deflecting opposition and hiding the true sources of power, Ogelsby claimed, that all "humanists" had to see that reforms, marches, or petitioning launched under the illusion that "the mighty can be reached" were hopeless. Instead, the only hope lay in an "unconditional" humanism.

The war yielded some of the best evidence of the pervasiveness of corporate liberalism and stood as the most dramatic example of how the system had become a moral monstrosity, even if run by men who were not themselves moral monsters. As Ogelsby charged, the multiversity had built cozy relationships with the military establishment, defense contractors, and the federal government. Nearly all of the major schools had their hands in the military-industrial kitty, some more than others. Penn, Berkeley, and Harvard all had important programs that variously related to defense work. The University of Wisconsin at Madison, which was rapidly becoming the "third coast" of New Left activism, housed a well-funded theoretical mathematics program for the Army that became a hated symbol of university corruption. Many schools held regular recruitment and job-placement programs for the CIA, FBI, and other arms of the government, and practically all schools had ROTC programs, which were now being reviled as symbols of militarism.

Naming liberalism as the enemy had enormous, yet contradictory, consequences for the New Left. The analysis yielded some of the most fruitful ideas since Port Huron. If liberalism was the enemy, then it was impossible to embrace the liberal myth of progress. The liberal illusions that affluence was permanent, that political progress was ensured by the smooth functioning of interest-group compromise, and that equality could be guaranteed by "a bigger and better welfare state" were all, as Todd Gitlin wrote in 1966, a "fantasy" that applied "aspirin to cancer." Potter explicitly denounced the faith in progress, which "has nothing to do with people or their needs." "Progress," he insisted, "is our enemy."

The critique of technology and progress could have become a major contribution to U.S. radicalism, but instead it was brushed aside. The bulk of the New Left moved toward a stiffer line of thinking that revised Marxism in the cause of student revolution; this stiffness doomed the high idealism of Port Huron. "The early spirit of pragmatism and experimentation," Hayden recalled, "was steadily being replaced by the adoption of more radical, abstract, and ultimately paralyzing ideology." As SDS grew, it became more attractive to the dogmatic left, which began to plot a takeover. Just as Harrington and the elders had warned, SDS was infiltrated in 1965 by members of the Progressive Labor party (PL), a tiny sect of Maoists so fanatical that they had been drummed out of the Communist party for "ultra-leftism." PL, a puritanical left-wing group, was as far removed from the messy anarchy of SDS as could be imagined. As if to prove its independence, SDS chose the 1965 national meeting in Kewadin, Michigan, to establish a nonexclusion policy, thereby ensuring a complete break from LID. As Gitlin writes, "who could believe there was anything to fear? . . . We were the *New* Left, vigorously antiauthoritarian, purely American, no suckers for a bunch of tightassed Stalinists."

The New Radicalism

Meanwhile, the new guard embraced an increasingly abstract radicalism based primarily on Franz Fanon and Herbert Marcuse. Fanon's *Wretched of the Earth* appeared in English in 1965, just at the time when the new guard was groping for a way to name the enemy. Whereas the Black Panthers embraced Fanon because of his faith in the dispossessed, white radicals were attracted to his theories of revolution, especially his claim that colonialism reduced its victims to psychological dependency, which could be broken through violent revolution. Violence was a cathartic act. Violence was freedom. *Wretched* arrived just as liberalism was choking on its own promises and spewing forth more war. At just the right moment, it justified left-wing violence in the Third World, while it provided a nearly perfect means of identification between student radicals and Third World revolutionaries: namely, they were all existentialists embarking on a confrontation in the name of psychological liberation.

The New Left's relationship with Herbert Marcuse, meanwhile, was full of misunderstandings. Marcuse's writings, especially *One-Dimensional Man* (1964), one of the books most central to New Left thinking, brought a feel of rounded sophistication that New Left thinking often lacked. Marcuse blended Freud's theories of the struggle between the life instinct of Eros and the death instinct of Thanatos with Marx's theories of surplus labor. To Marcuse, Freud's categories were not fundamental to human nature so much as determined by the social order, at least in advanced civilization; in that same civilization, people were driven to work far beyond what is necessary to survive not only by the desire to produce wealth but also by "surplus repression," the socially constructed demand that people put aside their desire for pleasure and engage in meaningless work. Marcuse believed that surplus repression was rooted in the organization of a scarcity society in which people were deluded into thinking that they still had to labor constantly, and where they did so, the life instincts were worn down and the "performance principle" reigned. People defied the performance principle when they let Eros loose in the form of art and eroticism, both of which were inherently alienated from and sparked opposition to the technological order. Together, they constituted the "Great Refusal."

The historic issue that Westerners faced, Marcuse wrote in *One-Dimensional Man*, was that technological society could conquer Eros only by providing some form of compensation. Consequently, it created the illusion of ever-greater freedom, bought off Eros, and imposed complete domination. In its consumer abundance, society pretended to offer unlimited choices for individual gratification but in reality dictated all the choices. Society was in the process of removing sexual taboos and granting license, but the sexual revolution replaced eroticism with indulgence. In contemporary society, Marcuse quipped, "sexuality turns into a vehicle for the bestsellers of oppression." In such a world, "guilt has no place," but neither does genuine freedom; the "Happy Consciousness has no limits," but neither was it liberated. This "controlled desublimation" established nothing short of totalitarian domination, a domination so pervasive that the possibility of escape was remote at best. Scattered expressions of genuine art might flicker momentarily but offered no grounds for optimism. Marcuse placed his only real hope for eventual liberation in the possibility that technology itself might do away with work completely, leaving people so alienated from the social processes that they might reassert the pleasure principle.

Marcuse's constant pairing of opposites could recommend his work to gay liberationists or to prudes (he was something of the latter), to revolutionaries or to technocrats. He was a great producer of wonderfully strident rhetoric, impressive to the ear: for example, he coined the phrases "repressive tolerance"; "euphoria in unhappiness"; "totalitarian democracy." Like any substantive philosophy, Marcuse's work could conveniently be read to say different things to different people, particularly on the issue of sexuality. As for the New Left, Marcuse's shift from the Marxist emphasis on class to the Freudian focus on the psyche offered a primer for radicals regardless of class and thus, as Allan Matusow astutely points out, "served well the new left prophets of middle-class liberation." Marcuse's theoretical detachment of Marx from Marxist class analysis fed the generation gap, for the agents of domination were not whip-wielding capitalists but tolerant parents and college administrators. Indeed real power, according to Marcuse, was hidden so deeply in bureaucratic administration that the slaves did not even know they were slaves. "Repressive tolerance" was exactly what Potter and Ogelsby had been getting at.

While Marcuse concluded for himself that individuals were powerless to change society, younger radicals took two strategies of active rebellion from him. One could take steps to alienate oneself completely, the farther the better. On the other hand, complete domination required complete revolution—revolution against the government, against the university, against the family, against reason, against the self.

By 1967 the New Left was applying Marcuse to a number of theoretical ventures of its own. As a result, they convinced themselves, first, that students were a legitimate revolutionary group, if not the vanguard itself; second, that the tolerant society was totalitarian and achieved its domination by providing affluence rather than by imposing poverty; and, third, that aggressive radicalism, perhaps even violent revolution, was the only way to break the chain. Once distilled, Marcuse was taken to mean that revolution did not have to be a struggle against poverty by or on behalf of the working class. Because the affluent society ensnared so many people, a new radicalism should look to recruit white-collar workers, bureaucrats, and especially college students, who, after all, were merely being trained at school to take part in the neocapitalist society. For that matter, each individual could—and should—be expected to launch a personal revolution. For the revolution against the affluent society was a psychological revolt, a conscious struggle against psychological repression and individual alienation. Revolution began with "the perception of oneself as unfree, as oppressed," as Gregg Calvert wrote. Calvert, who began to emerge as the late New Left's leading theorist, Hayden's successor, hoped that this new radicalism, designed to meet the new contradictions of "neocapitalism," would become a "libertarian socialism" that "regards the authoritarian structures of bureaucratized society as well as the taboos of repressive civilization as contrary to the health and freedom of people everywhere, and as obstacles to love, creativity, and real community."

With Calvert, the New Left came to an intellectual resting place far from Port Huron. Port Huron had renounced ideology; Calvert was ideology and then some. Port Huron had proposed that students were uniquely situated to act as radical catalysts in the larger society; Calvert's work implied that radical change began in the individual mind. Port Huron had envisioned a political strategy of engagement in which, like the civil rights movement, SDS would work in coalition with Social Democrats and liberals while holding dear to principles; Calvert renounced "liberal reformists" as guilty white liberals who sought only to ease the contradictions of neocapitalism. Politics, as a process of matching available means to desired ends, was dismissed out of hand. When Marcuse was mixed with Fanon, revolution became, as Calvert claimed, "the struggle for one's own freedom," and freedom was defined as a rejection of the psychological pressure of society. It followed that individual acts of rebellion brought individual liberation, but far from being a selfish act, individual liberation "unites one in the struggle of the oppressed, because it posits a more universally human potentiality for all men in a liberated society."

The logical strategy for the New Left to follow was to move from "protest to resistance," and it is no surprise that Calvert coined the phrase. The New Left had always sought action, but "resistance" in this formulation was action for its own sake. As its domination of the peace movement demonstrated, New Left resistance was based on the supposition that means were ends. It also hung on the most tenuous of justifications: that storming the barricades at Chicago or blowing up Army Math in Madison were acts of revolutionary solidarity with the Vietnamese, the southern sharecropper, the "wretched of the earth"—solidarity with everyone, that is, but the average American—and were, therefore, inherently "human" acts. Revolution did not have to be a matter of "objective conditions," as the tired old Marxists believed. In theory, it could be whipped up out of nothing more than vague discontent.

"You Don't Need a Weatherman to Know Which Way the Wind Blows"

By 1968 young radicals worldwide seemed pretty close to whipping up revolution on the strength of discontent. Radical students were bringing Paris to a standstill and were on the march in West Germany and Mexico. Czechoslovakians were thumbing their noses at Soviet tanks. Always tightly interwoven with the new radicalism, by 1967 the counterculture gave hints of the New Left's direction through new fashions and symbols. Protest music had gone electric, and Bob Dylan and Joan Baez, the popular poets of the early New Left, were now overshadowed by psychedelic rock from the Bay. In dorm rooms and crash pads, walls once adorned with

Beatles posters sported Che Guevara, Karl Marx, and Ho Chi Minh. Vietcong flag emblems nudged out peace signs as favored clothing patches. Mao's guerrilla primer, *The Little Red Book*, made the rounds. SDSers listened to Panthers explain how to load weapons. The authorities had become "Pigs." The *New York Review of Books*, influential within the Left but usually respectable, printed a picture of a Molotov cocktail along with instructions on how to make one and articles from Hayden and Andrew Kopkind embracing the violent example of black militants. "It is as if these intellectuals think that the [urban] riots are just an exercise in camp," LID secretary Rachelle Horowitz wrote in disgust to an acquaintance. She thought the New Left intellectuals had become "monsters." Many students took as an absolute article of faith that revolution was imminent; many in the establishment did too. FBI agents watching over the New Left began to wonder whether this was not the revolution that their hysterical director, J. Edgar Hoover, had been warning them about for years. A writer in *Fortune* in 1968 claimed that "these youngsters are acting out a revolution—not a protest, and not a rebellion, but an honest-to-God revolution."

In spite of this fevered condition, revolution was objectively impossible. Middle-class America was manifestly content with the comforts of consumer capitalism. When radicals tried to organize in working-class high schools, they were often chased out and occasionally beaten up. Ho Chi Minh was willing to applaud U.S. college students, but the Vietnamese usually counseled their impressionable American friends toward moderation. The claims of an international revolutionary union, like the claims about an imminent revolution at home, were grand in inverse proportion to how distant they were in fact. One organizational disaster after another indicated that the revolutionary coalition could never be more than a figment of the imagination. The Left could not even put together a multiracial, multiparty challenge in time for the 1968 election, a failure amply illuminated at the 1967 National Conference for New Politics.

Unmoored from practical reality, the New Left turned extreme, both in theory and in action, as it imagined a reality all its own. The movement suffered an "implosion," Todd Gitlin believes, and it is the only apt word. Increasingly self-contained, having traded politics for the liberating virtues of violence, there was no one to check them but themselves. Talk was cheap; now it was time for action.

Columbia

Such was the temper of the New Left when resistance moved from the Pentagon to Columbia University near the end of the 1967–1968 academic year. The school's SDS chapter led a student strike against the university's plans to build a new gymnasium in what was at the time a neighborhood park. The beginning of construction brought tension to the boiling point, and community militants allied with black and white students to take over the administration building. Not allowed to stay among the black protesters but not wanting to miss the action, white students moved into several other buildings and awaited the predictable police charge that resulted, just as predictably, in the beating of protesters. The administration settled on a hard line against the students, but the faculty was deeply split, some sympathizing with the students and others, such as the eminent historian Richard Hofstadter, appalled that the "young totalitarians" would attack a humanistic institution, whatever its faults. Although final exams were canceled, the university attempted a commencement, during which a contingent of students walked out on Hofstadter's address and held their own, well-planned "countergraduation."

Columbia was the scene of the most dramatic student action since the Berkeley Free Speech Movement, though more obscure in its goals. Columbia's SDS chapter had been taken over by an "action-faction" led by "ruthless" Mark Rudd, the son of a New Jersey real estate salesman and a mother who dutifully brought a home-cooked meal to campus. Rudd was a newer version of Mario Savio, except that he lacked Savio's speaking skills and could muster no more eloquence than to steal a line from a LeRoi Jones poem to sum up his intentions to the administration: "Up against the wall, motherfucker, this is a stick up!" Tom Hayden, who arrived at Columbia in the middle of the protests, found Rudd "a nice, somewhat inarticulate suburban New Jersey kid, . . . a young boy." Rudd was bored with speaking—even more so with thinking—and believed that action was the only thing that counted. He imposed the action-faction's will on fellow students who wanted only to humanize the school. This was a "faggoty, wimpy, tepid" goal, according to Rudd, that "implied capitulation to the liberal mythology about free and open inquiry at a university."

It was becoming the logic of things that, first, the loudest wheel brought the media attention and, second, the commitment to action gained strength within the organized New Left. Spring 1968 saw the beginning of New Left violence on campus; ten bombings or acts of arson were reported that term, most aimed at ROTC offices.

The Battle of Chicago

Political theatrics, the sense that the revolution was on, the illusion that individual liberation and world liberation were being acted on at once, all bound together in rage and frustration against the ongoing war, led to Chicago and the Democratic Convention in August. The agreement between several groups on staging protests in Chicago covered the disorganization within the movement and ensured that protests at the convention would be messy, if not violent. Several different leaders had hatched the idea of staging great protests, but each faction had its own agenda, its own goals, and its own measures of success. The hippies, re-unorganized in the "Yippie Party," proposed a "Festival of Life" to counter the Democrats' "Convention of Death." Hayden and Rennie Davis, old SDS comrades, were encouraged by Gene McCarthy's strong showings in the primaries and saw a week of demonstrations against the Democrats as a means of increasing the antiwar movement's leverage within the party, especially after Robert Kennedy's assassination. Dave Dellinger wanted MOBE to organize routine antiwar demonstrations of speeches, marches, and picketing. The PL, always alert to opportunities to insinuate itself into the movement, showed up to hunt for new recruits. The Panthers planned to participate. An East Village anarchist group, indelicately known as the Mother-fuckers, had pledged to attend. Many young McCarthy supporters expected to participate in respectable demonstrations in the hopes of tying the protests firmly to the convention.

Practically the only important group that hesitated to endorse the Chicago demonstrations was SDS, whose national leaders objected on a number of counts. They were not happy that the "old men" like Hayden and Davis were organizing on their own; nor did they care much for the Yippies, who were not serious enough about politics. Some argued that convention protests could only be based on the assumption that the Democrats would listen. Serious and legitimate concerns were also voiced about what Chicago could accomplish. Mayor Daley promised to turn Chicago into an armed camp, and he had to be reckoned with. On these grounds, Michael Rossman, a veteran of the Free Speech Movement, rebuked the Yippies for inviting kids to follow them like lemmings into a bloody confrontation. They were committing the only sin that hippies recognized, dishonesty, because the "Festival of Life" was going to be far from joyous. "Chicago in August," Rossman warned, "will harbor the nation's richest pool of uptight bad vibes, set to flash. Pack 200,000 kids in there . . . and it's sure to blow."

Whatever other objections were raised against Chicago, Rossman's was one to take seriously. Daley and his supporters were gearing up for confrontation, and the Yippie leaders Abbie Hoffman and Jerry Rubin angered them with their peculiar brand of political humor. Yippie was farce, and nearly everything the two said had to be taken as a joke. But Daley never joked about his town. As they negotiated over the Yippie request to camp in Lincoln Park, it became clear that the two sides did not speak the same language. When Hoffman announced that for $200,000 he'd leave town, Daley's people thought he was asking for a bribe. The Yippies made plans to put LSD in the water supply, but they did so for the benefit of the undercover agents who had infiltrated their meetings. The papers published rumors that the Yippies intended to poison food and drink, flood the sewers with gasoline, and kidnap delegates. All in good fun—but it was also Hoffman's way of baiting the establishment, and he may as well have marched into town with a band of armed marauders.

Both scared and stubborn, the city refused most of the permits that organizers requested and greatly narrowed the boundaries of legal demonstration. Daley an-nounced that the entire 12,000-member police force would be on twelve-hour shifts and could rely on help from 11,000 National Guard and regular army troops. Between Daley's police and federal authorities, thousands of undercover officers, some of whom acted as provocateurs, prepared to flood into the demonstrations. Later estimates held that one in every six demonstrators at Chicago was an under-cover officer. Police tails were put on all the demonstration leaders.

The city's stalling made Hoffman, Rubin, and Hayden all the more determined to engage in confrontations, and their defiance angered some of their colleagues.

Yippie leader Ed Sanders heatedly criticized Hoffman for "urging people to go out and get killed for nothing. Man, that's like murdering people." In his memoirs, Hayden writes of his "darkening mood" on the eve of the convention, but he had long been slipping toward the conclusion that violent confrontation was in the offing and probably necessary, a mood that belied his comparatively mundane political hopes for the Chicago protests. Dellinger, reading Hayden's mood, worried that the protests would turn violent.

The battle lines having been drawn, Chicago became a march to catastrophe, which was exactly how many participants thought of it. Only the most foolish, the most stout-hearted, or the most committed went. Where Hoffman had promised 200,000, no more than 10,000 gathered, only half of whom were from out of town. Daley seemed invigorated, rather than relieved, and was more determined than ever to teach the youngsters some manners.

The confrontations began almost immediately. Dellinger's pacifists were stationed in Grant Park, across the street from the Hilton Hotel where many of the delegates were staying; the Yippies went to Lincoln Park. Hoffman and Rubin moved ahead with the Festival of Life against constant police hassling. When they nominated their presidential candidate, a pig they named Pigasus, Rubin was arrested and the candidate packed off to the safer surroundings of an animal shelter. On the eve of the convention, the police enforced an 11:00 P.M. curfew in Lincoln Park by driving demonstrators out with tear gas. On the first full day of the convention, the police kept Hoffman from bringing a flatbed truck into the park for a stage and then cut off the electricity when a band began playing anyway. Some in the crowd began to taunt police while Hoffman tried negotiations; the poet Allen Ginsberg, the patron saint of the hippies, added his own touch by meditating to relieve the tension in the park. Slightly before the curfew was to take effect, the police moved in, singling out individuals for beatings, cursing back at the crowd, and forcing the demonstrators out of the park under a sky filled with tear gas. To frustrate police efforts to control the flow of the crowd out of the park, the fleeing demonstrators split up into small groups or ran on their own. Hoffman was amazed that the city preferred to have Yippies sneaking around town instead of containing them. It was, he figured, "about the dumbest military tactic" since the Trojan horse.

Much the same thing happened at Lincoln and Grant parks over the next two days. The police positioned themselves ominously around the demonstrators, randomly clubbing those who fell into their hands, harassing them when possible, and then driving them out at curfew time. The protesters continued their speeches and picketing, sneering back at police and carrying out any "guerrilla" actions they could get away with, which consisted mostly in nothing more deadly than homemade stink bombs or sneaking past police lines into the Hilton. On Tuesday, the protesters held an "un-birthday party" for Lyndon Johnson. Hoffman was arrested for obscenity: he wrote "Fuck" on his forehead because, he explained, he did not want to be hassled by the media. Hayden was arrested not once but twice and took to donning a series of improbable disguises, at one point including

In August 1968 police reach for an antiwar demonstrator as he attempts to "liberate" the monument of General John Logan in Chicago's Bryant Park.
[UPI/Bettmann Newsphotos]

a football helmet, in order to slip his police tail. Meanwhile, the Democrats were splitting among themselves. Many McCarthy delegates, sensing their defeat, began showing up in Grant Park and were gassed and Maced along with the less restrained demonstrators. When Julian Bond appealed to the delegates in the Hilton to turn on their lights in a sign of solidarity with the demonstrators, the hotel lit up like a Christmas tree.

On Wednesday, the Democrats nominated Hubert Humphrey, and the confrontation peaked. MOBE had been given an official permit for an afternoon rally in the Grant Park bandshell, across the river and north of the Hilton, but none of the leaders had firm control of their crowd or their strategy. In mid-day, the police charged into the crowd to prevent a young man from turning the American flag upside down; when he tried to intervene, Rennie Davis was smashed with a billy club. Dellinger decided to lead a nonviolent march to the convention site. But after he announced his plans, Hayden called on people to get into the streets and move, guerrilla-like, all over the city. Unable to secure the right to march to the convention amphitheater, Dellinger aimed his march toward the strip of Grant Park across the street from the Hilton.

The Battle of Chicago became a running clash between Dellinger's people, who moved back and forth looking for a way across the river, the police and National Guard, who tried to block their progress, and those who followed Hayden and moved on their own into the Loop. Dellinger's troops made it over one bridge, which inexplicably had been left unguarded, and moved down the narrow area along Michigan Avenue to the Hilton. It was early evening, and the television cameras were there to broadcast the battle live on prime time. After some jostling, the police took off their badges and charged the crowd, screaming "Kill, Kill, Kill!" The frontline demonstrators took the wave of beatings, while those behind them taunted police and chanted "The whole world is watching!" As the frontline was beaten and scooped up either for arrest or to be rushed to first aid, others moved up to absorb the police fury. Hayden, in disguise, was with his old Port Huron colleague Bob Ross and got stuck against the wall of the Hilton with perhaps fifty other people, mostly McCarthy supporters, reporters, "and plain ordinary citizens," as he recalls. The police had them trapped and turned on them viciously, spraying Mace and aiming clubs at their kidneys. The pressure was so great that the crowd blasted through the window of the hotel, where they spilled into the laps of drunken Democrats and unnerved employees slinging drinks in the Haymarket Lounge. Hardly skipping a beat, the police continued their charge into the hotel. Some demonstrators tried to escape by taking inconspicuous seats in the bar or the lobby, where they stood out like battered thumbs. Embittered McCarthy delegates took some of the injured up to their fifteenth-floor headquarters, only to suffer a police raid and beatings of their own later that night. Having occurred under the lights of national television, the "police riot," as the obligatory federal follow-up commission called it, finally brought the streets into the convention, where delegates broke into bickering, yelling, and cursing at one another.

The demonstrators were right: the whole world was watching. No doubt they hoped that international publicity would leave Daley and the Democrats shamed and repentant, but public sympathy ran toward Daley instead. Hayden's strategy had succeeded on one level: the demonstrations had forced the Democrats to face up to the issue of Vietnam. Unfortunately, however, they nominated a man committed to sustaining the war policy. Insofar as 1968 increased the power of progressive forces in the party, it did so only by driving many traditional Democrats out. Happy to measure success by the standards of farce, the Yippies chalked up Chicago as a great success. What counted for them was the extent of disruption and media exposure, and they got both in abundance. "Everybody played out their karma," Rubin exalted. "It was all perfect. We wanted to show that America wasn't a democracy, that the convention wasn't politics. The message of the week was of an America ruled by force. That was a big victory."

As unsettling as it was at the moment, Chicago only affirmed the direction of the New Left toward self-defeating confrontation and greater marginalization in national politics. It was but one of many dramatic moments in the movement's life, one of "a hundred aspiring preludes" to a future "not yet revealed to us," in Carl Ogelsby's estimation. It is true nonetheless that on an individual level the convention marked a sharp and momentarily complete break with America. Pessimism had been growing on the left for years, but Chicago led many to give up any hope of national redemption. Hoffman, Rubin, Hayden, and Davis readied themselves for the conspiracy trial stemming from Chicago. The future that the Old Left had warned of for SDS came to pass at the group's 1968 convention. SDS came to its end when a walkout by a spontaneous coalition opposed to a PL takeover in effect left the organization in the PL's hands.

The Weather Underground

All that was left was Weatherman, a tiny group of SDS extremists, including Mark Rudd, the charismatic Bernardine Dohrn, Cathy Wilkerson, John Jacobs, and a handful of others. They saw themselves as action-oriented, indifferent to theorizing, and engaged in a complete anti-American revolution, from denouncing "monogamy" to carrying out terrorist bombings. They took their name from a line in Bob Dylan's "Subterranean Homesick Blues": "You don't need a weatherman to know which way the wind blows" supposedly symbolized their rejection of PL party discipline.

Their one contribution to the movement was the "Days of Rage," a series of mini-riots they organized to coincide with the trial of the Chicago Seven in October 1969. Dreaming of organizing thousands of Chicago's young toughs, they put out the word that they were going to begin a rampage from Lincoln Park. A few hundred young gangsters showed up, and, after encouragement from a poorly disguised Hayden, they began several nights of wild vandalism along the city's prestigious Gold Coast, smashing shop windows, bashing cars, and flinging themselves headlong into battles with the Chicago police, who returned violence in kind. Besides the vain expectation that tens of thousands of working-class kids would join them, the only purpose of the Days of Rage was to fight. If one was lucky enough to get shot or beaten, all the better for one's reputation in Weatherman.

Never numbering more than a few hundred members, by 1969 the Weather Underground became the new symbol of radicalism on the strength of its propensity to violence. They inspired countless imitators: between September 1969 and May 1970 at least 250 bombings and fires were attributed to the New Left. In early March 1970, several Weathermen were preparing bombs in the basement of a fashionable townhouse on the edge of Greenwich Village when an explosion razed the home and killed three of the radicals. Police recovered enough explosives to destroy a city block. The biggest blast of all was the work of imitators in Madison, Wisconsin. In August, with school out of session and the campus relatively quiet, a terrorist group detonated a van full of homemade explosives underneath the Army Math Research Department. Nearly the entire building was destroyed, windows were shattered for blocks, including those in the hospital across the street, and an innocent young physicist, the father of two small children and himself a quiet opponent of the Vietnam War, was killed. The wing where Army Math was located was damaged least of all.

To Hayden and Gitlin, both members of SDS's "old guard," the roots of the violence in general and Weatherman in particular were to be found in flaws that the New Left carried along throughout the sixties. To Hayden, Weatherman was the result of SDS's indifference to formal structure and its devotion to "thinking and acting in new ways to change the world." Embittered by the confrontation with the establishment, the New Left "in just seven short years had fallen victim to every dire and cynical prediction ever made about revolutionary movements." Hayden strongly implied that the Weatherman underground was created by Chicago and, presumably, forced toward violence. In Gitlin's view, Weatherman resulted from ideological bankruptcy; the group was "an extension . . . of bad, abstract politics by other means. . . . They were the pure New Left in a way—self-enclosed, contemptuous of liberalism, romantic about Third World revolutions, organized in small squads, exuberant with will, courageous, reckless, arrogant, burning to act *as if* anything might be possible."

Hayden and Gitlin were right, but they also were taking too much responsibility for the failures of the movement that they did much to start. Weatherman symbolized not so much the specific failures of the New Left, or the impossibility of starting revolution in a nonrevolutionary context, or even the insurmountable difficulties of building a permanent and viable left in the United States. Rather, in a moment when peer judgment and open rebellion against parental authority were increasingly important to young people, and when these developments took place in an intensely political time, it is not hard to imagine that some people would see politics as the antidote to personal demons. Susan Stern described her commitment to the Days of Rage by posing it against her relationship with her father. "I resented my father not only because he had tormented me for the first twenty years of my life, but because he was a capitalist, and he was very prejudiced." Joining Weatherman brought a sense of power, however limited and illusory; it brought a personal mystique, and it soothed a yearning for acceptance. The Weather people, Gitlin points out, "were the children of the cornucopia par excellence" and hailed from families that were far better off than those in the early New Left. They had something to prove to a generation that had marked its distance from parents and from wealth and had to be all the more revolutionary because of their backgrounds. Weatherman and its imitators were not a product of soured radicalism but of the wreckage of U.S. society more broadly—the collapse of private authority, the political exacerbation of inherent tensions between children and parents, the cultural invitation to extremism. Weatherman was the United States' "worst nightmare" only because it was made up of its "best" children.

The End of Radicalism

Neither the bombing of Army Math nor the townhouse explosion was responsible for destroying the American left. Like it or not, from the beginning the left was intertwined with liberalism, and when the status quo returned with Richard Nixon's 1968 presidential victory, liberals and radicals were thrown even more closely on one another.

Two broad consequences emerged when the New Left expired. One-time activists scattered in countless directions: some to communes or private farms; others to corporate offices; a few, tragically, to despair, suicide, and homicide; and yet others took the New Left into left-wing academic careers, public interest groups, labor organizations, or storefront law offices.

The second post–1968 development was the emergence of several movements, clearly indebted to the New Left and yet independent of it, into the political mainstream. Radical feminism and the gay liberation movement were born of New Left parentage, and yet each stood up on its own. These movements increasingly blended with the liberal wing of the Democratic party, however regularly their members railed against mere reformism and tame politics. In both cases, the movements survived because they managed to take hold of some rock of safety in the mainstream—the women's movement in the case of radical feminists, and the sexual revolution and the liberal defense of privacy in the case of gay liberation. They were able to remain organized because they aligned with these other developments. In so doing, they became the interest-group residue of the New Left.

Radical Feminism

Radical feminism grew directly out of the New Left, where young women played essential roles from the beginning. The initial attempts to raise issues of gender repression and inequality grew out of the activism and openness of the New Left; yet radical feminism also emerged as a response to the indifference of men in both SNCC and SDS to women's issues.

Although there was no great eagerness to take up women's issues when they began to emerge, SNCC members considered in general good faith a women's manifesto that Mary King and Casey Hayden presented in November 1965. Rather than a challenge to the organization, King and Hayden saw their document as a logical outgrowth of SNCC. At that point, the organization was floundering in search of renewed purpose, and true to SNCC's democratic nature, the two women wondered whether some members might spend their energies exploring women's issues. In proper SNCC fashion, the two had no firm notion of "end results"; they merely wanted to be guided by the principle "that women should be able to define freedom in their own way." "To raise questions" about women's rights was to illustrate "that society hasn't dealt with some of its deepest problems and opens discussion of why that is so." Although it became renowned as the beginning point of feminism within the New Left, Hayden and King's "A Kind of Memo" was pure SNCC, down to the self-effacing title. And, indeed, the initial New Left advocates of feminism took up the cause not so much because SNCC or SDS ignored their pleas but in order to preserve some measure of the original spirit of the New Left.

Just as we have to recognize two cohorts of the New Left, it helps to define two sorts of radical feminism, one mostly political, the other primarily cultural. King, for one, had in mind an activism that might exalt the essentialist virtues of the woman's "perspective on birth and death, endurance, love, and basic human values. . . . We were just as concerned for employed mothers who were locked into low-paying, dead-end, meaningless jobs providing little means for caring for their offspring, as we were for women who needed the gratification of stimulating work for their sense of fulfillment and personhood." King took her inspiration more from Ella Baker than from Betty Friedan, and her spirit was more universalist than revolutionary. That universalism disappeared as the original spirit of the New Left turned more and more toward rebellion.

SDS was always more male dominated than SNCC. Although the movement gave women practical political experience, the white New Left systematically, and by 1967 quite aggressively, shouted down women who called for convention planks on organizational commitments to women's rights. Women were unrepresented in the national leadership, particularly as the New Left became media-conscious and power within the movement became associated, as one disillusioned woman activist wrote, with "having visibly dominated some gathering . . . or in having played some theatrical role." Women ran the offices while men made the speeches. The antiwar movement, which might have provided a stage for those who believed that women were uniquely suited to working for peace, instead spent its energies on the draft issue, the male nature of which was aptly summed up in the movement slogan, "Girls say yes to boys who say no." Women who called attention to the inequities were accused of whining about personal problems or of being man-hating fems trying to distract the movement from the business of real revolution.

Slowly and often with a pronounced ambivalence, some women began to mark themselves off from SDS. After 1966, SDS meetings commonly included discussions of the women's place in the movement, sometimes through formal discussion groups, other times in spontaneous talks, and still others in acrimonious exchanges with male colleagues. All along, many SDS women, whom feminists derisively named "politicos," continued to insist that women's issues were secondary to stopping the war. Others were pulled in two directions, feeling that they "shared the same radical tradition, rhetoric, heroes, dates, the whole bloody history of class war" with male radicals. "It is pitifully easy for radical women to accept their own exploitation in the name of some larger justice," Marge Piercy wrote.

When dozens of factions began splitting off from the imploding movement core, groups of radical women concluded that they, too, had to adopt the strategy of separatism. A group centered in Chicago came out of the Conference on New Politics, where Shulamith Firestone, trying to push through resolutions to give women controlling votes in the Conference, was told to "move on, little girl." While radical groups emerged in many major cities, Firestone and Pam Allen, both SDS veterans, organized the best known, Radical Women, in New York. In November 1967 Radical Women infiltrated a women's contingent during a Washington peace march. They exhorted marchers to split from the politicos and to follow them into a demonstration against "traditional womanhood." The following September, the New York group brought radical feminism to national attention with a protest against the Miss America pageant in Atlantic City. Taking a page from the Yippies, they crowned a sheep Miss America, auctioned off a Miss America dummy, and set up a "freedom trash can" where they tossed in bras, girdles, dishcloths, and steno pads. Later that fall, a group calling itself the Women's International Terrorist Conspiracy from Hell (WITCH) raided the New York Stock Exchange, leaving hexes as they went.

While they broke off from the New Left in both organization and goals, radical feminists built their case directly on the ideas of the late New Left. Radicals argued that women were an oppressed group whose liberation depended on immediate revolution. Women were the most oppressed people, for their subordination crossed the lines of class, nationality, race, and even history. There was no need to go chasing after obscure causes when the need for women's liberation was so obvious. As the "Red Stocking Manifesto," the 1969 organizational statement of the radical group that succeeded Radical Women in New York, insisted: "Women are an oppressed class. Our oppression is total, affecting every facet of our lives. We are expoited as sex objects, breeders, domestic servants, and cheap labor." Every relationship between men and women "is a class relationship, and the conflicts between individual men and women are *political* conflicts that can only be solved collectively."

Once they established themselves as a legitimately oppressed class, the radicals, still indebted to New Left dogma, argued further that women were a colonized people. They thereby established themselves among the panoply of oppressed groups whose revolutionary aims allegedly coincided with those of the Vietnamese, African Americans, Hispanics, and others. "Our bodies had ownership by many," one activist wrote, "men, doctors, clothes and cosmetic manufacturers, advertizers, churches, schools—everyone but ourselves." As Robin Morgan maintained somewhat later, women's bodies were colonized territory. Like any colony, women had been "mined for their natural resources"; and as Fanon wrote of colonial people, women, "the Wretched of the Hearth," either had been convinced of their own inferiority or, worse, convinced that they were not oppressed at all. Revolutionaries, Morgan wrote, had to brace themselves with Marcuse and be prepared for a dose of tolerant totalitarianism. "When slammed up against the wall, the Man will liberalize abortion and birth-control laws, and open up the professions to a few more token women."

Beneath the rhetoric, radical feminism went much deeper than conventional New Left thinking. Radicals were right about the universal subordination of women, and they were far more hostile than most late-decade radicals to consumer culture, which they also accurately saw as the source of many standard conceptions of sexuality. Yet radical women were never able to transcend the political calamities of the moment, and in some ways reflected the worst impulses of the New Left. They assumed that the revolution was on, but they had no mass base. While radicals could legitimately claim that 51 percent of the population comprised an oppressed group, they could not legitimately claim the allegiance of more than a tiny part of that group. Their "Third World sisters" never consistently saw their interests aligned with those of white radical feminists. Radicals could claim that too many women were submerged in false consciousness and had embraced their own oppression; they could contend that it was radicalism's job to shake women out of that slave mentality. But the revolution was no closer, and radical feminists were as far removed from the concerns of workaday women as the New Left was from workaday men.

In the face of insurmountable obstacles to revolution, radical feminists were doomed to a course that was little different from that of their male colleagues and the movement as a whole. They too began to fragment. Several different lines of analysis emerged concerning the issue of how women perceived oppression, whether they shouldered any blame themselves or whether, by virtue of their gender, they were blameless. Other differences arose over whether to break all ties or to do battle with men. Those who chose to break all ties—sometimes figura-tively, sometimes literally—disavowed practical politics, and, their critics charged, essentially retreated from revolution. By 1970 lesbianism defined the vanguard of the radicals and drove women into separate gay–straight camps. What one radical thought of as the "internecine hostility of any oppressed people" split activist women into a dozen different categories, each according to some fine shade of sexual self-definition. Some struggled to welcome the polymorphous nature of the radical wing of feminism, but having intensely politicized sexuality by locating the roots of oppression there, the radicals had to suffer the consequences when polymorphous sexuality became a political litmus test.

If radical feminism went the way of the organized New Left, still its adherents left their imprint on the mainstream women's movement. Above all, the younger, more radical women brought to feminism the emphasis on personal matters that the mainstream was determined to avoid until, in their hope for unity, NOW began to absorb the energy of the left. The radicals insisted that "the personal was political" and that no real answer to the subordination of women could be had without a fundamental revolution in the relationships between the sexes. If NOW remained uneasy about the sexual implications of radical feminism, nonetheless personalized politics laid the basis for the abortion-rights effort and reinforced the mainstream's criticism of consumer culture. The mainstream also benefited from the activism of the radicals, who brought direct action into the feminist movement and helped enliven the mainstream when it was caught in the doldrums of interest-group bargain-ing. The "consciousness-raising" groups that the Red stockings pioneered provided useful grass-roots organizational tools that helped democratize the women's move-ment from the bottom up. As the mainstream made use of such techniques, so did it provide a home for those radicals who maintained their political energy and who remained, then, to influence postmodern liberalism from within.

Gay Liberation

Radical feminists also opened an avenue for sexual radicals to enter the realm of activist politics. At least as a matter of timing, radical feminism attacked heterosex-ual male dominance before the organized gay liberation movement and in so doing legitimized issues of sexual identity on the left. As with radical feminism, gay liberation emerged among people both enlivened by radical politics and frustrated over its failures; as with radical feminists, homosexual activists committed them-selves increasingly to a separatist course as the promise of wider revolution evapo-rated. Gay liberation also shared radical feminism's theoretical reliance on the claim that polymorphous sexuality was inherent in human nature. The two move-ments overlapped in practical ways as well, as many radical lesbians fought for gay liberation as well as for women's causes.

Although gay liberation shared the sensibility of the New Left and was surely spurred on by the activist lessons of the sixties, its roots were far less in radical politics than in cultural radicalism and in the evolution of gay communities in larger cities. Within the anonymity that postwar urbanization provided, homosexuals began to congregate more or less openly for the first time. One new arrival in New York in 1963 was astonished to find that his homosexuality was not the "solitary perversion" that he thought it was but rather that there were evidently "millions of gay men."

In response to the apparent aggregation of gay communities, municipalities nationwide increased police harassment at gay gathering spots and heaped more antiperversion laws on the local books. In spirit if not in fact, such laws ran against the strong tilt of Supreme Court rulings on privacy rights and public morals, which in themselves had opened up more room for descriptions of homosexuality in fiction, theater, and film. Partly compelled by the extent of harassment, and partly emboldened by court rulings and the temper of the times, gay-rights advocates increased their activism. These first activists were mostly moderates by later standards; working out of the so-called homophile organizations, the lesbian Daughters of Bilitis and the gay Mattachine Society, they aimed to soften harassment and decriminalize private acts, while portraying homosexuals as modest, regular folks.

Only tenuously organized to begin with, the homophile movement remained moderate longer than other movements of the time, whether one compares it to the New Left, the civil rights movement, or even the farm workers. Gay liberation, the radicalization of the homophile movement, awaited several interwoven developments. First, the second stage of the sexual revolution, which took hold in the avant-garde communities of New York and San Francisco, slowly legitimized homosexuality among cultural radicals and also diminished the extent of harassment, at least in New York City. As with radical feminists, New Left activists who were gay responded to the implosion of the movement by moving down a similar path that began, as it did, for instance, in Carl Wittman's case in 1967, by raising issues of homosexual rights in the context of New Left universalism and that ended in an increasingly separatist determination to go it alone. Lesbian activists began to show up at homophile meetings and to push for more strident activism. As elsewhere in the left after 1968, the air wafting through gay communities was increasingly laced with pugnaciousness.

This was the general context out of which the gay liberation movement sprang. Its actual birth is usually cited as the day in 1969 when a police raid on the Stonewall Inn in Greenwich Village erupted in several days of rioting and marches. The Stonewall Rebellion was spontaneous in the sense that no one planned the riots, but in an age of sexual revolution and urban chaos, it was hardly surprising. The Stonewall itself was a symbolic point of embarkation. It was by all accounts a squalid dive, run by the Mafia in cahoots with the police, but the one bar in New York City where gay men could dance face to face with reasonable certainty that the place would not be raided. When police raided it anyhow on June 27, as part of a crackdown leading up to the mayoral election, the patrons struck back, trapped the police in the bar, and assaulted them with such vehemence that a riot squad had to free them.

The riot, as well as the marches that followed, marked the break between homophilism and gay liberation. Gay liberation activists worked on the separatist logic of the late New Left, insisted on their oppression as a particular group, and played up their distinctiveness. In the aftermath of Stonewall, radicals organized the Gay Liberation Front (GLF), a name intended to imply identification with the Vietcong; the GLF announced its dedication to destroying the "dirty, vile, fucked-up capitalist conspiracy." As had radical feminists, radical gays distinguished themselves as another of the system's victims and linked their cause to that of "all the oppressed: the Vietnamese struggle, the Third World, the blacks, the workers." Such rhetoric, together with the avowed aims of destroying the repressive nuclear family, were what put gay liberation on the political left.

That broad identification only repeated the illusions of the rest of the left. Gay liberation had no more chance to establish itself as part of a class-based revolution than radical feminism. In the long term, moreover, gays shared with women a general improvement in their place in U.S. society by virtue of their cohesion in political pressure groups rather than as part of a revolutionary coalition. They were able to move into the New Politics because they shared the sensibilities and the political methods of the remnants of the New Left. But as an interest group they had an inherent cohesion. To become an activist was to "come out" and to tie one's fortunes to the political success of the movement, which in turn ensured the long-term commitment of activists.

Together, radical feminism and gay liberation demonstrated that the New Left's survival after 1968 depended on a narrowing of focus and a nearly exclusive attention to separate interests. It seems indisputable, however, that such methods allowed more than mere survival; instead, both residual elements from the New Left served fairly well the purposes of their constituencies. The fortunes of some groups improved as the New Politics came to control the McGovern campaign and wield predominant influence within the Democratic party. But such narrow purposes were far removed from heady notions of universal revolution, and these movements demonstrated the larger failure of the New Politics on just that score.

CHAPTER 6

The End of Culture

 In an age of affluence, the economic grievances that had set the terms of social struggle for a hundred years or more yielded to cultural grievances. Consequently, the defining battle of the sixties was a cultural civil war that pitted a traditional culture born in an age of scarcity against a new culture that was more appropriate to the age of affluence. Traditional culture, as Philip Slater described it in his widely read book, *The Pursuit of Loneliness* (1970), comprised a set of values shaped by need and want: self-denial, the work ethic, and a faith in technological progress. It was the culture of the old generation—presumably everyone "over thirty"—and took as its "moral reference point" the values of the political right. The old culture was "authoritarian, puritanical, primitive, fundamentalist," and often violent. Like the youthful generation that had seized control of it, conversely, the new culture grew from the affluent society and counted as virtues open sexuality, pacifism, and egalitarianism. Its adherents yearned for natural utopias rather than technological progress. "Instead of throwing away one's body so that one can accumulate material artifacts," Slater wrote, the new culture called for people to "throw away the artifacts and enjoy one's body."

As Slater's simplified description of American culture showed, it had become dogma among the advocates of the new culture that young people were free of the "hang-ups" that burdened their elders and that the cultural revolution that they were leading was a thoroughgoing social transformation. The question for Slater and his fellow advocates of the new culture was whether or not young people would prevail and forestall a future doomed, in Theodore Roszak's term, to "totalitarian technocracy." Susan Sontag, writing in *Partisan Review*'s symposium on "What's Happening in America" in 1967, was pessimistic: "Today's America, with Ronald Reagan the new daddy in California and John Wayne chawing spare ribs in the White House, is pretty much the same Yahooland" that it had always been, except that the nation's "barbarism and innocence [now] are lethal."

The new culture found plenty of evidence that the forces of tradition continued to strangle American life. John Wayne was still making films; *Reader's Digest* remained an important part of the reading public's material; popular entertainers from Bob Hope to Pat Boone to the Serendipity Singers (one of Richard Nixon's favorite groups) upheld apple-pie virtues of blandness, conformity, and respect for authority. In rural areas, the gun-toting, stock-car racing vigilante culture of white America remained. The forces of tradition sneered at young people with long hair and colorful clothes. Even roadside billboards heaped instruction on young people: "Keep America Beautiful. Get a Haircut." Traditionalists continued to push for book banning in public and school libraries. Here was "yahooland."

It does not minimize the importance of the conservative aspects of American life to insist, however, that Sontag and the other new-culture advocates exaggerated both the power of what they called tradition and the extent to which they were actually breaking with mainstream America. The momentum in film, literature, music, art, and television clearly was running toward the new values. For every indication of tradition's staying power there were more indications of its withering. Even as he "chawed" White House spare ribs, John Wayne was beset by the cancer that eventually killed him, and his art, the western, was obsolete; his indelicate dining with LBJ, who needed all the friends he could get, was no indication of cultural sway. Of course, there were grumblings about the sexual promiscuity and rebelliousness of youth, but that was hardly unique to the sixties. Technology's champions included not only Pentagon hawks and IBM computer wizards but also the Yippies, who advocated cable television and machines that could "free [people] from the drudgery of work," and radical philosophers like Herbert Marcuse and Shulamith Firestone who could see no way to utopia without those machines. If we make the necessary distinction between cultural and political conservatism, it is hard not to agree with Paul Krassner, who worked to subvert cultural restraints through his satirical magazine, *The Realist*. Reviewing these tumultuous years, Krassner marveled that "over the decade the climate has changed so much that stuff I might once have published now appears in the *Wall Street Journal* instead, while Tom Hayden is a guest on the David Frost show, sandwiched somewhere between Henny Youngman and Tiny Tim."

The End of Modernism

U.S. culture in the sixties did not mark the conquest over "tradition" but, instead, it constituted the realm where the shift from modern to postmodern society was clearest, save that of work and industry. Since World War I, when modernist ideas began to percolate through the New York avant garde, art, literature, music, criticism—formal culture—all had been transformed. The modernist credo made it the artist's duty to challenge all conventions, redefine standards, and attack dogmas. The determination to break with the past and defy convention carried over into the postmodern culture beginning in the sixties, but there was a clear distinction between the two periods. The modernists remained serious about the transcendent importance of art; insisted that new but earnest definitions of great art and talent could be developed, if they were not self-evident; and scorned the marketplace. By the sixties, however, the modernist rebellion had itself become, as the art critic Harold Rosenberg often said, the "tradition of the new," and there was little left to rebel against except the modernist devotion to seriousness and taste. Postmodernists came to see even these qualities as stuffy conventions. They wanted art that was "relevant" rather than transcendent; they discarded all but the most minimal of standards in pursuit of cultural freedom; and they proceeded to sell themselves.

By the 1950s, modernism was wearing thin. James Joyce and William Faulkner had revolutionized the novel. Modernist composers like George Gershwin, Aaron Copeland, and Samuel Barber had tapped the mine of American folk music. The abstract expressionists had brought painting out of the realist rut with an outpouring of brilliant work that seemed to exhaust the possibilities of that medium. Artists and writers were beginning to face an extraordinary problem: nearly all conventions had been destroyed, and there was not much left to rebel against. Because art had already been taken to such extremes, it was no easy thing to do something "new." The last group of modernists, who came to maturity in the late 1940s and early 1950s, dealt with this problem by turning away from the intensely political art of the 1930s. It was a salutary direction that brought the artists' focus back to the work itself and promoted greater attention to method and skill. The abstract expressionists were a case in point. They mostly had been trained in New Deal art-for-politics-sake methods. Soon after World War II began, however, Mark Rothko, Jackson Pollock, Willem de Kooning, and others emerged as the most vital new forces in the New York avant garde. Shunning the methods as well as the cultural dominance of Parisian modernism, they broke form down entirely and experimented with the surface of the canvas. Pollock, for example, shattered the geometry of cubism, relying instead on free lines, "drips," and a lively blending of textures. Pollock was in search of "living" art, even surprise, that spoke to the confused and chaotic nature of modern life. The abstract expressionists proceeded in like fashion to reconceive painting itself. They became "action artists," as Harold Rosenberg called them, who maintained that art lay in the act of painting rather than in the finished product; the canvas became "an event." "The new painting," Rosenberg wrote, "has broken down every distinction between art and life."

In breaking down this distinction, the abstract expressionists conferred their one great source of influence on the sixties artists, who proceeded to attack all barriers between art and life in an effort to make art "alive" and "relevant." The development begs an obvious question, however: if art is life, then what, exactly, distinguishes "art" from any other part of life, say, drinking soda pop? The modernists had an answer: art was still that which serious artists produced by working in full regard for the past and with the intention of furthering the method and skill of the medium. "Every intelligent painter carries the whole culture of modern painting in his head," Robert Motherwell wrote in 1951. "It is his real subject, of which everything he paints is both an homage and a *critique*." They remained dedicated to art for art's sake, and the way they lived and worked—often hand-to-mouth, in the conscious exile from conventional society that had been the lot of all bohemian modernists since the 1920s—reflected their continuing commitment to serious work.

For a host of reasons, it proved difficult, if not impossible, to transfer this set of virtues to the next generation. Under certain circumstances, collapsing the distinctions between art and life could destroy the nature of bohemian self-exile, that mode of living that was so essential to the rigor of the modernist project. Indeed, the last group of bohemians, the "Beats," the most famous cultural outsiders of the fifties, eagerly sought to destroy the distinctions between bohemia and the rest of society. The Beats believed that society was full of hypocrisy, sexual repression, and conformity, but rather than rejecting society for those reasons, they set out to shake loose those encrusted evils, to make society itself into bohemia.

To do so, they wrote about subjects that were taboo: homosexuality, drug use, the black subculture, and insanity, among other things. They drew heavily from the methods of the late modernists, relying on action, emotion, and intensity rather than on controlled skill. The most famous poem of the period was Allen Ginsberg's aptly named "Howl" (1956). "I saw the best minds of my generation destroyed by madness," Ginsberg wrote, presaging, perhaps, the Port Huron statement, scorned in the universities, left to wander "the negro streets," or committed to the "madhouse with shaven heads and harlequin speech of suicide." The message of Jack Kerouac's book, *On the Road* (1957), was much the same, for it, too, implied that liberation and action were the same things. Written in a single 120-page paragraph, the book followed a group of hipsters on a mad trip crisscrossing the country, through the bars, lockups, and jazz joints that made up the underground's life. They did drugs, got drunk, and made love, but mostly they just moved, constantly and frenetically.

Both "Howl" and *On the Road* carried a dual message. On the one hand, they utterly rejected everything conventional. Yet the other, implicit, message was that the United States ought to begin appreciating its derelict genius and embrace its outcasts. "Howl" was at once a work of indignant alienation and a plea for acceptance; *On the Road* was a Beat version of the classic American tale of innocence on the lam, a postmodern western.

The Beats, in their determination to bridge the gap between fantasy and reality, madness and sanity, art and life, also began to erase the gulf between bohemia and civilization, an erasure that did more damage to bohemia than to society. Just being famous compromised the real rebel's integrity, for fame and the underground life were contradictions in terms. The painter Mark Rothko poignantly testified to this irresolvable contradiction: a deeply serious artist, Rothko lived through a life of troubles, only to find fame and wealth so unbearable that he committed suicide.

The contradiction was less acute for the Beats and their successors, the Pop Artists. These early sixties artists became famous not because of skill but because their pose of alienation caught the mood of young people coming of age. With the Beats, bohemia and mass culture intersected, and the infusion of people— physically into Greenwich Village and the Bay area, mentally through drugs, sexual experimentation, and rock music—enlarged bohemia, commercialized it, and destroyed its artistic soul. As Michael Harrington wrote in a perceptive essay on the sixties counterculture, "a Bohemia that enrolls a good portion of a generation is no longer a Bohemia. When the great majority of people were kept in the cultural darkness and the rulers were tasteless makers of money, the enclaves of art had to be refuges of an outcast minority of aesthetic aristocrats even when some of them were starving." Cruel as it was, starvation and artistic seriousness went hand in hand. Even "our phoniness had high standards," Harrington mused. "We postured about the first rate." As went bohemia, so went modernism.

Rejecting the Authority of Form

Best understood as constituting the end of the modernist epoch, the developments in U.S. formal culture in the sixties flowed directly from the modernist conundrum. How does one rebel against rebels?

Sontag

To begin with, it was useful to develop a new aesthetics, a task that Susan Sontag took up in the process of defending much of the new culture and synthesizing the developing standards of taste. Sontag rejected the expectation that art live up to preset critical standards, which, in her view, stifled creativity by forcing artists to adhere to accepted styles rather than move with their instincts. The tyranny of the critic, of the compulsive insistence that art be "interpreted," was "the revenge of the intellect upon the world," she wrote, for "to interpret is to impoverish, to deplete the world." By turning art into an intellectual activity, interpretation denied the artist access to everything that could not be rationally understood, which is to say, nearly everything that comprised life itself: nature, impulse, desire, madness, passion. "A work of art is an experience, not a statement or an answer to a question."

As an alternative to that tyranny, Sontag recommended "an erotics of art" that defied the intellect and aimed at the heart. Art should present itself as "an instrument for modifying consciousness and organizing new modes of sensibility." It should escape the shackles of style and revel in sensuality. Above all, the new art had to become "the extension of life . . . , the representation of (new) modes of vivacity." In Sontag's view, a culture built on such aesthetics held out hope for vast improvements in the formal arts and, most important, in society at large. Freed from the tyranny of interpretation, artists would not presume to judge and, therefore, would never see formal art as superior to popular culture. The new culture was therefore pluralistic and egalitarian. "If art is understood as a form of discipline of the feelings and a programming of sensations, then the feeling (or sensation) given off by a Rauschenberg painting might be like that of a song by the Supremes." Because she assumed that authority repressed passion, then it followed that to heed one's impulses was a first step toward cultural rebirth. In spirit, Sontag's "new aesthetic" was not much different from what had prevailed among modernists, save perhaps her stronger emphasis on the erotic and her easy willingness to equate popular and formal culture, an equation that modernists scorned. She knew that for decades critics and artists had been saying similar things. That she had to ignore the past simply to make a case for innovation was itself a strong hint that the possibilities for innovation were running dry.

In many other ways, the practitioners of formal culture in the early sixties engaged in the similar pretense that they could depart from modernism, mostly using modernist strategies. One of the prevailing impulses, for example, was to sustain the modernist assault on form in an ongoing effort to break down the distance between art and life.

The Assault on Form in Art, Literature, and the Stage

Yet painters were finding quite early that this strategy had reached the point of diminishing returns. Jasper Johns, Robert Rauschenberg, and others tried to transcend abstract expressionism; like their forebears, the sixties painters were determined to collapse the distinction between artist and the art object in order to overcome what they deemed the artificial boundaries that separated feeling from expression. But the possibility of doing anything genuinely new was daunting. Ultimately, Rauschenberg and his colleagues managed nothing more than scattered innovations in method and form; as a group, they had little coherence and engaged mostly in "accelerated broken-field running," according to one critic, "in which precocity and technical brilliance . . . mingle with promiscuous switches of approach."

Artists in other areas had more success, at least in presenting work that challenged still-standing conventions. The composer John Cage, for example, continued the radical innovations that made him widely known in the fifties. Having begun his career arranging notes in haphazard fashion in an effort to "demanipulate" sound, he started to employ percussion to escape the reliance on pitch, and he used dice and other means to arrange his sound in completely random ways. In 1961 he recorded "4'33," four minutes and thirty-three seconds of total silence. His justification was that listeners would be regaled, not by predetermined music, but by the sounds that remained around them. Much as Jackson Pollock had turned painting into a random act, Cage's music was to be spontaneous and surprising.

For writers, rejecting form was more difficult, inasmuch as they still had to rely on language. As Ken Kesey put it, "we are ruled by an imaginary teacher with a red ball-point pen who will brand us with an A-minus for the slightest infraction of the rules." Kesey abandoned writing altogether in favor of less restricted forms of expression, but many more determined writers skirted the rules and befuddled the "imaginary teacher." One strategy was to use the printed page differently, arranging words in various shapes or breaking up the text as Marshall McLuhan did in his influential books on media. Others ignored basic conventions of grammar and punctuation. Tom Wolfe became the foremost chronicler of popular culture during the sixties with a prose style that one reviewer described as a mixture of "jukebox bursts of exclamation points, italics, dots, hip rhythms and pop idioms." Kurt Vonnegut begins *Slaughterhouse Five* (1969) with a rambling account of how he decided to write the novel, which consequently becomes part of the novel; and he adorned *Breakfast of Champions* (1973) with mock advertisements. The most sophisticated attack on fictional form appeared in the works of Thomas Pynchon, whose dark, difficult works became standard reading among new-culture advocates. *V.* (1961) was a technical masterpiece; superficially a sort of mystery novel, *V.* is a book about language more than anything else, so that the clever use of hints, names, places, and "v" words eclipses the plot.

Perhaps what best distinguished the postmodern assault on form was how widely the impulse was felt during the sixties. It appeared, in one form or another, throughout U.S. culture. In jazz, Miles Davis's *In a Silent Way* (1963) was a minimalist composition held together only by a subtle rhythm, and John Coltrane introduced African influences, especially polyrhythms, into his work. On the stage, the Living Theatre attempted to collapse the distinction between artist and audience with innovative acts of what has since become known as "performance art." The Living Theatre enjoyed immense respect among the New York avant garde, not only for its theatrical innovations but also because its founders, Julian Beck and Judith Malina, were active pacifists who became cause célèbres when the Internal Revenue Service shut the group down in 1964.

The Living Theatre's guiding principle was that traditional theater maintained an artificial distinction between the players and their audience. Although the group performed a wide repertoire of avant-garde plays, it was best known for performances in which the audience was variously enticed, tricked, and browbeaten into becoming part of the performance. Once the distinction between the performers and audience was breached, the next step was to take performance out of the confines of buildings and into the real world, as in 1968 when Beck and Malina took the sexually explicit *Paradise Now* into the streets of Avignon, France. Their purpose was, they claimed, to teach the townspeople to enjoy the freedom to "live without money," to smoke pot, to "love or to live without clothes." "They are not really performers at all," wrote one enthusiast, "but a roving band of Paradise-seekers, defining Paradise as total liberation. . . . Their presence and function are in direct opposition to that repressive totalitarian state called Law and Order."

That there was something concocted about "staging" real life or being self-consciously spontaneous never seems to have dawned on Beck, Malina, or the other practitioners of "guerrilla theater," who remained convinced that turning "real life" into theater allowed artists to shock, confront, and liberate people from complacency. "Guerrilla theater" is what the Living had in mind, though other groups that emerged were better in theatrical confrontations. San Francisco's "Diggers," for example, considered themselves performance artists and had their origins in a local mime troupe. The Diggers became prominent in the Haight-Ashbury district where they ran, among other things, a "free store" that distributed goods scavenged or stolen from other shops—property, after all, was a crime. The Diggers saw themselves as anarchist artists determined to prove that both art and people could exist completely outside the system, needing neither power nor money.

Anti-Art

The collapse of the distinction between art and life was meant to be the basis for a redefined aesthetics, one that rejected the old notion that art had "to be something." Taken to its logical end, it amounted to a rejection of artistic purpose and led to "anti-art," typified, for example, in sculptor Robert Morris's 1963 claim that his work had no "aesthetic quality and content." Where art had no "content," it could not be judged, and therefore cultural authority was completely undermined, as Sontag intended. Art could be anything the artist wanted it to be, and anything was good. Here indeed was a point of departure from modernism.

The champion of anti-art was Andy Warhol, whose Pop Art representations of everyday objects made him the most famous artist of his day. Warhol was known for his silk-screen depictions of soda cans, Marilyn Monroe, and other objects of mass culture. Whereas the modernists consciously alienated themselves from mass culture, Warhol and other Pop Artists immersed themselves in the objects of consumer society, much as Ginsberg and the Beats tried to bring bohemia to the mainstream. Warhol's choice of subjects went hand in hand with his rejection of painting. Most of his work was silk screen, which made him, Harold Rosenberg pointed out, a painter who did not paint. By 1970 many prominent artists had followed Warhol's lead and refused to work in "dead media" like sculpture and painting, preferring, among other things, environmental art and "earth art."

Anti-art flowed quite inexorably out of the logic of modernist rebellion. If there were no more schools of method, if there were no more conventions, there was nothing left but to renounce art itself. That renunciation could well begin in a sincere effort to create new form, as when the composer John Cage defended his minimalism with Sontag's call to overthrow the domination of the mind over art. "One has to stop studying music," he told students at Julliard, who might have wondered then what they were doing in school. "One has to stop all the thinking that separates music from living. . . . The wisest thing to do is to open one's ears immediately and hear a sound suddenly before one's thinking has a chance to turn it into something logical, abstract, or symbolical." And yet the only logical result of that renunciation was a retreat from the modernist injunction that obliged the artist to create something new; anti-art was an admission of failure, an admission that nothing new could be done. By mid-decade, Cage was abandoning composing just as painters were fleeing the canvas. He was "less and less interested in music," he wrote, not only because he found "environmental sounds and noises more useful aesthetically than the sounds produced by the world's musical cultures, but [because], when you get right down to it, a composer is simply someone who tells other people what to do."

Amateurism

New-culture advocates had to look elsewhere for a rich new movement of ideas and forms, one potential source of which was the flood of amateur artists and new forums. The new culture provided a congenial atmosphere for amateurism, which blossomed into a cultural entrepreneurialism that included a host of new faces and a glut of new places for them to show their work. The holdover Beats established *Avant Garde* and *Evergreen Review* for short fiction, criticism, and poetry; the *New York Review of Books* opened in 1963 as a forum for cultural and political analysis; and both Paul Krassner's *The Realist* and the *Village Voice* emerged as major voices for the new culture. *Ramparts*, a sleek publication begun as a liberal Roman Catholic journal, became influential in progressive circles and one of the period's finest publications. The scene was so fluid and the prevailing standards so loose that what Peter Schrag called a "cultural prison break" took place; any number of people were enticed into thinking that they too could become cultural figures. "Hundreds of thousands of 'creative' people," Schrag wrote, "have proclaimed themselves artists and poets, a million amateurs have entered the culture biz, and God knows how many gurus, cultists, swamis, and T-group trainers [have] hung out their shingles." From garage rock bands to mimes, the amateurs flourished, most abundantly in underground newspapers. Nearly every community of consequence saw papers pop up, so that the underground press enjoyed its greatest years and became essential to the reproduction of new-culture values. Some of the organs became legendary—the *Berkeley Barb*, the hippie paper, *Oracle*, Detroit's rock newspaper, *Creem*, New York's *Rat*—but obscure voices like the *Dallas News* were just as important in their own way. There was even an underground wire service, the Liberation News Service, that provided its constituents with left-wing versions of events and stories that the established services would not touch.

The quality of work produced in the cultural prison break was at best uneven and often quite awful. The amateur quality of the underground press, for example, was hard to miss. The writing throughout the underground put a greater premium on vulgarity than on subtlety. The most troubling aspect of the underground press, however, was its thoroughgoing mediocrity, a kind of counterculture conformity. To read through one—with its glorification of new values, its trendy use of profanity, its cries for revolution—pretty much was to read through all of them. Something of the same thing can be said about rock music, which became so important to the period partly because it was accessible to amateurs. Simple, even primitive, in form, rock made it possible for any group of friends with instruments to start a band. Some turned out good, some not so good. "No one can expect most of them to be good, or even serious," Schrag contended. "The wildcatters are working new territory, and a lot are going to go bust." But, then, to fall short of quality work was not a shortcoming among people whose principal objective was to rattle conventions. Chasing after professional quality would have been self-defeating.

If this amateurism were the cultural equivalent of participatory democracy, then Sontag was right to declare that the new culture was egalitarian. But the real test of the new aesthetics and, by implication, of the new culture, was whether a coherent and democratic direction could replace cultural authority. Otherwise, what seemed egalitarianism might have been nothing more than an artistic failure of nerve, a refusal to build new and more democratic standards of cultural judgment. Sontag was the first to warn that the new aesthetics should not be taken as a call that all standards be destroyed. But she only begged the questions: how, then, were new standards to be set and how was art to be judged?

The Artist as Star

Postmodernists never satisfactorily resolved these issues. Moving the measure of value from the work of art to the act of creating art, as Harold Rosenberg argued, meant that the new aesthetics judged the artist rather than the work, and the artist accordingly became the marketable object. Warhol again is the best illustration. Art was whatever he decided it was, and he needed only to sign his name—wherever, on whatever, he wished—to turn an object into a collector's item. Once he stacked several paintings of Marilyn Monroe together and let an acquaintance shoot a pistol through them. "Marilyn Monroe looked marvelous after she'd been shot," one of Warhol's friends recalled. "Just beautiful. . . . Andy sold them, of course. There's nothing he doesn't sell." Those who decried Pop Art's employment of everyday objects, from bullet-riddled pictures to toilet seats, missed the point: the object had become meaningless. The artist, Rosenberg wrote, "has become, as it were, too big for art."

Museum curators, critics, and collectors accommodated these developments, for they, too, were in the business of selling the new. The more they could inflate the artist's appeal, the more they stood to gain from exhibitions and purchases. Warhol, Rosenberg wrote, had something for everyone: "for gallery-goers easy art; for collectors a signature." It made sense for him to employ as objects the very same things that advertising agents were pushing on consumers; at least he was not a hypocrite.

The inflation of the artist was not confined to painting. The novelist Norman Mailer, bedeviled by the elusiveness of popular acclaim after the grand reception of his first work, *The Naked and the Dead* (1948), turned from fiction to journalistic accounts of his personal adventures; he became his own protagonist. *Armies of the Night* (1967) and *Miami and the Siege of Chicago* (1968) were important books and well worth reading, but there is no denying Mailer's self-promotion. The "star" system of rock music was another case in point. It was an indication of the pervasiveness of the star system that it infused even New Left politics. Reflecting on the trial of the Chicago Seven, Tom Hayden wrote of his discomfort with having become a star. "Too many people looked up to us," he lamented. They "regarded us as rock stars." His description of how he rose to stardom is much like the rise of Warhol and Mailer: "You begin to monopolize contacts and contracts. You begin making $1000 per speech. With few real friends and no real organization, you become dependent on the mass media and travel in orbit only with similar 'stars.' "

The star system was a consequence of cultural dynamics driven by the marketplace, and culture itself became style rather than substance. By mid-decade, embracing popular culture had became fashionable in elite circles and cultural slumming became chic. This, surely, was what made Tom Hayden so uncomfortable with his notoriety. The commitment to living the life of the avant garde and to accepting the pain of alienation for the higher purpose of art was subverted as the values of the avant garde became increasingly popularized. Alienation was impossible where alienation itself became fashion. Warhol and Mailer indicated not rebellion so much as they showed that alienation had become domesticated, which meant that the sixties witnessed the exhaustion of the avant garde. For the discomforting fact was that artists never before had been so widely accepted in U.S. society.

Popular culture, meanwhile, was enriching only to the extent that it remained spontaneous. But success spoiled it too. By the end of the decade, rock had achieved a technological sophistication well out of proportion to both its musical simplicity and its simple origins. Where once the start-up costs were very low, by the end of the decade a group needed a vast array of sound equipment and noise effects to compete. As in painting and fiction, popular music became enmeshed in personality cults and the "star system." As one observer wrote, "at this stage, the stars merely exist; nobody cares what they *do* anymore." More and more bands began to rely on the recording studio. The Beatles made the transition with great success in ways that improved their music, but the path-breaking *Sgt. Pepper's Lonely Hearts Club Band*, released in 1967, was strictly studio work. The Grateful Dead, to their credit, never enjoyed recording success because they could not translate their famous informality onto a record. In their failure, the Dead helped to show that the increasing technical sophistication of popular music undercut the spontaneity that was the best part of amateurism and that had made it appealing in the first place.

The most serious flaw in Sontag's new aesthetics, then, was that in her effort to overthrow the tyranny of the critic she left herself no way to fend off the corrupting force of the marketplace. Where all accepted standards were brushed aside—however necessary and good it was that they be abolished—critical judgment, the cultivated sense of what is good in art, was reduced to mere "taste," the equivalent of the consumer marketplace wherein a producer tells a consumer how to choose among the indistinguishable items pouring from the cornucopia. Rather than encouraging cultural democracy, the repudiation of judgment in formal culture created a new kind of snobbery where the marketplace, represented by "experts," decided what was art and what was not. In popular culture, meanwhile, what sold was also the decision of advertising agents, record producers beholden to investors, and the corporate establishment that allegedly upheld traditional culture.

The Critique of Rationality

The ascendance of the new culture in the sixties generated a set of values that fused the avant garde with mainstream popular culture in the misnamed "counterculture." Although these values eventually proved politically ambiguous, they were meant to dovetail with the radical criticisms of U.S. society. Like the New Left, cultural radicals condemned the United States as a rationalized, overly bureaucratized society dominated by technocrats. When people decried "the system" or "the establishment" they were not thinking in conspiratorial terms but rather about a world that seemed to have contempt for human needs and was indifferent to human action. Corporations ran the economy and controlled both workers and consumers mostly through subtle manipulation. The universities had become huge animals whose benign appearance masked rigid rules that thwarted creativity. The establishment liberals who governed the United States were well-intentioned captives of the bureaucracies they had built. Behind all of this, there loomed the bomb and the military-industrial complex.

There was considerable substance to this description of the United States, and the political and economic critiques of the rational society were the most important intellectual products of the sixties. But what of the cultural critiques? The use of psychedelic drugs, the adoption of countercultural styles of dress, the popularity of oriental religions, the appearance of communal living—all were ways of defying the rationalized world. Along with these forms of dissent, we can trace a line of more or less formal attack that began with the contention that the United States was rational only in that it obeyed a rigid line of rules that made no real sense; the rational society actually created a mystifying world. Thus, "we seem to be living," Charles Reich wrote, "in a society that no one created and no one wants."

Take the military, where rules were supposed to strengthen the virtues of self-discipline, efficiency, loyalty, and honor. When rules became ends in themselves, according to new-culture advocates, they became irrational. Such, for example, was the message of Kenneth Brown's play *The Brig*. Performed by the Living Theatre in 1963, *The Brig* examined the senselessness of military discipline as it worked itself out in a Marine jail. While being detained, the prisoners are forced to undertake any number of meaningless tasks—cleaning the quarters, washing the lavatory, standing in line for a single cigarette—simply because they were ordered to do so. The rules in *The Brig* only serve to demean the men in the name of discipline and are not only senseless but at bottom also a form of control.

The issue of bureaucratic control emerged both in critiques of the military and in the widespread use of supposedly benign institutions, such as the university and the mental hospital, as subjects. In *Giles Goat-Boy* (1966), John Barth added the university to the list of bureaucratic and technological monsters. Trapped in a cold war with the other superpower university, Barth's New Tammany College rests atop a supercomputer that protects the campus by turning enemies and transgressors of the rules into simpletons through a sort of electronic lobotomy, and it thereby controls the lives of the student body, faculty, and administration alike. Meanwhile, other works depicted the asylum as a death camp of institutional control. Doctors and nurses of mental institutions were supposed to help patients, but, as Ken Kesey maintained in *One Flew over the Cuckoo's Nest* (1963), they were really in the business of exercising power. In Kesey's book, the Big Nurse with the phony smile and an iron hand rules the ward full of quiescent patients, always insisting that the rules were carefully designed for the patients' therapeutic benefit. Similarly, Peter Weiss's influential play, *The Persecution and Assassination of Jean-Paul Marat As Performed by the Inmates of the Asylum of Charenton under the Direction of the Marquis de Sade* (1966), includes a running clash between Sade, the aggressive critic of conventional rationality, and the asylum director, who attempts to "protect" the inmates from overexcitement.

Many of the works that focused on mental instability criticized not just institutions but the psychiatrists who ran them. Certainly, Kesey's hospital staffers are no angels of mercy. Saul Bellow's Professor Herzog discovers that his psychiatrist spent more energy trying to seduce his wife than in helping him cope with encroaching madness. At best, the psychiatrist was patronizing. "Doctor Dear," Vera Randal had one of her women inmates in *The Inner Room* (1964) quip, "I know that you are an anti-Freudian, anti-any-other-school-of-psychoanalysis person. . . . [But] if you won't talk to me about how I really want to murder my mother (which I do) . . .

will you please tell me why Mrs. French in the sewing room at O.T. gets into such a sweat when a needle is missing."

Caught in their ivory towers, men of science failed to understand that the soul heard sounds other than the voice of reason. Those determined rationalists never saw that people were too complex, too driven by impulse to fit into a neat world. The critique of rationality dismissed not only the mental health professions on this score but such disciplines as history and political science as well. Both of Barth's major works rejected historians' faith that history could be arranged neatly. *The Sot-Weed Factor* (1961) was, as Morris Dickstein has pointed out, a satire on history in general; Ebenezer Cooke, the poet laureate, concocts grand visions of a noble Maryland when in fact the colony was nothing more than a hovel full of whores and thieves. So too, as Dickstein notes, Joseph Heller's *Catch-22* (1955) and Vonnegut's *Slaughterhouse Five* attack a specific bit of history, World War II. Renowned as the "good war," World War II emerges in those books as neither neat nor good. Thomas Pynchon rejected the basic assumption that history moved in linear fashion toward some irresistible human progress. *V.* (1963) moves back and forth across time, and the even more difficult *Crying of Lot 49* (1966) attacks the notion of human progress by insisting on an unbreachable gulf between chaos and order.

To renounce the rational was also to encourage levity, the so-called black humor of satirists such as Lenny Bruce, and absurdist critiques of rational society. Joseph Heller's *Catch-22*, though written in the midfifties, became one of the most influential books of the sixties because it set the tone for satire and absurdist expression. Heller's book is a compilation of jabs at "the system"; set in a World War II army compound in the Mediterranean, the book pokes fun at corporations, Christianity, capitalism, and technology. In Heller's military nothing makes sense. It is populated with fools like Colonel Cargill, "a self-made man who owed his lack of success to nobody," and the even more vapid Major Major Major, whose father named him as a joke. His lack of effort to the contrary, Major Major Major is promoted, to Major of course, "by an I.B.M. machine with a sense of humor." To Milo Minderbinder, the quintessential capitalist who trades in everything from plum tomatoes to chickpeas, the great cause at hand is profit, and where there is no enemy but charity, he could trade with the Nazis or have the Americans bomb their own base, all with a clear conscience.

The broad message was that the best laid plans of the rationalist world no longer promised humane progress. It was precisely in its powerful presentation of this message that Weiss's *Marat/Sade* affected U.S. audiences. The play was an account of the Marquis de Sade's stay in an asylum, where he was known to have produced plays with and for the inmates. Weiss's production put a play within a play and examined not only Sade's existentialism but also how the rejection of rationalism resounded through the institution. The play that Sade has the inmates perform concerns the assassination of the radical French revolutionary Marat, although Sade's purpose is to show that the grandiose promises of liberal rationalism led inexorably to political murder. Just as the promise of psychological cure had devolved into institutional control, so political rationalism led to violent repression.

To some degree, this line of reasoning resembled the views that Cold War liberals had of communism: what once held out great promise had turned to terror. But new-culture advocates insisted that the Cold War distinction between liberal systems and totalitarianism was no longer acceptable, given the ample evidence of liberal corruption. The only tenable position, therefore, was that all systems, rooted as they were in the erroneous faith that the mind could construct a blueprint that human beings would contentedly inhabit, were corrupt. Even solid opponents of totalitarianism could not be trusted if they were too determined in their opposition. Heller's protagonist says of the character Clevinger, the anti-Nazi ideologue, that "there were a good many things in which Clevinger believed passionately. He was crazy." Where Cold War liberals had decried the "closed systems" of totalitarianism, new-culture advocates insisted that all systems were "closed." For that reason, they attacked not just prisons but hospitals, universities, and liberalism itself.

Arrogant, violent, and bent on control, the rational society ignored the importance of the less calculated aspects of life and squelched what was best in people. The rational society was incompatible with love and emotion. Indeed, "normal" society seemed determined to define these better impulses as insane. When Vonnegut's Eliot Rosewater, heir in a long line of wealthy robber barons, politicians, and other thieves, decides to give away the family fortune bit by bit, his family has him committed. His father, the senator, thinks that Eliot has ruined the word *love* because he takes the Golden Rule literally. "Eliot did for the word *love* what the Russians did for the word *democracy*." Whereas Eliot Rosewater sheds the cynicism of "normal" adults in order to become "insane," the protagonist in Edward Albee's stage adaption of James Purdy's *Malcolm* (1965) is from the start innocent and harmless but falls into the clutches of exploitative "normal" people. Even where the insane tried to emulate normal society, they botched the job because they were incapable of ruthlessness or cynicism. Kesey's patients in *Cuckoo* show as much. So, too, do the asylum inmates who spilled out into town in *The King of Hearts* (1967), a French film that enjoyed underground success in the United States. Left to fend for themselves by the retreating German Army, the citizen-inmates go about their business oblivious to the surrounding war. *What's So Bad About Feeling Good* (1968), a sappy American comedy, offered a twist on the theme with its story of a virus that makes hostility and aggression disappear among normally surly New Yorkers. The city fathers, accordingly, deem it a great threat and set about to quarantine happiness.

At the extreme end of the critique of rationality rested a defense of insanity. If it were not a means to a better life, at least insanity should be seen, R. D. Laing argued, as a place on the continuum of mentality that was no less legitimate than the place where the "normal" lay. Laing's defense of insanity as an alternative state of mind, outlined in *The Politics of Experience* (1966), tied so many strains of thought together that it stands with Norman O. Brown's books and Sontag's writings as a major new-cultural expression. Laing argued that in the ideal state of mind, the "outer world" of normal behavior harmonized with the "inner world" of emotion, fantasy, and feeling. Rationalized society intentionally blocked that union, he argued, and deadened people to their inner world. "Normal" parenting, for instance, was a relentless assault on the child's sense of adventure and play.

Denied access to their inner world, people were turned into "murderers and prostitutes"; "normal men have killed perhaps 100,000,000 of their fellow normal men in the last fifty years."

If what was defined as normal could not be trusted, then the definitions of insanity could not be taken seriously. They were just labels: at best mere "value judgments," at worst "a political event." Schizophrenics, Laing claimed, were completely maladjusted to the normal world, but their behavior had a logic of its own, developed in response to private experiences. Because the ideal mentality united experience and emotion, the outer and inner worlds, schizophrenia, and any other state of mind (drug use, religious experience) that grew from the inner world were entirely legitimate if they brought on that union. "Madness need not be all breakdown. It may also be breakthrough," which meant, conversely, that "our sanity is not 'true' sanity." We "have to blast our way through the solid wall" separating the two worlds, Laing concluded in terms that imitated the conflation of art and life, "even if at the risk of chaos, madness, and death."

The Quest for Intense Experience

The new-culture advocates believed that rejecting the authority of form and reason would emancipate the senses, unleash instinct, and provide the widest possible access to experience. They defined liberation, not in political or economic terms, but as release and encounter. Liberation consequently assumed a number of specific and overlapping forms: the sexual revolution; the use of psychedelic drugs; and the interest in oriental religion.

Changes in Censorship Laws

It is true that the sexual revolution was not merely a cultural development. Its origins were various and can be located in as general a condition as the growing complexity of urban life and as specific an event as the mass marketing, beginning in 1960, of the birth control pill. It is difficult, however, to exaggerate its importance within the new culture. Taboos against public displays or discussions of sexuality were the foremost aspects of the repressed culture of the past and thus the foremost targets of repression's enemies.

One measure of the pervasiveness of the attack against sexual taboos was its prevalence in American fiction, an area in which frank depictions of sex had only begun to appear, to considerable challenges, in the fifties. At the same time, it was an indication of how widely accepted sexual explicitness had become among U.S. writers that, as early as 1960, John Barth's The Sot-Weed Factor, from the beginning to the end a romp, could appear without challenge. By the end of the period, what was acceptable had changed so much that Philip Roth's Portnoy's Complaint (1970), the subject of which was adolescent masturbation, became a best-seller.

New-culture advocates were convinced that puritanical censors were hiding everywhere outside Greenwich Village, but like so many other avant-garde targets, the hold of censorship was tenuous. A series of court battles had culminated in the *Roth* decision (1957), where the Supreme Court upheld the constitutionality of censorship but defined obscenity in such vague terms that the decision was a practical victory for free speech. The Court ruled that material appealing solely to "prurient interests" and that ran against "contemporary community standards" was obscene. By the midsixties, after the *Fanny Hill* case (1963), the Court had gone so far as to rule that no work could be banned unless it was "*utterly* without redeeming social value," as Justice William Brennan wrote. If it had any social value at all, then it did not matter if it "is found to possess the requisite prurient appeal and to be patently offensive." The burden of proof fell on the censor.

Not that the censors quit trying. Local school officials were often bombarded with complaints from conservative groups demanding the removal of books from library shelves. Congress considered several laws to empower the postmaster general to deny the mails to obscene material. In 1966 Californians considered a state initiative to outlaw pornography. Individual artists paid a price for transgressing "community standards." The comedian Lenny Bruce, for example, embarked on a crusade against local obscenity ordinances and was arrested several times in 1963–1964 for his efforts.

Advocates of free expression countered such attempts at repression with a whole host of arguments. The most common strategy was to argue that pornography should not be banned because intelligent people would avoid it and perverts would find it anyway. Another strategy was to politicize the sexual revolution and argue, as writer William Burroughs did, that inhibition of any kind added weapons to the arsenal of the political right. The answer to political repression was to do away with privacy all together: "When nobody cares, then shame ceases to exist and we can all return to the Garden of Eden without any God prowling around like a house dick with a tape recorder." Susan Sontag took an aesthetic tact and waved away the distinction between art and pornography; pornography, she insisted, operated by a set of rules no less legitimate than regular art, and, however degraded, it dealt in fantasy, emotion, and pathos. Finally, one could argue, as *New York Times* columnist Anthony Lewis did, that the courts would distinguish between art and pornography on the strength of advice from experts, which was, he maintained, as it should be—and as it turned out.

Ultimately, there was no doubt which cultural forces were prevailing. The California initiative lost by a ratio of 3 to 2. Defenders of free speech could rest assured that "today the voice of the sophisticated critic is dominant, and the Philistines are on the run," Anthony Lewis proclaimed in 1963. As Albert Goldman wrote in a particularly insightful piece on Lenny Bruce, there was room to doubt that the suffering and alienated artist existed any longer. The comedian's increasing vulgarity had come to resemble "the twitching of a damaged muscle" not because of repression but because

the steady relaxation of restraint exemplified in the Supreme Court liberalization of the definition of "obscenity" has a . . . frustrating effect on those whose social contribution is relentless challenge to established values. To meet protest with ever-expanding permissiveness is to refuse to feel its bite . . . , thus forcing the dissident into ever more extravagant gestures of defiance.

The developments that turned *Roth* into a victory against censorship had less to do with the "sophisticated critic" or the Supreme Court than with the marketplace, which displayed a seemingly inexhaustible taste for sexually forthright material. There was enough pressure from filmmakers on the Motion Picture Association (MPA), the organization responsible for the self-regulation of the film industry, that the MPA's long-standing censorship code simply fell apart. In the memoirs of his life as a Hollywood censor, Jack Vizzard writes that the moribund code was a "piece of Americana" from the 1920s. "It could never happen again." The MPA continued to allow the Catholic Legion of Decency to screen movies and make recommendations, but even this once-feared conscience was in increasing confusion. In 1965 the Legion condemned *The Pawnbroker* because of a crucial scene in which the old man, a Holocaust survivor, confronts a naked prostitute and is suddenly convulsed by the memory of a Nazi officer molesting his wife. At the same time, it approved the highly suggestive James Bond film, *Goldfinger*. The Legion's personnel increasingly comprised young, liberal clergymen, and the liberalizations of Vatican II (1962–1963) ended any substantial censorship role for the Catholic Church. "Whether or not a film receives a Code seal no longer matters much at the box office," the critic Joan Didion wrote in 1964. "No more curfew, no more Daddy, *anything goes.*"

The MPA hesitated to establish a firm rating code and do away with censorship altogether because it feared public outcries would spell box-office disaster. By the time a ratings system was formally adopted in 1968, filmmakers knew that quite the opposite was true: the system worked against films that were rated as the safest and most wholesome. "They want fucking—so we'll give them fucking!" the actor Anthony Quinn protested to critic Nora Sayre. He was just as blunt about the artistic consequences: "It's our own fault that people don't accept movies as an art form." What defenders of the old code of decency feared had come to pass. As Monsignor Thomas Little, one of the leaders of the Legion of Decency, fretted during the *Pawnbroker* controversy, accepting nudity would simply invite its widespread appearance. "Nudity would become just as common as blowing your nose." Both Monsignor Little and Didion were right: by the midsixties, daddy was gone and anything went.

Sexual Freedom in the Arts

With restraints removed, a wave of more or less spontaneous exhibitionism and experimentation appeared. What purportedly was the first live nude radio show was conducted in New York in 1968. It was "psychedelic burlesque," according to the *Village Voice*, and the participants felt liberated for having trespassed on taboos, particularly the women, who gathered in a circle and held hands "just to see how it felt." Berkeley was home to several groups dedicated to open sexuality, including the Sexual Freedom League, which held widely advertised nude parties that became, as the *San Francisco Chronicle* reported, an "unadulterated orgy." In theater, meanwhile, *Oh, Calcutta!* ran as the first all-nude play and as one of Broadway's most successful shows during the late sixties.

Such episodes were offered in a spirit of genuine experimentation, and the sense of release was powerful. But along with individual liberation came the commercial exploitation of the sexual revolution. Hugh Hefner's *Playboy* empire enjoyed dramatic growth throughout the sixties, so that by mid-decade his magazine claimed a readership of 3 million. Hefner shrouded his business dealings in the self-justifying philosophy that he was doing a national service, demonstrating that therapeutic arguments could justify any amount of self-interest. "I realized," he explained, "that just as it is possible for an individual to have a sick or neurotic view of sex, it's possible for an entire society to be sick and neurotic on the subject. Basically, I feel that's what America has been." He also convinced himself that the repression of sexuality was historically connected to the repression of women, implying thereby that his national sex therapy would emancipate the sex drive and women at the same time. It was an odd argument coming from a man whose nightclubs refused to pay their "bunnies" wages, making them exclusively reliant on tips, no doubt on the grounds that women should be liberated from needing money.

Hefner's glamorization of sex was but an exaggerated version of what appeared throughout popular culture. The combination of sex and glamor proved commercially successful in any medium—film, fiction, popular magazines. Ian Fleming's series of James Bond books partook of the *Playboy* credo that sex accompanied globe hopping and champagne. Fleming was enormously popular and counted John F. Kennedy among his fans. Jacqueline Susann, the single most successful novelist of the sixties, personified the multimedia appeal. A beauty queen and actress, wife of a successful television producer, friend and confidante of show business personalities, Susann had a string of pulp best-sellers, including *Valley of the Dolls*, *The Love Machine*, and *Once Is Not Enough*, that made her the steamiest romance novelist of the day. *Valley* was not really a dirty book, her husband-agent and self-confessed *Playboy* reader, Irving Mansfield claimed, "but every time a reviewer or a critic called it dirty, we noticed a spurt in sales." Definitely a man with an eye on the market, Mansfield wrote that when *Time* denounced *Valley*, "we cringed and secretly said, 'thank you.' " "The only way they could hurt us was by ignoring us."

Above all, the popularity of these books, films, and magazines underscored how powerful the connection between the sexual revolution and the consumer ethos was. Both shared the underlying assumption that restraint, whether in sex or in buying habits, was an abnormal denial of natural impulse that resulted in some vague neurosis. Sex and selling had been part of consumer culture for most of the century, but whereas advertisers used sexual allusion to sell products, Hefner and others reversed the order and sold sex with slick packaging and mass marketing.

Two Aspects of the Sexual Revolution

In theory, it was possible to detach the sexual revolution from consumerism. Without a doubt, the avant garde's definition of sexual liberation was different from the

Playboy version. Just as it is necessary to contrast liberals with radicals, however much they overlapped, so it is necessary to distinguish two parts of the sexual revolution—the first made up mostly of a liberal assault on censorship, and the second a more radical assault against male dominance, against sexual divisions of all kinds, and perhaps most important of all, against the very way in which the larger society intruded into the intimate mysteries of sexuality.

Norman Mailer stands out as an example of the first sort of sexual liberal. A stalwart opponent of censorship, he was obsessed, as Kate Millet pointed out in her influential *Sexual Politics* (1969), with upholding male potency against any sort of effeminization of life. Mailer believed that manhood was earned through taking up every fight and lost with every act of aversion. He associated cowardice with homosexuality and supineness with women—beliefs, incidentally, that drew Mailer applause from Eldridge Cleaver, among others.

Advocates of the second, radical wave of the sexual revolution hoped to disassemble the distinctions between male and female, heterosexuality and homosexuality. The radical vanguard rallied behind the ideas of Norman Brown, a mild college professor whose major works, *Life Against Death* (1958) and *Love's Body* (1966), set the theoretical defense of the radical sexual revolution. Working from Freud, Brown argued that moderns constantly repressed the instinct for pleasure and surrendered the natural desire for "polymorphous perversity." The result was a public neurosis in which society pursued only power; society extolled the "death" instincts of power and gain (Thanatos) over the "life" instincts of artistic sensibilities and sensuality (Eros). A truly healthy society would not repress instincts but synthesize them; it would blend Thanatos and Eros and permit the instincts to flow together into the realm of reality. Brown was interested, he maintained, in a spiritual dialectic that reconciled internal tensions and went above dualisms. "What the great world needs," Brown concluded modestly, "is a little more Eros and less strife," more poetry and less salesmanship, more philosophy and less statesmanship.

In one sense, Brown's was simply another call for society to become more humane. In another sense, it paralleled Beat radicalism. When he called on humanity "to live instead of making history, to enjoy instead of paying back old scores and debts, and to enter that state of Being which was the goal of [humanity's] Becoming," he sounded like an academic Kerouac and presaged Charles Reich.

In still another reading, *Life Against Death* was a serious coming to grips with how intimacy and consciousness were shaped in contact with society. Unlike Marcuse's *One-Dimensional Man*, which it resembled in many particulars, *Life Against Death* did not blame only contemporary capitalism for human ills. Brown instead located the source of repression far more deeply in the nature of culture itself; he saw a fundamental conflict between living as an individual and living as a member of society. He was not optimistic that the conflict could be resolved, but he believed that the only hope for reconcilation lay in the widest exercise of polymorphous perversity. Because Brown rooted the human conflict so deeply, he was not much interested in theories about capitalism or even about political change. The battle was to be won in culture only; all other fields of struggle were peripheral.

As the similarities between Marcuse and Brown show, the radical edge of the sexual revolution paralleled the New Left, in that it, too, issued from male-dominated demands for liberation to wider, more heterogeneous paths. The radical feminist assault on "the boys' movement" included not just a condemnation of male supremacy but a challenge to the New Left's version of sexual liberation. Their charges that the New Left had become essentially a vehicle for male radicals to indulge themselves at whim was accurate enough that they continued to leave honest radicals like Hayden and Gitlin sheepishly recalling that the women indulged too. As for radical feminists, if there were to be no more mimeographing, neither would there be any more "sex on demand for males," as Robin Morgan wrote in her broadside, "Goodbye to All That." "The so-called Sexual Revolution," she continued, "has functioned toward women's freedom as did the Reconstruction toward former slaves—reinstituted oppression by another name." Goodbye to Hefner. Goodbye to Abbie Hoffman. Goodbye to Paul Krassner.

The denunciation of the first wave of the sexual revolution led to a call, much in the spirit of Norman Brown, for polymorphous perversity, which theoretically would destroy the dominance of male heterosexuality. "The end goal of feminist revolution," Shulamith Firestone announced, "must be . . . not just the elimination of male *privilege* but of the sex *distinction* itself." The real sexual revolution therefore meant the ascendance of homosexuality, bisexuality, "pan-sexuality"—the inner drive, in short.

Firestone was politicizing here what had been an undercurrent of the sexual revolution all along—the burgeoning of polymorphous perversity. Ginsberg's "Howl" was hardly the sole forthrightly homosexual work of the time. Throughout the period, the treatment of homosexuality in both serious and pulp fiction shifted from the lurid, "problem" novels, in John D'Emilio's words, toward the incorporation of "gay characters and subplots." Grove Press included a number of books with male homosexual themes on its lists by mid-decade, and according to one survey, 348 books with plots that revolved around female homosexuality were published in the year 1964–1965, more, D'Emilio points out, than were counted in another survey of 2,500 years of Western literature. Meanwhile, "camp," a mostly gay style that celebrated the tastelessness of mass culture, represented both an effort to identify with the mainstream and to steal into it. According to some observers, young people were heeding the calls to abolish sex distinctions through unisex clothes like blue jeans and long hair styles for men, which Sontag interpreted as the healthy "depolarization of the sexes."

In this stage of the revolution, sex was reduced to its purest elements: to "the deep experience of pleasure, and the possibility of self-knowledge," in Sontag's words. As if to endorse these developments, Norman Brown reemerged in 1966 with *Love's Body*, the foremost call for the eradication of sexual distinctions. Brown insisted that "the prototype of all opposition or contrariety is sex." Human beings constructed distinctions, he maintained, in an effort to grapple with the fundamental psychological problem of separation from the womb, the return to which we all ambivalently seek. All human distinctions, "the rents, the tears, splits and divisions," manifested at their worst in the grasping after political power and in war, were attempts to stave off that reunification. The "way out" was to rid ourselves of ambivalence and "to make one again; to unify or reunify: this is Eros in action." Reunification meant the eradication of all distinctions, but especially sexual differences, since sex was at the heart of the matter. Thus, "if we are all one body, then in that one body there is neither male nor female." Just as the transcendence of barriers supposedly made it possible for artists to express themselves more honestly, so the removal of sexual distinctions would liberate the deepest emotions and finally remove artificiality and dishonesty. "To make in ourselves a new consciousness," Brown wrote in a clear parallel to Sontag's call for an erotics of art, we need "an erotic sense of reality."

Regardless of the extent to which radical liberationists wiggled to disengage themselves from the first wave of sexual revolution, they were still fundamentally dependent on the liberal challenges to anti-obscenity laws. Although they might denounce the way *Playboy* or advertisers reinforced conventional categories, the sexual radicals were captives of the marketplace because like postmodern artists, their rejection of all but the most mimimal standards left them with no real defense against exploitation. Where all restrictions were discarded as attacks on free speech, it was impossible to build a sound argument against harmful pornography or sexual exploitation or, for that matter, to defend polymorphous perversity on any grounds other than the psychological theorizing, easily turned to dogma, of Brown and Firestone.

So the two branches of the sexual revolution were united in their rejection of censorship in all forms, which, in sex and in aesthetics, issued in a general retreat from the need to build new distinctions. The will to distinguish between "life-affirming" sexuality of genuine love and the "death instincts" that underlay sexual violence and exploitation made sense on the individual level, where people, gays and lesbians especially, felt able to heed their instincts. On the larger social level, however, such minimal distinctions were far too weak to restrain less constructive impulses. Having exalted natural instinct as ethically superior to "repressive reason," new-culture advocates could hardly backtrack and admit that sexuality harbored a dark side.

Sexual liberationists such as Robin Morgan denounced not only the male radicals in SDS but also the editors at Grove Press because of their readiness to exploit women in their ads as well as their publishing list (and indeed in the office). She and others reproved the radical group Weatherman whose sexual liberation justified mate-swapping and rape. Liberationists derided the Rolling Stones for hits like "Midnight Rambler," which extolled the adventures of a knife-wielding rapist. They condemned Eldridge Cleaver for excusing rape as a political act in *Soul on Ice* (1967). They had to wince when, in the bohemian mecca of the counterculture, the Haight-Ashbury district in San Francisco, the sexual revolution included the raffling off of a young woman incapacitated by a drug overdose. Morgan quite rightly argued that this destructive sexuality was, in her mind, antirevolutionary. But at the very least they were indications that the sexual revolution, like most revolutions, was messy and prone to destructiveness.

One might argue that the destructive impulses appearing in the midst of the sexual revolution would conceivably pass away in time. Charles Rembar, the lawyer who defended the most important obscenity cases in the late fifties and sixties, regretted that his work quickly created "a lip-licking, damp-palmed age" obsessed with filth that he considered "anti-sex." Nonetheless, he had every faith that "the present, distorted, impoverished, masturbatory concentration on representations of sex will diminish as the restraints recede." Radical liberationists argued on similar but more firmly dogmatic grounds that sexual terrorism would pass away with white heterosexual male domination, since that form of rule was responsible for all of the anguish, repression, and ugliness of contemporary life. The evidence weighed against any such optimism and seemed to suggest that Brown was wrong: Thanatos and Eros could not be uncoupled; with the liberation of angels came the emancipation of demons.

Psychedelic Drugs

Sex was the basic intense experience, but it was not the only one. Psychedelic drugs provided another means toward the same end, and if there were a number of sociological causes of widespread drug use—alienation, peer pressure, disrupted home lives—the advocates of LSD and marijuana use stressed the drugs' capacity for producing mind-opening experiences.

As with the sexual revolution, self-promotion and promises of a new world through expanded consciousness mingled among the advocates of psychedelics, particularly in Timothy Leary and Ken Kesey. Leary was a Harvard psychology professor who discovered peyote during a trip to Mexico and returned a changed man. In the early sixties, he began to promote the use of drugs in a controlled environment as a means of reaching spiritual growth, was drummed out of Harvard as a menace in 1963, and proceeded thereafter as an independent advocate of LSD. In 1965 he founded the League for Spiritual Discovery, which had pretensions of mixing science and religion in an experimental spirituality. Although Leary attempted to capture the new-culture temper in his famous dictum, "turn-on, tune-in, and drop-out," his angle on the movement was always self-promoting. He played on his professorial background and cloaked his message in the guise of scientific enterprise, even though he considered his League a religious organization dedicated to "psychedelic celebration" and "the death of the mind." Ultimately, he was too serious and self-important to realize much more than a minor cult following, even after an arrest and jailbreak in 1970 turned him into a bona fide fugitive.

Leary's main competitor, Ken Kesey, was a more appropriate symbol of the psychedelic experience. Kesey was an ill-fitting character everywhere he went, whether at Stanford or among the world of prominent authors. He soon squandered the early success he achieved with *Cuckoo's Nest* by overseeing a mediocre Broadway production of the book, which he followed with a mediocre novel, *Sometimes a Great Notion* (1964). In contrast to Leary, Kesey was bent on crusading and carousing at the same time. In 1964 he collected a small group of followers, the "Merry Pranksters," bought an old school bus, and set off on a cross-country tour not unlike the mad trip chronicled in Kerouac's *On the Road*.

The Pranksters intended to shock people everywhere out of their complacency by confronting them with a stoned band of cultural rebels. "This wild-looking thing with wild-looking people," wrote Tom Wolfe in his chronicle of Kesey's adventures, "was great for stirring up consternation and vague befuddling resentment among the citizens. . . . But there would also be people who would look up out of their poor work-a-day lives in some town, some old guy, somebody's stenographer, and see this bus and register . . . delight, or just pure open-invitation wonder." The whole trip, Wolfe came to believe, "had great possibilities for altering the usual order of things."

Returning home near San Francisco, Kesey organized "acid trips" through which he and his cohorts invented psychedelic culture. Acid trips were happenings, gatherings of hundreds of people to whom free LSD was distributed; rock bands, often the Dead or Jefferson Airplane, played for free; and gradually, through the inventiveness of rock promoters such as Bill Graham, the wild lighting that became the stock props of rock culture was introduced.

There were those who regarded Kesey as a self-promoting windbag. Some of his one-time neighbors at Stanford thought that he had turned their close-knit bohemian community into a conformist nightmare. "There had to be sex parties, marijuana smoking, and you had to dress and speak in a certain way," one recalled. Thanks to Tom Wolfe's exuberant *The Electric Kool-Aid Acid Test* (1967), however, Kesey's reputation as a genuine advocate of new-culture virtues has held. Kesey was a rebel by disposition, much like R. P. McMurphy, the leading character in *Cuckoo's Nest*. In his open and occasionally aggressive flouting of the law, Kesey betrayed the impulses of someone who was a loser and wanted it that way.

The Religious Experience

Intense religious experience was harder to come by than sex and drugs, but many people looked to Eastern religions as a means of gaining new experience. Yet another cultural development rooted in the Beats, the interest in the East began with Alan Watts, a one-time Protestant clergyman who began to popularize an easygoing brand of Zen Buddhism in the 1950s. Watts claimed that Zen did away with artificial distinctions that prevented people from living a "real" life. Where Christianity distinguished between daily life and salvation, between the soul and its surroundings, Zen was concerned with "what is." Watts, too, sought a "unified" person that was "one process in an infinite number of processes, all of them working together in harmony." Like Norman Brown, he believed that the world was in terrible shape because the wrong mind-set had captured it. Those given to "puritan pomposity," he claimed, "act from the feeling that man is *separate* from the natural universe—either pushing it around or being pushed around by it."

Watts, therefore, embraced Buddhism, using familiar arguments, and it is hardly surprising that Eastern religions grew more popular as the avant garde extended its reach. Many cultural figures made pilgrimages east. Allen Ginsberg, the Beatles, and Timothy Leary all made treks for religious inspiration, and all brought back some favorite bit of spiritual baggage. Ginsberg could be encountered, as Wolfe found him

178

at Kesey's party for the Hell's Angels, dancing about, chanting h
playing finger cymbals. Leary, ever the scholar, imported his favo
Tibetan Book of the Dead. The Beatles simply brought back their own gu
Mahesh Yogi, who evidently hoped to take the magic of commercial suc ⎯ ⏤ιe
Beatles. The Maharishi came to the United States and established his Transcenden-
tal Meditation movement, which by 1968 claimed 20,000 U.S. followers (though by
then it could no longer claim the Beatles among the faithful). The atmosphere bred
other cults, not least the Hare Krishnas, and it gave rise to less austere practices such
as yoga, which spread through the amateur setting of the new culture and made small-
time gurus out of countless advocates of altered mentalities.

Rock Music

In a culture searching for intense experience, it was no coincidence, as *Ramparts*
editor Warren Hinkle pointed out, that psychedelic drugs and electrified music
went hand in hand. Music itself became such an important element of sixties
culture because it relied more on spontaneity than the calculated arts of fiction
and painting. Music was inherently a sensory experience. Here again, the appeal
of rock was that it was a music of instincts rather than training. Rock depended
on its ability to evoke a physical response, which it did not only through sexually
suggestive lyrics but also through its sheer physical nature. In contrast to folk
music, which had more direct political content, rock prompted listeners to dance,
or at least to move. The greater sensuality of electric music was what separated it
especially from folk, a division that the outcry over Bob Dylan's conversion to the
electric guitar in 1965 symbolized.

As it shrouded itself in psychedelic paraphernalia, rock music displaced other
music among new-culture advocates; even John Cage preferred it to jazz. Bands like
the Doors established themselves as the quintessential pursuers of experience. Lead
singer Jim Morrison became renowned for behavior that ranged from LSD trips on
stage to indecent exposure, the latter of which landed him in jail. "The Doors
always make it real," wrote one excited critic. "Morrison . . . is the most subversive
dude on the planet, sounding innocuous . . . , [then] whipping his cock out in
Miami, Phoenix, or Baltimore." Morrison, like Jimi Hendrix and Janis Joplin, was
also self-destructive, and he represented the nihilistic end of the quest for experience. Where reason was tossed aside and the instincts were unleashed, after sex and
drugs, there was not much left but violence and destruction. True, the rock culture
managed to produce one last hurrah in the Woodstock Music Festival in 1969, a
peaceful happening that brought together many of the biggest acts for the benefit of
several hundred thousand people. But shortly thereafter, the Altamont concert,
billed as the West Coast Woodstock, broke down in violence and death when the
Hell's Angels, hired by the Rolling Stones as security guards for $500 in beer,
rampaged through the crowd, killing a young man who touched one of their
motorcycles and beating up others, including one of the singers for Jefferson
Airplane. As Todd Gitlin has written, the entire "ambience" at Altamont "felt like
death. . . . It wasn't just the Angels," but the people interfering with doctors trying

to help people on bad acid while others pushed and shoved to get a better view of the stage. Rock culture thus ran its course quite like the sexual revolution and the New Left: it liberated the senses and yet failed to draw a line that should not be crossed.

On Heroes and Anti-Heroes

Gitlin writes of Altamont as a disappointing ending to an age of promising cultural and political ferment. Altamont was even more than that, however. It symbolized the conquest of the anti-hero, whose struggle against the traditional good guy of U.S. culture had been ongoing for years. Mick Jagger, after all, had billed himself as "his satanic majesty" in the late sixties, and the Hell's Angels were the United States' most notorious bad boys. It was fitting that they should come together, for they exemplified that part of the new culture that renounced the services of the traditional hero, the omnipotent or resourceful carrier of mythical virtues, the guy in the white hat. The protagonists of sixties culture were anti-heroes, some of whom appeared as bumbling fools, as opponents of rationalized society, or as violent rebels.

The hero, like God, died, and for some of the same reasons. In the midst of a messy period, it was difficult to have faith in the hero anymore. When Simon and Garfunkle asked "Where have you gone, Joe DiMaggio," in the theme song to *The Graduate* they caught precisely that difficulty. The nation "turned its lonely eyes" to the Yankee Clipper, but he was nowhere to be found.

The hero was also boring. As Jeff Greenfield, a journalist and speech writer for Robert Kennedy pointed out, the United States' last real hero was Dwight Eisenhower, and look what he became. A warrior-king to the older generation, he was, to the baby boomers, the "President as Dumb Grownup . . . , a flesh-and-blood equal of Howdy Doody's Phineas T. Bluster, a Very Old Man with a great deal of power, and an air of befuddlement."

Worse, the hero was downright dangerous. To many new-culture advocates, the hero defended repression in the name of foolhardy beliefs. The hero was a dogmatist who believed in meaningless pieties and wanted everyone else to believe in them as well. Under the surface, the hero was closer to insanity than your typical schizophrenic and more destructive because he wanted to drag someone else down with him. Thus, John Barth has Max Spielman react with shock when his Goat-Boy explains that he wants to be a hero. "What's this hero? What kind of hero?" Sure it was okay to be a genuine hero, Max explains, but there were too many professional heroes running about in search of dragons to slay. "They decide they're heroes first and then go looking for trouble to prove it; often as not they end up causing trouble themselves . . . I got no use for heroes like that. Heroes! Bah!" Eldridge Cleaver saw that young middle-class whites "are rejecting the panoply of white heroes. . . . They recoiled in shame from the spectacle of cowboys and pioneers . . . galloping across a movie screen shooting Indians like Coke bottles."

The hero was in disrepute across the board, and even where he should have enjoyed some strength, in those old pockets of traditionalism—children's books, westerns, and sports—he was disappearing by decade's end. Some vestiges remained, for example, in the stock-car racer Junior Johnson whom Tom Wolfe dubbed the "last American hero," or in professional wrestling. But comic book heroes like Superman, the hero of the fifties and early sixties, yielded to the odd upstart, Batman. Not only was Superman too patriotic—no good existentialist would fight for such absurdities as "truth, justice, and the American way"—but he never gave in to Lois Lane's obvious attempts at seduction. He could have had his way with her, but, like the mad general in "Dr. Strangelove," he was sexless. Superman, sixties dogma would have said, heeded the "death instincts." Batman, on the other hand, was more mysterious and a bit campy, at least as he appeared in his television show. His enemies were scarier, as Jules Feiffer pointed out in *The Great Comic Book Heroes* (1965), and his relationship with Robin was pretty peculiar for a superhero. Here was the wealthy Bruce Wayne, living with his "ward," Dick Grayson, amidst surroundings that touched on the too-refined and included no women other than the flighty aunt. "It is like a wish dream of two homosexuals living together," wrote one observer.

Westerns

Westerns, meanwhile, the quintessential vehicle for American hero mythology since Owen Wister published *The Virginian* in 1899, collapsed of their own obsolescence and gave way to a genre of antiwesterns. Filmmakers continued to make traditional westerns, true enough, and even attempted some epics. It is revealing that perhaps the most important standard western was not a western at all but John Wayne's sorry attempt to justify the Vietnam War, *The Green Berets* (1968). Shot in Georgia, where the autumn foliage made for a rather different background from what one would expect to find in semitropical Vietnam, the movie was a stock western, down to the circle-the-wagons battle against the nonwhite savages won with the cavalry's timely arrival. Only the horses were missing. The movie was self-parody, a sign that Wayne and the western had nothing to say to Americans in the midst of upheaval. Wayne himself stuck to his myths, but the new culture was invading even his own family in the form of divorce and the temptations facing his daughter Aissa, who writes in her memoirs that she could not help but be attracted by marijuana, boys, and the antiwar movement.

To spite its tradition, the western, like art itself, became its own negation. In *Little Big Man*, the film adaptation of Peter Berger's caustic 1964 novel, the Indians won and the old heroes, Wild Bill Hickock and General George Custer, were revealed as duplicitous and insane. The Old West of American mythology was not the land of the white man's progress but, as in Barth's story of colonial Maryland, the tempestuous home of the impure. In *McCabe and Mrs. Miller* (1971), Warren Beatty and Julie Christie brought the sexual revolution to the West by trespassing on the myth of the good cowboy and pure schoolmarm. It is not implausible to see *Midnight Cowboy* (1968) as an antiwestern, since it was a modern story of the western boy come to the Big Apple, the complete reversal of the traditional western. The Academy Award winner was a perverse play on the genre: Jon Voight, the cowboy, comes to New York expecting quick riches, tries his luck as a gigolo, and ends in a relationship with homosexual overtones with Dustin Hoffman's pathetic but aptly named Ratso Rizzo. In films where the plot remained in the West, the plot lines changed considerably, as in Sam Peckinpah's tribute to outright lawlessness and violence, *The Wild Bunch* (1969). The western was turned into light comedy in *Butch Cassidy and the Sundance Kid* (1969) and musical comedy in *Paint Your Wagon* (1969). It is testimony to how far the traditional western fell into disrepute that many westerns were made in Italy, where Clint Eastwood began his rise to fame as the "man with no name," or that the genre moved to television in "Bonanza." Eastwood's various films elaborated on the theme of *The Wild Bunch:* there were no good guys; there were only survivors.

Sports

The traditionalist in search of heroes could not even look to sports as the sixties wore on. At the beginning of the period, there were a number of classic figures, such as Mickey Mantle. Mantle's career was effectively ended by debilitating knee injuries; his one-time teammate, Jim Bouton, proved that nothing was sacred when, in *Ball Four* (1970), he exposed the sexual escapades of major league ballplayers and detailed Mantle's drinking career. The New York Mets became baseball's version of anti-art in 1962 when they boasted that they were the worst team in history (which they were) and in so doing cut considerably into the Yankees' monopoly on New York fans. "The Mets are so bad you've got to love them," Jimmy Breslin wrote. In football, the foremost sensation was Joe Namath, a long-haired upstart braggart who committed the greatest football heresy when he led the American Football League New York Jets to victory over the more established National Football League Baltimore Colts in the 1969 Super Bowl, thus precipitating the merger of the two leagues.

Of all the athletes, Muhammad Ali became the foremost anti-hero. As Cassius Clay, he had won the 1960 Olympic Gold Medal and proceeded to make waves in professional boxing with both his ring skills and his irrepressible mouth. With each success his claim to fame grew, and as early as 1962 he dubbed himself "the greatest." He was to sports what Warhol and Mailer had become to their respective professions: an artist whose personality overshadowed his art and thereby accelerated his fame. "A southern colored boy had made $1 million just as he turns 22," he once said. "I don't think it's bragging to say I'm something a little special." By the midsixties, sportswriters routinely referred to Ali's antics as performance art—the "Muhammad Ali Repertory Theatre," *Village Voice* writer Joe Flaherty called it. Many magazines likened his 1967 fight with Ernie Terrell, whom he taunted mercilessly, to "theater of cruelty." And his 1967 imprisonment for refusing the draft solidified, in a serious way, Ali's anti-heroism. As Eldridge Cleaver wrote, Ali angered the establishment because the heavyweight champion, a symbol of American masculinity, was supposed to be powerful but stupid, talented but compliant.

"A racist Black Muslim heavyweight champion is a bitter pill for racist white America to swallow."

Reincarnations of the Hero

After being buried in the assault on tradition, the hero emerged in at least three reincarnations: the schlemiel, the picaro, and the rebel. The schlemiel was an outgrowth of Jewish literature, where he appeared as a hapless character who survived through something like accidental tenacity. Although pure versions of the schlemiel were not widespread, a bit of him appeared in countless places. Pynchon's Benny Profane, whose career path takes him from the Navy to a job shooting the mythical alligators in New York City sewers, and Vonnegut's Billy Pilgrim, the feckless optometrist in *Slaughterhouse Five*, both had bits of the schlemiel in them. Dustin Hoffman's Jack Crabb in *Little Big Man* boasts that he was a "frontiersman, Indian scout, gunfighter, buffalo hunter, adopted Cheyenne," but his life is one big misadventure. Kidnapped by Indians as a child, adopted by a less-than-pure missionary, Crabb winds up as a guide for General George Custer at the Battle of the Little Big Horn, which he survives through sheer luck.

The schlemiel resembled the innocent schizophrenic in that both were harmless, except perhaps to themselves. The picaro similarly meant no harm but was sophisticated and cynical; where the schlemiel was too innocuous to be self-interested, the picaro turned self-interest into an existentialist virtue. His credo: where firm beliefs were based on discredited rationality, then it was best not to have beliefs at all. At least self-interest was honest. Besides, it was more fun. The picaro was inclined toward romping, after the manner of Tom Jones, the hero of John Osborne's 1963 film of the same name, who drinks and cavorts his way across the English countryside. The old man in *Catch-22*'s Italian brothel, in his dialogue with the young American, Nately, assumes the type when he wonders at the absurdity of patriotism. "What is a country?" he asks. "A country is a piece of land surrounded on all sides by boundaries, usually unnatural. . . . There are now fifty or sixty countries fighting in this war. Surely so many countries can't *all* be worth dying for." When Nately insists that there are things worth dying for, the old man answers that "anything worth dying for is worth living for," which meant watching out for one's own backside more than one's ideals. In the end, the real victor would not be the heroic nation but the conquered one. "Italy is really a very poor and weak country, and that's what makes us so strong. Italian soldiers are not dying anymore. But American and German soldiers are. I call that doing extremely well."

Neither the schlemiel nor the picaro posed an ominous threat to mainstream society, but the development of the anti-hero gave rise to a cultural type whose stock-in-trade was violent confrontation. The rebel was the most precise mirror image of the traditional hero. Whereas the hero typically was too good for society and therefore detached, the rebel was, according to the trite justifications that warmed his path, an "alienated" character lashing out at the society that refused to nurture him. The hero's grand cause justified his violence; the rebel's victimization justified his.

To some extent, Muhammad Ali fit this type, but more important, herein lay the attraction that Cleaver and the Black Panthers held for white liberals and radicals. Victims of racial injustice, the Panthers were of course violent, according to their liberal defenders, and it is clear that Cleaver and his colleagues understood that their allies wanted to see them as modern Robin Hoods. The Panthers became another means to intense experience for their white hangers-on, and Cleaver's writing was embraced by mainstream intellectuals for essentially the same reason—it was "real" and "gut-wrenching."

Much the same sort of temper surrounded the cult of the Hell's Angels, the California motorcycle gang that roamed the fringes of San Francisco's avant garde. Because the Angels were dirtier, drunker, and more violent than any other gang, they became an object of hand-wringing in the mainstream press, which in turn meant that they became a new-culture fascination, and all the more so after hip journalist Hunter S. Thompson detailed their habits in a 1966 book. Their reputation grew in proportion to the anxiety they provoked in civilized society, and they made natural allies with Ken Kesey's Merry Pranksters. As Tom Wolfe tells it, Kesey was the first person to accept the Angels without fear or nervous condescension, and the Angels in turn intensified the Prankster experience. Kesey made the Angels a hit in new-culture circles in town; they became musts "on guest lists at Berkeley hipster parties," wrote one observer, with "young sociology instructors passing joints around and questioning these Great Society dropouts about 'alienation.'" According to Wolfe, the "intellectuals were always hung up with the feeling that they weren't coming to grips with real life. . . . Well, the Hell's Angels were real life. It didn't get any realer than that."

The Angels did not symbolize alienated youth; they didn't give a damn. The rebel was a fighter, not a lost soul. Ultimately, he was political because of his refusal to seek acceptance. Again, therein lay the Panthers' attraction, but perhaps a better example of the politicized anti-hero was the guerrilla, a figure who not only enjoyed cultural resonance but also symbolized the political struggle against the establishment. The guerrilla was irreconcilable, dangerous, and effective. The cult of Che Guevara was ample testimony to how the figure cut. Che had been an associate of Fidel Castro, which was enough to make him an enemy of the U.S. liberal establishment, which in turn had him assassinated. Che was not only a guerrilla but also a martyr and thus the leading anti-hero on a list that included Ho Chi Minh, Castro, Mao, Regis Debray, and Franz Fanon.

Despite the left's attraction to the rebel, this cultural type could be turned in other political directions. Nowhere was this political ambiguity more obvious than in Clint Eastwood's films, whether his *High Plains Drifter* (1973), which infused a *High Noon* plot with a spree of violence, or his Dirty Harry Callahan films. Eastwood turned the anti-hero into a defender of tradition, playing as he did on the widespread backlash against public disorder. And here, finally, it is possible to see how the new culture was not politically decisive. For Eastwood's Dirty Harry was the anti-hero who despised the bleeding-heart liberal, the spoiled-brat radical, and other representatives of the political left, the very people who had spent a decade encouraging anti-heroes.

Notes on the Politics of Culture

Eastwood thereby demonstrated, as the Hell's Angels did at Altamont, that the anti-hero was no more loyal to the cause of revolution than he was to the effeminate status quo. In that sense, they pointed up the fundamental flaw in the program for radical change through cultural rebellion. With too few distinctions between what was healthy and what was not, between reason and irrationality, the new culture had no way to ward off the worst elements of human behavior other than the well-intentioned but ineffectual pleas for people to love one another.

The quest for the unified personality and unified art paradoxically muted the radicalism of the new culture. Indeed, where the quest for cultural radicalism was strongest, political commitment tended to be weakest. Norman O. Brown disavowed political intentions and chose to believe that cultural change would make political change unnecessary. Many cultural radicals took this political indifference to heart, especially the hippies, the loose-knit group of cultural dropouts who gained attention in mid-decade for their colorful lives, open sexuality, and drug use. The hippies drifted into centers such as San Francisco's Haight-Ashbury, Greenwich Village, or any of the smaller imitations that popped up in most major cities. To the mainstream press, they symbolized the new culture and dramatized the widespread disaffection with American life; the press focused so earnestly on the hippies that they were confused as the leading edge of the new culture. It got to the point, Joan Didion wrote, that "there were so many observers on Haight Street from *Life* and *Look* and CBS that they were largely observing one another."

Of course, the more the mainstream press worried over the hippies, the more young people sought to emulate them. Behind the energies of many cultural entrepreneurs, the hippies became trend-setters and their "style" ballooned, as Todd Gitlin has written, "into a whole cultural climate." Men with long hair and beards, women without cosmetics or styled hair meant "a turn from straight to curved, from uptight to loose, from cramped to free. . . . Clothes were a riot of costumes" that included, for example, "India's beads, Indian headbands, cowboy-style boots and hides, granny glasses, long dresses, working-class jeans and flannels; most tantalizingly, army jackets." The hippie style, which Gitlin aptly calls an "anti-uniform," became standard apparel not only in bohemian meccas but also, ever so gradually, in Kansas, Ohio, North Carolina—quite literally throughout the nation.

It is doubtful that the majority of those who constituted hippie culture had ever made the conscious decision to be radicals. Many political radicals embraced the style as an act of defiance, but for other young Americans, the hippie life was less a cultural statement than a temporary refuge or a last resort. They may have been rejecting society, but it is likely that those were personal rejections, the sloughing off of parents, of older community ties, of unfulfilling personal pasts. Given the constant turnover of people and general instability of places like the Haight, Joan Didion's portrait of the hippies seems most tenable. "We were seeing," she thought, "the desperate attempt of a handful of pathetically unequipped children to create a community in a social vacuum. . . . They are less in rebellion against the society than ignorant of it, able only to feed back certain of its most publicized self-doubts, *Vietnam, Saran-Wrap, diet pills, the Bomb.*"

Still, it seemed natural to stake out an alliance between cultural rebellion and political radicalism, and the hippie style was a natural instrument for welding the two together. That was the hope, at least, of Jerry Rubin and Abbie Hoffman, two men whose penchant for high-profile foolishness made them partners in radical chic. Rubin, a Cincinnati native who wound his way to Berkeley, took up radical politics, partly under the inspiration of Fidel Castro and Che, and, with less alacrity, the hippie life. "Berkeley radicals saw [the hippies] as a diversion from politics," Rubin recalled, "hippies saw the radicals as up-tight politicians. I saw the hippies as the true political expression of the breakdown of the affluent society."

Rubin's hopes for fusing the two peaked during 1967, which began with the January "Human Be-In" in Golden Gate Park, which in many ways was the high point of the Bay area counterculture. Leary was there to expound on the glories of acid; Ginsberg led the crowd in Buddhist chants; the Dead and Jefferson Airplane, among others, played; the Angels provided security; and finally there was Rubin, fresh out of jail, ready to speak on politics. Although he received a "cool reception," as he put it, the connection between politics and culture was made at least on some. The San Francisco *Oracle* summed up the be-in as "a union of love and activism previously separated by categorical dogma and label mongering."

Along with Hoffman, who had been similarly evolving in New York, Rubin combined the two streams into political theater. Media-wise, the two instinctively sensed that the absurd and outrageous made news and that the media could be manipulated. In 1966 Rubin appeared before the House Un-American Activities Committee, the McCarthy-era red-hunting committee that was the bane of civil libertarians, wearing a Revolutionary War uniform and playing the part of Tom Paine. Security guards tossed him out as he yelled, "I want to testify!" In August 1967, Hoffman and Rubin executed an assault on the New York Stock Exchange, where they set off a scramble by tossing dollar bills onto the floor and then held reporters' attention by burning money. Together, the two were irrepressible media geniuses and could pick their targets. In 1968 they founded the Yippie party, which took the slogan "Abandon the creeping meatball," and set off to lead protesters at the upcoming Democratic National Convention in Chicago.

Rubin and Hoffman succeeded in their first hope—organizing spectacles of absurdity. In so doing, they brought cultural radicalism into politics, but they never intended to be serious. They chose the name Yippie, for example, because it sounded silly. "Can you imagine the President warning the country about the danger from the 'yippies'?" Rubin asked. "Nobody would take him seriously, and the whole country would be reduced to one big joke." Like Pop Art, the meaning of Yippie was to have a good time at the expense of the uptight establishment.

That purpose was based on the widely shared supposition that cultural rebellion translated into political radicalism and a better world. The essential argument, as Theodore Rozsak, Philip Slater, and Charles Reich distilled it in their respective books, was that the new culture marked a watershed of change as important as the industrial revolution of the nineteenth century and the corporate-managerial revo-

At a 1968 Easter Sunday "love-in" in Miami's Greynolds Park, thousands of hippies share and celebrate their communal and informal lifestyle.
[AP/Wide World Photos]

lution of the early twentieth. Associated with yet another phase of social and economic transformation, the age of affluence, the transformation of culture was an inextinguishable part of a profound alteration in U.S. society, and it was just a matter of time before the alterations transformed the U.S. political landscape. As Reich wrote, the coming revolution "will originate with the individual and with culture, and it will change the political structure only as its final act. . . . Its ultimate creation will be a new and enduring wholeness and beauty—a renewed relationship of man to himself, to other men, to society, to nature, and to the land."

It was an article of faith that the new culture would be one of love, empathy, and "wholeness." Just as the acquisitive culture of the nineteenth century reflected the unbridled pursuit of profits, so would the affluent society encourage a mentality of abundance that had no need of greed or violence. In Reich's flight of fancy, the new mentality—"Consciousness III," he called it—would value warmth, honesty, cooperation, and tolerance. "There are no 'tough guys' among the youth of Consciousness III," he fantasized. "Hitchhikers smile at approaching cars, people smile at each other on the street, the human race rediscovers its need for each other." In the new world, "people all belong to the same family, whether they have met or not. It is as simple as that."

No doubt the society of consumer abundance was undermining the traditional restraints on sex and the acquisitive drive, but no one was clear why it would give rise to Reich's utopia. Indeed, it is curious that Rozsak, Reich, and Slater all published their defenses of the new culture at the end of the sixties, at a time when such claims were so clearly exaggerated that one had to wonder what they were looking at. Perhaps they should have been with Todd Gitlin at Altamont, who came away from that new-culture spectacle with a far more realistic conclusion: "Who could any longer harbor the illusion that these hundreds of thousands of spoiled star-hungry children of the Lonely Crowd were the harbingers of a good society?" Perhaps they neglected to note how Charles Manson, the unnerving mass murderer, clung to the values of "Consciousness III." Maybe Reich was not talking about Weatherman, who followed Bernardine Dohrn in adopting a three-fingered salute in praise of the fork that one of the Manson children had stuck in the stomach of a pregnant victim.

Those who confused cultural rebellion with political change misunderstood the nature of both, but most particularly how the United States' consumer culture easily made use of the most basic elements of the avant garde. It was wrong to think that the power of the nation's political and economic establishment rested on cultural repression, and that power would change hands, and even its very nature, once that repression was blasted away. The U.S. establishment could ultimately accept cultural revolution because sex and rock-and-roll were so eminently marketable. Particularly in the country's strange political culture, it was easy for establishment figures to use new cultural themes for their own ends. John Kennedy was not just king of Camelot; he was also the tough-nosed Irishman whose sexual escapades were no secret. And Richard Nixon, the born loser, saw himself as an anti-hero who wanted power more than dignified respectability. What other president would have appeared on Rowan and Martin's "Laugh-In," a new-culture comedy hour, to say "sock it to me"? It helps to remember, in this regard, how the age ended: with Richard Nixon, embroiled in the Watergate scandal, looking for momentary distractions, sitting down to a special viewing of Clint Eastwood's *Magnum Force*.

CHAPTER 7

The Urban Crisis

In the early hours of Sunday, July 23, 1967, a Detroit police vice squad raided a "blind pig," an after-hours liquor joint on Twelfth Street, the "nastiest street in town." During the hot, muggy night, a crowd of eighty-five people or so, all black and about half women, had gathered to toast some local soldiers. At 3:00 A.M. on a Sunday morning the police force was at minimum manpower; nevertheless, the officer in charge decided to arrest all of the revelers. It took well over an hour to load everyone into police vans. Meanwhile, some two hundred spectators gathered. The crowd was a varied lot: ordinary folks on their way to work, "drunks and drifters," gamblers and prostitutes. There were also some angry young men, who whipped up the crowd. One young man issued a call to arms: "Black Power. Don't let them take our people away. . . . Let's get the bricks and bottles going." When police loaded up their last wagons and pulled away, the crowd sensed that it had driven the police out of the neighborhood, and thus emboldened, began a week of rioting that claimed forty-three lives, led to 7,200 arrests, and did $45 million in damage.

The Detroit riot was noteworthy but hardly unique. U.S. cities during the sixties became cauldrons of recurring and violent "civil disorders." Beginning with the 1965 Watts riot in Los Angeles through July 1968, over one hundred cities experienced riots. According to survey statistics compiled by the Senate Subcommittee on Government Operations, 189 people were killed, 7,614 were injured, 59,257 were arrested, and nearly $160 million in property was damaged. Erupting at a point when the civil rights movement was floundering, mostly confined to African-American neighborhoods of northern cities, the riots mocked the integrationist promise of Martin Luther King, Jr.

The riots were only partly a result of the nation's legacy of racism. They were even more a consequence of the nation's accumulated urban woes, which collected as the cities underwent a uniform process of decay in the years after World War II. The vast postwar construction of suburban housing had directed new building away from the areas where it was most needed and drew middle- and upper-income people out of urban cores. The tax base of the cities declined while the shortage of decent housing worsened. Industries that first had beckoned working people into the cities near the beginning of the twentieth century reduced their dependence on unskilled labor through automation and, therefore, their need for expanding blue-collar employment, even in the boom times of the sixties. Corporations began to locate new plants either in suburban areas that offered tax breaks or in Sunbelt cities of the South and Southwest that offered nonunionized labor as well as tax breaks. City government had become a juggler's art, as the traditional political machine yielded to a mélange of interest groups. Whatever their faults, the machines had been vehicles for assimilating immigrants into the American mainstream. In the absence of both of these important vehicles, the cities were unable to accommodate the millions of postwar immigrants, mostly blacks from the rural South, but also Appalachian whites, Mexicans, and Puerto Ricans. The urban crisis was in the largest sense the default of the traditional function and promise of the city, and in the "post-city age," as one writer described the sixties, the city became a grim holding area for the nation's superfluous people, its poor, its minorities, its elderly, its incompetent, its "pathological."

Urbanization, Housing, and the Segregated City

To some extent, the United States would have faced urban problems in the sixties even if all else had been ideal. Depression and war had diminished urban construction; the housing stock was inadequate and aging; and office and public buildings were showing wear. Aging cities shouldered the additional burdens, pollution and traffic congestion, which came with the nation's wasteful reliance on automobiles. Pittsburgh was so polluted that the architect Frank Lloyd Wright recommended that it be abandoned after World War II, and the air of Los Angeles was already notorious. Cities like Dayton, Ohio, and Phoenix, Arizona, which had never experienced pollution problems before, were forced by 1960 to institute smog alerts; Cincinnati adopted a "soiling index" that warned people when it was inadvisable to hang their wash out to dry.

These problems hardly discouraged the long-term flow of rural Americans toward the cities. By 1960 nearly three-quarters of the nation's population lived in metropolitan areas (defined by the census as 250,000 people or more). The process of urbanization was most notable among African Americans: by 1960, 73 percent of this traditionally southern and rural population was urban; by 1967, almost half of all African Americans lived in the North. Between 1940 and 1960, 2.75 million blacks left the South, for all intents and purposes, for the cities. New York's black population increased two and a half times in those twenty years; Philadelphia's doubled; and Detroit's tripled. Chicago had a black population of 890,000 by 1960.

In the so-called Sunbelt, from Atlanta to Los Angeles, metropolitan growth exploded. The region's population increased 112.3 percent from 1940 to 1980; twelve of its communities grew from modest cities into major metropolitan areas. Phoenix grew from 65,414 people in 1940 to 584,303 in 1970, while Houston doubled its size to nearly a million people over the same period. Although warm weather and cheap labor made the region attractive to employers, the real impetus for growth in the Sunbelt was the federal government, which favored the region with a disproportionate share of defense spending, NASA, highway construction, and other forms of largess.

When these statistics are scrutinized, they bear out two of the most important developments of postwar social history, the growth of the suburbs and of racial and class segregation. From 1950 to 1960, 75 percent of metropolitan growth took place in the suburbs, which increased population five times faster than the cities they surrounded. The truly urban population increased only 1.5 percent, which, considering the overall rate of population growth, was no growth at all. Indeed, forty-one northeastern cities lost population; fourteen of them lost over 10 percent of their population. Those leaving the city were primarily white, middle class, and upwardly mobile, their urban places taken by the postwar migrants. Given the influx of southern, rural blacks into the central cities, suburban growth foretold a society that was increasingly segregated by race and by class.

Housing

The pronounced urban segregation was no mere accident or matter of choice. The federal government led the way in promoting segregation almost as soon as it developed a national housing program. In the late 1930s the Federal Housing Administration, the bureaucracy that doled out low-interest mortgages and building loans, advised appraisers to lower ratings and even reject loans for homes in neighborhoods where "inharmonious racial or nationality groups" mixed. FHA policy recommended using restrictive covenants in mortgages that would prevent owners from selling dwellings in white communities to members of those "inharmonious groups."

The Supreme Court ruled that such covenants were illegal in *Shelly v. Kramer* (1948), after which outright government discrimination in housing dissolved. By then, however, the FHA had set the tone for the private housing market and continued to encourage the market's tendencies to promote further segregation. The FHA continued to set guidelines for what constituted suitable construction, which clearly favored new housing. As a consequence, well into the sixties FHA-insured loans overwhelmingly went to suburban areas. Builders were encouraged to ignore the central city and the low-income market, and middle-class whites responded in predictable fashion by moving to new suburban housing made cheaper through government loan guarantees. In setting the guidelines for low-risk mortgages, the federal government encouraged the practice of "redlining," through which private lenders refused loans within areas on maps marked off with red lines. Whole neighborhoods—even entire cities—were denied loan guarantees. As Illinois Senator Paul Douglas discovered while chairing the National Commission on Urban Problems in 1968, "even middle-class residential districts in the central cities were suspect, since there was always the prospect that they, too, might turn as Negroes and poor whites continued to pour into the cities, and as middle and upper-middle class whites continued to move out."

Under pressure from the civil rights movement, numerous open-housing laws were established, until by 1970 there were some 370 local open-housing laws. But they provided little help, for they did not override local zoning laws that made it possible for suburbs to prevent construction of multiple-family units or homes on small lots, both of which might have provided low-cost housing.

The liberal administrations of Kennedy and Johnson made overtures to improve the nation's housing situation. An urbanite himself, Kennedy had an instinctive interest in urban problems and often spoke of the housing crisis during the 1960 campaign. Even if it took him over a year to outlaw segregation in public housing "with one tick of the pen," he did improve federal policy. His first move was to appoint Robert Weaver, a well-respected urban economist who had been fighting for decent minority treatment in public housing since the 1930s, to head the federal housing finance agency. Weaver, a strong integrationist, sought to provide mortgages to lower- and middle-income buyers that required little down payment, limit suburban sprawl by providing federal incentives for long-range construction, and promote land-use planning for park and recreation development. The administration's 1961 Housing Act improved mortgage conditions for lower-income buyers, but fewer than 13,000 single-family, low-income units were built in 1962 and 1963, and the supply of new housing in the area of greatest need remained entirely inadequate. Not even FHA attempts to promote renovation and direct mortgage money to minority purchases, which began in earnest in 1966, eased the situation. Indeed, writes historian Kenneth Jackson, "the primary effect" of liberalized FHA policy "was to make it easier for white families to finance their escape from areas experiencing racial change."

Considering the damage its destructive policies had done to the cities, the federal government might have reversed them by actively promoting urban housing or by refusing loans for suburban construction. But no groundswell of support emerged for withdrawing FHA support from the suburbs. Even in the heyday of sixties liberalism, federal officials were wary of interfering in private enterprise, even though its earlier meddling had promoted segregation. It was much safer to stay with those programs that either spread federal money around to as many sources as possible or that dealt in areas that the marketplace ignored. Accordingly, federal efforts went mostly into urban renewal and public housing.

Urban Renewal

Like the FHA mortgage program, urban renewal had been part of federal policy for some time, established under Title I of the 1949 Housing Act. Intended as a program of revitalization, Title I provided money to local communities for slum clearance and new housing. The cities were to organize redevelopment agencies to identify sites, plan clearance and construction, receive bids, and apply for federal money. After a sluggish response in the early fifties, project completions began to mount, partly because the administration increased Title I money in the 1961 Housing Act. By 1963 there were 588 projects in some stage of execution, and most major cities were making use of Title I.

Despite the initial intentions behind it, the urban renewal program only exacerbated the urban housing situation. Nothing in the program limited new construction to low-cost housing: 24 percent of the new building was in public works, such as New York's controversial Lincoln Center; and only 56 percent was new housing, most of which was in the form of luxury apartments. City governments needed the tax revenue that would come from expensive new buildings, private developers had little interest in dabbling in low-cost housing, and the leaders of the redevelopment agencies, particularly New York's Robert Moses, often preferred projects for their glamor rather than their utility. Some of the areas that were cleared were slums only by the urban planners' definitions. Boston's west end, which Herbert Gans made famous in his splendid book, *The Urban Villagers* (1962), was the best example of a neighborhood destroyed simply because its residents were working class. As Jane Jacobs argued in her bitter critique of urban policy, *The Life and Death of Great American Cities* (1963), city planners preferred "middle-class housing projects which are truly marvels of dullness and regimentation" to cohesive and vibrant ethnic neighborhoods.

Begun as an effort to ensure livable housing for the United States' urban have-nots, urban renewal actually reduced the amount of private, low-income housing available and displaced the very people it was supposed to help. Urban renewal destroyed 140,000 low-income dwellings, which it replaced with 40,000 new units, only 5 percent of which low-income residents could afford. Not only were there fewer low-cost units, but also the decline in the supply raised the cost of all housing. Under federal guidelines, cities were supposed to provide relocation assistance to the estimated 609,000 people who were displaced by 1963, but this side of the program was the last planned and the most poorly executed. Only about half of the displaced received any compensation for moving expenses, and probably fewer still received assistance in finding new housing. Public agencies did not follow up on many relocations, and thus the guesses about the fate of those displaced varied widely. By 1968 federal officials had marshaled statistics to show that relocation had been almost completely successful, but their claim that 93 percent of the displaced had been successfully placed in standard housing was dramatically at odds with most other studies. Peter Marris's mid-decade estimates, for example, were that between 15 and 50 percent moved into substandard housing and perhaps as few as 10 percent into public housing. For their trouble, according to Marris, the displaced probably paid between 17 and 25 percent higher rents after moving. Four out of five were nonwhite, which led civil rights leaders to dub the program "Negro removal." Some observers noted the genuine pain of separation, something akin to grief, as the displaced pined for their "lost homes," even when they ended up in better housing. Meanwhile, the loss of neighborhoods had ripple effects across the inner cities, for it led to overcrowding and deterioration elsewhere. The Twelfth Street area where the Detroit riots broke out had been just such a neighborhood: poor but respectable, only to be inundated with displaced residents of Detroit's renewal programs. Against criticism of urban displacement, New York's renewal czar, Robert Moses, sneered: "Look, in ten years you will have forgotten all about these people, and you'll have me to thank for the project."

Few believed that urban renewal was the cure-all of the housing situation, and it always went hand in hand with other strategies, especially public housing and rent supplements. In its 1965 Housing and Urban Development Act, the Johnson administration tried to include a program of rent subsidies to lower-income people who did not qualify for public housing—essentially the urban working class. Congress limited subsidies to those who already qualified for public housing; in other words, subsidies were provided to those already subsidized. Robert Weaver continued to fight for working-class subsidies on the grounds that a clear gap existed between what the government defined as poor and what it took to live in any major city. Testifying before Congress in 1965, Weaver claimed that the majority of those displaced by urban renewal earned between $3,000 and $6,000 annually, which meant that they were hard-pressed but not poor enough to meet the federal level for aid ($3,000 a year, money income). Congressional Republicans, however, opposed rent supplements, ostensibly because they smacked of "socialism" but mostly because they feared that the program would make it possible for some of those working people to move into older sections of suburbia—near them, in other words.

The only market that the federal government actively entered, therefore, was in constructing public housing for the truly poor, an area that private builders shunned. Johnson characteristically spoke of the need for tremendous increases in such construction. The 1965 Housing Act called for 200,000 new units over four years, but actual construction peaked at 23,660 in 1967, a paltry 5 percent of the multifamily housing starts that year and obviously short of the 135,000 units mandated by the 1949 Housing Act.

Given the abysmal condition into which much public housing chronically fell, the curious planning that went into it, and the inability of housing authorities to police projects, those units that were built were mixed blessings at best. In some ways, they were improvements. Many residents of the Pruett-Igoe projects in St. Louis told sociologist Lee Rainwater that they appreciated the reliable heat, the regular attention to maintenance, and the periodic treatments for roaches and rats that came with project housing. Elaine Brown, a later leader of the Black Panthers, recalls moving from an old North Philly ghetto neighborhood into a housing project, where her mother at least could lock out the rats and roaches. Whatever its faults, public housing allowed low-income people to escape that bane of the sixties ghetto, the slumlord.

On the other hand, housing projects failed to reproduce the street life that prevailed in poor neighborhoods, and not always to the good. Because more units could be packed into a small area by using high-rises, many projects were huge buildings that prevented parents from watching children at play and that provided rowdy children with too many places for misbehavior—elevators, staircases, and hallways. As Jane Jacobs argued, the experts who designed such projects were under the illusion that park areas, wide walkways, and the like, would foster a healthy environment regardless of the character of the buildings themselves. In projects that had turned bad, however, the open areas often became gauntlets of teen violence that older residents and young children had to run. Many projects were governed by rules and admission regulations, and their quality often hinged on how well those guidelines were enforced. Chicago's two most notorious projects, Cabrini-Green on the north side and the southside Robert Taylor homes, were both reasonably civil places to live, according to Nicholas Lemann, until city housing officials, in a rush to fill vacancies, dropped or simply ignored screening procedures. Both became living nightmares of drugs, gang violence, and impoverishment. The Robert Taylor homes became a "seventy-million dollar ghetto," one critic wrote, whose inhabitants nicknamed it "the Congo Hilton." "The projects are hideous, of course," James Baldwin sardonically wrote in Nobody Knows My Name (1964), "there being a law . . . that popular housing shall be as cheerless as a prison." "The Harlem projects," he continued with his usual flair, "are hated almost as much as policemen, and this is saying a great deal." As Rainwater's St. Louis study demonstrated, the projects made the steadiest, most decent families prisoners in their homes. Public housing became large holding cells for the urban poor, indiscriminately imprisoning struggling working people along with criminals, drug users, and incompetents.

The End of the City

Middle-class flight from the central cities imposed great hardships on urban areas, most immediately by reducing the tax base, which in turn reduced city services, cut school funding, and forced cities to raise taxes on those who stayed—thereby driving out more people. Boston was the most dramatic example. After losing 13 percent of its population through the 1950s, the city was left with a tax base in 1960 that was 25 percent less than what it had been before the Great Depression. So bad were city finances that its bond rating dropped. Even after fiscal reform in 1969, New York found itself with a $500 million shortfall. The cities collected a tiny fraction of all tax revenues, most of which came through property and income taxes, the most direct and painful forms of taxation. As inflation began to eat into the standard of living, increased taxes were all the more straining for working-class people, who often tended to blame the poor for the fiscal plight of the cities. In this circular way, the erosion of the urban tax base contributed in no small part to the increase of racial and class tension by the midsixties.

Death of the Political Machine

Wrestling with metropolitan financial and social problems was made inestimably more difficult by the fragmented nature of political power and civic authority. Although the "city" in the abstract included a whole metropolitan community, on average, eighty-seven independent units administered government in metropolitan areas. Metropolitan Chicago alone contained 1,060 communities in the midsixties. A 1972 Census Bureau study counted 78,218 different local governments in the United States. Within cities, fragmentation was increasingly the rule. Indeed, one of the most striking urban developments, rarely noted at the time, was the decline of the great political machines, nearly all of which had fallen apart by the late sixties. The Irish machine of Boston's James Michael Curley, the Baltimore machine of Thomas D'Alesandro, and Kansas City's Pendergast machine passed from power. New York's Democratic party, historically associated with Tammany Hall, fell into fratricidal war. In many cities, the machines were replaced with good-government reformers, as in Philadelphia and Milwaukee. Detroit, too, elected a reform mayor, Jerome P. Cavanagh. Unlike the old machines, the reform administrations had to rely on temporary and unstable coalitions that joined, for example, urban professionals with African Americans against the ethnic coalitions of the machines. In the Sunbelt cities, the old-line segregationist types yielded—quietly, for the most part—to moderate, probusiness forces.

Two notable exceptions served only to prove the rule. Chicago's Richard Daley and, to a lesser extent, Sam Yorty in Los Angeles were traditional machine pols, but they were the last of a dying breed. Daley was a classic character. He boasted only a modest Irish upbringing, which he never left behind. He lived his entire adult life in the same modest home in the same working-class Irish neighborhood; he attended church several times a week. He won the mayor's job in 1955 by aligning with South Side blacks and needed their help again in 1963. Yet he never took Chicago's blacks seriously, and he ignored their growing electoral clout, eventually to his peril. By allowing, even building upon, residential segregation, by turning a deaf ear to demands for improved schools in the black neighborhoods, and by insisting that blacks participate in the machine on his terms, he set himself up for the inevitable confrontation with independent black leaders that only began with Martin Luther King's 1966 efforts in Chicago. If in the last half of the decade, Daley survived as a national symbol of white backlash, that symbolism did nothing to guarantee the survival of the machine. No machine could live long by abusing a group that comprised more than a quarter of the population, and without black support, the Democratic machine sputtered out in the early seventies.

Daley's unwillingness to concede justice to blacks makes it impossible to pine for the passing of his machine. But destroying the machine did not bring many improvements or justice. By the end of the decade, urban blacks had begun to establish their political power in most cities and had taken formal power in some metropolises with the election of Richard Hatcher in Gary, Indiana, and Carl B. Stokes in Cleveland. However, the urban crisis was too complex and profound to be reversed simply by black electoral success. Furthermore, the traditional machines had certain virtues that their successors lacked. As noted earlier, they were important means by which immigrant groups assimilated to urban life, and their demise took away city patronage jobs and other forms of largess that might have gone to urban blacks. Second, like it or not, the machines provided administrative coherence to city government—not always honest, to be sure—so that one at least knew how things could be accomplished or whom to criticize for the lack of accomplishments.

The default of the machines left the cities to the caprice of interest-group competition, and the result was that municipal authority was difficult to muster for good or ill. When Los Angeles mayor Sam Yorty, facing Robert Kennedy in congressional hearings after the Watts riots, blamed his inaction before and during the riots on fragmented local administration, he did so with some legitimacy. The fragmentation of authority also hampered black politicians and was one of the important reasons why electoral success did not translate into rapid improvement for the black urban poor. Getting elected was one thing, but because power rested in many different hands, getting something accomplished was quite another matter entirely.

Fragmentation: Proposed Solutions

The rational solution to fragmented authority was metropolitan government, such as Miami organized in 1957, or even wider, regional governments of the sort the philosopher Lewis Mumford recommended during the sixties. Although regional planning commissions and similar forms of comprehensive administration emerged, no major metropolitan area followed Miami's lead. The suburbs had little incentive to bow to urban government, particularly if they had a large enough tax base of their own to provide municipal services. The worse urban problems became, the more tenaciously suburbs held on to their autonomy in a futile effort to immunize themselves from blight, poverty, and violence. Metropolitan government was a solution, but one, Robert Weaver regretted in 1965, that appealed only to "professional students of urban problems."

Another solution to fragmentation was to have the federal government assume command of metropolitan policy. The Kennedy administration, hoping that urban policy would be better coordinated if a cabinet-level bureaucracy were established, proposed the Department of Housing and Urban Development (HUD) along with its housing act in 1961. Congress knocked HUD out of the legislation, in part because both suburban and rural representatives saw HUD for what it was: a bureaucracy whose main mission was to work in the interests of the central cities. Meanwhile, southern congressmen opposed HUD because they assumed that Kennedy would appoint Weaver its first head. By 1965 southern opposition was weaker, congressional opponents focused more attention on rent supplements, and HUD was established as part of Lyndon Johnson's urban program. The president then appointed Weaver as the first secretary of HUD, making him the first African American to hold a cabinet post. Weaver's considerable talents helped to rationalize metropolitan policy, but HUD still was unable to override local autonomy consistently.

Causes of the Urban Crisis

The urban crisis was in no small way a result of housing patterns, shaped by racial and class bigotry, laid down by the private market, and shaped by federal policy. In a broader historical sense, however, the urban crisis was entwined with the development of what the sociologist Daniel Bell termed the "postindustrial society." Capitalism, Bell pointed out, had reached that stage of technological development at which it relied less on producing goods than on thinking or on service occupations. In *The Coming of Post-Industrial Society* (1967), Bell, like John Kenneth Galbraith, argued that modern capitalism had moved beyond the age of scarcity and that work in the postindustrial world would probably center on intellectual pursuits, especially those of applied science, administrative tasks as in government, or work in the consumer or "service" sector. Although Bell was concerned principally with how capitalism had gotten to such a point and with who would rule postindustrial society, the developments to which he called attention had been altering the metropolitan landscape and, in the bargain, shaping American lives.

Postindustrial society undermined the modern city's historic economic and cultural purposes. A society that was no longer based on manufacturing no longer needed cities to serve as manufacturing centers. And because the postindustrial economy no longer depended on the labor of unskilled immigrants, the cities no longer had to serve as melting pots of ethnic assimilation.

The nature of the postindustrial society created the paradoxes of affluence, for if measured by general statistics on growth, income, and employment, the economy of the sixties was robust. Kennedy inherited a sluggish economy in 1961, and although his tax cuts probably stimulated enough activity to initiate a long period of growth, the real economic acceleration came from military spending associated with the Vietnam buildup. The war added an estimated 1 million jobs to the private sector from 1965 to 1967. Unemployment, over 6 percent when Kennedy assumed office, fell to under 4 percent for much of 1966 and ran at that level through 1969. The affluent economy put record numbers of people to work in the sixties and record numbers of all people—skilled and unskilled, black and white, male and female. Even the manufacturing sector employed record numbers, achieved a fairly impressive rate of productivity from 1960 to 1966, and at least in union plants provided regular wage hikes. Detroit's healthy auto industry helped reduce unemployment to 1.6 percent for white workers and 3.4 percent for blacks, which meant practically full employment.

The fate of the cities, however, was bound up with what sort of jobs were being created, and the statistics here demonstrate what the postindustrial society had in store. The number of people employed in manufacturing industries increased from 15,241,00 in 1950 to 19,564,000 in 1970. Within manufacturing industries, that rise in total employment was primarily an increase in white-collar work; from 1953 to 1965, white-collar jobs in manufacturing increased by more than a million, while blue-collar production jobs declined by a million. The proportion of the work force engaged in manufacturing, meanwhile, declined while the proportion engaged in service industries rose to 60 percent.

The decline in the growth of blue-collar employment went along with a steady increase in worker productivity, which provided evidence that the technological improvements that U.S. industry began to introduce in the early 1950s were paying off. Automation allowed industries to do more with fewer workers. Although some industries suffered a terrific decline in employment from automation—railroads, steel, coal mining, oil refining—prosperity generated enough demand for labor in service industries that those who were displaced could find other work. In good times when consumer demand was high, as in 1965, industries could have automated productivity and still retain a great many workers, as in the auto industry. Still, automation limited demand for unskilled labor; the unskilled were therefore forced into the service sector—retail sales, personal services, tourism, entertainment, janitorial work, maintenance, and, finally, health care.

Although a high demand for labor increased wages faster in service industries than in manufacturing, especially where service work was unionized, these were portentous developments for the established cities. Defense-related production jobs were far more plentiful in Sunbelt cities, and thus the urban working class in the East and Midwest experienced a regional decline in the market for manufacturing labor. More important, automation allowed manufacturing to flee the cities along with the middle class. Because industries no longer required large pools of unskilled labor, they located plants according to new considerations. Suburbs offered attractive tax deals and cheaper land. Furthermore, most major cities followed Boston's lead and built some sort of outer highway ring that offered easy transportation. Some business leaders wanted their work to be close to where they now made their homes. Without doubt, some businesses felt driven out of the cities during the decade and became refugees from crime, vandalism, and declining services. Still others, the *Manpower Report of the President* concluded in 1971, moved to the suburban rings simply because others had done so. Whatever the motive, the trend was notable. Between 1960 and 1965, 62 percent of the nation's new industrial building was constructed outside the central cities, and the vast majority of new manufacturing employment, such as it was, went with it.

The relocation of manufacturing, combined with the declining growth of manufacturing employment, coincided with the arrival of a huge wave of rural migrants that staggered the inner cities. The people who most needed decent, unskilled work were least likely to live near such work. The whole process of deindustrialization weighed most heavily on the inner-city poor, and, because they were disproportionately represented among this group, African Americans felt the effects most harshly. True, African Americans made substantial economic gains after World War II. Black income rose much faster in the postwar period than did that of whites, and blacks made occupational gains as well. Throughout the sixties, blacks made greater relative gains in the skilled trades than did whites, and black women made important gains in professional, clerical, and managerial jobs. Overall, unemployment among African Americans dipped to below 8 percent in mid-decade.

Yet alongside these gains were signs of retrogression. Much of the improvement was statistical wizardry produced by the mere fact of migrating from appalling conditions in the rural South. Despite income growth, the black share of the national income did not change significantly. Relative to whites, the rate at which blacks moved into white-collar work actually fell from the midfifties to the midsixties. Black unemployment was almost always twice that of whites. The unemployment rate among certain sectors of the black population, especially young men aged 15 to 24 ranged as high as one in four; it had actually been lower than that for whites of the same age in the late 1940s. Over a brief period, that kind of dismal situation clearly discouraged many young men because the labor force participation of black men under age 30 began a long-term decline in the early sixties. Clearly, many were just giving up, and those who kept up the struggle continued to hold a disproportionately high number of the lowest level jobs, such as janitors or domestics, that promised next to nothing in the way of real upward mobility.

Perhaps this state of affairs would not have been cause for too much concern in cities of an earlier day. Other immigrant groups had also begun at the bottom. But the rungs that had been there for earlier immigrants had moved to the suburbs or had evaporated entirely. Education was therefore absolutely critical for black upward mobility; yet inner-city black children typically were forced into the worst schools. Alone among the immigrant groups, African Americans came into the cities at a time when industrial employment was disappearing. Bayard Rustin neatly summed the problem up:

> When the migration of Negroes to Northern and Western cities was at its height during World War II, factory jobs were available at decent wages. With the advent of advanced technology eliminating many semi-skilled and unskilled jobs, and with the movement of plants from the central cities to the suburbs . . . urban Negroes suffered rising joblessness or employment in low-paying service jobs.

Some observers rejected Rustin's claims that blacks faced an urban situation that was fundamentally different from that into which earlier immigrant groups came. Some scholars promulgated a whole line of argument stating that the urban crisis was the invention of romantic intellectuals. Edward Banfield, one of the most productive scholars from the Harvard–MIT Joint Center of Urban Affairs, went so far as to suggest that the urban crisis did not exist. For taking this view, Harvard's "young totalitarians" hounded him from his position. Banfield insisted that housing was better and more readily available than ever before; that the problems associated with the urban crisis—poverty, illiteracy, hunger, and so forth—were more prevalent in rural America than in the cities; and that what problems existed affected only a small minority of urban residents. Nor should it be alarming that most of that "small minority" were African Americans or Puerto Ricans. They were poor because, for the most part, they were but the latest of the many immigrant groups who came to the cities without skills, education, or money, and they would be the latest to work their way up into the mainstream. Banfield could only conclude that the urban crisis, such as it was, had been created out of impossibly high expectations. "Our performance is better and better," Banfield wrote, "but because we set our standards and expectations to keep ahead of performance, the problems are never any nearer to solution. . . . There is a danger that we may mistake failure to progress as fast as we would like for failure to progress at all."

Banfield was among a whole group of skeptics, which included Herbert Gans, Roger Starr, Nathan Glazer, and Daniel Patrick Moynihan, who by the end of the sixties were dubbed "neoconservatives." Although they were critics of the War on Poverty, the label does not describe them well; they were less conservative than complacent or optimistic that the day's urban problems were neither new nor comparatively severe. Starr, who took a post in the Nixon administration, argued that the free market, especially in housing, would do more to ease the urban crisis and help marginalized groups than anything the liberal state could dream up. Gans rounded out the theme of antiliberal thinking when he began to defend the sub-urbs. For most people, "suburbia means more housing space at less cost, a backyard and an up-to-date community—all of which make raising children significantly easier." "This urge for suburban life," he remarked, "is not limited to the middle class. . . ; the poor would leave the city as well if they could afford to go." To the optimists, the forces at work were as inexorable as the free market and the innocent desire for a healthy family environment, and no amount of intellectual hand-wringing, liberal guilt, or militant violence could change the course of metropolitan development. "For all the chorus of protest," wrote Raymond Vernon, one of Banfield's colleagues, "most Americans seem strangely unaroused. Each year, they buy a few hundred thousand more picture windows, seed a few hundred thousand more lawns. The decay of the central city barely concerns them."

The value of these arguments rested on the premise that the same natural process that had assimilated previous immigrants into the U.S. mainstream would continue to work for blacks. The flaw in the optimistic argument was that suburban-ization in the larger context of technological decentralization represented not a healthy adaptation but, as one writer put it early in the decade, "the withering away of the city." The postindustrial marketplace, the very force that neoconservatives assumed would revive the cities, was draining them of economic purpose. "The modern city," Don Martindale wrote, "is losing its external and formal structure. Internally it is in a state of decay while the new community represented by the nation everywhere grows at its expense. The age of the city seems to be at an end."

The Anti-City

It was possible to say that the city was not just withering away but that postmodern society was hostile to true urban life. Postmodern society, the philosopher and architectural critic Lewis Mumford maintained, was constructing the "anti-city": a vast glut of space filled with cement, asphalt, shopping malls, and suburbs that blurred the integrity of city after city. The anti-city, Mumford wrote, was a result of the United States' heedless acceptance of the automobile, the free market, and technological abundance. The dispersion of the city was not issuing in a revival of happy neighborhoods and a reconnection of people to the earth but rather was leading to the avoidance of human relationships and the destruction of mutual interdependence that the true city inherently demands. The anti-city had emerged as "an incoherent and purposeless urbanoid nonentity, which dribbles over the devastated landscape"; it was "the form that every modern city approaches when it forgets the functions and purposes of the city itself and uses modern technology only to sink to a primitive social level."

Mumford chose the term *anti-city* carefully and fully meant it to convey the underlying similarities between what was happening to the physical existence of the United States and the anti-art that was passing for high culture. Indeed, the younger architects and planners, Mumford perceived, had gotten from contempo-rary art the idea that "randomness, accident, deformation, fragmentation . . . have the same order of value as function, purpose, integration, health, moral character, or esthetic design." The anti-city reflected the avant-garde sensibility that "the only order possible is willful disorder. . . . If a chimpanzee, a psychotic, and a museum-qualified painter are equally capable of achieving a 'modern' painting, the forces that are now vomiting the wreckage of the city over the landscape are doubtless sufficient to produce the 'modern' form of the city." Whereas sixties artists had destroyed the integrity of cultural authority, the sixties developer was destroying the integrity of community; and as in the art world, this destruction had produced a formless freedom that left real power to the marketplace. The urban crisis was therefore another part of the United States' national incontinence, the only real cure for which, Mumford was sure, was not just the commitment to some political strategy or to economic equity but the recovery of moral will.

The Cities and the War on Poverty

Instead of the moral reaffirmation that Mumford had in mind, the urban crisis gave birth to the liberals' war against poverty, surely one of the most curious episodes of a most curious time. Convinced that the inner cities presented the single greatest domestic problem, sixties liberals proceeded to build a program that avoided com-monsense solutions in favor of social experimentation. Determined to achieve unconditional victory over poverty, they decided to fight the policy equivalent of guerrilla warfare instead of confronting the enemy directly. Put less metaphorically, sixties liberals decided that poverty was not primarily economic but cultural and political. Having come to see the whole host of urban problems as the result of a stodgy establishment that denied minorities and the poor participation in the affluent society, they designed a program that would attack the establishment, only to realize that they *were* the establishment. In attempting to deal with the urban crisis they excited expectations that they could not meet, encouraged political discontent that they could not quell, contributed to the Democratic party crisis of 1968, and solved next to nothing for their troubles.

The self-destructiveness of the liberal War on Poverty is all the more difficult to comprehend when we remember what superb politicians both Kennedy and John-son were. But, then, overt political motives did not play a dominant role in the program's creation. Kennedy believed he paid his dues to the civil rights movement with his "one tick of the pen." Martin Luther King, Jr., had yet to turn his attention to the North when Kennedy insiders began to formulate an antipoverty program. The New Frontiersmen evidently assumed that big-city mayors would jump at the chance to have more federal money, but only one, Detroit's Jerome Cavanagh, showed any enthusiasm for the program.

The New Frontier's Poverty Initiatives

The origins of the poverty program have to be traced to considerations outside of politics. A city boy himself, Kennedy, as we have seen, was attentive to urban problems. There is no reason to question the sincerity of the Kennedys' concern for the poor. If nothing else, it was another way for them to sympathize with outsiders and mock the Wasp establishment. Whatever other motives went into the poverty program, the Kennedy people had a straightforward desire to do good. Adam Yarmolinsky, a key member of the administration's domestic team and later one of Robert Kennedy's close advisors, recalled that the motives were "99 and 44/100 percent noblesse oblige. . . . This was entirely a matter of 'this is what we've got to do because we're good fellows.' "

If, as Yarmolinsky claims, there was a genuine concern about the downtrodden in the cities, the New Frontiersmen did not think poverty was a serious problem. They predictably saw poverty as a challenge that they could overcome with the right technique and the latest ideas. It is safe to say that their initial understanding of the issue came from Galbraith's *Affluent Society*. Because Galbraith convinced Kennedy that poverty was nothing more than a regionally specific "disgrace," Kennedy probably would have been content with the many social programs that he pushed in 1961 and 1962: the minimum-wage bill, the juvenile delinquency program, the job-training bill designed to ease technological displacement, and the accelerated urban renewal program. As long as poverty was understood as a festering pool in the nation's stagnant backwaters, the logical solution to it was a program like the 1961 Area Redevelopment Act, which aimed at directing business loans and other aid to depressed areas.

After becoming familiar with Michael Harrington's far more critical book, *The Other America* (1963), Kennedy concluded that poverty was a more urgent problem than Galbraith had maintained. Harrington agreed with Galbraith that U.S. poverty was contained in pockets, but he argued that the impoverished regions were huge and that perhaps as many as one-third of all Americans were poor. Working from that assumption, the president encouraged his domestic policy team to consider solutions. The poverty fighters came from several different places in the executive bureaucracy: a few were New Frontier foot soldiers; others came from the Bureau of the Budget, the Council of Economic Advisors, the Labor Department, and, most important, the Office of Juvenile Delinquency (JD). This last group was the most interesting and in time the most influential. None of the JD people had substantial political stakes in formulating the program. Their motives were, if anything, intellectual; that is, they had accepted, or in the case of JD's Lloyd Ohlin, they had done much to advance the prevailing social science theories about race, poverty, and social disorder. They were intellectuals in government, committed to their ideas, contemptuous of bureaucrats, and devoted to the cause of social reform. They were exactly the sort of people with whom bureaucrats can never rest easy, which is why the Kennedy brothers liked them.

The working theory behind the antipoverty program was that poverty was the product of culture. Anthropologist Oscar Lewis, in his study of the Mexican poor, coined the term *culture of poverty* to describe the collection of seemingly antisocial habits, behaviors, and attitudes that pervaded the lives of the poor. Criminality, violence, drug and alcohol abuse, spousal and child abuse, indifference to work and education were neither temporary nor natural; they were part of a subculture, created and sustained by the conditions of poverty, that provided, in however degraded a form, the rules of human interaction and even psychological security. The behavior that comprised the culture of poverty made it very difficult for the poor to blend into the mainstream, even if the opportunity presented itself.

Lewis invented a catchword more than a concept, for these ideas had become common in U.S. social science and were commonly accepted as well, in simplified form, by political liberals. In common usage, the culture of poverty became a shorthand means to account for why the black urban poor seemed increasingly poor while mainstream America enjoyed unparalleled affluence. Liberals did not want to concede the conservative charge that the poor were victims only of their own improvidence, incompetence, or corruption, and the culture of poverty helped counter that argument. The "pathological" state of the poor provided reasons why government should act, rather than why the poor should be ignored, and hence it provided the rationale for state activism.

Another reason why the culture-of-poverty concept was intriguing and powerful was that it defined poverty according to a population's abstract, even stereotypical, subcultural behavior. Defining poverty as a cultural rather than an economic condition gave rise to an expansive definition of what poverty was. Every serious observer of the day recognized that poverty in the United States was relative. But if poverty were a matter of cultural maladjustment, then urban blacks, juvenile delinquents, Appalachian and Hispanic migrants, practically everyone most vulnerable to the harshest parts of the urban crisis, might be considered poor and in need of help. Partly for this reason, the concept appealed most strongly to those New Frontiersmen whose interests lay outside the normal social programs, housing, employment, and the like, for it provided them with a justification for expanding their pet programs.

Generated by no pressing political needs, informed by a social-science concept that defined poverty as cultural rather than economic, the urban poverty program was, in a sense, contrived. It was, as Martin Rein once described it, "a program in search of a political constituency." Kennedy liberals knew as much too, and they therefore cautiously envisioned only a modest effort that would complement, rather than replace, the administration's other social programs.

The JD's Role

The foregoing all helps explain the Office of Juvenile Delinquency's central role in the War on Poverty. It was this office, rather than one of the bureaucracies more traditionally related to urban issues, that initiated the momentum and developed the unique strategies behind the poverty effort. Like the poverty program itself, JD was not part of any established bureaucracy. As the head of the program, David Hackett, stated in retrospect, "There was no constituency, there was no pressure, there was no interest in delinquency other than in professional organizations." Hackett personified what JD was about. As a prep student at the Waspish Milton Academy, he had befriended Robert Kennedy when no one else would, and Kennedy in turn brought his chum into an administration that expected to turn Wasp America on its ear. Hackett had no particular expertise in juvenile delinquency or anything else in government. He was sincere, loyal, and hard-working and had little patience for the bureaucratic fools who populated the government.

He was a good Kennedy man, and he went about his task accordingly. First, he discovered who the leading experts in the field of juvenile delinquency were and what they had to say. The most serious work was that of a group of renegades from the University of Chicago Sociology Department, especially Lloyd Ohlin and Richard Cloward. In *Delinquency and Opportunity* (1960), the authors argued that delinquency was not so much wrong as a violation of norms that the status quo had set; it was, they wrote, "behavior that violates some conventionally sanctioned set of social expectations." For those caught in the cycle of poverty and denied legitimate outlets and opportunities, the most important "norms" were set by their slum subcultures. Delinquents were rational young men engaged in a deviant sort of upward mobility within their gang or peer group. The upshot of Ohlin and Cloward's work was that delinquency was misguided energy that could be rechanneled into respectable paths if only the opportunities were there. Another assumption at work—unstated but a matter on which the activists were quite clear and practically united—was that delinquency was fundamentally entwined with poverty, and specifically with urban poverty among African Americans.

Hackett set in motion the juvenile program with a minuscule $2.1 million budget, which President Kennedy announced in May 1962 after a ten-minute meeting with Ohlin. The size of Hackett's program showed its experimental nature, but his eagerness, his ability to wrench more money out of the government, and the basic implications of the Ohlin–Cloward thesis all gave the program a life of its own. Hackett knew that his money would not last and that Congress was not about to give him more. So he placed staff members in various federal bureaucracies, where they were to siphon off funds toward the delinquency program. "Hackett's guerrillas," as they called themselves, were essentially "anti-bureaucrats," according to Daniel Patrick Moynihan, "living off the administrative countryside, invisible to the bureaucratic enemy but known to one another, . . . making off with the riches of established departments."

Like most guerrilla wars, Hackett's produced irregular results but succeeded just enough to keep the delinquency effort alive. He launched a series of small, cautious programs designed to test various approaches to the issue. Set up in sixteen different cities, the programs were based on the Ohlin–Cloward thesis that the poor were poor because they lacked the political savvy to secure opportunity. In other words, poverty was primarily a political and cultural problem, not an economic one. The consequences that followed from this position were momentous. First, the assumption was that the interests of local institutions—welfare agencies and traditional social-work institutions, schools, and city governments—and the interests of the poor were at odds and that the poor had to be organized so they could hold their own. Here was the thinking behind JD's "community-action" program.

Sometime in the fall of 1963, as the civil rights movement began to turn its attention from segregation to the general issues of employment and housing, Kennedy decided to develop a comprehensive antipoverty plan that he wanted to have in place by the 1964 election. He met with bureaucratic infighting and a notable lack of enthusiasm from his secretaries of Labor and Health, Education, and Welfare, even from Galbraith. The bureaucrats' lukewarm response left Kennedy's key economic advisor, Walter Heller, to seek counsel from Hackett's guerrillas, who were the only people in the administration doing anything specific about urban poverty and who were more than happy to oblige. By design or not, the activists found themselves strategically placed to shape any emerging legislation.

The Great Society's Poverty Program

Just as the administration began to sort the issue out, the president was assassinated, and the poverty program became the heart of Lyndon Johnson's Great Society. Indeed, it was Johnson who declared the "war on poverty." When he declared his allegiance to liberalism during his November 23 meeting with Heller (see Chapter 1), Johnson not only embraced the program but also characteristically proceeded to expand it. In January he accepted a report from Heller's Economic Advisory Council that called poverty a startling problem and urged $1 billion in new spending. Hoping to trade on the postassassination Kennedy mystique, Johnson appointed Sargent Shriver, a Kennedy in-law and the director of the successful Peace Corps, to formulate an ambitious urban policy and later to head the bureaucratic agency that administered the program. When he did so, Johnson dramatically altered the experimental nature of the program as Hackett's guerrillas had been devising it.

The mandate of the Shriver task force was as unfocused as it was wide. Shriver, aware that the new president simultaneously wanted something ambitious, glitzy, politically salable, and electorally helpful, generally aimed to do something about the urban crisis, particularly the inner-city ghettos. By all accounts, LBJ had in mind something like the New Deal programs that he had run in Texas in the 1930s, a sort of new National Youth Administration that would provide a bit of work in hard-pressed neighborhoods. It would not have hurt if, in the bargain, ghetto restlessness were eased or some money were to find its way to urban supporters. Johnson's only firm instructions to Shriver were to keep the program clean—in his words, to keep out "criminals, Communists, and cocksuckers."

Community Action

The only program at work, however, was JD's community-action program—the effort to organize the poor for political activity. Heller had already embraced community action, and although Shriver thought it would "never fly," as he told Yarmolinsky, he was a salesman willing to peddle whatever the activists put in his hands. Thus, the Economic Opportunity Act of 1964 was written to include a community-action component: the act called on cities to organize local agencies that would serve directly the particular needs of the local poor. Moreover, the local agencies were to include representatives of the poor in the decision-making process; the poor were to be guaranteed, in the now-famous phrase, "maximum feasible participation." When mixed into the expansive nature of the act, community action immediately became a part of urban politics. As Allan Matusow writes, "In one stroke Johnson escalated community action from an experimental program to precede the War on Poverty into the very war itself." Community action had its advantages: it was cheap; it traversed the entrenched bureaucracies; it could be sold as a means of empowering southern blacks; and it had the Kennedy sex appeal. Because it did not give money directly to poor people, the program could be defended as, in Sargent Shriver's words, "a hand up, not a hand out." Johnson defended the program on exactly these grounds when the Economic Opportunity Act was passed in August 1964. "Our American answer to poverty," he claimed, "is not to make the poor more secure in their poverty but to reach down and to help them lift themselves out of the ruts of poverty. . . . The days of the dole in our country are numbered." Even those who had ambitious plans like Warren C. Haggstrom, the Syracuse University professor of social work who administered one of the more controversial programs, defended community action as an innocuous and entirely American approach to poverty: "Ours is a philosophy of self-help," he explained.

But community action surely had its pitfalls. No one bothered to define what "maximum feasible participation" was, although Shriver, when pressed, had hinted that about one-third of any agency should comprise representatives of the poor. But who represented the poor? No one expected to hold local elections, where voters who qualified by virtue of their impoverishment would choose their leaders. These questions merely glossed over the radical ideas embedded within the act. It was assumed that the poor would stand up to established institutions, which meant, in practice, mostly Democratic local governments. In this fashion, the Democratic administration in Washington put itself in the business of fomenting organized opposition to its own power base.

This curious state of affairs developed because Johnson never thought through the logic of the program and because some activists expected the organized poor to join forces with, rather than fight against, Democratic mayors. There were also those insiders, such as Richard Boone, whose sympathies lay with the poor and not with the Democratic party and who wanted exactly this contentious result. The mayors, meanwhile, were dumbfounded that Lyndon Johnson, the most politically attuned of men, would sponsor such a program, but when community organizers bolstered by Office of Economic Opportunity (OEO) funds began to descend on their communities in 1965, they reacted vigorously and immediately. San Francisco's Democratic mayor, John F. Shelly, was convinced that community action was "undermining the integrity of local government." Authorities in Syracuse similarly charged that the local community-action project, which combined the talents of Saul Alinsky, the most notorious urban radical of the day, with the Ford Foundation and Syracuse University, was engaged in nothing less than Marxist revolution.

Without question, the biggest clash between OEO and urban government came in Chicago, where Mayor Daley decided that if the federal government was going to spend political cash in his town, it would have to go through him. The president was solicitous of the powerful mayor, and Shriver, who nurtured hopes of running for the Senate from Illinois or for governor of the state, could hardly afford to oppose Daley. Daley was so brazen in his domination of the program, however, that he drew widespread criticism, and OEO activists gently pleaded with him to allow real participation. In turn, Daley joined an angry group at the 1965 U.S. Conference of Mayors in St. Louis and denounced community action for "fostering class struggle." Only then did Johnson begin to sense the implications of community action, and in an effort at damage control, he dispatched Vice President Humphrey to reassure the mayors.

It was too late to prevent damage, for the program had raised the expectations of radicals, militants, anti-establishment social workers, and some urban poor. Shriver was bombarded by heated charges from local radicals and former activists alike that he was selling the program out. To Saul Alinsky, community action had become a form of "political pornography," in which funds were spent "as a form of political patronage." Poverty funds, Alinsky charged, were being used to "suffocate militant independent leadership," and the concept of maximum feasible participation had become "a fraud." The more the urban establishment refused to abide by maximum feasible participation, the more many programs became connected with or infused by black nationalism. In Oakland, the Black Panther party spun out of the community-action office, where the party's leader, Bobby Seale, had been working; in Harlem, the powerful congressman Adam Clayton Powell appointed a less than competent crony to head the agency, which eventually became such an administrative mess that fringe radicals were being paid to stay out of the way of programs that seemed to be working. In San Francisco, militants stormed the mayor's office and extorted $45,000 for summer youth employment. Whatever will for organizing the poor that was left in the political nexus connecting Washington with the cities, the infusion of black militancy into the program killed it by 1966.

A reasonable defense of community action could still be made. The activists were no doubt right to believe that the interests of the black poor ran against those of city hall. Real change necessarily required some change in the distribution of urban political power. Furthermore, why shouldn't radicalism pursue just such ends? Although there unquestionably were examples of poor administration, the program was new, its budget large, its mandate vague, and mistakes were inevitable. Congress squashed the effort before it had much of a chance to prove itself.

The real failure of community action was not that it rocked the boat but that, by design, it was rigorously indifferent to the basic sources of the urban crisis— suburban flight, housing segregation, and deindustrialization. By any reckoning, fighting poverty by proposing to organize the poor for diffuse and unspecified political action was a peculiar strategy. Their radicalized version of the culture of poverty led administration liberals to hope that politics, in and of itself, would have a cathartic effect on the poor, enlivening them, leading them to shed despair in exchange for productive lives—all of this when the real problem was the lack of decent jobs and affordable housing. The poor themselves sensed as much, for they were notoriously apathetic to the community-action efforts.

Problems in Defining Poverty

It was not as if there were no information on the problem. Instead, the program ignored most of what was known about poverty at the time. Not much scholarship existed on the problem when the effort began; in fact, Shriver's task force worked with a bibliography that ran less than two pages. After 1964, the study of poverty became such a dynamic growth industry among scholars, pundits, and policy types that the money spent on publishing, research, and conferences might have gone some distance toward eliminating poverty. The bulk of the work reached the not very surprising conclusion that poverty was an economic problem—namely, that many Americans, probably over 30 million, did not have enough money to obtain good housing, food, or education.

The Council of Economic Advisors (CEA) reached these figures when it calculated that an urban family of four needed at least $3,000 in annual money income to live. The CEA based its poverty level on rational assessments of costs, but still the figure was problematic. The cost of living varied from city to city; anyone whose income was $3,001 was officially defined out of poverty; some of those who lived under the level, mostly senior citizens living on social security, owned homes and other assets that surely meant they were not poor. The grave inadequacies of the poverty-level conception, therefore, provoked the obvious objection that poverty was relative. True destitution was rare in the United States, and where and when it did occur, it was certainly an idiosyncratic rather than a systemic matter. The American poor, as conservatives liked to point out, typically drove cars, watched television, and ate regularly. Moreover, the scholarship on poverty pointed out again and again that 70 percent of the poor were white, and while the rate of poverty was higher among African Americans, about 40 percent of whom met the definition, the majority of poor blacks lived in the South rather than in northern ghettos.

Conversely, if the rigid definition of poverty failed to account for the comfort of the modern American poor relative to the desperate poor of past eras, so, too, it failed to take note of how many Americans struggled to get by with incomes that were above $3,000 but far below affluence. By 1968, for example, the Bureau of Labor Statistics estimated that an urban family of four required $9,376 to live decently. But 69 percent of such families earned less than that; only 9 percent of Americans earned $15,000 or more.

Job Programs

If this was the nature of poverty, then the only logical solution was to redistribute wealth through progressive tax programs and public-works programs, a solution that both Kennedy and Johnson categorically rejected. Such an approach might have provided needed income, replaced the manufacturing jobs that were drying up, and avoided the explicitly racial character of community action. Yet the whole focus of the Economic Opportunity Act was set on urban blacks, whose objective interests called not for political organization but for fair housing, decent schools, and respectable jobs. The Economic Opportunity Act perversely contained very little that would produce economic opportunity.

When the evidence, political prudence, and the objective requirements of justice all recommended a job-producing program, why then did liberals fail to develop one? For their part, the New Frontiersmen assumed that economic growth would take care of whatever problems existed. According to Adam Yarmolinsky, the Shriver people made a "tactical decision" to emphasize community action over a jobs bill because they anticipated that the 1964 tax cut would generate new jobs that the poor could take if only they were prepared. The most aggressive proponent of an outright jobs bill, however, was Labor Secretary Willard Wirtz, a temperamental, old-line establishment sort who had none of the political finesse necessary to sell Johnson on such a program. In February 1964, both Shriver and Wirtz made the mistake of proposing a large-scale jobs program that would be based on sales-tax increases, only to have Johnson utterly ignore them.

The one jobs-related program that was launched turned bust: the Job Corps program, which Shriver himself insisted on running. The "family communist" among the Kennedys, Shriver wanted to do for the Job Corps what he had done for the Peace Corps. The Job Corps theoretically met Johnson's conceptions of a good program, inspired as it was by the Civilian Conservation Corps of the New Deal. The program was supposed to take needy young men out of the slums and teach them specific job skills in a healthy, disciplined environment. Shriver tried to enlist 10,000 young adults in the first year and 45,000 by 1966. The effort was hampered, however, by much administrative confusion, inadequate candidate screening, poor supervision, and poorer community relations. Some enlistees proved difficult to control, and riots, burglary, and sexual misconduct scarred the program's public reputation. Critics calculated that the Corps was spending more per year for each enrollee, $8,000 in 1967, than it cost to send a person to Harvard for a year. Smug congressmen began to refer to the camps as "country clubs for juvenile delinquents." Corps officials rightly pointed out that they were dealing with extremely difficult young people and that it was unfair to expect such students to master much of anything in a short time. One former Corps director offered to pay personally for any Job Corps enrollee whom Harvard accepted—he lost no money on the challenge. Simple mismanagement was behind much of the Corps' generosity, and the leadership, rather compromised by its own incompetence, could not afford a congressional fight to justify high costs.

The decade's most comprehensive and ambitious jobs program was proposed not by administration insiders but by Bayard Rustin, A. Philip Randolph, and the League for Industrial Democracy, who were searching for the means to cement their "coalition" movement. Their "Freedom Budget," first proposed in 1965, called on the Johnson administration to commit itself to full employment rather than to the political and cultural strategies of the War on Poverty. Administration policy, they wrote, had the "tendency to place *excessive* emphasis upon the personal characteristics of the poor" and threatened to "generate resentment and reaction by lifting expectations much more rapidly than they are being fulfilled." Instead, they recommended a massive public works program that spent an initial $100 billion and $300 to $400 billion up to 1975 in order to employ people in everything from building low-cost housing to education and health services. Full employment would mean 4.6 million new jobs in 1967, 9.3 million in 1970, and 16.6 million by 1975—so many that all areas and all people would benefit. The authors stressed how widespread and generalized the benefits of the Freedom Budget would be, but Rustin elsewhere put the case for its benefits to blacks in exactly the right context. "From the end of the nineteenth century up to the last generation," he wrote, "the United States absorbed and provided economic opportunity for tens of millions of immigrants." But the participants in the Great Migration of African Americans from the rural South "have entered an economy in which there is less and less need for unskilled labor [and] cannot be compared with these immigrants of old. The tenements which were jammed by newcomers were way stations of hope; the ghettos of today have become dead ends of despair."

It was truly a sign of the times that the Freedom Budget was met with cold indifference in Washington and hostility from black militants. The black militants dismissed it as one more "reform," this one drawn up by "Mr. Sleeping Car Porter," as Eldridge Cleaver contemptuously called Randolph. The Johnson administration believed Rustin was asking for too much money, given the escalating costs of the Vietnam War.

Nixon's Poverty Policies

Ultimately, Richard Nixon came closer than either of the liberal presidents to redistributing wealth. In part because of his own intellectual and cultural insecurities, Nixon brought into his administration the maverick liberal Daniel Moynihan, whose pet scheme by the late sixties was the guaranteed annual income, a negative income tax that would provide cash grants to citizens on the basis of income. Given the real options for reducing poverty, Moynihan explained to the Ribicoff Committee in 1967 that "income maintenance" was cheaper and more efficient than full employment and sustained retraining. "We are the only industrial democracy in the world that does not have a family or children's allowance, and we are the only industrial democracy whose streets are filled with rioters each summer. We seem to be unable to recognize that what it means to be poor is not to have enough money."

The Nixon White House toyed with the guaranteed-income plan for reasons that had little to do with any desire to help the poor. The program was attractive, as Nicholas Lemann has shown, because it would reduce or replace the welfare system, and it required no commitment to the messy business of racial integration. Moynihan may have hoped that the program would stem the flow of black migrants from the South, for it would eliminate the economic incentive behind the trek. Nixon was no fan of government social initiatives, but the guaranteed income gave him a trump card to use against his imaginary enemy, the snotty liberal who treated him as a rube. This was his reason for bringing Moynihan in to begin with. As it was, Nixon shed no tears when the plan twice failed to get through Congress, where southerners and welfare-rights organizations joined forces to knock it down.

Burn, Baby, Burn

It is possible that a proposal like the Freedom Budget would have addressed poverty, put a brake on the hemorrhaging of the cities, and eased racial tensions as well. It probably would have done little to ease metropolitan segregation, but the serious needs of African Americans—jobs and housing—would have met some redress. At the same time, it is difficult to see how even the best government program could have saved the cities from exhausting their traditional functions. The anti-city generated no compelling political or economic imperative for well-off Americans to support even the minimal programs of the Great Society, much less the best of programs.

Indeed, the lesson of the recurring riots within inner-city black communities, if not the lesson of urban life in the sixties altogether, was that the cities could be written off to indifference. Contrary to the conclusions that government review committees invariably reached, the riots were not simple cause-and-effect episodes. They were varied and multifaceted results of the entire urban crisis, violent flares fired off by the careening descent of the cities. The simple explanation that racism and poverty generated the riots cannot stand against the clear evidence that it was not the most impoverished or racist cities that had riots. Instead, the causes included everything from unemployment to racism to neighborhood overcrowding to inescapable ghetto squalor to a mysterious stranger called "the new ghetto man."

The Heightened Expectation Theory for the Riots

The most complete explanation for the unrest held that the Great Society and the civil rights movement generated rising expectations among urban blacks, and when those expectations were continuously frustrated, especially among the young, tensions rose. Solid, though general, evidence rests behind this explanation. It accounts for why riots broke out in places and among people who were objectively not the most hard-pressed. Los Angeles, for example, liked to boast that it was the best place in the nation for blacks to live, and if one looked at the city's expansive black middle class that claim was not idle. Detroit was governed by one of the nation's most progressive administrations, had made extensive use of War on Poverty money, and had a buoyant economy. Plainfield, New Jersey; Buffalo, New York; Cambridge, Maryland; Dayton, Ohio: none of these cities was the worst example of poverty and racism, but each experienced serious rioting. The most riot-prone areas tended to be located between the "ancient, emptying ghetto cores" and middling neighborhoods, as one study found, areas populated by "people with intense expectations who found the relative deprivation gap widening when it should have diminished."

Heightened expectations not only accounted for why relatively decent areas witnessed riots but explained individual motivation as well. The most common rioter, according to many observers, was a social type dubbed "the new ghetto man." Relatively young, better educated than many of his neighbors, and typically employed, the new ghetto man was a son of the urban ghetto rather than a migrant from the rural South. Studies done on behalf of the Kerner Commission, which ultimately accepted the new ghetto man theory, found that 74 percent of the rioters in Detroit and Newark had been raised in the North, a slightly larger proportion than their nonrioting neighbors. Over 90 percent of the rioters in those cities had received some high school education—again a higher proportion than nonrioters. Unemployment was also lower among them. The new ghetto man had listened to the liberal promises of social justice only to see precious little change. As the Kerner Commission concluded, he "feels strongly that he deserves a better job, . . . takes great pride in his race, . . . and is substantially better informed than Negroes who were not involved in the riots." It was a prototypical "new ghetto man" who explained to Robert Coles that he could no longer share the values of his aunt, a migrant to Boston who raised him and whom he loved dearly: "All the time my aunt used to say that: be good, be real good. You know what she meant? She meant to do whatever they tell you, the white teachers and the white police and the white landlord and the white store people. Black people live here, but it's the white who own us. They'll always own us until we stop them—and that means it'll come to a fight."

The experience of such young men bore out one of the most oft-stated realities of ghetto life. Ghetto residents did not compare themselves to other poor people, either over time or in other places, and the young ghetto residents did not find solace in comparing their conditions to the conditions their parents had endured in the segregated South. Kenneth Clark described their embittered perspective at the outset of his famous work, *Dark Ghetto* (1963), by insisting that "the residents of the ghetto are not themselves blind to life as it is outside of the ghetto. They observe that others enjoy a better life, and this knowledge brings a conglomerate of hostility, despair, and hope. . . . The discrepancy between the reality and the dream burns into their consciousness." When blacks considered their housing, employment, and educational situations, they compared their lot with what middle-class life offered, and the grievances they aired during the upheavals testified to this sense of relative deprivation.

The Great Society promised some relief for this keen sense of injustice, and its failure to pay off undoubtedly increased frustrations. Every riot was infused with a political edge, with some participants determined to shape the violence into a revolt against the white establishment. The Newark riot especially exhibited the political characteristics of classic mob violence. Rioters spared black-owned businesses and refrained from arson, which in other riots had destroyed the homes of black residents. Watts, meanwhile, contained elements of class antagonism between ghetto residents and upwardly mobile blacks, and rioters gave established black leaders, including Martin Luther King, Jr., a rough handling when they called for peace.

Yet, as substantive an explanation as it is, the heightened-expectation theory fails to account for the complexities behind urban violence. To begin with, it cannot explain why some people rioted and others did not—and it is important to appreciate that even in the largest outbreaks, the vast majority of neighborhood residents did not riot. Ultimately, the situations of rioters and nonrioters were similar, and furthermore, many of the studies relied on examining arrestees, the

In August 1965 National Guard soldiers assist firefighters in a battle against fires set by arsonists in riot-torn Watts, Los Angeles.
[UPI/Bettmann Newsphotos]

vast majority of whom had been arrested for tame curfew violations rather than for some act of violence.

Other Causes of the Riots

What determined whether or not a person participated in a riot was as varied as the rioters themselves. Young men participated to a much greater extent than young women, and certainly young male aggressiveness played a role. In his comprehensive study of Detroit, Sidney Fine shows that many rioters simply got caught up in the sheer exuberance of the moment and rioted for the "joy" of it. Some of the more carefully controlled studies found, in contrast to the Kerner Commission, that the sense of deprivation was not particularly high among rioters. As Fine writes, "although the arrestees appraised their overall condition something less than favorably, . . . they were not, on the whole, a despairing lot." Nor can the conditions of the ghetto explain the actual riot, because so many of the area's residents remained behind locked doors, feared for their own security and safety, and subscribed to law-and-order attitudes that would have made George Wallace blush. The Detroit riot, Fine concludes, was spontaneous and accidental and was caused primarily by the general tension between police and Twelfth Street residents.

Still, accumulated general grievances—racial, economic, political, the urban crisis in its totality—caused the riots. Whether relatively healthy or not, cities from

Detroit to Cambridge had experienced the process of urban disintegration. In Los Angeles, for example, the inner-city areas had become increasingly crowded and more segregated from the mid-1950s to the great conflagration of 1965. Watts was 90 percent black, and nearby Avalon 96 percent. Without doubt, segregation resulted from heavy redlining: FHA loans in Los Angeles were awarded to only about 1,200 buyers a year in minority neighborhoods, in a market of about 180,000 potential homes. Of the 330,000 new units built in the Detroit metropolitan area between 1950 and 1960, only 3 percent had been made available to blacks. Other than one large project that isolated blacks near white working-class neighborhoods, Dayton's black community was confined to the city's west side. Buffalo committed itself heavily to slum clearance, but in the ten years before its riot in 1967, construction lagged some 2,000 units behind demolitions. Although the riots ran their course during good economic times, unemployment in riot areas ran as high as Watts's rate of 34 percent. In Detroit where unemployment was very low, blacks still worked mostly in low-skilled jobs. The city, working in conjunction with the state and the auto manufacturers, organized a model job-training program that was hailed as the best in the world and that primarily served African Americans. But even in a city with an apparently firm job base, there was not enough demand to soak up the recipients of job training; 44 percent of those unemployed at the time of the riot had been through some training program.

When a riot erupted, it was usually in response to some specific event or a specific grievance. The single most important, frequent, and notorious spark for unrest was local police action. Some specific police action set off the riots in Harlem, Watts, Newark, and Detroit. Police behavior in inner-city communities constituted the foremost grievance for African Americans, according to the Kerner Commission. The police neither protected nor served the black community. Opinion polls showed that blacks were every bit as concerned with "law and order" as whites, but their concern was far more real than the paranoia of suburbanites. The police, who may well have been understaffed and overworked in inner-city precincts, were routinely inefficient in meeting the needs of black residents, and at the same time routinely harassed and occasionally brutalized them. It is unfortunately easy to pick out horror stories: the shooting of an eight-year-old boy in Los Angeles; the killing of a Detroit prostitute stubbornly resisting arrest—each community could tell one. Police departments traditionally had been vehicles for the employment of lower-class white ethnics, the sort of men whose economic vulnerability made them notoriously racist. Police power, moreover, was never given up without a fight. Widespread efforts to form civilian review boards usually incurred the opposition of police unions and political windbags alike, even though such inner-city demands were reasonable and moderate.

The riots were also, to some extent, reactions against the intrusion of authority in the form of white police into the inner city. For this reason, many analysts wanted to see them not as riots but as "revolts," self-conscious outbreaks of violence with clear political ends. Black militants and white radicals took the riots as proof of the "colonial" nature of the ghetto. According to this analogy, the ghetto stood in relation to white society exactly as colonies to imperial powers: they were sources of cheap and exploitable labor; what resources they had were extracted for the benefit of the status quo; and, finally, they were deprived of any genuine political independence.

There was a certain persuasiveness to this view, particularly at a time when the cult of the anti-establishment guerrilla and left-wing affection for the Third World were at their height. Black militants, whose black power ideology was rooted substantially in the messages of Black Muslim separatism, saw themselves as cadres in the Third World revolution. White radicals, preoccupied with the Vietnam War, easily imagined, as Tom Hayden did, that "American foreign policy differs very little in essentials from the domestic colonial policy." And radicals of both races embraced the analogy in the optimistic expectation that ghetto residents would be as successful at revolution as the Cubans and the Vietnamese had been. Even the Kerner Commission accepted a sanitized version of this view in its lengthy and much-publicized report, which itself was a strange mix of impressive data gathering, political symbolism, moral evasion, and liberal self-flagellation. "What white Americans have never fully understood—but what the Negro can never forget—is that white society is deeply implicated in the ghetto. White institutions created it, white institutions maintain it, and white society condones it." The "basic conclusion" of the report was that "our nation is moving toward two societies, one black, one white—separate and unequal."

To come to such a conclusion was no small feat. Doing so demanded that the commissioners ignore the many urban problems that their own abundant data helped bear out. While the United States' racism was indeed implicated in the urban crisis, it was so in ways that could be addressed through intelligent reform, such as through federal housing policy, and in other ways that only a fairer distribution of wealth could address.

The premise, shared by liberals and radicals alike, that the ghetto was sustained by "white institutions" grossly oversimplified reality. Ghetto residents legitimately complained about paying high rent for substandard housing and about price-gouging by food merchants, but slum landlords were not often representatives of "white institutions." They were more frequently sleazy characters like Manny Gelder, the typical lower east side landlord whom Richard Elman writes about in The Poorhouse State (1966). Ghetto grocers were overwhelmingly small independents whose costs were higher no matter what their location but whose prices were raised even more by the high insurance and theft losses that were part of doing business in the ghetto. Elman found ghetto grocers who survived only by extending credit and then fighting with welfare agencies in order to collect from defaulting customers. Caught, Elman writes, "in a backlash of wretchedness," some grocers had to push their wives on welfare.

By singling out racism as the cause of the urban crisis, the Kerner Commission seized on a dramatic theme but embedded the crisis in the context of race relations, where it was most likely to evoke heated emotion and least likely to yield real solutions. Both the Kerner report and the radical view of inner cities as colonies failed to come to grips with the essential nature of the urban crisis. The logic of the postmodern economy made it possible for corporations to do business without exploiting unskilled labor because they needed less and less of it. Tom Hayden waved off this objection in a flight of apocalyptic fantasy that was so characteristic of the late New Left: "In the old forms of colonialism, brutality rarely became genocidal because the colonists needed the slaves for production; but in a new form in which slaves are economically useless, what is to prevent genocide when the colonist becomes irritated by the slaves' demands?"

Even a cynical conclusion in retrospect would have to conclude that genocide was evidently too much trouble. The Kerner report's self-righteous denunciation of white racism missed utterly what genuinely distinguished the sixties ghetto from its predecessors: far from being an impoverished appendage of the mainstream, the ghetto was the repository of society's economic outcasts, increasingly isolated and on the verge of becoming a world of its own. The moral crime inherent in the urban crisis was not racist exploitation but sheer indifference, and the riots, which accomplished little save provoking a great many government review committees and giving work to a great many social scientists, testified to that indifference by their flailing impotence.

CHAPTER 8

Beyond the Melting Pot

The process of suburbanization, and the urban crisis generally, stretched and attenuated community life. Both as a defense against the destruction of community and as a form of adjustment to post-modern society, Americans began to identify themselves as parts of national communities that depended not on proximity or interdependence but on self-identification. These new communities provided some means for group advancement and, because they were supposedly culturally distinct, protected their members from becoming part of the undifferentiated mass of consumer society.

As a means of collective self-protection, movements based on ethnic consciousness grew first among working-class or impoverished people—the Black Muslims and Cesar Chavez's Chicano farm-workers' movement, for example. Yet because group identification was the key to involvement in liberal interest-group politics, ethnic consciousness proved valuable for middle-class organization and promotion. By the late sixties, cultural nationalists, whether African, Italian, Polish, or even Native, tended to be middle-class and professional people or were aspiring to be. In fact, for some people, political organization was itself a way to move into the middle class. The "rise of the unmeltable ethnics" produced a subtle paradox. Those who most loudly proclaimed their cultural distinctiveness and announced their refusal to "melt" were often middle-class people fully engaged in the process of political and economic assimilation. Conversely, self-conscious cultural nationalism had less of a hold on those people who remained most rooted in older communities, mostly in the ethnic working-class enclaves, where some genuine cultural distinctiveness remained.

Did the Wasps Decline?

The 1960 presidential election, in the person of John Kennedy, brought an endorsement of the United States' ethnic diversity. Kennedy overcame the handicap of being an Irish Catholic in a political system supposedly dominated by Anglo-Saxon Protestants, but he did so only by renouncing any political allegiance to the Church. In contrast, his ethnic heritage was not much of a handicap. If Catholics were a minority, they were a sizable one that voted regularly and that was not put off by Kennedy's assertion of independence from the Vatican. If he qualified his Catholicism, he did not attempt to make himself less Irish, less the immigrant.

Kennedy, in fact, had been among various congressmen in the 1950s who worked to overhaul the national immigration restrictions that since 1924 had based quotas on national origins. In arguing for a new policy, Kennedy complained about the poorly coordinated set of laws that oversaw immigration. He also argued that the national-origins policy was based on Anglo-Saxon attempts to maintain ethnic dominance. This interpretation was surely accurate, but it is a rather interesting one for a presidential aspirant to make.

Much as he had symbolized resurgent idealism, Kennedy inaugurated a wave of ethnic consciousness that repudiated the melting pot as a national ideal and denied White Anglo-Saxon Protestant (Wasp) cultural and moral authority. Indeed, the repudiation of cultural authority had an ethnic component to it from the first. In the same way that older cultural standards were falling, so too was Wasp supremacy on the decline. As a cultural figure, the Wasp had grown awfully shabby by 1960. He had been aging, not so much gracefully as imperceptibly; when the sixties hit, his cultural authority shriveled up. His traditional authority had always rested on his claims that he represented reason and maturity in public life, but the sixties culture dethroned both reason and maturity as virtues. His authority was built on the acceptance of certain moral standards, but his own children (or more accurately, perhaps, his grandchildren) defied those standards. He was a lover of the arts and a patron of artists, but artists sneered at his tastes and sought patronage from philistines (though museums scrambled for his collections when he finally died). He was formally religious, but God was dead. He liked to think of himself as racially enlightened and wanted to help "Negroes," but black nationalists mystified him and Malcolm X terrified him. Most unnerving of all, it seemed as though the last loyalists to the Wasp ethic of work and self-discipline were working-class and lower-middle-class whites. Almost embarrassed by this loyalty, the Wasp turned on the working class with a vengeance, and the bewildered working class turned to demagogues.

The decline of the Wasp seemed so evident that some observers considered it the main explanation behind the social chaos of the times. "The WASP was the landlord of our culture," the journalist Peter Schrag wrote, "and his values, with rare exceptions, were those that defined it: hard work, perseverance, self-reliance, puritanism, the missionary spirit, and the abstract rule of law." This predominance ended in the sixties, Schrag maintained, in part because "the central, integrating ethic of American life," the developmental ethic of the western pioneer, had been exhausted. Vietnam, hopefully the last U.S. missionary effort, signaled that exhaustion, for the war destroyed the Wasp illusion that the United States had a special mission to humanity. The civil rights movement, black separatism, self-conscious Irish Catholics in South Boston, and Wasp children who renounced their heritage made it painfully clear that the Wasp was no longer the nation's cultural master. He could not even prevent ethnic studies from displacing Western Civilization from college curricula. The Wasp was a sissy, and his declining self-confidence and sense of mastery only further eroded his social authority.

It was a sign of how badly eroded the influence of the traditional American elite was that the term Wasp came into usage in the first place, for it implied that his was just another ethnic group. By the end of the decade, the term was so common that it lost its capitalization and usually appeared simply as "Wasp" rather than WASP. In 1964 E. Digby Baltzell was the first to use the term in his work, *The Protestant Establishment*, and there he referred to the nation's traditional ruling class, which he believed faced certain decline because it refused to accept new blood into its ranks. The establishment continued to gather in its clubs, board-rooms, and public offices but faced a "moral crisis," according to Baltzell, because of its exclusion of Jews and African Americans. In order to adjust to "our heterogeneous and rapidly changing world," Baltzell wrote, the establishment itself had to become more heterogeneous.

Undeniably, Peter Schrag was right about the collapse of a central American ethic and the transformation of culture. The question, however, is whether this "decline of the Wasp" was more than a transformation of moral codes and values, whether in fact the traditional American elite lost genuine power. For all of the obvious cultural change, there is little evidence that the Wasp lost economic status. As part of its 1970 survey of the United States' 500 largest corporations, for instance, *Fortune* magazine found that Wasp rule remained firm. Nearly 80 percent of the corporate chief officers were Protestant. *Fortune* also reported that 35 percent graduated from Ivy League colleges and over 40 percent from other private schools. Although many of them had voted against Barry Goldwater in 1964, most continued to identify themselves as Republicans. The vast majority were of "comfortable middle- and upper-middle-class" backgrounds, and nearly half were sons of men who themselves had been heads of businesses.

The Wasps, meanwhile, continued to dominate other institutions. They ran museums, for instance, even though they supposedly were being pushed out by the destruction of artistic convention. They presided over the universities—only one major nonreligious university was run by a Catholic president—and their dominance was unshaken by campus unrest. They led the charitable foundations.

The Wasps were no longer a genuine ruling class, for they had lost political and cultural dominance. Yet it is all the more interesting that, as G. William Domhoff concluded in his late-decade study of power in the United States, the Wasps still controlled "a disproportionate amount of the country's wealth" as well as the nation's institutions. Given this persistence, one has to wonder whether all of the talk concerning the Wasp's decline did not do more to obscure, and in so doing sustain, his economic and institutional power.

The term itself became increasingly obscure as it became associated with culture and ethnicity instead of economics. In Baltzell's usage, Wasp was a synonym for the establishment, the only usage that made any real sense. Yet the term's meaning was transformed over time. Where once the Wasp was considered a prudish snob, by mid-decade he was painted as a cultural imperialist who demanded that all other Americans shed their ethnic heritage and embrace his. In this definition, the Wasp became nearly everyone's enemy, from intellectuals of Eastern European descent to black nationalists. Several years later, as the politics of ethnicity intensified, Wasp came to mean any white American Protestant. But white Protestants had never been ethnically coherent. They may have been Northern and Western Europeans, which meant that they were Boston Yankees—and Swedes and Scots and Finns and Welsh and Scandinavians. They may have been Protestant, and among them genteel New York Episcopalians figured prominently—as did liberal Presbyterians and conservative Baptists and isolated Amish and idiosyncratic Mormons. There was no logical precision to a term that ignored the regional and historic differences between New England's white ruling class and Birmingham segregationists. The redefinition of the Wasp as an ethnic type was so sloppy that when liberal activists discovered—much to their surprise—that the impoverished mountaineers of Appalachia were actually Anglo-Americans, they had to try to convince these objects of pity that they actually were an oppressed and distinct "minority." It startled others to learn that the white Protestant economic elite had spent much of the nineteenth century oppressing the white Protestant working class. As one observer wrote, in this guise the Wasp "is not a very clear target, much less a scapegoat."

Black Nationalism and the Quest for Community Control

We cannot account for the rise of ethnic consciousness, therefore, by suggesting that it emerged to fill the void left by the Wasps' decline. The most intense expressions of ethnicity grew out of class-based movements and were responses to economic difficulties and social disarray more than cultural change.

The connection between ethnic politics and economic conditions is most clearly seen in the development of black nationalism, which in its initial form took root mostly among working-class people intent on creating a stable, respectable society in the midst of ghetto life. In the urban environment, working-class blacks were already in the "melting pot." The absence of formal segregation was small comfort to people vulnerable to the ravages of the larger society—unemployment, underemployment, market-driven forms of discrimination. They had their churches, their "blocks," and other semblances of community, but in the cities, working-class blacks did not control their schools, they did not have an independent economic base, and they lacked much control at all over their communities. It was out of this atmosphere that black nationalism, in its many guises, sprang, here where its principles of race-pride and local control provided a potential basis for the reconstitution of community life.

The Nation of Islam

In terms of its class basis, inner-city character, and appeal, the Nation of Islam should be understood as the best example of black nationalism. Although the Nation predated the sixties, it enjoyed tremendous growth in notoriety, if not in actual size, during that decade. First organized in depression-era Detroit, the Muslims were linked to northern urban blacks. In thoroughly rejecting white claims to racial superiority, the Muslims called on their faithful to renounce the "ghetto lifestyle" that they believed blacks had been duped into adopting in exchange for an austere life of self-reliance, the patriarchal family, and avoidance of drugs, alcohol, premarital sex, and buying on credit. They advocated a race-conscious version of the traditional American work ethic, which led some observers to say that they were "more like the white 'old American' than any other subgroup in America." Their followers were originally rural migrants, but the proportion of urbanites grew steadily after World War II; they were, as C. Eric Lincoln describes them, "domestic and factory workers, common laborers and the like," and they were predominantly young males, the most marginalized of ghetto inhabitants. The Muslims drew from the population that had come to symbolize the ghetto, and while the rigors of Muslim life surely limited their appeal, they were able to organize sixty-nine congregations in twenty-seven cities by 1960.

After 1960, Lincoln writes, the Nation of Islam had "its ups and downs," and even at its high-water mark was never large. Still, the Muslims provided an intangible psychological lift to working-class blacks. According to Lincoln, acquiring a sense of community was the foremost reason why people joined the Muslims, but even those who never joined learned from the Muslims to respect their race. The Nation insisted on a strict and well-ordered patriarchal family life—they understood what the ghetto was doing to black men and the black family well before the infamous Moynihan Report described the beginnings of family breakdown—and offered a means by which black men could reclaim a sense of worth. Taken together, these strengths made the Muslims a prominent part of some inner-city lives.

The Muslims gained their greatest fame through Malcolm X, the minister of Harlem's Mosque Seven. Born Malcolm Little and raised in Lansing, Michigan, as a teenager he moved to Boston and then went to Harlem where he lived as a hustler. He substantiated the Cloward-Ohlin theory of juvenile delinquency: denied legitimate opportunity, he learned to make the most of illicit ones. His formal education ended at the eighth grade, but he was intellectually gifted, energetic, and uncompromising—attributes that Islam, to which he converted while in prison for burglary, shaped and disciplined. He understood his constituency like few others and was therefore an effective missionary. "The ghetto people knew that I never left the ghetto in spirit," he wrote in his *Autobiography*, "and I never left it physically more than I had to. I had a ghetto instinct . . . , and I could speak and understand the ghetto's language." It did not hurt his effectiveness that New York, publicity capital that it is, provided the forum he needed to develop a wide reputation for his relentless attacks on white society.

Particularly after he appeared in Mike Wallace's 1959 television documentary, "The Hate That Hate Produced," Malcolm X discovered that publicity was two-edged. It brought notoriety but also enemies; it disseminated his message but often distorted it. Subtlety not being one of his strong points, he outraged the mainstream when he mocked middle-class blacks as Uncle Toms, civil rights liberals as hypocrites, and whites in general as "blue-eyed devils." Most unnerving to liberals was his rejection of integration as a ruse whereby whites satisfied their consciences by allowing a few "integration-mad Negroes" to eat at their country clubs or live in their neighborhoods. Instead of integration, he argued that "the American black man should be focusing his every effort toward building his *own* businesses, and decent homes for himself." Economic self-determination based on the individual work ethic was not a dangerous, radical program, but the media made Malcolm a black counterpoint to King and in so doing gave far less attention to what he said than how he said it.

While he remained the most famous early black nationalist, his break from Nation leader Elijah Muhammad in 1963 and his famous pilgrimage to Mecca fostered a growing universalism. As the story goes, Malcolm discovered that Eastern Islam was a cosmopolitan faith, which included people of all races and nationalities. The trip marked his maturation, his awareness of a world beyond Harlem where Islam's universality proved powerful enough to gather distinct cultures in a harmonious common faith. He noticed "that people who looked alike drew together and most of the time stayed together. This was entirely voluntary; there was no other reason for it." He resolved that "when I returned home I would tell Americans this observation: that where true brotherhood existed among all colors, where no one felt segregated, where there was no 'superiority' complex, no 'inferiority' complex— then voluntarily, naturally, people of the same kind felt drawn together by that which they had in common."

The keys to employing these observations to bring practical change for Malcolm's constituents remained more economic and political than cultural, and if his beliefs softened, his strategies changed very little. When he formed the Organization of Afro-American Unity (OAAU) in the summer of 1964, he brought his pragmatic focus together with his economic radicalism. Part of the OAAU's rationale was to build a distinctly black political organization that would work like a traditional interest group. "U.S. politics is ruled by special interests and lobbies," he wrote, every one of which pushed its way into Washington and seized favors; some, like farmers, even got their own departments. "There ought to be a Pentagon-sized Washington department dealing with every segment of the black man's problems," but obviously blacks were going to have to build pressure through their own efforts. "The demanding voice of the black lobby should be in the ears of every legislator who votes on any issue." The "black lobby" would not be integrationist or integrated. Malcolm continued to distrust whites who were eager to join black political organizations; they reminded him of the whites who would sneak uptown to partake of Harlem's illicit pleasures. Sincere white people would instead work on their own and, in so doing, "actually will be working together" with blacks.

Black Power

It became a stock assumption among black nationalists that Malcolm X was just about to divulge his systematic plans for black America when he was assassinated in 1964. This was a romantic hope, however, driven by the ongoing inability of black nationalists to define just what it was they wanted and how they were going to get it. The nationalist movement—black power—that emerged after Malcolm X's death and that presented itself as an alternative to King's movement was plagued from the beginning by political splits and the very vagueness of goals. The nationalists put themselves forward as the champions of the black masses, but the uncomfortable fact was that black nationalism was more appealing to the black middle class in most forms other than the Nation of Islam. It was, in this sense, the alter ego, rather than the true opposite, of integration.

The difficulties of laying out a program can be seen in Stokely Carmichael's attempts, along with Charles V. Hamilton, to define a nationalist strategy in 1967. In *Black Power* (1967), the two maintained that, although some united front between poor whites and blacks was eventually possible, blacks had to reject assimilation into the white middle class, move away from the liberal coalition, and redefine themselves through cultural revival and historical exploration. Only then could they participate with confidence in an "open society." Like Malcolm X, Carmichael and Hamilton were convinced that psychological liberation was the first task of black power, and it was to be followed by a movement from the masses, which could not be clearly defined because it was still in the making. The best they could do was to point to some examples of what seemed like welcomed developments—New York parents demanding "community control" of schools or voters in Chicago aligning in racial solidarity to wrest control of their ward from Mayor Daley's hands.

Cultural Nationalism

That Carmichael and Hamilton avoided a blueprint for black nationalism is not a criticism, except that the movement badly needed a core of ideas to keep its cultural and economic wings in healthy tension. By late decade, separatist ideas of cultural nationalism began to eclipse talk of economic change, in part because affecting African folkways was so much easier. Cultural radicalism became radical fashion, with many aspirants to publicity or power attempting to outdo their competitors. In this spirit, Ron Karenga, a pudgy southern Californian, led a spiritual back-to-Africa movement that fed the growing interest in the Swahili language and, among other things, introduced "Kwanzaa" as a traditional African holiday. Black Studies programs began to appear on college campuses, either in response to students' demands or in fear of them; the programs typically included African history and language courses. On the popular level, African dress and natural hair styles emerged in trends that paralleled the loosening of styles among young whites. "Black people," as one activist wrote, "were addressing each other as 'brother' when they passed in the streets; 'soul food' restaurants became a matter of community pride; 'black history' the all-consuming topic, Malcolm X the authoritative source. Even seven-year-old black children seemed to know a phrase or two of Swahili."

The drive for cultural independence arguably gave rise to the greatest outpouring of ethnically conscious art in U.S. history, even greater than that of the Harlem Renaissance. For that matter, the movements in African-American literature and poetry that were inspired by black nationalism represented the most coherent body of writing since the nineteenth-century transcendentalists. Although writers, especially Ralph Ellison, Richard Wright, and James Baldwin, had been an integral part of the modern civil rights movement, the late sixties witnessed a flowering of younger, ardently nationalistic talent. LeRoi Jones had by then changed his name to Imamu Amiri Baraka and had moved from Harlem to Newark, where he established a black culture center; another poet, Nikki Giovanni, gained fame with a collection, *Black Feeling, Black Talk, Black Judgment* (1970), dedicated both to race-consciousness and violent rhetoric. Ishmael Reed began to ply his unique style of satire and commentary, and Toni Morrison began her extraordinary publishing career with a modest novel, *Lula* (1973). The encouragement cultural nationalism gave to black artists cannot be overestimated, not least because in rejecting the cultural aspects of white domination, the nationalist movement among writers offered one of the best examples of how the new culture might be redefined along democratic lines.

As a cultural movement, however, nationalism contained huge flaws. The identification with Africa took little account of the vast discrepancies—both historical and contemporary—between Africa and African Americans. Pan-Africanism, the union of the world's black people, never succeeded past the level of rhetoric. Karenga's movement helped people learn about Africa, but that they knew so little in the first place was an indication not of "cultural genocide" but of the sheer weight of time and distance. "The African return" was a spiritual and psychological balm, but, as Albert Murray argued in *The Omni-Americans* (1969), one of the most sensible books of cultural criticism to emerge in the sixties, it ignored that most of the genuinely unique American cultural forms were created by African Americans—especially jazz, the popularity of which suffered as commercialized soul grew.

Cultural nationalism was at best politically ambiguous and was indifferent, even hostile, to issues of class. Karenga himself insisted that "race rules out economics because whites are racists, not just capitalists," an argument that freed up entrepreneurs to cash in on cultural nationalism. The movement was particularly susceptible to capitalist charms. The first major black power conference, held in Newark in July 1967 only days after the great riot, was funded by a number of major corporations, organized by a black Republican, and held in a posh, white-owned hotel. The following year in Philadelphia, the Clairol Company co-sponsored the event. Far from threatening the white power structure, black power under these circumstances was something even Richard Nixon could warm to. "Much of the black militant talk these days," Nixon announced in 1968, "is actually in terms far closer to the doctrines of free enterprise than to those of the welfarist thirties. . . . What most of the militants are asking is not separation, but to be included in—not as supplicants, but as owners, as entrepreneurs—to have a share of the wealth and a piece of the action." By 1970 hair products, clothes, music, cigarettes, alcohol, and countless other products were being targeted directly at black buyers.

Whatever radical content nationalism originally possessed was drained away because the very nature of the movement made it vulnerable to political appropriation by nonradicals. When growing urban clout began to result in the elections of black candidates, for instance, the radicals discovered that the calls for racial unity could be used against them and in effect could bring nationalists into confrontation with other black leaders. Something of this dynamic was behind the "Battle of

Cleveland." In August 1968, a group of nationalists ambushed some city police-men, and in a hail of gunfire, three policemen and seven radicals were killed. It might have been another episode in the continued urban violence, but the city was then under Carl Stokes's administration. Stokes moved to prevent any further violence in the city's ghettos by charging all but the most militant black leaders with responsibility for keeping the city quiet, thus putting radical nationalists on the defensive in their own communities. "It is a move," the radical Julius Lester observed, "which takes advantage of the calls for unity based on blackness rather than unity based on class and ideology. . . . Under the guise of black unity, the black community is being divided." Stokes himself thought the militants who had initiated the conflict were charlatans and was convinced that using blacks to police black neighborhoods was both an act of decency and necessary to keeping the peace. Even then "it meant the end of Carl Stokes as hero."

Certainly, Stokes could not afford to seem "easy" on violent radicals, but at the same time the nationalists could not condemn Stokes or other more moderate black politicians without being inconsistent. It made no sense to justify cozying up with white corporations and then condemning black elected officials for playing main-stream politics.

Yet that cooperation certainly worked against black political independence. Just as the road to economic independence and cultural autonomy seemed to lead inexorably toward assimilation, so, too, did the struggle for political power. It was fitting that black power culminated in the convening of the National Black Politi-cal Assembly at Gary in March 1972. The largest all-black political convention in U.S. history, the Assembly brought together 12,000 activists from all strains of the national community who united for the moment in a spirit of racial solidarity and committed themselves to working for the election of black officials. Gary was both the high point and the end point of the nationalist movement, for once they committed themselves to electoral politics, they committed themselves as well to the Democratic party. This was a far cry from the aspirations to political indepen-dence. As Vincent Harding has written, after Gary the activists "turned back to politics-as-usual, turned aside to the demands of self-interest, or wandered off into unclear, necessarily solitary ways, searching for their own best responses to the new time."

The nationalists faced a predicament that was irresolvable by their own terms. It is difficult to see how they could have built any economic independence except through capitalist strategies, which inevitably meant the development of an entre-preneurialism and, just as inevitably, the emergence of a black middle class. Carried out through the exploitation of consumers, that entrepreneurialism also meant assimilation into mass culture and the destruction of genuine cultural autonomy. Under those circumstances, black nationalism in America was doomed to be a program of economic and political assimilation gilded over by a facade of contrived, exaggerated, or nostalgic cultural expression.

By way of contrast, it is helpful to note the Panthers' hostility to cultural nationalism. To the Panthers, real revolution was multiracial and class-based. Cul-tural nationalists, especially Karenga, practiced "pork-chop nationalism," in Huey

P. Newton's derisive phrase, because unless the system were changed, it would replace white oppressors of the masses with black oppressors. Cultural nationalists were racists who stooped "to the low, scurvy level of a Ku Klux Klansman," Bobby Seale wrote. Although the Panthers were too loose-knit to keep cultural nationalism out of the party completely, the party line always opposed it. "In our view it is a class struggle between the massive proletarian working class and the small, minority ruling class. Working-class people of all colors must unite against the exploitative, oppressive ruling class," Seale insisted. "We believe our fight is a class struggle and not a race struggle."

Awakened Minorities

Regardless of its own internal inconsistencies, black nationalism awakened the sense of cultural identity and political grievance among numerous groups. Particularly for Native and Hispanic Americans, whose historic condition in some ways paralleled that of blacks, the sixties provided the opportunity for pressing claims and redefining their place. In different ways, the rise of ethnic consciousness within these two groups illustrated the competing stresses of assimilation and isolation. The emergence of a Hispanic consciousness showed even more clearly than black nationalism how a group might establish a national presence on the basis of cultural identification, even though that identification was contrived. Native Americans, meanwhile, demonstrated that cultural distinctiveness was possible only by way of a thorough renunciation of mass culture, something that few groups were willing to undertake.

Hispanics

If one includes Puerto Ricans, Mexican Americans, and other Latinos as an ethnically coherent group, Hispanics were relatively poorer than blacks. The average annual income of New York's Puerto Ricans, for example, was $4,000 a year in the late sixties, $1,000 under the average nonwhite income; more than one-half of the Hispanics in New Mexico lived below the poverty level; and Chicano unemployment in Los Angeles was higher than that of blacks. In the Southwest, Hispanics were associated with labor migration that drew them into urban areas, especially Los Angeles, which had a Mexican-American community of nearly a million by 1970; in California as a whole, over 85 percent of Hispanics lived in cities.

In the barrios of southwestern cities, they endured the double burden of the urban crisis and racial discrimination. Originally communities of agricultural laborers, the barrios were engulfed by the growth of Sunbelt cities. Like the segregated black communities in the South, they were culturally coherent. Yet because they were maintained through segregated housing practices, the barrios took on many of the problems of urban ghettos, especially unemployment, underemployment, and police brutality. "Hemmed in from the outside by the heritage of anti-Mexican racism and built up from the inside by the cultural pride of La Raza," Stan Steiner wrote, "the barrios were a paradox of poverty and strength"—that is, until urban renewal programs brought interstate highways or, in the case of Los Angeles, a baseball stadium for the city's new major league baseball team.

Sunbelt Hispanics had been educated in segregated schools, which instituted active steps to eradicate their ethnic heritage. It was common practice from Texas to California to punish children—sometimes through mockery, sometimes through corporal punishment, sometimes through "Spanish detention"—for speaking Spanish in school. The language issue united Hispanics across class and national lines, and provided so much fuel for grievances that they forced a component to the 1965 Elementary and Secondary Education Act that made Spanish "acceptable" in public schools and provided federal aid to districts to develop bilingual education programs. Like the rest of the act, the bilingual component was better in theory than in practice. Although hundreds of districts applied for funds for Spanish education in the years after the act was passed, only a handful received part of the meager money that had been appropriated, and not all of those that received funds used them wisely. Partly in frustration over the failure of the act, some 15,000 students struck against the Los Angeles schools in March 1968.

Although the comparison is simplistic, Hispanics offered their version of Martin Luther King, Jr., and Malcolm X in Cesar Chavez and Reies Tijerina. Like King, Chavez was deeply religious, raised among the people whom he eventually led, and committed to a cause the justice of which was indisputable. Tijerina was, like Malcolm X, raised in a large, impoverished family and went on to lead a small uprising based on uncompromising cultural nationalism.

For his leadership of a nonviolent campaign to organize California farm workers, Chavez drew widespread sympathy and attention. Chicano farm workers typically worked for an hourly wage plus a piece rate, which added up to little more than $10 a day and $1,300 a year. Their working and living conditions were shabby, unsanitary, and overcrowded. And they were not organized. The CIO had failed in its attempts to organize the farm workers, in part because the workers were extremely transient and insecure but also because the bureaucratic, industrial unions were out of place in the southwestern countryside. The organization of farm workers was finally made possible when Congress refused to extend the bracero system at the end of 1964. A labor recruitment program, the bracero system allowed U.S. growers to import seasonal workers from Mexico under the protection of the federal government; thus, they were provided with a ready supply of compliant, poorly paid labor. The end of the system provided just enough labor scarcity for Chavez, who had been trying to organize for several years, to bring pressure to bear on the growers. In May 1965 Chavez's National Farm Workers of America (NFWA) attempted to organize in the heart of California's rich central valley, beginning with a strike against several of the largest growers in Delano. Five years later, after sporadic violence, international boycotts against California products, a challenge from the Teamsters Union, a necessary merger with the AFL-CIO, and a long Chavez hunger strike, NFWA had won but partial victories.

Chavez built his movement from the ground up by effectively appealing to ethnic and religious unity—a "triple magnetism," as one activist put it, when these

Cesar Chavez fasted for 23 days in 1968 to protest unjust working conditions for farm laborers. Robert Kennedy (left) helps the union leader break his fast. *[UPI/Bettmann Newsphotos]*

two qualities were added to labor unity. NFWA marches were accompanied by prayers, priests, and symbols of the Virgin Mary. Workers rallied around the Spanish cry of "Huelga!" and used an Aztec eagle on its flag. "Chavez's secret," one grower perceived, "is that he has the utter loyalty of the Mexican workers." The NFWA was not "a trade union. They're a racial and religious organization." "The revolt in Delano is more than a labor struggle," one participant wrote. "There is the desire of a New World race to reconcile the conflicts of its 500-year-old history." Chavez even played on white stereotypes. Placid and quiet, he was an unlikely agitator, but his demeanor proved an effective organizing tool: it made it hard to oppose him without seeming anti-Christian, and it also led opponents to underestimate him. As another grower saw it, "Our biggest mistake was to think Chavez was just another 'dumb Mex.' "

He also knew the temper of the times. He caught the imaginations of Martin Luther King, Jr., and Robert Kennedy and parlayed their sympathy into effective public relations for the organizing drive. He played the liberal line, carefully avoiding inflammatory behavior while not exactly condemning it in others. He used his anti-establishment image to court help from countless activist groups, from liberal Catholics to SNCC and CORE workers to student radicals. Drawing from SNCC's strategy in Freedom Summer, Chavez welcomed the help of "summer volunteers" from Berkeley and elsewhere, even though, it turned out, the student volunteers were "appallingly ignorant" of the region and its people, as John Gregory Dunne wrote.

Like King, Chavez cannot be understood outside his ethnic subculture, yet he never accepted nationalism as an end in itself. This was not the case with Reies Tijerina. Tijerina was a one-time evangelical preacher who in 1967 founded the Alianza Federal de Mercedes (Federal Alliance of Land Grants) in order to re-claim title to land taken from Mexican nationals by Anglos in the nineteenth century, much of which was allegedly in the hands of the U.S. Forest Service. He earned a moment in the national spotlight in June 1967 when a group of his followers raided the courthouse in the tiny northern New Mexico town of Tierra Amarilla to protest police harassment. They escaped into the mountains, and it took more than 2,000 law enforcement agents to arrest the men, including Tijerina. Tried for kidnapping, assault, and over 150 other charges, he defended himself, won acquittal, and was hailed by Hispanics as the "Robin Hood of New Mexico."

To Tijerina, reclaiming land would mean economic independence for some of New Mexico's desperately poor Chicanos, many of whom were idle and on welfare in small towns that bordered national forests. From their perspective, there was no good reason why both they and the land should remain idle, especially if they could stake some historic claim to it. And the land issue ran deeper than mere economics. Reclaiming land was an act of cultural redemption, a way to recover a proud past of magnanimous and prosperous landholders who had been ground into poverty by generations of Anglo-American thieves. Although much of New Mex-ico had been stolen by Anglos, there was a good deal of mythologizing in Tijerina. Little matter, however, for to his followers, who were estimated to number from "300 to 30,000" according to the New York Times, the man was the Prophet. His own intention was nothing less than to discover "the lost identity of my people." To those Hispanics who were not his followers he was either an unnerving or an inspiring figure. Tijerina scorned the assimilationist strategies of the middle class, the "Tío Tomases" whom he accused of forsaking their heritage. Some establish-ment types considered him variously a communist stooge and a rascal taking advantage of the ignorant poor. Joseph Montoya, New Mexico's Democratic sena-tor, thought Tijerina an "exploiter, discredited charlatan, imposter, and racist." Few middle-class Hispanics minded seeing Tijerina stick it to the Anglo, but the surge of ethnic consciousness raised difficult questions about their own assimila-tion. "You know what that bastard Tijerina has done to me?" one man expounded to Stan Steiner. "He has questioned my whole life. All my life has been based on my denying I am a Mexican to myself. My life has been a denial of what I am. Now I have to decide whether I am lying to myself. Now there are two sides of me and I have to decide which one I am." "I hate that bastard," he went on. "Who appointed him my conscience?"

Tijerina was influenced, if not by Malcolm X directly, at least by black nationalists, with whom he had contacts. He often referred to black political strategies in his speeches and claimed similar aspirations: "The Negroes are expecting this great change. That's why they are jumping, breaking the barriers, and yelling, and respecting *nothing* that gets in their way." Like black nationalists, Tijerina gradually outgrew a parochial perspective, adopting an international view of both his movement and U.S. social conditions. He organized beyond his original Alianza when he helped found La Raza Unida (the United People), which was meant to be an ethnic interest group quite like Malcolm X's OAAU; he often preached his nationalist message to college students; and he led a contingent in the 1968 Poor People's March to Washington. His record of accomplishments was similar to Malcolm X's: there were few hard-and-fast successes, but he had a psychological influence that is not easily measured, especially among young Hispanics. He directly inspired student activists in the region's universities, and the Brown Berets, a loose-knit nationalist movement, also looked to him as a source of inspiration.

Like black nationalists, Hispanic activists sought a flowering of ethnic self-consciousness. As one Brown Beret put it, "we're not in the melting pot sort of thing. Chicanos don't melt." The truth, however, was that Hispanic Americans were melting, brown power notwithstanding, and the very creation of the "Hispanic American" was itself a sign of national assimilation. At the very least, it marked attempts to organize people of some shared lineage in order to realize national political clout. But what was a Hispanic American? There were tremendous differences between Hispanic groups—between, for example, Mexican Americans in Los Angeles and South Texas, between Cubans in Miami and Puerto Ricans in New York, and even between Tijerina's rural land claimants and the urban middle class. There was a terrific gulf between fifth-generation Mexican Americans, long established in San Antonio, Austin, or San Diego, and the migrant worker who crossed back and forth over the border in search of work. And yet, much as with black nationalism, the creation of a Hispanic movement obscured class differences. As with black nationalism, the Hispanic movement settled down into a routinized, bureaucratized form of interest-group politics that more often benefited middle-class professionals than the rural poor, the wandering migrants, or urban youth.

Native Americans

Both Hispanic and African Americans demonstrated that political organization along racial lines was an effective way for members of their groups to gain clout, but only at the cost of assimilating. Only Native Americans had the sort of separate existence within the United States that other ethnic nationalists seemingly aspired to. Like other ethnic minorities, they found themselves fighting off poverty, discrimination, and ill health. But adverse conditions and misery had been constants in native life since the end of the nineteenth century, and it is indicative of how the climate of the sixties encouraged organized, group-conscious grievances that Native Americans began to reassert themselves after so many years. Detached though they were from the U.S. mainstream, they, too, experienced generational conflict, first as men returning from military service in World War II and later as college-educated young people demanding political militancy against the "Uncle Tomahawks" who had been complacently representing them. Spurred to action, they held "fish-ins" and "hunt-ins," occupied the abandoned Alcatraz Prison in San Francisco Bay in 1968, and stormed the Bureau of Indian Affairs in 1973, all under the rallying cry of "red power." They rewrote history, most notably in Dee Brown's important revisionist work, *Bury My Heart at Wounded Knee* (1970), and saw the emergence of nationalist intellectuals like Vine Deloria, Jr.

If grievance alone were enough to drive a people to rebellion, Native Americans would have been the most rebellious of all. They were, Vine Deloria, Jr., often pointed out, "the only people who have a history of getting the shaft from the federal government." By 1960 Native Americans constituted the poorest of all ethnic minorities. The average household income was near $1,500 but much lower for the 380,000 who lived on reservations, where unemployment ranged from 45 to 98 percent. An estimated three-quarters of those on reservations lived in substandard housing. Infant mortality was two to three times higher than the national rate, and life expectancy was only 46 years. These conditions were so degrading as to be virtually impervious to any of the standard solutions—jobs, new housing, and the like. Such programs were not much help for those who had fled to the cities, but they were all the more ineffective for those who remained on the reservations.

It made sense to Indians at any rate that, rather than counting on the federal government, they should help themselves. Like Tijerina and his followers, they focused on reclaiming land that was once legally theirs and otherwise going about the business of staying alive. Economic survival meant hunting or fishing in restricted areas. When thousands of Indians launched fish-ins in the Pacific Northwest in the midsixties, they did so knowing that they would be arrested. Comparing themselves to civil rights activists, fish-in leaders insisted that "when there is a problem the only thing that takes care of it is direct action," even if that meant "filling the jails with Indians." While they tried to do just that, their claims made their way through the Supreme Court, which, after prodding from the Justice Department, offered limited recognition of tribal rights. When the fish-in movement caught on and eventually included Florida Seminoles, Nebraska Winnebagos, Dakota Sioux, and others, it became, as one spokesman announced, "the first full-scale intertribal *action* since the Indians defeated General Custer on the Little Big Horn." When the federal government sided with them, it seemed to demonstrate the value of solidarity.

Beyond these actions, both the immediate and long-term interests of Native Americans were directly at odds with the standard solutions that the welfare state offered. To accept welfare, job training, and low-income housing was to accept assimilation and thus to acquiesce in the further destruction of their heritage. Resurgent Indian nationalism was more than a response to the failures of the United States; it was a refusal to accept the promises that the nation held out—the promise of economic development and the protection of the social safety net. Indian nationalists insisted that Native Americans did not want to be "developed"; rather, they hoped to be left alone. Nowhere was that desire better demonstrated than when the federal government attempted to address the housing problem on the reservations by building low-income garden apartments or townhouses, only to have Indians refuse to move into them because the dwellings were "un-Indian." On one reservation after another, people laughed or shook their heads in disbelief when they saw what the government had built. Accustomed to dispersed living, they could not see where the improvement lay if it meant living on top of one another. "If we want to live like that we can go to Chicago," Vine Deloria, Jr., scoffed, and often only Indians returning from cities would occupy such apartments. Others noted the absurdity of paying contractors $25,000 per unit when they could build homes to their own liking much more cheaply. One young activist on the Chippewa Turtle Mountain Reservation in North Dakota built a small house of his own on a lake shore for $1,500 and held it up as an example of what Indians would do if they were given construction funds themselves. The government, he was told, did not do things that way.

More than other ethnic nationalists, Native nationalists presented a thoroughgoing critique of mass society and recognized that real nationalism could be achieved only through the pain of cultural isolation. One of the main reasons why young Indians were returning from college to take up roles as reservation activists was that they had seen the mainstream and concluded that it was bankrupt. "They look at the mainstream, and what do they see?" asked Deloria. "Ice cream bars and heart trouble and neurosis and deodorants and getting up at six o'clock in the morning to mow your lawn in the suburbs." Native Americans were the original critics of the mainstream, of mass man, and of the "establishment." "When you get far enough away from the reservation," Deloria explained, "you can see it's the urban man who has no identity."

In his nationalist manifesto, *Custer Died for Your Sins* (1969), one of the sharpest critiques of assimilation written in the sixties, Deloria was quite clear about what Indians would have to do in order to build a united political front. At a time when Indians were struggling to redefine themselves, Deloria believed, whites were insisting that they continue to represent the Indian of western lore. The most meddlesome whites were the social scientists who descended on the reservations every summer to do "applied research" on the "Indian problem," although Deloria suspected the real motive was to advance their academic careers. Federal policymakers and many educated Indians—"workshop Indians," Deloria called them, the Indian analogue to the middle-class black-power advocate—unfortunately listened to these experts, so that behind every "program with which the Indians are plagued . . . stands the anthropologist." Deloria was appalled at the experts' tendency to blame the "Indian problem" on some cultural maladjustment. Rather than blaming poverty or the denial of Indian autonomy, anthropologists focused on such factors as the frustrated "warrior tradition," as one study of the Oglala Sioux concluded. "The very real and human problems of the reservation were considered to be merely by-products of the failure of a warrior people to become domesticated," Deloria observed. Poking fun at the predictable liberal programs that were sure to ensue after such a study, "some Indians . . . suggested that a subsidized wagon train be run through the reservation each morning at 9 A.M. and the reservation people paid a minimum wage for attacking it."

What Native Americans wanted, Deloria wrote, was "a cultural leave-us-alone agreement." Deloria hoped to build Indian unity through the National Congress of American Indians and use the organization to secure long-range financial stability for cooperating groups.

But his group was eclipsed by younger and more radical Indians. During 1968, a group of young men, acquaintances from reform schools and prisons, organized a self-defense group in Minneapolis to protect Indians against police brutality, emulating the Black Panthers. Calling themselves the American Indian Movement (AIM), these activists quickly branched out through northern and western cities with large Indian communities. In 1969 they hit upon the idea of occupying abandoned federal property from the West Coast to Washington, D.C.—the settlement of the frontier in reverse. They began in November by occupying the abandoned prison of Alcatraz and announced their intention of turning it into an all-Indian university. The federal government let them alone, and they slowly left the island. The trail ended in Washington in fall 1972 when AIM supporters occupied the Bureau of Indian Affairs (BIA), doing $2 million damage and making off with BIA records that allegedly showed fraud and conflict of interests among agency bureaucrats. The Nixon administration had been under the illusion that it had improved government-Indian relations by restructuring the BIA and encouraging Indian self-determination. Miffed by the occupation, the administration covertly paid the occupiers' travel expenses home and then instructed federal law enforcement agencies to plot AIM's destruction.

Always prone to overkill, the Nixon administration probably did not need to plot AIM's destruction, for the movement was quickly reaching an impasse of its own. One of AIM's principal grievances was that the BIA, in accord with agency-approved tribal governments, continued to sell Indian property and mineral rights to large gas, coal, and chemical corporations. This exploitation, added to the increased power of the tribal governments under the administration's self-determination policy, raised the stakes of tribal control and pitted Indians against one another. The most famous of all AIM occupations, the seventy-one-day siege at Wounded Knee in 1973, grew principally out of a conflict between AIM members and the tribal government on the Pine Ridge, South Dakota, reservation. There, AIM had organized a community of members whose interests regularly clashed with those of the tribal head, a ne'er-do-well named Dickie Wilson, who believed that "the only major Indian problem is AIM. . . . They're just bums trying to get their braids and mugs in the press." In late February, AIM occupied the small BIA office in the hamlet of Wounded Knee, the scene of the last great massacre of Indians in 1890, taking eleven hostages and demanding an uncompromising redress of Indian rights. As at Alcatraz, federal authorities decided to wait AIM out, a tactic that diluted the effectiveness of their confrontational, "it's-a-good-day-to-die" tactics. Wounded Knee became a clumsy media circus; the hostages turned out to be participants who were being held "voluntarily" by city-bred Indians who spoke of reclaiming Indian tradition by reclaiming autonomy but who largely seemed in search of their own roots.

Rise of the Unmeltable Ethnics

Minority groups typically received regular support from enlightened Wasp politicians honoring *noblesse oblige*, Wasp clergy practicing a new social gospel, and Wasp college students searching for personal authenticity and political justice. These same Wasps, however, were not so sympathetic with Irish, Poles, or other ethnic groups who had difficult histories of their own. White ethnics were not the poorest of the poor and generally did not want liberal sympathy. Many were Catholic and therefore easy for Protestants to overlook. When they celebrated their ethnicity, they did so in places—churches, families, neighborhoods—that were far less exotic than the ghetto or the reservation.

As the elite began to demonstrate its sympathy for the disenfranchised, they turned their own prejudice against white ethnics, and working-class whites found themselves the objects of what one observer termed "respectable bigotry." Negro jokes went out of fashion and were replaced by white ethnic jokes: "What's the first thing a pink flamingo does when he buys a house? He plants a Pole in the front yard." At a 1969 party for New York's quintessentially Wasp mayor, John Lindsay, then locked in a tight race against the conservative Italian, Mario Procaccino, the actor Woody Allen quipped that Lindsay's Italian opponent was at home "in his undershirt, drinking beer and watching Lawrence Welk on television." The joke in the Lindsay camp was that if Procaccino won he would replace the rugs in Gracie Mansion with linoleum. When a conservative Italian announced his mayoral candidacy in New Haven, a Yale professor reportedly told his dinner companions: "If Italians aren't actually an inferior race, they do the best imitation of one I've seen."

Respectable bigotry was both morally and politically serviceable. No longer employers of labor, elites could strike the easy moral pose because it cost them nothing. "The upper class," Michael Lerner observed, "has reached a plateau of security from which its liberal-radical wing believes that it can mock the politics of the policeman and the butcher and slight their aspirations while still living genteelly in the space between them." It also provided the grounds on which elites could blame someone other than themselves for the failure of reform. Arthur Schlesinger, though no Wasp himself, spoke for many when he surmised that the apparent split between reformism and conservatism was at bottom a split between "the poor, uneducated who tend to be the most emotional and primitive champions of conservatism" and "the affluent and better educated . . . [who] tend to care about identity, reform, and progress."

With the demise of the melting pot ideal, the ethnic assertion of minorities, and the degree to which both Wasps and minorities criticized working-class whites, it was probably inevitable that white Americans would begin asserting themselves along ethnic lines. Indeed, Robert Coles believed that underlying working-class resentment was not merely envy of the attention minorities were receiving. "They also envy," he wrote, "the black man his success at finding a protest movement that persists and commands a degree of attention. *They* need a protest movement of sorts too." Coles doubted that they knew how to organize one, but a "movement of sorts" did emerge, though it was by degrees haphazard, disingenuous, and ineffectual. By the late sixties, ethnic organizations like Americans of Italian Descent, the First Catholic Slovak Union, even the Jewish Defense League, appeared. Ethnic intellectuals led the way, defending the "white ethnics," calling for "a quiet revolution of consciousness aimed at creating a new pluralism," and applauding expressions of the "new ethnicity."

As proof of ethnic consciousness among whites, advocates of the new ethnicity pointed to two signs: the substantial ethnic neighborhoods that could still be found in most older cities from Baltimore to Boston to Chicago, and the persistence of ethnic voting habits. Urban scholars like Herbert Gans, Nathan Glazer, and Daniel Moynihan set the tone for ethnic studies with important books in the early sixties. In *Beyond the Melting Pot* (1963), Glazer and Moynihan concluded that ethnic consciousness was increasing—at least in New York City politics. It was remarkable, they wrote, that "in 1963, almost forty years after mass immigration from Europe to this country ended, the ethnic pattern is still so strong." For Jews, the Holocaust and the emergence of Israel generated greater attachment to their heritage and encouraged a vigilant ethnic defensiveness. Because Jews had been more committed to assimilation than most groups, their increased solidarity was all the more notable. African Americans were a more solid bloc than ever, and Catholics united behind the Church's strong anticommunism and the prayer-in-schools issue. Although they speculated erroneously that white Protestants would meet the ethnic challenge by strengthening their own sense of solidarity, Glazer and Moynihan nonetheless provided a glimpse at the rest of the decade in New York, which included not only extensive white-black tension but also the bitter fight between blacks and Jews; the emergence of Mario Procaccino on the ruins of the city's Democratic party in the late sixties; and the tenuous hold of John Lindsay.

What Glazer and Moynihan found in New York City, other scholars discovered to be true more generally. Political scientists and political historians alike began to view voting and political loyalties according to ethnicity rather than, say, region or class. In his early sixties' study of ethnic politics, Raymond E. Wolfinger found that ethnic voting patterns were stronger in the second- and third-generation immigrant than in the first, a clear sign that the impulse to assimilation was stronger in the original immigrants than in their progeny. Social mobility, once considered the great homogenizer, may have encouraged greater ethnic identification, Wolfinger argued, because voters had less reason to vote along class lines. If Wolfinger was right, then the affluent society was more likely to exaggerate ethnic differences than to obliterate them.

Whatever underlying explanations there were for the new ethnicity, it was more a product of middle-class intellectuals than a genuine grass-roots reclamation or celebration of ethnic heritage. Writers like Andrew Greeley, the scholarly Irish-Catholic priest, Geno Baroni, who directed an ethnic think-tank in Washington, and Michael Novak, a philosopher-theologian who wrote the most controversial book about the new ethnicity, were all second-generation immigrants who had moved into academia. They came of age as scholars just as the myth of the melting pot was losing its holding power; thus, it became legitimate, even trendy, to defend their ethnic backgrounds.

If Greeley was the most prolific advocate of the new ethnicity, Novak was the angriest. A second-generation Slovak, Novak wrote on behalf of the PIGS—the Poles, Italians, Greeks, and Slovaks—whom white liberals and black nationalists condemned as racists. His *Rise of the Unmeltable Ethnics* (1972) was a compilation of grievances—against the past, against liberals, against mainstream intellectuals, against blacks, against the very politics of ethnicity that Novak seemed to be working. For Novak, ethnicity continued to provide a buffer against the loss of identity and allowed white ethnics to sustain cherished values like the work ethic, religiosity, and patriotism. Wasps had renounced those values and turned on the ethnics; the ethnics simultaneously were being asked to surrender their ethnicity and were being told to discard the values they always associated with being American.

Novak's book evoked predictably angry reviews, accusing him mostly of a backhanded form of racism. Journalist Garry Wills described it as an "immoral book." Agnes Moreland Jackson wondered at the hypocrisy of people who had accepted the melting pot ideal for decades, only to denounce Wasps now that blacks and other ethnic minorities had begun to win concessions. A more substantive criticism of Novak might have suggested that the new ethnicity was a concoction of middle-class intellectuals served up to ease their own sense of lost identity. Rather than a description of working-class reality, it was more a matter of wishful thinking. Some aspects of the new ethnicity were clearly artificial attempts to recapture a lost past. Novak sentimentally recalled his grandmother's ethnic cooking, while Rudolph Vecoli romanticized his Italian father as an opponent of the melting pot because he grew his own vegetables and made his own wine. For many, ethnicity was a weekend indulgence, something to partake of through a ride into Little Italy from Long Island on Saturday, as the journalist Nicholas Pileggi wrote. Pileggi's "Saturday Italians" came into the city "not only for the bread, tiny bitter onions, bushels of snails, live eels, and dried cod, but also to enjoy a weekend heritage that their education, blonde wives, and the English language have begun to deny them." Ethnicity in this sense was another commodity to be enjoyed at one's convenience.

Part of Novak's purpose was to call necessary attention to the class bias embedded in the liberal criticism of white workers, but his focus on ethnicity served largely to obscure the one part of his book that made sense. If the so-called white ethnics could register any real grievance, it was along class rather than ethnic grounds. Novak and the other spokesmen were wrong to assume that working-class whites felt specifically ethnic resentments; they found themselves speaking most often about working-class people simply because the working class had been relatively immune to mass homogenization and had retained, therefore, stronger ethnic ties.

"Everyman" in the Sixties

In contrast to how Novak sought to describe them, working-class whites most keenly felt their own powerlessness with regard to their economic and social destiny and not any particularly ethnic sensibility. It seemed to them that the Wasps had reneged on a long-term social contract whereby, it might be said, the ethnics were to be provided steady work and respectful acknowledgment in exchange for their embracing Wasp rule and some Wasp values. The working class had two antagonists: minorities, especially blacks, whom they believed were getting rewards they did not earn; and the liberals who were dishing out those rewards. "They want all they can get—for free," one man told Robert Coles. "They don't want to work. . . . They seem to have the idea that they're entitled to something from the rest of us." But who was to blame? "The rich ones out in the fancy suburbs, they're the ones—the bleeding hearts, always ready to pat people on the head and say you're wonderful and we love you."

Working-Class Grievances

Working-class frustration spilled out intermittently through the midsixties, as it did in Chicago when Martin Luther King planned his march into Cicero. There all of the material for racial tension was at work. The Chicago suburb was overwhelmingly ethnic—Sicilians, Poles, and Slovaks—and many of its residents worked at Western Electric's giant Hawthorne plant. Cicero was a community of homeowners, but that is about all the townspeople could claim by way of affluence. They had watched as the west side ghetto, which King had adopted as his home, crept steadily toward them and engulfed the white working-class neighborhood of Lawndale. The racist barrage launched at King and his fellow marchers in 1966 has to be seen, for all its ugliness, as an effort in community control, the very thing that other ethnic nationalists were demanding. Cicero was a case in which the legitimate grievances of African Americans clashed with the legitimate concerns of the white ethnics, and as one observer noted, "The true sadness of this state of affairs is that it admits of no easy solution. . . . The fact is, the cards of neglect, discrimination, and obtuse social policy have been shuffled for more than a half-century, and Cicero has been dealt a bad hand." In ignoring Cicero's side of things, the media, liberal politicians, and King himself all but guaranteed bitter opposition.

Many political commentators took Cicero as evidence that the race issue was the principal motive underlying working-class behavior. Yet it is doubtful that specifically ethnic grievances did working-class whites any more good than they did African Americans or Hispanics. Any claim that their own past was just as oppressive as that of African Americans and Native Americans was dubious. But the white ethnics could advance legitimate complaints on economic grounds. Working-class whites were not poor by definition, but their income hovered between $5,000 and perhaps $10,000. The higher end, of course, was composed of the skilled workers and members of the industrial unions like the autoworkers. For most others, that income level had made a two-income family a necessity well before middle-class families accepted it as a symbol of a progressive marriage. Although the widespread image among elites was that these workers were "blue-collar aristocrats" with boats, big cars, backyard barbecues, and paneled basements, the reality was that most owned nothing more than their homes, which they protected with a desperate seriousness. "The Negroes say they have nothing," an Irish woman admitted to Robert Coles. "Well, we have more, that's true. . . . But it's as hard as can be just living and staying even with everything. . . . You have to be an owner of something or a professional man to have an easy mind today." Like their black peers, working-class whites knew that affluence was unattainable. "The auto assembly line worker who owns a five-year-old Chevy he bought second hand," wrote Andrew Levinson, whose father, Stanley, had been Martin Luther King, Jr.'s close friend and advisor, "spends eight or nine or even ten hours a day building Cadillacs or Torinos he will never buy. . . . Social inequality is not abstract for these people. It is a visible daily reality."

Beyond their fear of economic insecurity, working-class whites harbored a host of political and moral grievances, best summed up by Barbara Mikulski, "the first lady of the white ethnic movement," in her 1970 "Bill of Frustrations." Mikulski, a Polish-Catholic from urban Baltimore, daughter of a small grocer, began a search for authenticity that took her back to her roots. Starting as a Baltimore social worker, she gained a reputation as a brash defender of working-class ethnics. "The ethnic American is sick of being stereotyped as a racist and a dullard by phony white liberals, pseudo black militants, and patronizing bureaucrats," she proclaimed. "He pays the bill for every major government program and gets nothing or little in the way of return. Tricked by the political rhetoric of illusionary funding for black-oriented social programs, he turns his anger to race—when he himself is the victim of class prejudice." The melting pot was in reality "a sizzling cauldron for the ethnic American who feels that he has been politically courted and legally extorted by both government and private enterprise."

George Wallace

The particulars of Mikulski's "Bill of Frustrations" generated the white backlash, advanced and symbolized by the emergence of George Wallace as a figure to be reckoned with. A classic demagogue, Wallace was a very careful student of political resentment and had shaped his career accordingly. After losing as a racial moderate in the post-*Brown* atmosphere of Alabama politics, he determined to play the race issue better than anyone else. He race-baited his way to becoming governor of Alabama in 1962, where he made his fame with his grandstanding plea against the integration of the University of Alabama: "Segregation now, segregation tomorrow, segregation forever!"

Wallace would have been the run-of-the-mill southern politician except that he was ambitious and he was the first politician to conclude that the race issue was not confined to the South. "It is as if," NBC correspondent Douglas Kiker mused, "somewhere, sometime a while back, George Wallace had been awakened by a white blinding vision: They all hate black people, all of them. . . . They're all Southern! The whole United States is Southern!" Thus inspired, Wallace decided to dabble in the 1964 Democratic primaries, advancing a flimsy message that combined opposition to the civil rights bill, a states' rights platform, and anticommunism. Yet he surprised—and frightened—many observers when he did well in those few areas where he expended any real effort. He did well in the steel-working city of Gary; he took almost a third of the votes in the Wisconsin primary; and he nearly won the Maryland primary, having swept the working-class areas of east and south Baltimore.

Both of the major parties took notice and maneuvered to limit Wallace's power in 1968. Under the presumption that Wallace's strength was purely and solely his appeal to racism, the leading contenders for the respective nominations tried to placate the southern establishment. Wallace knew that he had no future in either party and therefore established his own, the American Independent Party (AIP). Running as a third-party candidate, Wallace reasoned, was a long shot, but certainly no longer than attempting to gain nomination through regular channels. Besides, a third-party candidacy had its virtues: he could avoid wasting money and effort in primary fights, and he was free to run the campaign his way, which meant maintaining the inventive financing through which he tapped the state of Alabama for funds and personnel. Poll results in late summer 1968 showed that Wallace could take as much as 20 percent of the vote, more at the expense of the Democrats than of the likely Republican nominee, Richard Nixon. His themes, sharpened since 1964, turned less on race-baiting than on liberal-baiting and a paradoxical criticism of the federal government's meddlesomeness in domestic affairs and its ineptitude in Vietnam. The themes worked until Wallace chose Curtis LeMay as his vice-presidential nominee. A former general and an ardent hawk, LeMay immediately proceeded to prove everything the press was saying about Wallace by announcing his support of nuclear attacks against North Vietnam. From that point, Wallace's appeal shrank as voters took a longer look at him, as the other two candidates got out their own messages, and as unions and other organizations stepped up their anti-Wallace campaigns. Still, he did remarkably well for a third-party candidate, taking four states (all southern) and almost 10 million votes, accounting for about 13 percent of the total. Nixon thus won by plurality.

Pundits were quick to link Wallace with the blue-collar aristocrats as partners in racist politics. As one writer put it, Wallace carried "the scent of hurry and hair oil" and was all but "indistinguishable from the lowest of the crowd." Pete Hamill wrote that Wallace proved how "the masses, those cabdrivers, beauticians, steelworkers, ironworkers, and construction men so beautifully romanticized by generations of dreamy socialists, are really an ugly bunch of people. If the campaign of George Wallace has its ugly and racists aspects, it is because George Wallace is the creation of the people."

But the profile of Wallace voters was not noticeably different from the profile of the voters for the other candidates. Wallace supporters tended to be slightly more rural, southern, working-class, conservative on foreign policy, and racist, but not significantly so. Their one significant characteristic, according to Jody Carlson's close study, was that, more than voters for the major-party candidates, they professed to a sense of powerlessness against the state of things, symbolized in their opposition to forced integration. Ironically, they were among the most alienated in what was supposed to be an age where the politics of alienation was welcomed and legitimate. Wallace himself was racist beyond doubt, but that did not mean that people supported him for that reason. Wallace's appeal to many working-class voters more likely lay in his folksy confrontation with "pointy-head intellectual morons" and liberal bureaucrats "who can't park a bicycle straight." Wallace was the only candidate to speak to the popular distrust of liberal reformers and the only one to appreciate the widespread sense of inequality. Those pointy-head policymakers "all come from the multimillion dollar tax-exempt foundations . . . who are making fortunes on tax loopholes while the little man is bangin' his head against the wall tryin' to pay his taxes." Those who would make racist reactionaries of the Wallace voters had to ignore the reality that many of these same voters had been attracted to Robert F. Kennedy before his assassination, for like Wallace, Kennedy had been on the side of the "little guy." One local Wallace leader in Minnesota explained to a reporter that RFK's assassination, "plus that of Martin Luther King, pointed up for me just how sick it was in this country." As Edward Kennedy sympathetically remarked while trying to woo support back to the Democrats, the Wallace voters "feel the established system has not been sympathetic to them in their problems of everyday life and in a large measure they are right."

Convergence of Black and White Opinion

What can be said of the Wallace voter can be said of working-class whites generally. Nearly all the important studies of opinion conducted in the late sixties concluded that working-class people did not deserve the stereotypes with which they had been branded. They consistently agreed that blacks had endured the harshest lot in the United States and consistently agreed that blacks were not demanding that change come too fast. Non-southern blue-collar respondents agreed by 80 percent and more that schools should be integrated and that blacks should be free to move wherever they could afford to and take whatever job they were qualified for. Poll results show, Brenden Sexton wrote, that workers "appear to be a tiny bit more progressive" than their better-educated, wealthier fellow whites. Sexton pointed out that these results were easy to understand. Far more than any middle-class or elite whites, blue-collar whites were more likely to work side by side with blacks and to interact with them on a level of equality in a score of other ways.

Understood in this fashion, working-class white opinion overlapped more with working- and middle-class black opinion than with that of any other group. Opinion polls that studied the black everyman revealed a widespread distrust of white liberals, an aversion to black militancy, and an ethnocentric desire to be left alone—all quite similar to the common attitudes of whites. In general, blacks overwhelmingly looked to King and mainstream organizations such as the NAACP as their leaders, and they believed as strongly that things were improving for their race. According to some polling data, they overwhelmingly approved of school and residential integration—though the extent of their integrationist convictions depended in part on how and when the questions were asked. In a mid-decade study, Gary Marx found that blacks favored school integration by as much as 79 percent in Birmingham to 96 percent in New York City. In later polls, conducted after the controversies over forced busing began, Lou Harris found much less support for integration; indeed, a small majority disapproved. Timing mattered, as did the question.

These results seem to reflect a good deal of ambivalence, but a closer examination of what people said suggests another conclusion. Insofar as they sought integration, working-class blacks did so because they considered it an implicit recognition of racial equality by white society rather than a means of moving into the middle class. For that reason, they strongly objected to the way blacks were characterized in the media, and they especially resented the sappy sympathy that many white liberals gushed at them. They understood and partly approved of nationalism, but like King, they saw racial separation as a foreclosure against equality rather than a means to it.

Malcolm X was accurate, then, when he remarked that the black masses did not want integration into the white middle class; they wanted "human rights. Respect as *human beings!*" "I don't want to live next door to the white man," one Philadelphian told Peter Binzen. "I just want my equal rights." Thomas Coolidge, a young resident of Pruett-Igoe whom Lee Rainwater interviewed, expressed the same sentiment. Coolidge imitated the nationalists and the Muslims, Rainwater wrote, but he wanted a chance to develop his own skills and lead a decent life. He wanted "to find a home, to be a man, and to search out valid ways of expressing himself," Rainwater concluded. Nowhere do such attitudes come through more clearly than in the interviews that Robert Coles conducted among Boston's working-class blacks. One man's comments were typically forthright: "I am called a black man. The fact is, mister, I work in a factory, and I have a wife and three children. . . . We don't want to live with white people, and we're happy with our own people, and that doesn't mean we're Afro-Americans or for black power or any of that. Hell, I work with white people, and I'd like my kids to go to school with them. . . . I'm just a plain guy—and there are thousands like me right in this section of the city. Why don't people talk about someone like me?"

The convergence of opinion among working people, white and black, refutes the claims to deep racial cleavage made by liberals, militants, and ethnic nationalists alike. Yet that convergence was obscured by the political usefulness of ethnic identity in U.S. political culture. Those who were most intensely organized were heard. And the foremost reason why this harmony of opinion did not rise above the shrill cries of nationalists was not only that there was so little organization across racial lines but also that it served the political interests of ethnic militants to mute that harmony.

Attempts to Organize the Appalachians

One might even say that to fail to organize along ethnic lines was to be disenfranchised by the late sixties. The so-called white ethnics fit this category, but the point can be made more strongly by applying it to Appalachian immigrants into the cities. In the years from World War II to 1965, mechanization in the coal industry and other economic pressures encouraged a massive migration of poor whites—not well educated, mostly unskilled by urban industrial standards—that depopulated Appalachia. Exactly how many migrated is not known because the Appalachians tended to be very mobile and often went back and forth from city to their old homes. But some estimates suggested that by the late 1970s six million people either born in Appalachia or whose parents were born there lived outside the region. Whether they moved to Pittsburgh, Detroit, Chicago, or Dayton, they went in search of industrial jobs; some succeeded and many others did not. And those who did not succeed were poorly equipped to adjust to urban life or to adopt the political strategies necessary to force urban life to adjust to them. Having lived isolated from mainstream society, they had developed a history and culture of fierce independence. As a group they hated taking welfare; it bred dependence, it was dishonorable, and it broke up families. They hated being talked about as poor people; they knew they were poor, and they hardly needed social workers or Ph.D. students coming around telling them that. Many activists, social workers, and scholars found them exceedingly fatalistic; they were at once invariably pitiable and sincerely proud.

Indeed, many of the social workers committed to helping them believed the Appalachians were too proud for their own good. Instead of taking the welfare that was there for them, they relied on one another, on relatives or old neighbors who were also in the city. "All they want is work," one case worker told Robert Coles. "All they want is a chance to be independent and make their own way through the world." Oddly, this determination was no virtue in the view of the case worker, who was frustrated with the mountaineers' refusal of help. "What kind of pride encourages parents who need money for their children to turn their backs on that money?" Perhaps, she surmised, it was an "almost perverse honesty."

The same qualities that bred this "perverse honesty" also made them devilishly hard to organize. There were some temporary successes, such as SDS's JOIN, the community-action group that organized Appalachians in Chicago's "uptown" neighborhood. Many scholars and activists tried to get Appalachians to think of themselves as members of a distinct ethnic group so that they might "increase their power to compete as a group for goods and services which cities distribute." "I try to remind them at every turn that they are a political group," another activist told Coles, "that they are *Appalachian whites*, and like *blacks* and *Chicanos* and *Indians* and *migrant farmers*, they have got to pull themselves together, become a force, become their own advocate and lobbyists, just as other groups in this society have learned to do." The trouble was that they continued to think of themselves not as a minority group but as "mountaineers": "They have been thinking that way for generations; it's an opiate, a word like 'mountaineer.' "

Among such activists, the liberal condescension that characterized much of the white contact with urban blacks was missing. They were committed to helping the Appalachians learn how to help themselves. And there was a good deal of truth in the organizers' chiding: aligning themselves as a minority group may well have "increased their ability to compete." It was true that the mountaineers stopped short of seeing their daily problems as part of a larger issue of exploitation. "I'm trying to make them more conscious of the *political* problems, their *class* position in American life," Coles's organizer explained. The real tragedy here was that in order to do so, in order to take the steps necessary to ease that exploitation, some softening of their "class position," the mountaineers would have had to give up the very qualities that made them unique in the first place. Justice, in their case, could not really be done, because justice in any meaningful definition would have entailed both economic improvement and a respect for their values. Thus, the same irresolvable predicament that bedeviled black nationalists confronted Appalachians as well.

The upshot of ethnic politics of the sixties was the silencing of a large part of the population that was not racist, that lived the inequalities of U.S. society, that was not particularly keen to embrace consumer culture, and that struggled to hold on to values in disrepute—independence, hard work, patriotism, and pride among them. The unrepresented in the sixties were that oft-mocked repository of decency, common Americans, white, black, Hispanic, Appalachian, and otherwise, who held to the work ethic, saw through liberal hypocrisy and militant boasts, and wanted simply to be given room to live. For all the notoriety that militants, liberals, racists, and radicals alike achieved, "everyman" or "everywoman" most probably saw the United States much as did Henry Rollins, who told Robert Coles: "I'm a poor man, I know it; and I'm black, or a Negro, I don't care which it is they go and call me. But to Hell with being called everything under the sun! I'm Henry Rollins, that's my name and that's who I am."

CHAPTER 9

The Crisis
of Authority

 The ambiguity of life in the sixties was nowhere more pronounced than in the "crisis of authority," the widespread sense that, for better or worse, forms of authority in public and private spheres of national life had lost their relevance, effectiveness, and legitimacy. The authority under fire was at once governmental, parental, and moral—and more. Depending on which commentator one read or listened to, the crisis of authority was either a necessary good, a healthy refusal to obey without questioning, or an unfortunate evil, which stemmed from growing irresponsibility and a declining national will.

Even in retrospect it is hard to measure the consequences of the crisis. Many forms of authority had proved their bankruptcy. At the outset of the sixties, it is not too much to say, many Americans believed that government was always right and never to be questioned; by 1974, after the Vietnam War and the Watergate scandal, many, if not most, of those same Americans had lost respect for the integrity of their own government. The great gift of the sixties to the future was the lesson, learned only through terrific strife, that democracy needs a skeptical citizenry.

A number of institutions—churches, families, and schools—that had historically mediated between the state and the citizen felt the brunt of the crisis of authority. Partly, these intermediary institutions came under fire in the generalized assault on cultural and moral authority. Liberal-minded people, who were primarily, though not entirely, middle class, rejected conventional religion, the nuclear family, and traditional education, much as they denounced the censor and scorned the Wasp. They believed that discarding institutions promised liberation. For people of the lower classes, however, these intermediary institutions brought spiritual sustenance, stability, and hope for upward mobility. For the working class and the poor, churches, families, and schools were necessary to a decent life. Yet the new liberal values filtered down into working-class society and changed the ground rules of social conduct.

The decay of the intermediary institutions was not a result of the middle class imposing its notions of liberated living on working-class people. The economic and social environment within which the nation's most vulnerable population lived was a more significant factor. The impoverishment of families and schools in particular was another consequence of the general urban crisis. If the crisis of authority teaches a lasting lesson, it is that, for all their resiliency, families, neighborhoods, and local and tight-knit communities, are fragile institutions that need stable surroundings. When stability is lost, the most vulnerable pay the highest costs, in our case, in the form of decaying neighborhoods, disintegrating families, crime, and drugs.

The Death of God

In April 1966 *Time* magazine ran a cover story that, according to the editors, had "been approached with more deliberation" than any other story in the magazine's "forty-three years of publication." *Time* asked, "Is God dead?"

But why? Americans long had been the most religious people in the Western world, and they evidently continued to be. Ninety-seven percent of respondents to *Time* polls said they believed in God, 120 million Americans claimed some religious affiliation, and forty-four percent attended church weekly. It hardly seemed that Americans lacked religious commitments. But by *Time*'s own accounting, less than half of the people in what had once been a universally religious society regularly attended church services. Barely more than half confessed to a particular affiliation, and roughly a third of those who did were Roman Catholics. When coupled with the almost universal belief in God, it would seem that it was organized religion, not God, that was dead.

In an age that questioned the relevance of institutions, organized religion was bound to engender criticism and doubt. The death of God, on one level, was the assertion of contemporary demands that institutions address obvious needs, become "authentic," shed their hypocrisy, and aid in finding solutions to social problems. People increasingly found organized religion irrelevant. "I love God . . . but hate the church," one teenage girl explained. In the face of this disillusioned state of affairs, leaders of religious institutions confessed to a sense of impotence and questioned their own usefulness. No less a figure than the Episcopal dean of the National Cathedral told *Time* that he was "confused as to what God is."

To many observers, such confusion was the healthiest possible response to the institutional crisis. Some liberal theologians argued that organized religion may well have no place in an enlightened society. In his influential book *The Secular City* (1965), Harvey Cox claimed, for example, that organized religion was a curious casualty of urbanization and not one to be mourned particularly. Cox applied the conventional ideas of establishment liberalism to answer the question that modernist theologians had been asking since the 1940s: "How do we speak of God without religion?" The best way, Cox implied, was to understand religion in essentially the same way postwar intellectuals had come to regard ideology. It was a holdover from a darker, less sophisticated age, best left behind because when mixed with modern technology it became destructive. The urban dweller, steeped in cosmopolitan culture, had no need for religion. City folks weren't antireligious; instead, they had matured beyond God, Cox suggested. The role of the church was little different from the role of the liberal state. The job of the church was to escape tradition and become "Jesus's avant garde"; it should destroy prejudice through "cultural exorcism"; it was responsible for helping the oppressed of the city. God—once detached from calcified churches—was a liberal, it seemed.

Cox offered a reassuring balm for those worried about the upheaval of U.S. society, one that soothed a variety of anxieties. Those who wanted to be contemporary, liberal, and Christian at the same time could see that such a feat was possible. Those who were worried about God's death might see that Christianity would survive. Those who feared Christianity could rest assured that it posed no threat to social progress. Above all, religion could meet that watchword of the day and remain relevant.

Even among those who wanted to consider themselves religious, then, the tilt was toward Cox's secularization of creed. However many Americans confessed to an ulimate belief in God, it became increasingly embarrassing to admit it in public. In polite circles, a clear disdain for those who were intensely religious prevailed. Christian fundamentalists were edged or forced out of the major denominational governing bodies and left pretty much to their own devices. When traditionalist Jews in New York City began to assert themselves against both the growing secularization of American Jews and the alleged anti-Semitism of the city's black nationalists, they evoked condescending contempt from midtown Wasps and embarrassment from midtown, assimilated Jews. The Catholic Church's loyalty to the United States' Cold War policy and its continued opposition to abortion and contraception made it appear to be the true bastion of reaction.

Conversely, more liberal sympathy was forthcoming for crusading atheists, of whom Madalyn Murray O'Hair was the decade's most infamous. O'Hair was a Baltimore psychologist whose teenage son complained about having to engage in compulsory Bible readings in his public school. According to her account, she felt compelled to support her son because she had always taught him to stand up for his principles. She therefore proceeded to challenge the Maryland state law that made prayer compulsory, and she won her case in 1963. For her efforts, her fellow Baltimoreans denounced her, harassed her, and finally drove her out of town, but not before she struck back with a campaign to revoke the tax-exempt status of religious organizations. Meanwhile, the court challenge to compulsory prayer paralleled the increasingly liberal bent of the Supreme Court and, when taken along with decisions striking down censorship, dealt another blow against traditional authority. Within three years, according to one survey, Bible reading became rare in public schools; by 1970 no more than 5 percent of the schools in the nation engaged in those activities. The exception to the rule was the South, where half of the public schools continued to read the Bible in spite of Court rulings against the practice.

Mainstream churches responded to the pressures of secularization by liberalizing rules and doctrine. The Roman Catholic Church led the way in this liberalization. Throughout 1962 and 1963, the Second Vatican Council revolutionized the Church, with dramatic consequences for the United States' 43 million Catholics.

In spite of those cynics who quipped that Vatican II brought the Catholic Church into the seventeenth century, the council rewrote governing laws and individual moral codes, took new and more progressive stands on peace, human rights, racism, and nationalism, and accepted the notion of theological diversity within the Church itself. The Latin mass was dropped—an astonishing change for young Catholics forced to memorize church ritual in a dead language—and even priests and nuns began to trade religious clothing for secular dress.

For the Church in the United States, Vatican II was as much a recognition of reality as a reform. The Church's long-standing association with the political right destroyed its legitimacy for many progressive Catholics. Michael Novak, who was a modest professor of religious studies before the *Rise of the Unmeltable Ethnics* made him infamous, criticized the bureaucratic rigidity of a faith stuck in the hands of a few prominent bishops. Reluctance to change, he argued in shades of Harvey Cox, only drove Catholics to voice their concerns over the urban crisis and racial injustice in purely secular terms. "The great irony," Novak wrote, was that "the most sensitive and inquiring young Catholics are presently finding the spiritual values represented by American secularism more compelling than the spiritual attitudes of the Catholic clerical establishment." The Vatican Council was thus "yielding to the sunshine of American liberties and the brisk winds of American realities." Vatican II encouraged a wave of social activism among church faithful, from nuns marching with Chavez in Delano and King in Selma to the Berrigan brothers and the radical pacifists in Baltimore.

Speaking through secular and left-wing Catholic journals like *Ramparts*, political progressives applauded such changes. There is little question that the Church was making urgently needed strides toward modernity. But the Christian God was on His way to postmodernity, which in theological terms that aped cultural critcism, meant that He was, as *Time* announced, dead. The quest for relevance, whether through Catholic reform or through Cox's embrace of the secular city, could not save Him.

Indeed, the most important development in Christian theology in the sixties was the "death of God" movement, a "post–Christian" body of thought that proclaimed the death of the transcendent God as a means of liberating Christians from their distracting concerns over the afterlife, their obsession with following rules, and their belief in fallen humanity. To accept the death of God was to enliven one's Christian morality in this life. "We do not ask God to do for us what the world is qualified to do," wrote the leading radical theologians, Thomas Althizer and William Hamilton. "We trust the world, not God." "Christian atheists," as Althizer described them, were existential Christians, "liberated from all attachments to a celestial and transcendent Lord."

Althizer and Hamilton evidently hoped to free up people to act now, much in the spirit of the New Left. But their intellectual strategy was closer to Susan Sontag's repudiation of cultural authority. By casting off the transcendent God, they presumed they were liberating Christians. Much as with cultural radicalism, however, religious radicalism could survive only when it had something to fight against. What made Madalyn Murray O'Hair's challenges to school prayer so important was that she faced the intense opposition of her neighbors. Once theologians pronounced God dead, once the leaders of national denominations admitted that they were no longer sure who God was, then it was impossible to mount challenges against Christianity that had any power. Althizer argued that Christian atheism meant reveling in the profane. He did not see that the profane depended on having the sacred alive as its antithesis: if nothing was sacred, than nothing was profane. To declare God's death, then, was truly to kill Him, but God's demise made the challenges to religious authority irrelevant, which in turn made nonsense out of radical theology's attempt to create a religion of the relevant.

Notes on the Generation Gap

Partly, the crisis in mainstream Christianity revolved around the infamous generation gap, which evidently was at the heart of the institutional crisis in the churches. Young people were impatient with ritual and authority; they sought immediate answers to the ultimate questions. Novak suggested as much when he approvingly quoted a 14 year old who walked into a prayer meeting only to be disappointed at what she found: "They're talking about Scripture and liturgy. But I came here to find out *whether there's a God*."

This generational chasm pervaded public consciousness in the sixties and was usually chalked up as a natural consequence of the baby boom. Without a doubt, the baby boom gave the United States a remarkably youthful population profile in the sixties. Beginning in 1942, the American birth rate reversed a centuries-old pattern of consistent decline, topping out in 1957 at nearly 123 births per thousand. By the end of the period, well over half of the U.S. population was under 30 years of age, 24 million between 18 and 24 years old. The boom was most immediately a result of a growing number of people marrying at an earlier age. Partly but not wholly in response to the dislocation of wartime society, the trend continued well after World War II and is usually explained as an indication of how earnestly Americans sought to return to a stable existence after two decades of depression and war. The baby boom was part of the age of affluence, and it was, therefore, associated with suburbia, the automobile, television—all under the reign of the traditional nuclear family.

The boom seemed to revitalize the traditional family, one in which father worked and mother tended the home. Many women returned home after moving into the wartime work force, and younger women began marrying straight out of high school and college—or sometimes while still in school. Popular culture, political rhetoric, and social science alike called on adults to see the nuclear family not only as the best vehicle for personal happiness but also as a serious contribution to the nation's well-being. "The family is the center of your living," one advice book intoned. "If it isn't, you've gone far astray." Women were urged to forget about careers, lest they spoil themselves in futile efforts at becoming "masculine." Men, too, were called on to hold up their end of the family bargain. For any adult to avoid marriage was to invite insinuations about homosexuality or immaturity. David Riesman's 1957 interviews with Ivy League college students bore out their commitment to the norms. "I want someone who would stay home and take care of the children," one young man told Riesman of his hypothetical wife. "But on the other hand I want someone who can stimulate me intellectually, and I don't know if those things are compatible. If a woman goes to Radcliffe and takes up economics, she isn't learning how to bring up children." Across the board, the statistics tell a story of compliance: divorce rates declined; average family size increased; and a record number of Americans married.

If this was the environment out of which the sixties generation grew, it is hardly any wonder that young people rebelled. The indications were that the generation gap was opening quickly. It was first noted as a distinct "problem" with the rise of late-fifties "alienated youth," which was a trendy focus of popular culture years before sociologists began to poke around in the generational divide. Capitalists, those aggressive explorers, uncovered it first in the process of tapping the mother lode of the youth market. The number of young people, more and more of whom lived in middle-class comfort, created a market segment that spent an estimated $9.5 billion annually by 1960, more than the total annual sales of General Motors; in 1970, 18 to 24 year olds spent $40 billion. With advertisers and producers jostling one another for a slice of that pie, U.S. mass culture overflowed with appeals to youth. The resulting deluge of advertising inflated the cultural importance of youth in general. This development, in turn, brought the natural process of youthful self-assertion into public life and indeed made a commodity out of it. Youth culture took on the character of a national, very public, generational conflict in part because it had become commercialized. Rock-and-roll was the most obvious and powerful of the items in mass culture's grab bag for young people, which also included a host of anti-heroes: James Dean, Marlon Brando, and Elvis Presley.

The attractions of the marketplace were by no means a complete explanation of why sixties children rebelled or were gripped with a sense of alienation. In one of the period's formative books, Growing Up Absurd (1960), Paul Goodman wondered why young people growing up in the United States could be anything but estranged. In past societies, Goodman claimed, young people were brought to maturity through established rites of passage against which they tested their mettle. There being nothing worthwhile in modern America to test themselves against, young men (Goodman's book was about youthful masculinity) were at a loss to direct their energy to constructive pursuits. Instead, they grew "alienated."

This notion of alienation, a concept uppermost in the minds of the existentialist founders of the New Left, was at once so vague and so easily employed that it provided the catch-all explanation for the behavior of young people. As early as 1960, sociologists like Kenneth Keniston were suggesting that the generation gap was built into modern society and that some measure of alienation was inevitable. Forced to stay close to home much longer than in the past, yet under intense pressure from consumer culture to give into impulse, the younger generation naturally chafed at parental control. Under these circumstances, one scholar wrote, the United States had become "one of the extremist examples of filial friction in human history." Less excitable investigators were similarly convinced that an adolescent subculture had emerged by the early sixties. A host of them plunged into the study of adolescence, claiming it to be the definitive moment in the socialization process.

By the midsixties, alienation—and the generation gap along with it—had become political. Whereas early sympathizers like Goodman and Keniston had treated alienated youth with a gentle paternalism, later sympathizers looked to alienated youth as the saviors of the world and in so doing helped to exaggerate the existence of the gap. Once rebellion became politically fashionable, U.S. academics lavished praise on the alienated young, not just on the famous Diggers or Yippies, but on the wandering hordes of the counterculture. It was almost as if the intellectuals thirsted for vicarious thrills. The renowned anthropologist Margaret Mead, in her last book, *Culture and Commitment* (1970), argued that the rebellion of young people was unprecedented. The young cultural rebels were setting the tone of culture and shaping values that others, even their parents, would soon find themselves following. Whether or not the older generation followed, Mead thought that such an enormous gulf separated children from their parents that the young could only think: "You were never young in the world I'm young in." Once treated as a pressing problem, indicative of some deeper malfunctioning of society, alienation became praised as a virtue, a healthy response to an unreasonable, illegitimate world. It was to be hailed, not cured. Hollywood celebrated it in the 1967 film *The Graduate*, where an alienated young man played by Dustin Hoffman, with nothing but time on his hands, rejects the advice of his father's associate to go into "plastics" and instead strikes up an affair with a much older women.

A number of problems were inherent in this talk about the generation gap and youthful alienation. First, the two did not necessarily go together, and, second, both applied to only a small minority of young people. In his study *Young Radicals* (1967), a widely read if not uniformly admired book about the student activists who ran Vietnam Summer in 1967, Kenneth Keniston concluded that a sense of powerlessness and a loss of life's meaning, even a tortured adolescence, did indeed characterize student radicals. Yet there did not seem to be anything one could call a generation gap between Keniston's radicals and their parents. For the most part, the activists were not children rebelling against authoritarian homes. Their upbringings were mostly normal. Their parents were mildly political and usually liberal; they had taken a keen interest in their children's education and interests. By and large, Keniston's radicals enjoyed warm family relationships.

Although there certainly were differences in generational attitudes, the most systematic studies of the generation gap demonstrated that those differences were better understood as part of a continuum rather than as a sharp break. On matters of childrearing, for instance, the parents of the sixties, having been under the gentle guidance of Dr. Spock, were more permissive than their parents before them; their children, the alleged young rebels, intended to be even more permissive. College students were more likely to be more tolerant of divorce, open sexuality, and marijuana use than their parents, but only by matters of degree. The students were not a very religious generation, but neither had their parents been.

Without question, the baby boomers were a unique generation that inherited a uniquely troubling world. Not only were they materially better off than their parents had been, but also they were the best educated generation in human history. They were the first television generation and the first to be enmeshed in technology within the home. They were the first generation weaned on mass culture, which accelerated children's familiarity with sex and other previous taboos, introduced new codes of conduct, and encouraged young people to identify with their peer group rather than with family, trade, or community. Just as the breakdown of distinct ethnic communities encouraged the formation of ethnic groups along distended national lines, so young people were massed into a category of their own. In his study of the early sixties, James S. Coleman showed that as the middle class abandoned most of its long-held standards, high school students became more prone to identify with peer groups and to disregard parental injunctions. The growing sophistication of children and their readiness to identify with peers provided the ammunition with which children could negotiate with their parents. With children well armed, the negotiations between the generations helped transform many homes into war zones, where, as one minister who specialized in intergenerational counseling wrote, fighting "continued until each has become so defensive and battle-scarred" that "meaningful communication" essentially stopped.

Though no doubt painful, such combat was more honorable than the alternatives. Some parents avoided war simply through surrender, which rendered family relationships meaningless; others ignored the fight altogether and refused to compromise. Rather surprisingly, the intensity with which the generation gap was experienced did not have much to do with the intensity of the war at home. Children whose parents capitulated seemed to run away as often as those whose parents fought to the bitter end. Why stay at home, after all, if you did not have to?

The weight of the sociological evidence suggests that the generation gap depended on the extent to which a particular child was enmeshed in mass culture. Middle-class children, whose relatively comfortable upbringings included massive doses of television and popular music, were far more likely to suffer from "alienation" than were working-class kids. Keniston's young radicals were all of the middle or upper class, just as his earlier "alienated youth" were Ivy Leaguers. At least in urban and suburban areas, Coleman found, middle-class families were more willing to "release" their children into "the adolescent culture." One consequence of this "release" was an estimated 500,000 to 1 million children who ran away from home annually by 1972, the majority of whom were "middle-class dropouts." One such youngster told author Christine Chapman that she ran away because "I hate living in the suburbs. There isn't anything to do and no one to talk to. My brother's away and my parents and I never talk. . . . I'll probably end up with a psychiatrist again."

The Sixties Family

That the generation gap intensified during the period demonstrated that mass culture made the natural and universal process of coming of age a public matter, one caught up, in fact, in the process of production and consumption.

Maturation became an item for sale. As such, the generation gap indicated that the family as an institution was losing what had been its primary function since at least the early 1800s and probably long before that: the nurturing of children in a private environment isolated from the processes of production and commerce.

From any number of directions, critics, having noted the decline in the capacity of families to nurture children, argued that the institution had outlived its usefulness and was now likely to produce tension, mental illness, and maladjusted youth. Intergenerational tension was taken as evidence not of the invasion of the private sphere by mass culture but, quite the contrary, as an indication that the family itself was an irrational barrier to the proper rearing of children, a source of deep mental anguish, and a fundamentally repressive institution.

The Fifties Family

The critiques of the family that flourished in the sixties and that denounced the patriarchal family resembled the cultural critiques of Wasps and puritanism. But the patriarchal family, ruled by the iron-handed father who demanded obedience from the children and submission from his wife, was in no better shape than the censor. The patriarchal family had been disappearing since World War I, and this was one development that the baby-boom era, the Golden Age of the nuclear family, did not reverse. The fifties cult of the family was not truly a revival of the nineteenth-century cult of domesticity: in the earlier form, the woman was to find fulfillment by subordinating herself to her husband's will; in the fifties, fufillment was gained vicariously, through the development of the children. By 1960, one had to conclude, as Robert O. Blood and Donald M. Wolfe maintained in their influential book *Husbands and Wives* (1960), "that the patriarchal family is dead."

By the fifties, the middle-class marriage had become what sociologists called the "companionate" ideal. The companionate marriage joined men and women who had much in common, were usually of the same religious faith and economic class, and shared roughly the same educational background. The homes that such couples established were no longer the castles of dominating husbands but joint enterprises where men and women were friends and lovers as well as husbands and wives. Modern marriage, pop singer Pat Boone claimed with characteristic blandness in 1958, was a "fifty-fifty deal."

The companionate ideal of marriage was complemented by an intensified obsession with the upbringing of children, an equally subtle shift away from older middle-class norms. Whereas the patriarchal family of old was designed to nurture children in firm morals and to breed character, the "filiarchical" family was preoccupied with making children happy. According to the sociological stereotype, the suburban middle-class family, often transplanted from one suburb to another with numbing regularity, organized itself around the children's ball games, schools, dance classes, and so forth, and thereby convinced children that they were the center of the universe. Quite in contrast to the stern hand of patriarchy, filiarchy was indulgent and permissive, its leading theorist being not St. Paul but Dr. Spock.

The child-centered home of fifties lore was thus very much like the companionate marriage in that both were exaggerated efforts to salvage initimacy in a bureaucratic, impersonal world. Both, in other words, were advanced as antidotes to alienation. In the absence of supportive communities, however, the family was left to carry the impossible burden of insulating its members from mass culture.

It is reasonably clear that the middle-class family was in no position to serve such a purpose. If anything, middle-class parents worked at cross purposes with themselves. Their families were tied to suburbia and corporate America, and yet it was here where the obsession with nurturing was most intense. Many parents tried to reconcile these competing characteristics by embracing the latest childrearing techniques, much of which offered instruction in indulgence. Such a strategy was self-defeating; for if the purpose of the family was to protect the individual from the outside world, it made little sense to guide the family according to the advice of outsiders. Yet that is exactly what many middle-class parents, perhaps for lack of credible options, resorted to. No wonder "middle-class parents," the sociologist Melvin Kohn wrote, "seem to regard child-rearing as more problematic than do working-class parents." No wonder, too, that middle-class children could so regularly dismiss parental supervision as hypocritical and irrelevant. Weakened by its own compromises, the middle-class family was in a sorry state and deserving of criticism.

The Women's Movement Critique of the Family

The most telling criticism came from the mainstream women's movement. The most important work from this direction, Betty Friedan's milestone *The Feminine Mystique* (1963), did not confuse the contemporary family with the patriarchal monster of old. If anything, the middle-class woman had more comfort and more superficial freedom than ever before. Far from the victim of iron-fisted repression, she was "the envy of women all over the world. . . . She was healthy, beautiful, educated, concerned only about her husband, her children, her home. . . . As a housewife and mother, she was respected as a full and equal partner to man in his world. . . . She had everything that women ever dreamed of." These were all superficial freedoms. The agonizing truth was that as middle-class women gained more comfort and latitude in the home, their public roles were actually decreasing.

The difficulties of the middle-class housewife were ultimately not very different from what confronted her children: she, too, was alienated. Like Paul Goodman's teenage boys, the contemporary woman was denied the use of her skills and deprived of outlets for testing her mettle. The "problem that has no name" ensnared women and left them emotional wrecks, usually wondering what perverse sexual problems they had because sex was what the experts always blamed for vague feelings of discontent. The middle-class home had become a "comfortable concentration camp" in which women were "progressively dehumanized." Contemporary housewives were "dependent, passive, childlike." Yoked to the "monotonous, unrewarding" chores of housework and childrearing, "they have given up their adult frame of reference to live at the lower level of food and things." The hideousness of grinding so many human beings into degradation was compounded by the consequences, not only of the mental dislocation of women themselves, but also of the growing dehumanization of children who were condemned to be raised by such women. The mother, Friedan was suggesting, was the vehicle through which contemporary society was funneling alienation into the home.

But what was the solution? "We need a drastic reshaping of the cultural image of femininity," she wrote, "that will permit women to reach maturity, identity, completeness of self, without conflict with sexual fulfillment." That meant a culture that did not narrow the acceptable image of women to the doltish housewife; educators who expanded the visions of their women students rather than shoving them into home economics courses; and women who recognized that they deserved expanded horizons.

Friedan's moderate plea for women to take an acceptable public role begged an obvious question, which radical feminists leveled by the late sixties: if alienation was rooted in the family and tied to the constraints on women, then why not redefine the family or simply do away with it altogether? Although they sympathized with Friedan's insistence on a public life for women, radicals argued that "the heart of woman's oppression is her childbearing and childrearing roles." These fundamentally oppressive roles were only partly defined by the mass media or fifties culture, Shulamith Firestone argued in the best radical critique of the family. The historic oppression of women had to be rooted in the biological functions of sex and childbearing. "The patriarchal family was only the most recent in a string of 'primary' social organizations" that narrowed women's role because of her "unique childbearing capacities," Firestone wrote. Because it remained powerful even though it had lost most of its economic and political justification, the nuclear family "intensifies the psychological penalties of the biological family." Thus, the ultimate end of revolution was to allow women to escape biology "by every means available," and if this were achieved, the puny nuclear family would shrivel away as well.

The biological function was not so easily done away with. Emancipation by any means available implied that, if women were to do away with men altogether, they would have to rely on artificial insemination and other new technologies, which in turn raised doubts about how democratic and far reaching this emancipation would be. Firestone was wary of technology, as long as it emanated from corporate capitalism, and her wariness was well founded, given the story of the birth control pill. Hailed as a virtually fail-safe contraceptive when put on the market in the early sixties, responsible for a good deal of the sexual revolution's momentum thereafter, the pill was the result of a decades-long collaboration of entrepreneurial scientists and drug companies. Because the taboos against their work made it difficult to test the pill, the collaborators conducted a short series of inadequate studies with women residents of a Puerto Rican low-income housing development. Knowing that a tremendous market awaited, the Searle drug company rushed the pill into production with little consideration for long-term health effects, the existence of which took twenty years to prove.

Alternative Institutions to the Family

Beyond the problems that technology presented stood the questions of what institutions, if any, should replace the family. The most impressive-sounding alternative offered by the radical critics of the nuclear family was the commune, of which there were an estimated 4,000 in North America by 1970. The commune had several virtues, according to its advocates. Housework and childrearing were shared. Sex was detached from power and dominance, because no one ruled in a commune. The commune did away with the feminine mystique because women did not have to live vicariously through the children, whereas the children could benefit from having a number of role models. The home would no longer be a battleground. For when "adults other than the mother are important as models for these children," one advocate contended "we find ourselves growing into 'deputy parents' [and] develop a community of households which trust one another and to whom angry, hurt or bored children (or adults!) can go without the trauma of leaving home."

For those too conventional to try out commune life, there was the alternative of "open marriages." Because marriage served as a brake on indulgence, many commentators assumed that it was the cause of great tension in an age of sexual liberation. Marriage turned people into criminals and cheats simply for following their natural impulses. The conventional marriage was inherently hypocritical. And sex was not the only aspect of life that marriage spoiled. As Nena and George O'Neill argued in *Open Marriage* (1972), "the rigid role behavior dictated by fiat in the closed marriage can be just as destructive, just as inhibiting," as conventional sexuality. Men felt obliged to live up to their masculine roles, whereas women chafed against the expectations of standard femininity. They become defensive, and "by cutting themselves off from all possibilities of growth, they cut themselves off from their own potential selves and finally from one another."

The best alternative to this sad state of affairs, according to the O'Neills, was "open marriage," a "relationship of peers" in which "mutual liking and trust" replaced "dominance and submission" and provided each partner "enough psychic space . . . to become an individual." Unlike the "trap" of the closed marriage, the liberated relationship attended to individual "growth" by allowing each partner to experiment. It was essential that neither partner see the marriage itself as the all-consuming aspect of life. Those who invested themselves totally in marriage were engaged in a pathetic search for security, when the only way to realize one's potential was to live for the "here and now." Especially in matters of sexuality, experimentation was essential. "Despite our tradition of limited love, it is entirely possible to love your marital partner with an intensely rewarding and continually growing love and at the same time to love another or others with a deep and abiding affection." Possible, that is, if couples settled on contracts for "non-binding commitments." A few Americans evidently adopted the O'Neills' view of things. When

Psychology Today conducted a survey of its readers in 1970, it found that 5 percent engaged in "wife-swapping" and another one-third liked the idea.

It is self-evident that the O'Neills were sixties creatures; their ideas, from the existential relationship to the frank claim that sex without love was a fine thing, were obviously drawn from the contemporary environment. Yet the "open-marriage movement" was more than just a collection of ideas used in the war against the patriarchal family. The main target of the O'Neills' book, and indeed of most other assaults on traditional marriage, was not patriarchy so much as individual commitment. Although the O'Neills' program seemed to call for the expansion of relationships, in reality they advised people to reduce their dependence on others, to take care of themselves first on the grounds that self-fulfillment was the basis of "your capacity to give openly of your love." Where the "filial" family of the fifties turned in on itself and poured its energy into the isolating relationships of the home, open marriage was a recommendation for that isolation to be taken one step further, to isolate the individual even from familial commitments. It is both illuminating and astonishing that the O'Neills barely mention children in their book. "If you happen to have any," children, too, would presumably benefit from the parents' enlarged capacity for love. The possibility that children are in deep need of predictability, security, the intense affection of biological parents—in short, all of those limitations on adult growth—was evidently beside the point. Here indeed was the end of the bourgeois family.

Divorce Trends

The radical critique of the family, the postmodern communards, and the open-marriage advocates, of course, did not destroy the family, any more than advocates of the second sexual revolution destroyed heterosexuality. The vast majority of U.S. adults continued to get married, pretty much as they always had.

Still, by any conventional measure, change was brewing. The divorce rate continued to climb: by mid-decade an estimated 25 to 30 percent of all marriages ended in divorce. Here again, the condition of the sixties family was part of a long legacy; divorce rates had been rising consistently since the late nineteenth century. When mixed into the cultural disarray of the sixties, however, the high divorce rates signaled important shifts in attitudes and in law. In some quarters, divorce was hailed as a good thing, the legal antidote to the "closed marriage"; in most quarters, it was accepted with increasing tolerance. The old song that unhappy couples should stick it out "because of the kids" hardly played in the age of liberation.

On the grounds that an enlightened society would accept the tentative nature of marriage and the need for "flexibility," Americans reformed the whole approach to the question of divorce by applying to marriage the same legal strategies that had been used to loosen tradition's grasp in other areas. Like the anti-obscenity laws, the nation's divorce laws were deemed to be downright primitive. "In few areas of American law," one advocate of liberalized divorce wrote in 1966, "does there exist a body of precepts less logical, less reflective of actual mores, and less respected and observed than our divorce laws." And the case was a good one. New York had the most notorious divorce laws; as late as 1966, when a long-running battle between the Catholic Church and liberals finally ended in reform, New York law allowed divorce only on the grounds of adultery. This had been a liberal law when it was originally written—in 1787 by Alexander Hamilton. By the sixties it was rather out of step with popular practice. Couples seeking divorce regularly perjured themselves and admitted to adultery. Those who could afford it went out of state—as Mrs. Nelson Rockefeller did when she divorced New York's governor in 1962. Meanwhile, many states permitted divorce on only a few grounds beyond adultery.

As with obscenity statutes, the restrictive divorce laws were swept away. California, a state whose conservative leader, Ronald Reagan, was himself a divorced actor and in no shape to obstruct reform, led the way by establishing no-fault divorce by 1970. Iowa, a state not known for loose morals, followed quickly, and within four years roughly half the states adopted no-fault laws. Divorce reform was less a result of the lonely fight of dedicated reformers against an entrenched establishment than it was a recognition of popular sentiment—of the marriage marketplace, one might say. In New York the law was so regularly flouted that it was an embarrassing joke, and as for the Catholic Church, it lost its will to resist change after Vatican II. In California, the no-fault system was embraced mostly to make the already widespread resort to divorce less traumatic. As one reformer put it, "it was impossible to make divorce easier in California than it already was."

The Working-Class Family

The importance of the sixties family lay far less in how its condition was related to the bourgeois family of times past than in how it set the tone for the indisputable impoverishment of the family in the years that followed. The "silent revolution" in the American family was a transformation of values, carried out partly in the cause of feminism, partly through the loosening of sexual restraints, and partly under the supposition that individual well-being was hindered under a regime of marital fidelity. As with the cultural transformation generally, this shift in values emerged from the middle class, and to some extent the critique of the nuclear family became another front in the clandestine war against the working class, whose commitment to traditional family relationships, in the eyes of many observers, was of a piece with its racism. Before World War II, liberals and radicals alike had taken a rather tolerant view of working-class families, which they assumed were less repressed than those of the bourgeoisie. In the years after World War II, that stereotype was transferred to African Americans, who were then thought to be more casual about extramarital affairs and less given to restraint—in short, they were licentious. The white working-class family was thereafter assumed to be the repository of violent drunkenness, authoritarian fathers, and terrorized women and children.

By nearly all accounts, the working-class family was both laggard in accepting the new values and less influenced by mass culture. With regard to childrearing practices, for instance, the experts regularly pronounced working-class parents backward. Even when controlled for ethnicity and religious affiliation, according to

Melvin L. Kohn in 1963, "the empirical evidence clearly shows that being on one side or the other of the line that divides manual from non-manual workers has profound consequences for how one rears one's children." "Working-class parents lagged behind" the middle class in embracing permissive techniques. They were more likely to use corporal punishment and to insist on strict obedience to adult authority of any kind, not caring about the child's motives for misbehavior. The working class, Mirra Komarovsky wrote, "retained a pre-Freudian innocence about human behavior," where misbehavior was taken as a sign of insufficient discipline, and the goals of childrearing were "expressed in moral terms." Komarovsky, a sociologist who did the most extensive studies of working-class values in the sixties, revealed her own biases when she wrote that her interviews with parents propelled her backward "from the world of the twentieth century—transported as if by a Wellsian time machine into an older era."

Most investigators concluded that the class discrepancies in childrearing resulted from the working class's isolation. Working-class parents ignored the advice of childrearing experts. Middle-class parents, Kohn wrote, "are far more likely than are working-class parents to discuss child-rearing with friends and neighbors, to consult physicians on these matters, to attend Parent-Teacher Associations meetings, to discuss the child's behavior with his teacher." Komarovsky believed that working-class parents wanted to raise children to be decent human beings: "They do not speak of 'emotional security,' 'creativity,' 'capacity to grow,' or of 'relating to others.' " "Insulated from contemporary currents of thought," Komarovsky lamented, such parents had not gotten wind of the ideas that the middle class had absorbed through "college courses and child psychologists." Beyond that, working-class Americans were simply more conservative; having achieved some measure of economic comfort, they no longer saw external authority as a class enemy. They "are willing to accord respect to authority," Kohn believed, "in return for security and respectability," and they taught their children accordingly.

The unspoken assumption was that middle-class childrearing was superior. There was no discussion of the possibility that middle-class parents were in the process of instructing their children in the development of self-absorption, no discussion of how permissive childrearing taught children that the family was itself an obstacle to their "growth," and no discussion of the possibility that middle-class parents were offering lessons in how to limit the ties of intimacy to "nonbinding commitments." Helen, the Boston maid in the enlightened Cambridge household (see Chapter 1), saw no virtue in such parenting. Her employers believed that children who were taught to respect authority were enslaved to the status quo, but to Helen, children raised in a permissive household never learned the virtue of mutual respect. "In that house," she told Robert and Jane Coles, "the kids speak back to their parents, act as fresh and snotty as can be. I want to scream sometimes when I hear those brats talking as if they know everything."

A similar gulf stood between the classes' distinct views on marriage. Komarovsky, who found working-class people extremely hard to interview because, unlike her middle-class subjects, they refused to engage in self-analysis, characterized the blue-collar conception of marriage with characteristic bluntness: it was "primitive," she concluded. And yet the marriages that she described were not patriarchal in the strict sense of that term. She found what she called "patriarchal" attitudes in situations where both men and women believed that the woman's place was in the home and that men should be dominant in a relationship. By her own definition, however, men dominated in 45 percent of the marriages in her study, women in 21 percent, and in 27 percent power was equally shared.

Meanwhile, conventional attitudes, where they continued to hold sway, were a "great distance" from the strict patriarchal arrangement. Wives increasingly worked outside of the home, principally to earn extra income for consumer goods, but also to get out of the house; blue-collar women were less likely than middle-class mothers to express guilt about working. Housework continued to fall heavily on the wife, but over half of the husbands regularly cared for the children. Men resented their wives' insistence on their doing household chores more than they disliked the chores themselves. They resisted doing dishes or washing floors, Komarovsky found, not because these chores were "unmanly" but because they did not want to yield to demands. In any case, working-class men probably did more of such work than their middle-class counterparts, although it must also be said that a large portion of Komarovsky's women subjects believed that they worked harder in marriage than did men. As for sex, blue-collar couples were neither prudes nor the stereotypical brawling, abusive husband and suffering wife. Most of Komarovsky's subjects, both men and women, took for granted the importance of mutual fulfillment and the healthiness of desire.

In many ways, then, the blue-collar marriage was essentially the same as the middle-class marriage, and in some ways it was slightly more "enlightened." When she called it "primitive," Komarovsky could only have meant that blue-collar couples were culturally deprived. The women remained close to their mothers, from whom they took most of their ideas about family life. Komarovsky's explanation for why women should demonstrate an "untroubled acceptance of housewifery" was that they suffered from "the lack of exposure to certain values." The men remained close to their buddies, with whom they socialized, if they socialized at all. The "companionate marriage" was rare in the working class; men and women did not marry in order to be friends. Marriage was not a means to growth; it was itself a form of movement into the adult world, an end in itself. Her subjects often shied away from the sort of open communication that middle-class couples were convinced was essential to a healthy relationship. Instead, they suffered from a "trained incapacity to share." "The restricted environment and the low cultural level of the [working-class] home," she concluded, promised to retard the development of children and ultimately frustrate any reforms designed to help the working class catch up, "socially as well as materially," with the "salaried middle class."

It is striking how clearly Komarovsky's blue-collar marriages resembled the working-class culture that more sympathetic observers found in other studies. Her subjects could have fit comfortably into Boston's west end among Herbert Gans's "urban villagers." In that sense, the assault on the working-class family was a sort of cultural urban renewal. For the shift in values surrounding intimacy, marriage, and childrearing demonstrated another instance by which the middle class repudiated long-standing beliefs that it once had insisted the working class live up to. Instead of condescending to them as primitives driven by impulse and in need of self-control—as nineteenth-century guardians of morality had—middle-class advocates of liberation of the sixties rebuked working-class Americans for their "primitive" devotion to discipline, their acceptance of authority, and their uptight refusal to follow their impulses.

It is little wonder that working-class Americans took umbrage at remarks about their "primitiveness," and it was not hard for them to see middle-class hypocrisy in such scorn. At the very least, Komarovsky and other observers could have admitted the ambiguities in or the range of legitimate interpretations of allegedly traditional values. Devotion to marriage, to sexual restraint, to the work ethic—all these values were arguably stifling. But to working-class people, they were often essential not only to their sense of self-esteem but also to the reality of practical independence. To have a mother at home instead of at work was not just a sign of the father's virtue, but proof that the family itself was at least one step away from economic disaster. The working-class home was geared toward facilitating the effectiveness of the main wage earner and thereby sustained an overall cohesiveness in which the household stood as a functional unit. Many of those working-class women who did work outside the home envied their peers who did not. Their envy was far less a result of their "lack of exposure to certain values" than of their constant exposure to onerous and unsatisfying work.

Another fault with the middle-class view of humble families was that, in spite of their evident attempts to remain isolated, working-class Americans were being drawn into postmodern society. The desire for consumer goods was strong among all Americans, not just among those who could afford them, and the search after consumer goods, as Lee Rainwater and others observed, often "encourages receptivity to the social models embodied in the mass media and acceptance of the authority of the media as purveyors of the social, cultural, and material goods available to an American who 'has made it.' " Moreover, much as in the middle class, mass culture seems to have induced alienation among those working-class Americans who embraced new values. Consequently, where Komarovsky found culturally isolated people, other observers found people locked in "pervasive anxiety" and engaged in "compensatory consumption," the acquisition of goods in an effort to make up for blocked upward mobility. Patricia Sexton insisted that the working-class wife was deeply discontented with the family's economic status. While "her tastes run to 'modern' in everything," her pocketbook "leaves her with the look of the discount store. She is firmly opposed to installment buying, but has no alternative." Two-thirds of the women Sexton interviewed reported being in debt and feeling guilty about it. "Workingmen's wives" floundered between traditional culture and mass culture; their anxiety and alienation was supposedly a result of being caught in the middle. Their "whole previous lifetime training was built around a different conception of how to live," Rainwater wrote in a study of the consumption patterns of working-class women. They simply "don't take on new habits automatically."

However debilitating or liberating mass culture was for working-class families, their economic position was ultimately far more important in dictating their fate. If wives lived in anxiety, it was probably a result of economic insecurity. They were far more pessimistic about the state of the economy than middle-class women, even in the boom times. The opening of the workplace in response to the demands of the women's movement did not promise much for them, not in an economic climate that had less use for unskilled and semiskilled labor. Moving into the work force meant moving into service jobs or the lowest paying branches of industrial work, very little of which was unionized. Women moved inexorably into the labor force regardless of their class status, so that they made up more than a third of the overall work force by 1970. But several new developments became clear by 1968. More mothers, including mothers with young children, were going to work; working-class wives of men who earned between $3,000 and $6,999 annually were going to work more often than either those above or below them; and more of these women were working full time.

These developments can be accounted for in two ways, both of which demonstrate that the working-class family was no longer isolated in a "pre-Freudian" state. Given the increasing acceptability of working women, endorsed by federal legislation and defended by the women's movement, working-class women moved into the work force in part to gain personal independence and to supplement the household income so that their families might participate in the consumer society. Necessity was probably just as important, however, especially for those families living in expensive cities as inflation began to increase. What at the time appeared to be a healthy transformation of the working-class family out of its patriarchal rut was, in retrospect, an attempt to fend off poverty.

The Moynihan Report

The damage that economic hardship inflicted on families in an affluent society given over to the new values was too little appreciated, something that the furor over the so-called Moynihan Report bears out. The report, which detailed the growing problem of single-parent, female-headed households among African Americans, had its origins in the bureaucratic turf war that was fought over Great Society programs. In an attempt to wrest some War on Poverty money out of the OEO in spring 1965, Assistant Secretary of Labor Daniel Moynihan prepared an internal document that was to set the backdrop for an upcoming national civil rights conference and that would provide the rationale for the Labor Department to administer a jobs program.

For many reasons, the Moynihan Report deserved neither its infamy nor its prominence. Not only was its main purpose bureaucratic, but also it was neither particularly comprehensive nor, ultimately, an important influence on policy. Moynihan's thesis was simple: the foremost problem in the urban United States was the breakdown of the black family. Almost a quarter of urban black women lived apart from their husbands, and women headed roughly the same proportion of households. The rate of illegitimacy in 1963 was 23.6 percent and clearly on the increase; only a minority of black children reached age 18 having lived their lives with both parents. "There is a considerable body of evidence to support the conclusion that

Negro social structure," Moynihan wrote, "in particular the Negro family, battered and harassed by discrimination, injustice, and uprooting, is in the deepest trouble. While many young Negroes are moving ahead to unprecedented levels of achievement, many more are falling farther and farther behind." In locating causes, Moynihan pointed to slavery's brutality against the family, the emasculation of black men under Jim Crow, the difficulties of the abrupt transition from rural to urban life, and the "racist virus that still afflicts us." African Americans continued to pay the costs of hefting this historical burden, which had now taken the form of family breakdown, welfare dependency, criminality, educational problems, and the absence of male role models. Given these broad implications, the crisis of the urban black family "is the single most important social fact of the United States today."

Once the report circulated through War on Poverty officials, it made its presence felt. In an important address at Howard University in June, President Johnson suggested that the upcoming conference would focus on the problems of black families. Thereafter the report's particulars leaked out bit by bit. Civil rights leaders became suspicious when they heard about this secret memo, which, according to some sources, blamed the economic plight of blacks on their moral failures. Their hackles up even before the fall conference, they warned the administration that they had better not hear any nonsense about black depravities. By the time the conference met, civil rights leaders had exerted enough pressure on the administration to have Moynihan all but banished. His exile duly became known when conference director Berl Bernhard assured the participants that he had been "reliably informed that no such person as Daniel Patrick Moynihan exists."

The wider importance of the Moynihan Report had far more to do with the reaction to it than anything the report itself said. Mainstream white liberals, led by New York psychologist William Ryan, accused Moynihan of a series of unpardonable sins: "blaming the victim," ignoring white racism, and calling for individual responsibility. In fact, Moynihan did none of these things. CORE director James Farmer attacked Moynihan's description of the black family as caught in "a tangle of pathology." Farmer charged Moynihan with fueling a "new racism" and of "suggesting that Negro mental health should be the first order of business in a civil-rights revolution." Moynihan never made such a suggestion. Still other critics condemned Moynihan as a cultural imperialist bent on imposing white middle-class values on lower-class black families. Others maintained that the matriarchal family was an extension of West African customs and should be respected as a legitimate part of ethnic subculture. But the most curious readings of all came from those who broached the possibility, much in the spirit of the Cloward and Ohlin thesis on juvenile delinquency, that the matriarchal family was a predictable and quite possibly a healthy adaption to the ghetto environment. Before he understood what his friend Moynihan was getting at, Bayard Rustin wrote that "what may seem to be a disease to the white middle class may be a healthy adaption to the Negro lower class."

Certainly, sound criticisms of the Moynihan Report were issued. For one thing, Moynihan's attention to "pathology" was far too much in keeping with the culture-of-poverty school of thought within the administration that had led to the disaster of community action. His exaggerations aside, Farmer rightly pointed out that Moynihan probably underreported the extent of illegitimacy among whites and failed to account for the greater availability of contraception and abortion to middle-class white women. Andrew Billingsley, meanwhile, showed that family breakdown was clearly associated with income level. Where annual income was above $3,000, the rate of broken families fell to only 7 percent, still higher than the rate for whites in comparable circumstances but hardly a national crisis. Below the poverty level, however, the rate rose to 36 percent. The Moynihan Report, Billingsley argued, rested on a stereotyped overgeneralization of black life and neglected to note similar trends in black and white family structure when income was considered.

The most curious aspect of the whole episode was that the report reinforced the assault on the nuclear family by focusing attention on the overheated elements of race and culture and by lending a polemical edge to the assault that it otherwise lacked. White liberals who could not treat white working-class families with much equanimity were quick to see in the desperate straits of ghetto families a model for cultural liberation, much, it might be said, as white radicals chased after the Panthers in a giddy effort to capture the authentic life.

The cultural polemics then and since have obscured what the Moynihan Report actually was. It was not a report on the historical maldevelopment of the black family. It was not a very good study of a contemporary crisis. Rather, it was a prediction of the future, and "its dire predictions," Nicholas Lemann plaintively writes in retrospect, "all came true." It was a prediction, moreover, not of the inevitable collapse of the black ghetto family but of the potential impoverishment—morally, socially, and economically—of all urban, working-class families.

"Our Children's Burden"

The amount of energy that activists showered on children in U.S. schools during the sixties was in inverse proportion to the absence of concern over children in the debate on the nuclear family. It was almost as if liberal-minded people took for granted that the public schools would assume the burden of childrearing. Few, if any, commentators on the quality of education—or lack thereof—made any such claim. Nonetheless, much of the writing on public education transferred to the schools many of the sentimental notions of childrearing that had governed the filial family.

It has become nearly an inflexible rule that Americans excuse their most pressing problems by blaming public education. Not surprisingly, then, educational activists pushed child-centered education as the solution to the urban crisis and racial segregation. "The burden of the urban future," journalist Peter Schrag wrote, "is the burden of the urban school. . . . In the city, the center of all that is presumably modern and dynamic, public education often remains the sluggish legacy of another age."

In 1967 Jonathan Kozol's impassioned *Death at an Early Age* set the tone for activist criticisms of urban schools, his dire view aptly expressed in the equation of poor education with death. In 1964 Kozol began a six-month stint as a substitute teacher in Boston's inner city, amid practically medieval conditions. Corporal punishment was not only accepted but honed to a secretive art by teachers and administrators who relished beating children. Overwhelmingly white, the teachers either had been banished to ghetto schools for incompetence or were awaiting better positions. There was no doubt that they were bigots; they routinely referred to their charges as "animals" and the schools as "zoos." They taught out of textbooks that depicted all the world's people as advanced and sophisticated—except Africans, who appeared as "half-naked, . . . beating on drums and puckering out their mouths and looking truly strange." Nearly all the teachers seemed to believe the textbooks. Where the physical plant was safe, it was dilapidated. Otherwise, it was downright dangerous: windows fell off walls, and blackboards crashed near students. Kozol took it upon himself to alter the situation when he began assigning essays on the neighborhood and had the students learn Langston Hughes's "Ballad of the Landlord." For his pains he was fired, but his book inspired many other diatribes against the "tyranny of schooling."

Though more passionate than most, Kozol's critique typified activist thinking about education because he placed the lion's share of blame on two primary culprits, bureaucracy and racism. Educational critics contended that urban school systems had become fortresses of privilege and incompetence. In some cities, the school bureaucracies had become stepping stones to political careers and therefore attracted people whose interests were less in education than in taking the winning side in high-profile disputes. New York, where the school system had become a "model of bureaucratic pathology," in David Rogers's words, was typical. In New York, no one was ever fired for incompetence, seniority ruled, power was centralized, and the whole system was isolated from the people it was supposed to serve. Professional bureaucrats promulgated long lists of rules and regulations for individual teachers and principals to follow but had little contact with the schools themselves. Innovation was not only difficult, but it was often impossible without breaking the rules and hence endangering the innovator's career. According to Rogers, "there are countless incidents involving professionals with imaginative new curricula who have not been able to get their materials into the classroom or have been harassed when they did."

Decentralization

The logical solution to bureaucratization was decentralization, which came in various forms. Detroit, for example, was one of the first cities to construct semiautonomous districts within the larger system in the hopes of tying the schools more closely to the neighborhoods and the parents. A deluge of new ideas about school organization and pedagogic method arose in mid-decade, from "anti-schools" to Montessori programs to the special programs for troubled youth.

Decentralization often accompanied the dismantling of curricula and ran along with the strategies of progressive education. Detroit was also one of the first large districts to implement the "nongraded school," where students ideally worked at their own pace without the judgments of grades hovering over them. In his romantic account of a "free school" on New York's lower east side, George Dennison and a few other hardy teachers taught two dozen problem students and offered them a destructured curriculum that took as its main object "the present lives of children." Field trips, walks through the city, and unsupervised play made up the bulk of the lessons. Dennison's hope was that the free school could build relationships between caring adults and deprived children, and in so doing breach the frightful isolation, imposed by impoverishment, that made it impossible for the individual children to swim in the mainstream.

Part narrative, part brief for progressive education, Dennison's *The Lives of Children* (1969) was also aggressively antibureaucratic. The very nature of the standardized schooling process, Dennison believed, was deeply antagonistic to learning because it eclipsed individuals: students looked at teachers as representatives of "the system" instead of as people with whom they might develop an instructive relationship. Children came to believe that even ideas were the property of the school system, rather than something they could hold and develop on their own. In such systems, the "schoolchild's chief expense of energy is self-defense against the environment," a point also made by teacher John Holt in his two books, *How Children Fail* (1964) and *How Children Learn* (1967).

As a strategy for teaching, progressive education in decentralized schools held out indisputable promise. No one could argue that low student-teacher ratios were undesirable or take issue with the wisdom of building humane relationships. It may have been difficult to implement across the nation, but its practicality was mostly a matter of public will. Decentralization, moreover, was the only notion of school organization that took into account the importance of family and neighborhood in the educational process.

As a means to liberal ends, however, decentralization left something to be desired. If it benefited Dennison's students, it was also the sort of strategy that had become the last refuge of southern segregationists. Decentralized schools on the lower east side might be models of humane education; in lower Mississippi, or more to the point, in midtown, they could be bastions of race privilege.

The ambiguities of decentralization worked themselves out around just such crisscrossing goals in New York's bitter teachers' strike of 1968, one of those extraordinarily messy situations so characteristic of the times. Two of the city's most prominent Wasps, Mayor John Lindsay and McGeorge Bundy (Bundy had left his post as national security advisor to head the Ford Foundation), united in support of black radical demands against unionized teachers, 55 percent of whom were Jewish. Lindsay was cresting at the peak of his national reputation, whereas Bundy had gone from fighting a war against community control in Vietnam to funding a war for community control in New York. The teachers' strike created fissures across the city, pitting blacks against Jews; working-class Jews against upper-class Jews; and black militants against some black teachers and probably many in the black community.

The roots of the school crisis lay in the problems of the overly bureaucratized system. It was hard to be too critical of the school bureaucracy, so unresponsive had it become. Teachers who were indifferent or burned out, incompetent or racist, were protected by a system that had fired fewer than fifty teachers from a faculty of 60,000 in the previous five years. The schools were unhinged from their neighborhoods. In 1964 and 1965, after the Harlem riots, several groups representing mostly middle-class black parents and community activists began to press the school system for racial desegregation. Over and over the school system feigned concern, only to ignore the requests. Integration would not have been easy in a system where 75 percent of the students were non-white, but the school administration's flippant response to legitimate demands made enemies.

In 1966 black militants prevented the school board from opening a new middle school in Harlem and demanded the replacement of white staff members. The board capitulated and then proceeded to consider a further decentralization of school administration. Decentralization was an appealing idea for many. Nearly everyone admitted that the administration was a dinosaur and needed reforming; militants saw it as an opportunity to exercise real community control; and John Lindsay saw it as a moral imperative. But as Charles Morris notes in his study of New York politics in the sixties, school decentralization was too much like maximum feasible participation: it sounded fine but no one knew what it meant. Lindsay turned to Bundy and the Ford Foundation to study and recommend decentralization procedures.

The teachers' union, the United Federation of Teachers (UFT), was acutely interested in decentralization. Any changes in administration automatically affected work conditions for teachers, especially those dealing with transfer and promotion, not all of which were governed by written agreements. The UFT was heavily Jewish and had helped make the school system a vehicle of economic security for working-class Jews. Its heritage was in the liberal trade-union movement, and its members liked to think of themselves as part of one of the nation's most progressive unions; they had sent volunteers to Mississippi Freedom schools, marchers to the Memphis sanitation strike, and a contingent to Resurrection City during the Poor People's March. UFT President Albert Shanker was an early member of CORE and an associate of Bayard Rustin. But like the white ethnics, working-class Jews were growing nervous about events swirling around them—not just rising crime and declining city services but the wider, even international aspects surrounding the Six-Day War in the Middle East. When they heard black militants denouncing Whitey, they detected strains of anti-Semitism.

Initially, the UFT was not opposed to decentralization. Union representatives helped some parents organize in anticipation of gaining more control over the schools. In one case, a UFT member, who was also a former CORE member, helped parents secure a modest grant from the Ford Foundation to offset organizational costs. This particular group was hoping to take control of the schools in Ocean Hill-Brownsville, "a tiny piece of urban blight," as one writer described it, stuck between two vast Brooklyn slums, Bedford-Stuyvesant and Brownsville; "it is a no-man's-land between two no-man's-lands." With this help, Ocean Hill parents put together a local school board in summer 1967 and chose a veteran teacher, Rhody McCoy, as board chair. McCoy's eighteen years of trying to climb the administrative ladder had earned him nothing more than an acting principalship at a school for delinquents. McCoy had become friendly with some of Harlem's aspiring black nationalists, including Malcolm X. He eagerly accepted the Ocean Hill invitation in the hopes that it might be a place where blacks could gain control of their institutions. Ultimately, he hoped to turn all of Ocean Hill, including the local community college, into a black-controlled district.

McCoy and the parents began to act on those hopes in September 1967. The UFT had decided to strike the city schools for reasons unrelated to decentralization, and Shanker personally asked McCoy to support the strike. Instead, McCoy told his board that "if you're not going to operate, you've already acknowledged the fact that somebody else controls you. . . . These are our schools. We decide what the hell we're gonna do." McCoy kept the schools open for the duration of the two-week strike by hiring hundreds of scab teachers, mostly new college graduates hoping to avoid the draft. He named new principals, whom he chose according to the board's own procedures rather than from a union-approved list of potential candidates. Among the new administrators was Herman Ferguson, a nationalist then under indictment for conspiring to kill NAACP head Roy Wilkins and Urban League director Whitney Young.

From that point on, union–board relations soured. Some UFT members transferred out of the district, and the union lobbied the state legislature to block decentralization altogether. In May 1968, the board judged nineteen district teachers incompetent and transferred them out of the district without benefit of a hearing. Lindsay and Bundy continued to support Ocean Hill. When the Bundy committee released its report that summer it called for thorough decentralization of New York schools into some sixty districts that would engage in maximum community involvement. With Manhattan aligned with the Ocean Hill radicals, Shanker decided to strike the entire system.

From late August to mid-November when the New York board revoked most of the Ocean Hill board's powers, the city's schools were shut down in an intensely bitter conflict that demonstrated how irreconcilable the legitimate goals of groups were. McCoy plodded along as best he could, visiting classrooms, hiring hundreds of local citizens as teachers' aides, and earning the loyalty of those teachers, blacks and Jews alike, who continued to teach. For the union teachers, the issue boiled down, as Michael Harrington wrote in their defense, to job security, not only in the immediate controversy but also in the larger sense of collective-bargaining rights. That was exactly the problem with the teachers' position, some critics claimed: for the UFT the controversy was simply a battle in a larger trade-union war, whereas for the district it was a battle for community survival. The teachers were acting "like plumbers," some charged; their behavior "makes you think of Irish dock workers or Polish and Czech steel and auto workers." But what were they supposed to act like, one UFT member asked, missionaries? "The public school teachers in this city are in the main a 'lower-middle-class' group of people," wrote Patrick Harnett. "If they have to act like members of an electricians' union . . . they will."

In August 1968 about a hundred members of the Bedford-Stuyvesant Parents Association of Brooklyn picket the Educational and Capitol buildings in Albany, New York, demanding that the education commissioner end the teachers' strike and open New York City schools at once.
[UPI/Bettmann Newsphotos]

As the confrontation wore on, it grew increasingly racial, and once it became an ethnic clash there was little hope of reasonable mediation. The extremes, prodded by media attention, became more pronounced. Both sides claimed the allegiance of black teachers, although the evidence points to an understandable ambivalence among them, forced as they were to choose between a cause that might benefit their race and a union that benefited their class. There were also white teachers who left the UFT on the grounds that it was abandoning both its responsibilities to the children and progressive principles. In such a situation, as one union defector explained, "the traditional trade union concept is [not] relevant any longer."

In such a heated atmosphere, decentralization was hardly the ticket to improved education. Even in the ideal it was an incomplete way to brighten African-American prospects, and in practice it merely obscured the more fundamental needs of the black community. As Michael Harrington argued, decentralization "avoids the uncomfortable point that there must be a social investment of billions of dollars in physical plant, in upgrading facilities, and, above all, in replacing the tenements with decent housing." "WASPdom" supported decentralization, he maintained, because it avoided social justice and skirted collective bargaining at the same time. Consequently, decentralization amounted to nothing more than "black control of black misery and white control of the nation's wealth."

Desegregation

Decentralization, moreover, was diametrically opposed to the other urgent educational hope of liberals, school desegregation. There was no way that the two aspirations could be squared. Although segregationists and black nationalists alike detested the idea, liberals believed that the justice of integration was beyond question. Not only was it in line with the spirit of the civil rights movement, but also the available evidence argued that integration improved the educational performance of minority students. In 1966 an HEW report by James S. Coleman and others found that minority students put into white schools improved their performance slightly, while white students whose schools were integrated performed as they had before. Generally speaking, educational performance was more closely associated with the quality of the school for minority students than for white students. If this were the case, then there was additional reason to recommend school integration: none would be hurt, and some would be helped.

The Coleman Report was not an inspiring document, or a clear rallying call for integration. Harvard professor Christopher Jencks compared it to "an Agriculture Department bulletin on fertilizer." None of its findings were dramatic, and some were bound to trouble its liberal readers. It found that educational achievement was not inherently related to spending per pupil, which suggested that spending more money on schools would not help much. More troubling still, and most routinely ignored, was the evidence that socioeconomic status was more important than race in determining performance. If that were true, then integration would work only if inner-city students were mixed with well-to-do students, who were increasingly found in the suburbs; logically as well, poor white students deserved to be included in any program of integration. For that matter, as Jencks pointed out elsewhere, the evidence suggested that "poor blacks would benefit as much from going to school with middle-class blacks as from going to school with middle-class whites." Tepid though it was, the Coleman Report was reinforced by further studies and by the less ambitious work of observers like Robert Coles, who found that improved schools did have a salutary effect on the lives of children.

The report, however, offered no resolution of the contradiction between decentralization and integration. As Peter Schrag pointed out, insofar as it was accurate, the report suggested that New York's decentralization scheme "is a step backward." The report showed that the advocates of decentralization were more interested in political power than in education. Thus, Schrag thought, "parents whose children attend decentralized schools may (with luck) learn more about political action and school management than their children learn about reading and mathematics." And yet integration did not seem to improve classroom performance either. All things considered, school desegregation could be defended only on the unsubstantiated hope that things would improve, as if by magic, simply through the act of integration. Integration was "morally important," Schrag insisted, and "any alternative to integration is, despite immediate attractions to the contrary, unthinkable."

Busing

Clearly, liberals were at an impasse. If giving up on integration was "unthinkable," the next question was how to achieve it. Especially in a political climate fascinated with community control, it was necessary to face the possibility that integration would have to be forced, and nearly everyone but middle-class black parents desperate to save their children from the corruptions of ghetto subculture opposed the idea of compulsory integration. Too many liberal-minded parents reconciled their fear of compulsion and their desire for racial justice by applauding plans to integrate every school but the one their children went to. Radical thinkers like Jencks came down on the side of decentralization, or as he put it, on the side of freedom of choice. Forced integration, he argued, was based on the implicitly racist assumption that blacks could not run their own schools, that black schools were *"by definition inferior."* Whatever the vexing difficulties, the courts settled the question by compelling school systems to integrate for racial balance and, if necessary, by forced busing. Just as it was difficult to take issue with the humane, if romantic, visions of child-centered schools, so it was hard to be critical of judicial logic, even though court-ordered busing did incalculable damage to urban school systems, was carried out in fundamentally antidemocratic fashion, and ignored altogether the greater importance of class against race. Liberals went along for the ride, and it was a bumpy one.

The momentum toward court-ordered busing rested in the long-lived southern resistance to *Brown*, which obliged federal courts to level increasingly determined rulings on desegregation. Had whites not been so stubborn, the courts never would have considered busing. But as late as 1965, only 7.5 percent of black children in the South attended desegregated schools. For the next several years, school districts continued to hide segregation under the banner of free choice, but during that same time a number of federal circuit court judges, emboldened by the 1964 Civil Rights Act, rendered decisions that moved away from choice. In 1968 the Supreme Court ruled in *Green v. County School Board*, a case concerning rural New Kent County, Virginia, that school districts had "the affirmative duty to take whatever steps might be necessary to convert to a unitary system in which racial discrimination would be eliminated root and branch." Not only was the district obliged to take remedial steps against discrimination, but it was to do so immediately. Free choice, the government argued in a direction that carried with it some irony, given later thinking, was inefficient and irrational, and undermined neighborhood schools, because students were bused across the county in order to attend segregated schools.

Green set the Court's decisive direction for the future, so that even backsliding in the Nixon administration could not prevent further integration orders. Having made up its mind, the Court was obliged to offer remedies as well. It was by no means clear what the Supreme Court meant by racial balance, what sort of percentages schools would have to achieve before they were considered integrated, or to what lengths districts would have to go to achieve those ends. The Court did make clear its impatience, however: in *Alexander v. Holmes County Board of Education* (1969) and *Carter v. West Feliciana Parish School Board* (1970), the Court refused to tolerate any further delays.

Then in *Swann v. Charlotte-Mecklenberg Board of Education* (1971), the Court ordered extensive busing in a large school district, thereby marking to the logical end of the judicial process. Whereas the government had held in *Green* that choice was irrational because it resulted in students being bused from one end of the county to the other, in *Swann* the justices insisted that busing across town was desirable because busing had always been part of the educational process. If racial balance became an end in itself, if it was not enough for a school district to have a policy of free choice, than all districts were vulnerable to court-ordered busing, not just those that had once practiced formal segregation. The neighborhood school was no longer inviolable; the decentralization movement essentially was dead.

The courts arrived at this point in good faith, though a bit nettled at having to order districts to desegregate more than a decade after *Brown*. Still it is astonishing to see how narrow the rulings and how wide the repercussions were. In the latter cases, the courts took the educational value of integration for granted, when, in fact, the best evidence warranted prudence rather than rashness. The importance of the neighborhood setting and the ability of parents to become actively involved in their children's schools were brushed aside. Perhaps most of all, the Supreme Court gave no heed whatsoever to the nature of the sociological realities of the urban crisis and the Great Migration. In following the Court rulings, we would conclude that racial balance became the purpose of public school education. Perfectly understandable as a matter of law and morally desirable, Court-ordered busing was politically reckless and, at best, pedagogically inconsequential.

Forced busing made bitter and immediate antagonists of parents in a number of cities—Dayton, Ohio; and Pontiac, Michigan in particular—but the busing conflict was sharpest in Boston, where it took on the distinct tones of ethnic rivalry, much as did the New York teachers' strike. The origins of the battle lay in the city's wider difficulties. Organized around heavily ethnic neighborhoods to begin with, Boston became increasingly segregated as the Great Migration increased the city's black population by 342 percent from 1940 to 1970. Coupled with white flight, the migration increased the black proportion of the population from 3 to 16 percent. During the 1950s Boston's black middle class was, according to Ronald Formisano, enjoying its best years in a century. Those very people whom Malcolm X mocked for their upward mobility in the *Autobiography* feared that the inundation by southerners would drag the whole African-American community down. Black professionals and native Bostonians began to chafe at residential segregation and impoverished schools that threatened their future and their status. Spurred specifically by state legislation passed in 1965 to encourage school desgregation in Boston, the city's mainstream African-American community began to search cautiously for ways to push the public schools toward improvement.

Meanwhile, the local school board had long been in the hands of the city's

Irish, who used the School Committee as a vehicle for patronage and a ladder for political careers. Through the crucial early years of the controversy, the School Committee was under the leadership of the irascible Louise Day Hicks. Well before George Wallace, Hicks discovered that "standing up" to black demands and defying liberals all but guaranteed election. Accordingly, she led the committee to shoot down even the modest attempts to address the school situation. Political beings that they were, the committee's Irish members were inclined to see any black demands not as simple requests for decent education but as part of a strategy to wrest control from them.

In his study of the school crisis, Formisano shows that the initial black demands were reasonable and modest and that the School Committee deserves the major share of blame for generating a destructive controversy that could very well have been dealt with in its early stages. When the courts stepped in to impose integration, however, they created a substantive antibusing movement. For ten years after 1965, the city fought the courts and the state, the black community fought the working-class Irish and Italian communities, and Boston's urban residents fought suburbanites until the state forced through a plan that paired South Boston High, the coveted institution of Irish South Boston, with black Roxbury. Nothing could have been better designed to inflame racial conflict, and the plan completely ignored the evidence from Coleman that educational improvement was possible only when students crossed socioeconomic barriers. Throughout the long conflict, demagogues rose and fell, and indignant blacks leveled blanket accusations of racism against all of white Boston. Through it all, the suburbs, especially prosperous Brookline and ultraliberal Cambridge, shook their fingers in shame at working-class Bostonians.

The dynamics at work in Boston were never simply racial. Boston undoubtedly had its share of snarling race hatred, but forced busing could in no way be construed as either democratic or pluralistic. White Boston believed that it was only defending its community institutions, and as Formisano shows, they assumed that they were only applying the lessons of anti-establishment participatory democracy that the sixties had taught. Nor is it clear that black parents wanted busing for its own sake. Their foremost concern was to improve the abysmal quality of their children's education, and for their trouble their children got sent to the worst white schools. Busing did them no favors.

The only possible solution to this dilemma was metropolitan integration that mixed economic groups. Although some suburban communities participated in modest exchanges, on the whole Boston's suburbs avoided responsibility. The hypocrisy of the suburban liberals was obvious, and for Boston's working-class Irish, liberals were the real cause of conflict. An Irish school teacher, speaking to Robert Coles, concluded that the "intellectuals and our rich liberal types" hate white workers but "like to champion the Negro or the Indian or the people in Africa and Asia. . . . They are trying to pretend they love everyone, but the ones they love are the ones who are different from themselves and don't live near them. Well, you don't have to be so smart to figure out what's going on." As Coles concedes, this comment holds an unnerving grain of truth.

CHAPTER 10

Revenge of the
Status Quo

"The Age of Nixon," the radical critic Andrew Kopkind sighed in anticipation of Richard Nixon's inauguration. "The phrase does not exactly seize the mind with a sense of historical moment. It looks to be a sober season."

Kopkind caught the obvious irony in Richard Nixon's rise to power in 1968. After everything the nation had gone through, the sixties was destined to run its course with the election and eventual dishonor of an instinctive right-wing politician who spent most of his life trying to be conventional. New Politics liberals were apt to see Nixon as proof that the United States was hopelessly reactionary and that both the white backlash and the death instincts of Main Street had prevailed. To the professional political observers, Nixon had managed the remarkable feat of turning a tarnished image and a string of failures into success by appealing to the vast, unorganized middle of America, the renowned "silent Americans." That he undoubtedly benefited from George Wallace's third-party candidacy in 1968 seemed less important than that Nixon appeared to be a genuine voice of moderation. To Republicans, Nixon was a moderate who could mend the long-running rift between eastern liberals and western conservatives. Kopkind was right on this level: Nixon was a breath of stale air that the intoxicating winds of change left behind.

Yet Nixon's rise to power was more symbolic than his image as the champion of middle-class respectability suggests. He was more instinctively an anti-hero than the thousands of self-invented "guerrillas" who popped up in the New Left. He had the qualities of the born loser. He never had to renounce his status, for he never legitimately had much to renounce. Nixon was a con man by temperament, and his confidence game was to reinvent himself as political expediency demanded. He was the true existential man. If, as journalist and Nixon biographer Garry Wills wrote in 1973, the sixties was an age of the hustle and the huckster, then Richard Nixon was fit to call the period to its conclusion.

Origins of the New Right

Even before the 1960 election, some liberal commentators on U.S. politics wondered whether the Republican party was not dead. Dwight Eisenhower had been the dominant politician of his day, but it was doubtful that his success could translate into long-term power. Eisenhower's strength was his unflappable moderateness, coupled with his heroic reputation. The Republicans had no one comparable in the wings, and the president's indifference to his potential successors only called attention to their inadequacies: Nelson Rockefeller was too liberal; Henry Cabot Lodge, Jr., was too cultured; and Nixon—well, he was just inadequate.

The Republican Conservatives in 1964

It was not just that Eisenhower was irreplaceable. Rather, the Republicans had never overcome the split between western conservatives and eastern moderates. The moderates had a long past in the party, tended to come from old money, had Ivy League connections, emphasized the importance of European security and a cautious defense in foreign policy, supported civil rights, and accepted, out of a sense of *noblesse oblige*, the moderate welfare state. They were Wasps in politics. Conversely, the conservatives represented new wealth realized from oil and other extractive industries, defense industries, real estate, and the entertainment world, all of which predominated in the West and Southwest. Having recently acquired wealth and power, they saw themselves as modern-day pioneers with no use for the welfare state. They were bitterly anticommunist, in part because the Cold War, by necessitating defense expenditures, was profitable.

This kind of conservatism was fairly new in U.S. politics and raised anxieties among liberals from both parties, who simultaneously believed that the far right was politically pathetic and extremely dangerous. They assumed that conservatism was the irrational impulse of traditional social groups, small-town and middle-class whites, lonely entrepreneurs, and merchants unable to adjust to the pace of industrial society. Modern America, as the liberal historian Richard Hofstadter wrote, was so mobile that "many people do not know who they are or what they are or what they belong to or what belongs to them." Unable to adjust to change, these lost souls lashed out in furious attacks against the symbols of that change: big government, internationalist foreign policy, civil rights, and the cosmopolitan values of the city. The right-winger, Hofstadter wrote, "believes himself to be living in a world in which he is spied upon, plotted against, betrayed, and very likely destined for total ruin." According to the liberal stereotype, conservatives were rarely public servants, never college professors, by definition not union leaders; they were used-car salesmen, independent grocers, insurance salesmen, feverish Christian fundamentalists, or loony members of the John Birch Society, whose leader, Robert Welch, once denounced Eisenhower as "a dedicated, conscious agent of the Communist conspiracy."

Such was the liberal view of the right wing, and it is no wonder that liberals, indeed the vast majority of mainstream political observers, believed that the Republican party had gone mad when Barry Goldwater took the 1964 presidential nomination from better known and more widely appealing candidates. Dubbed "Mr. Conservative," Goldwater was more representative of the far right than any other prominent politician on the scene. He was a native Arizonan; his family had been in the West since the nineteenth-century Indian wars. When he was elected to the Senate in 1952, Goldwater gained a reputation as an energetic colleague of western conservatives like William Knowland and Joseph McCarthy. Like them, he was obsessed with the prospects of domestic communism. Although the rest of the country turned toward the responsible politics of Eisenhower and later to the New Frontier, Goldwater refused to temper his fanatical anticommunism, and as the tone of the nation moderated, Goldwater was left without the conservative surroundings that had once helped place him in U.S. politics. Although he already had become the darling of the Republican right, Goldwater approached the 1960 election ready to support his fellow westerner and brother-in-anticommunism, Richard Nixon. Nixon probably assumed that he had a lock on the conservative vote and so made no overtures to that segment of the party. His only opposition, he felt, came from the eastern wing in the candidacy of Nelson Rockefeller, who announced in May that he would accept a convention draft. Frantic to head off this potential threat, Nixon hashed out a compromise platform with Rockefeller that was distinctly liberal: it endorsed civil rights, government involvement in the economy, medical care for the elderly, and a vigorous national defense. Conservatives, with Goldwater leading the way, accused Nixon of selling out. Nixon further distanced himself from the far right by choosing the Boston aristocrat, Henry Cabot Lodge, Jr., as his running mate.

The "Nixon–Lodge disaster," as Goldwater termed the 1960 election, brought GOP right-wingers to two related conclusions: that the party could not succeed by trying to be more liberal than the Democrats; and that the best prospects for success, for conservatives in particular but for the party as a whole, lay in charting an uncompromisingly ideological course. These conclusions led back to Goldwater. In late 1962, a cadre of conservatives, including *National Review* publisher William Rusher, Ohio Congressman John Ashbrook, and F. Clifton White, secretly began to plot a party coup.

Goldwater himself welcomed the idea of a thoroughly conservative party and certainly had done nothing after the 1960 election to discourage talk of a presidential candidacy or to soften his stands. At the urging of close friends and advisors, he had published his views in *Conscience of a Conservative* (1960), a tract that sold an astounding 700,000 copies. In Goldwater's estimation, the party had become gripped with "me-tooism," a bumbling effort to appear as liberal as the Democrats. Because he continued to think of communism as a worldwide conspiracy, he saw Kennedy foreign policy as mere appeasement: the Bay of Pigs was a "betrayal" of the Cuban "patriots," and the Missile Crisis a "retreat." Liberals, meanwhile, continued to waste taxpayers' money on socialistic domestic programs.

Pushed by fellow conservatives, Goldwater began a campaign that was strange from beginning to end. Rather than accepting help from the core conservatives, he relied on old friends and fellow Arizonans to manage him, and, as he later admitted, they were not an experienced bunch. He wanted to stay out of all the primaries except for California, on the grounds that they were "political booby traps" that "can cripple a candidate's chances for the nomination." But his team did enter him in the New Hampshire primary, where he went in as the favorite but came out losing to an absentee candidate, Henry Cabot Lodge. Lodge had come to epitomize moderate Republicanism; indeed, he was then ambassador to Vietnam, a job that threatened to implicate the party in an enormous foreign policy disaster and drove conservatives to nickname him "Henry Sabotage." Although New Hampshire convinced party regulars that Goldwater was a loser, rank-and-file conservatives exerted strength in local and state caucuses, rallied together in the waning days of the all-important California primary, and gave him the nomination in spite of the party pros.

Taking over the party in 1964 was probably all that the conservatives hoped for at that point. They did not expect to beat Lyndon Johnson, and so they encouraged Goldwater to run for the future by sticking to an uncompromising course. The candidate never minced words, rarely hedged his claims, and often spoke thoughtlessly. In one slip he suggested that social security should be abolished, and his foreign policy views were so aggressive that he appeared trigger-happy. His supporters admired his unrestrained conservatism—Goldwater provided "a choice, not an echo," Phyllis Schlafly claimed—but those qualities frightened the uncommitted. When conservatives tugged at the voters' innate patriotism with the slogan, "In your heart you know he's right," the Democrats played on the even more innate fear of nuclear war: "In your guts you know he's nuts." Evidently, fear was more powerful than sentiment.

The Liberals' Misjudgment of the Conservatives' Defeat

Liberals interpreted Goldwater's defeat as a last gasp of conservative lunacy and as proof that conservatism, in Hofstadter's words, was "a revolt against the whole modern condition." Even in defeat, however, Goldwater demonstrated how thoroughly wrong the liberal view of conservatives was. The conservatives' political strategies and methods were thoroughly modern; they pioneered, for instance, in direct-mail fund-raising. Goldwater himself was no backwater fool, even if he lacked, as he once said of himself, "a first-class brain." His followers liked to see him as a counterpoint to Kennedy. He, too, was handsome, personable, and dashing enough to convince supporters that there was such a thing as the modern individualist. Clifton White claimed that he appealed to "the nation's mothers and grandmothers, the co-eds, the stenographers, the girls working behind counters in shops and department stores," because they saw in him someone "who would preserve the civilization and society they felt slipping out from under them."

With their vision hampered by their stereotypes, liberals blinded themselves to how formidable the conservative movement was. Conspiracy theories and paranoid anticommunism were not the only ideas to be found on the right. Their opposition to the welfare state might have betrayed a stinginess, but not many voters wanted to pay higher taxes for social programs they considered dubious. Average Americans were not as worried about the "communist conspiracy" as Goldwater was, but that did not mean that they trusted the liberal politicians who were sinking them into Vietnam. Conservatives had their intellectuals, too, who quarreled over doctrine among themselves but who managed to put up a consistently united front against liberalism and Democratic rule. And Goldwater had his youth wing as well, which was organized in the Young Americans for Freedom (YAF) after the 1960 convention and quickly claimed a membership of 27,000 on a hundred campuses.

Nor was Goldwater underwritten by small donations from the frightened or maladjusted. His support came from the likes of H. L. Hunt, the Texas billionaire, Douglas Stewart, head of Quaker Oats, George Humphrey, Treasury secretary under Eisenhower, Ralph Cordiner, chief of General Electric, and Lammot du Pont Copeland, Jr., of the Delaware du Ponts, among others. Conservatism had more than its share of heavy money behind it. Far from being the nonplussed small businessmen whom rapid technological change was burying, Goldwater's friends were drawn from the very corporate elite that was guiding and profiting from that change. And the reasons for their support did not have to be found in the political psyche. As Irving Howe wrote: "This politics rests on the desire of powerful men—Ralph Cordiner is not a mid-western automobile salesman, George Humphrey not a malaise-stricken petty bourgeois, H. L. Hunt not a bewildered storekeeper—to call a halt to social reform and then slowly to push it back."

To the continual surprise and bewilderment of nearly all liberal or left-wing observers, right-wing Republicans were evidently rational, well-educated, articulate, not noticeably anxious (almost entirely white) suburbanites. They were the parents of the young idealists who had come to Kennedy—or, conversely, occasionally they were the children of old Democrats in rebellion against the liberal establishment. As the liberal news magazine, *The Reporter,* editorialized about the second YAF convention, it resembled "nothing so much as a proud commencement day gathering." Michael Walzer noted that many reporters had gone to the 1964 convention fully expecting to see loonies, only to find "suave and aggressive college graduates, young corporate executives on their way up, upper middle-class professional men and women, confident, tough-minded, power-hungry."

The electoral equation surrounding the rise of Goldwater and surviving through his defeat was further indication that the liberals badly misjudged the right. One of the most important developments underlying the political emergence of conservatism was its growing strength in Dixie. Conservatives had been keeping an eye on the South throughout Eisenhower's presidency, and several developments began to dovetail and erode the Democratic lock on the "Solid South." The Republicans did not try to exploit massive resistance, and despite both the *Brown* decision and Little Rock, Eisenhower did well there. His strength rested on a new element in southern politics, the middle-class suburbanite who was quite new to the South and whose interests were rooted in the government-encouraged defense and oil industries. Republicanism was part of the so-called New South, its growth symbolized by the young, upstart politicians who found it much easier to move up through the fledgling Republican apparatus than through the encrusted Southern Democracy. Beginning with the election of John Tower, a Goldwater supporter, in the May 1961 election to replace Lyndon Johnson from Texas, the future of south-ern politics began to turn toward conservative Republicanism. The 1962 off-year elections, a disappointment for the Republicans nationally, were heartening for the party in the South: five new congressmen were elected; the party put up stiff challenges to powerful Democrats like Lister Hill and J. William Fulbright; and it began to break the Democratic monopoly on the state level in North Carolina and Georgia. Overall in the South, Republican voting strength grew 244 percent in 1962.

The New Right

In turning the South their way, the conservatives had to disregard the black vote. They winced at accusations that they were race-baiting, but they could not culti-vate the conservative and the black vote at the same time. Wallace's 1964 primary run helped Goldwater see a coalition in the making, one that would include middle-class white southerners, the wealthy, and working-class white northerners.

Incarnated as the "New Right," the members of this coalition were very much products of the sixties. In the minds of some young conservatives, being on the right was all the more exciting for being unpopular. "You walk around with your Goldwater button on," one young conservative remarked, "and you feel the thrill of treason." If there were obvious differences between the young conservatives and the New Left, there were similarities as well, particularly in their mutual contempt for establishment liberals and defense of small government. By the late sixties, conser-vatism metamorphosed into anarchism for some. Murray Rothbard, the foremost conservative-turned-anarchist, marveled at the transformation. Writing in almost apologetic tones, he claimed that he never changed his ideas; political fashion had merely turned him from a conservative to a radical. Karl Hess, Goldwater's main speechwriter in 1964, decided soon after that he (Hess) was really "a left-wing anarchist."

By belittling the conservatives as maladjusted extremists, liberals failed to prepare themselves for losing power. In 1964 it seemed inconceivable that the Republicans could retake the White House anytime soon. Four years later Richard Nixon moved in.

"Not a Little Boy That You Wanted to Pick Up and Hug"

Too zealous to admit defeat, conservatives read 1964 as a victory, for at least they had beaten the "radical leftists" in their own party, as Senator Strom Thurmond (R-S.C.) once called Rockefeller Republicans. A more accurate assessment was that they had established parity between the two wings of the party and that, hence-forth, mutual dependence, at least at the national level, would dictate party policy and nominees. Ideological zeal could not change the reality of 1964: Goldwater got thumped and took the party down with him. That reality posed a number of substantial problems, not the least of which was finding a successor to Goldwater, who had to retreat into the role of senior conservative.

One possibility was Ronald Reagan. An actor who had become involved in conservative politics through his role as celebrity spokesman for General Electric, Reagan had given a rousing speech for Goldwater on national television just before the election. The voting had barely ended before an active movement of "Republicans for Reagan" was organized. His stock rose when he won the 1966 California gubernatorial race in his first effort at public office. Although Reagan was even less likely than Goldwater to be accused of having a "first-class brain," he had many virtues. He was a dedicated conservative and improved his standing among right-wingers when he warned student radicals at Berkeley that they "observe the rules or get out." Disturbed over Berkeley's "sexual orgies" and the more troubling university practice of "subsidizing intellectual curiosity," he threatened university funds, helped force Clark Kerr from the presidency, and eventually ordered the National Guard to occupy the campus. Berkeley became Reagan's whipping boy. The state's seemingly endless economic boom, as Stephan Ambrose has observed, made it a no-lose job. In sharp contrast to Goldwater, Reagan was the consummate television politician because he never "shot from the hip"; he rarely spoke without a script. "Hero of the Late Show westerns," Richard Whalen wrote, Reagan "was an ideal television candidate, a fresh 'nonpolitical' citizen in politics."

Nixon's Return to the Political Scene

Of all the other potential candidates, only Richard Nixon had any appeal whatever for conservatives, although their commitment to him was lukewarm. He had begun his political career as one of them: a hungry young communist-basher from southern California. Nixon was placed on the 1952 ticket in order to balance Eisenhower with a representative of the New Right, but rather than acting as a conservative leader, he groveled for acceptance among mainstream Republicans. In the end, he received Eisenhower's barely concealed distrust, which only made Nixon seem the weaker for having sought approval in the first place. Posing as the candidate of party unity in 1960, he appealed to both wings, relying on his background and his California base to hold the right wing and playing up his role as Eisenhower's vice president to hold the moderates. Like the party itself, Nixon the candidate tried to push a vague mishmash of discordant positions.

Nixon's attempt at party mediation was as much an effort at personal metamorphosis as political strategy. He was an even more interesting study in political psychology than Kennedy or Johnson. His upbringing was as unspectacular as Kennedy's was glamorous and Johnson's was stark. Born in Yorba Linda, California, Nixon grew up in an environment notable only for its thorough commonplaceness. His father, Frank, had wandered from Ohio to California near the turn of the century, where he met and married the daughter of a prominent family in the Quaker community of Whittier. By most accounts, Nixon's Quaker mother, Hannah, was a "saint," a pious and quiet woman whose hallmark was a devoted reticence. The father was aggressive, at times surly, given to a certain degree of self-display. At times a railcar motorman, oil roustabout, lemon rancher, butcher, and grocer, Frank Nixon was a survivor who was frequently a tough disciplinarian with his children. If the parents had something in common, it was the yearning for upward mobility. The family was never poor, but to stay afloat, Frank had to work constantly.

On the surface, Nixon was his mother's son: undemonstrative, not shy but standoffish, and lacking in spontaneity. He had none of the politician's natural conviviality; many even agreed that he did not like people. Throughout his life, he had perhaps only two close male friends, who asked no questions and had no expectations of him. Publicly frigid, Nixon was often ruthless to political loyalists. He constructed his campaigns and his administrations in ways that intentionally pitted people against one another, fostering competition among them lest they should combine against him. His public image even at its best was as a cold, analytical, clever man. No matter how many hands he shook, how many Rotarian dinners he addressed, how many babies he kissed, he still appeared cold. One relative summed up his entire life with an observation of Nixon as a child: He "wasn't a little boy that you wanted to pick up and hug."

Like many strivers, Nixon had a perpetual chip on his shoulder, which gave rise, much as with Lyndon Johnson, to a paradoxical quest for acceptance in the establishment and a visceral contempt for respectability. He felt constantly snubbed. In one of his more interesting moments of self-analysis, he told his aide Kenneth Clawson that "what starts the process, really, are the laughs and slights and snubs when you are a kid. But if you are reasonably intelligent and if your anger is deep enough and strong enough, you learn that you can change those attitudes by excellence, personal gut performance while those who have everything are sitting on their fat butts." Struggling for a respectability of which he was contemptuous, Nixon constantly tried to remake himself. It became difficult even for insiders to keep track of who he was at any particular moment. "The trouble with most perceptions of Nixon," speechwriter William Safire wrote in comparing Nixon to a layered cake, is that "one layer or another is chosen as 'real' and the perceiver roots for that one layer's success. But the whole cake is the 'real' Nixon, including some layers I have not mentioned because I do not know." In the long run this constant reformation or relayering paid off in political success, not because of sincerity but because by 1968 he had revamped himself so many times that his public self was utterly vaporous, almost formless, perhaps like the middle class, without identity.

When the strategy of sheer effort failed, he lapsed into self-pity. Because he believed that hard work paid off, he could account for failure only by assuming that he had been the victim of misunderstanding or treachery. Unfortunately, these tendencies were reinforced when Nixon discovered that self-pity could be turned to political uses. In the midst of the 1952 presidential campaign, for example, he became embroiled in a scandal in which he was accused of having taken contributions to defray office costs. Faced with the possibility of losing his place on the ticket, Nixon went on national television and delivered his famous "Checkers" speech. In this long exercise in excruciating self-pity, he emphasized his family's modest financial condition, recalled his hard-working father, half-apologized for his wife's "respectable Republican cloth" coat, disavowed any wrongdoing, but asserted that, no matter what, he would never give up one gift—the family dog named Checkers. The journalist Walter Lippmann, watching the speech with English visitors, called it "the most demeaning episode in American political history." Evidently, however, self-degradation was politically astute, for the speech evoked an outpouring of public support.

Along with self-pity, Nixon was ready to blame everyone but himself for his failures. In his memoirs, he blamed his 1960 defeat on a media that disliked him and an opponent that "approached campaign dirty tricks with a roguish relish." As he saw it, he ran an honest and reasonable campaign that never abused the religious issue, never dredged up Kennedy's father, and never touched on his opponent's sexual escapades. He was the good guy, he was certain, and look where it got him.

Nixon's dealings with the press were never good. He saw reporters as adversaries, whereas the press found Nixon self-righteous, boring, cynical, or some combination thereof. In the famous press conference held after Nixon lost the California governor's race in 1962, he accused the media of willful distortion and unprofessionalism. His advisors nearly had to force him to attend the press conference; indeed, his press secretary had begun to read his concession speech for him when Nixon stumbled into the room. He launched an extraordinary harangue against the press, much of which was incoherent and therefore all the more unsettling for having come from a candidate who had always been so thoroughly prepared. "I leave you gentlemen now. . . . But as I leave you I want you to know—just think how much you're going to be missing. You won't have Nixon to kick around anymore." Of course, he did not keep his promise.

Nixon and 1968

Aggressiveness, secrecy, self-pity, lies, a hunger for power—all came to mark Nixon's career as it ran its course. It was not surprising that much of the nation, certainly the press, the intellectuals, and even many of his closest advisors, came to see him as slightly mad. Several of the first post–Watergate biographies focused on his upbringing on the assumption that he might have been psychologically unstable. No doubt Nixon had his strange aspects, but he was certainly not pathological. His upbringing was not markedly different from that of countless others; his aspirations, though more grandly envisioned and more aggressively pursued, were not qualitatively different from those of thousands upon thousands of his fellow Americans. Nixon collapsed under the pressure of the Watergate scandal, but in the end, he was not pathetically unbalanced. Rather, he was pathetically normal. He was not the independent pioneer but in many ways he was the homogenized middle-class American trying to distance himself from his past by joining the white-collar corporate set. Many Americans, especially politicians, journalists, and other members of the official set, needed to see Nixon as deranged because they could not bring themselves to admit that there was a bit of Nixon in all of them.

It is the hallmark of his career that his personality fit the political culture that prevailed in the Republican party. His surly side served him well as a representative of the Republican right; this side of his personality, apparently inherited from his father, was associated with anticommunism, his defense of the "silent majority," and his opposition to the welfare state. His refined side, associated with study and persuasion, conversely gave him the tools to move toward Republican moderates; he was a consistent moderate on civil rights, a supporter of an internationalist foreign policy, and pragmatic about domestic economic policy. Even the common bond that his parents clearly shared—a desire for upward mobility—was perfectly in keeping with Republican politics and provided Nixon with the middle-class temperament necessary to develop his uncanny feel for the pulse of that group of voters.

Nixon, then, was well suited to uniting the party. As he made his move toward the 1968 nomination, he resolved not to take the right for granted this time, and Goldwater gave Nixon his blessing at an early date, soon after 1964. From 1964 up to the 1968 election, Nixon was the steadiest critic of Johnson's war policies, which he viewed as insufficiently aggressive. Yet when he took decisive steps toward the middle ground, it was in the area of foreign policy. In a July 1967 meeting of top Republicans, Nixon suggested that the United States should pursue trade and arms negotiations with the Soviet Union, and then in an article in the influential journal *Foreign Affairs*, he hinted that U.S. policy should soften toward Red China, lest the Asian superpower be left "forever outside the family of nations." As always, he was careful to shape his message to fit the audience; to the Republican leaders he stressed the ongoing global necessity of U.S. moral and military strength; to the moderates who read *Foreign Affairs* he suggested that the United States should not be the world's policeman.

By 1968 Nixon had remade himself into several sorts of "new Nixons," so that conservatives heard in him the aggressive anticommunist that he had once been and moderates assumed that he was becoming a statesman. Outside the party, meanwhile, the quaking political terrain began to shift his way. He was able to present himself, in all his ambiguity, as the "new Nixon," the candidate of change. When Johnson dropped from the race at the end of March, 1968, Nixon's prospects brightened even more. He was the front-runner among Republicans, and the only way the other potential candidates, George Romney or Nelson Rockefeller, could catch him was to convince party members that Nixon could not beat the likely Democratic nominee. This was an inherently difficult task, for after Johnson's withdrawal it was by no means clear who that nominee would be. Reagan posed some concerns because of his strength in the South. Nixon therefore moved to enlist support from southern stalwarts like Strom Thurmond by promising support on textile tariffs. Nixon also expected to run well in the border states.

Nixon's position was enviable. He could afford to run a cautious campaign and content himself with general positions on issues that kept him malleable. He promised to bring "new leadership" to a "new majority" so it could enjoy a "new freedom." He was for "law and order," which many critics decried as having racist implications, but Nixon was careful to avoid any hint of race-baiting and usually countered with the correct observation that blacks were the most frequent victims of crime. With the economy overheating, he called for a return to simpler policies of lower taxes and less spending. He also pushed what he called a "new federalism," a reorganization of the federal government that would return power to the states and local governments. These were soft positions, and he hoped that they would allow him to build on that coalition for which Goldwater had provided the foundation. The "silent majority," the "millions of people in the middle of the American political spectrum who do not demonstrate, who do not picket or protest loudly," was his capstone appeal.

To execute the strategy of ambiguity, the Nixon campaign relied on a tightly managed series of public appearances and television spots. Knowing that Nixon's weakness was his lack of personality, his handlers had him address only large audiences made up, insofar as possible, of supporters and loyalists. The television campaign was directed by New York's leading advertisers and headed by Harry Treleavan, an executive from J. Walter Thompson, the nation's largest advertising firm. The team decided to air a series of staged "spontaneous" question-and-answer sessions in which Nixon matched wits with "real people." They would make him seem personable and friendly, but under circumstances that allowed maximum control of Nixon's image. The audience would be hand-picked, down to allowing a critical question every now and then.

By many accounts, Nixon had succeeded in remaking himself, the true existential man. Richard Whalen, a conservative writer and a man of substance and integrity, thought so after having met with Nixon in the fall of 1967. "Trivial discoveries about him," Whalen wrote after a long interview with Nixon, "assumed encouraging significance. There was no trace of the arrogant self-importance often found in politicians." Norman Mailer, who admitted that "Nixon's presence on television had inspired emotions close to nausea," discovered to his astonishment that the candidate who arrived at the Republican Convention in Miami had indeed been remade. Mailer speculated that perhaps Nixon's travails had humbled him. For whatever reason, Nixon was somehow "less phony now," Mailer decided. "That was the real miracle, he had moved from a position of total ambition and total alienation from his own person . . . to a place now where he was halfway conciliated with his own self. As he spoke, he kept going in and out of focus, true one instant, phony the next, then quietly correcting the false step."

The candidate's reformation notwithstanding, the Nixon campaign hit several major snags. Nixon, above all, feared the prospect of facing Robert Kennedy. Nor could much be done to control the third-party candidate, Wallace, who threw the entire, messy race into even greater uncertainty. It was not clear at the time how Wallace was going to affect the race, but Nixon saw him as a "spoiler" who would prevent him from taking a large mandate into the presidency. Nixon had to concede Wallace the Deep South, which he probably would have taken in a two-way race with Humphrey; on the other hand, many of Wallace's voters, as we have seen, were the white ethnics and northern workers. Nixon's strategy was to emphasize the law-and-order issue around potential Wallace voters and otherwise allow Wallace to make the most extreme appeals to base instincts.

The most difficult issue was the most important one: Vietnam. Nixon had done his hardest, most genuine thinking on the war, and his plan for isolating North Vietnam through diplomatic overtures to the Chinese and Soviets was at least original. His basic hopes, however, were not much different from Johnson's; both men wanted peace on U.S. terms. After hearing Nixon intimate that he would approach the war differently, the press began to suggest that he had "a secret plan to end the war," though he never really put it quite that way. For most of the campaign after Tet, he said as little as possible about the most momentous subject of the day, begging off any comments about the war with the excuse that he did not want to interfere with ongoing negotiations. Nixon was in a ticklish position. He agreed with Johnson's general goals, and to have been overly critical would have complicated his job if and when he became president. When Johnson finally released Humphrey from his war policies, Nixon broke his silence on Vietnam. But all he could do was await the polls.

Considering the closeness of the race, Nixon had to concoct an argument for a mandate much as Kennedy had. Instead of reading the vote as merely a tentative approval, he concluded that almost 59 percent of the voters—his and Wallace's— chose against the Democrats and "for change." He had a case here. Although the Democratic coalition had been dissolving at its edges since 1960, especially its southern edges, Nixon's election foretold a complete dismantling of that historic bloc. Nixon employed the so-called southern strategy more thoughtfully and systematically than previous Republicans, and along with Wallace, he denied the Democrats any victories there at all.

The Republican theorist and Nixon campaign worker Kevin Phillips argued that the southern strategy provided the means to forge a completely new coalition, including ex-Democrats from the South, traditional Republicans, and disaffected workers and ethnics. But Phillips's study of the election, *The Emerging Republican Majority* (1969), actually points to a somewhat different interpretation. Nixon had lost in the Deep South, but Phillips, like Nixon, chose to see Wallace's strength there as a sign of "an inchoate Nixon constituency." Nixon did very well not only in the border states but also in the metropolitan areas of the South; he did well with the transplants, the New South professionals, and the beneficiaries of the postindustrial growth of the region. He appealed to them not because he was a tactless racebaiter but because his conservatism was based on more wholesome values like anticommunism, antiliberalism, and procapitalism. The southern strategy, in other words, was not southern at all. If anything, it employed a variation of Wallace's insight: Instead of "they're all southern!" Nixon's victory suggested that "they're all suburban!"

The 1968 election marked the arrival of political homogenization, where regional politics were less important than metropolitan politics, where the politics of Dallas, Phoenix, or Atlanta were not much different from the politics of Detroit, Chicago, or New York. It was less an indication of backlash than of the full-blown introduction of major social forces—suburbanization, mass culture, and postindustrialism—into national politics. Nixon, the homogenized candidate, deserved to win.

The Nixon Presidency

Nixon took his theme, "Bring us together," from a sign that had caught his eye during a campaign swing. Like so much about him, it was a mix of insincerity and public relations. Instead of encouraging national reconciliation, Nixon's presidency was consumed with the same polarities that marked his whole career. He drew the war in Vietnam out through the whole of his first term, promised negotiations but invaded Cambodia, and initiated unprecedented bombing campaigns against North Vietnam in pursuit of "peace with honor." While playing the mad-bomber in Vietnam, he pioneered in the most important foreign policy innovations since World War II with *détente*, a policy of improved relations with both communist superpowers, China and the Soviet Union. In the domestic arena, he pursued a course that wavered between conciliatory new welfare policies and the nominations of segregationists to the Supreme Court. A lifelong believer in free enterprise, he angrily attacked his own Justice Department for its antitrust activities and then supported wage-and-price controls. Again and again he appealed for calm in the streets, and yet his law-and-order rhetoric and his dismissal of protesters as "bums" only invited more disruption. He pleaded for unity, but his appeals to the silent majority deepened the cleavages between the races and generations.

Foreign Policy Objectives

Nixon's foreign policy was based on several goals that were not easy to reconcile. He understood that he was stepping into the presidency at that moment when the United States' world dominance was ending and that the morass of Vietnam, Soviet nuclear parity, and the high tensions between the Soviet and the Chinese communists recommended an overhaul of strategic thinking. The reorientation of U.S. diplomacy began with a rejection of liberal globalism, something that Nixon's co-conspirator in *détente*, Henry Kissinger, actively advised. A Harvard professor with a taste for power, Kissinger had insinuated himself into the recesses of foreign policy during the sixties, using his credentials as an expert on nuclear strategy and relations with Europe as a passkey. He was a diplomatic realist, who believed that foreign policy should be guided by calculable, rational interests rather than vague moral commitments or nagging anxieties. He traveled to Vietnam twice during the Johnson years and became privy to the secret negotiations. Meanwhile, he pinned his hopes for a governmental position on Nelson Rockefeller. When the New York governor lost in the primaries, Kissinger began feeding the Nixon campaign information about the Vietnam negotiations.

Nixon chose Kissinger for his national security advisor for several reasons. The two men had a roughly similar understanding on Vietnam and on the importance of improved relations with the communist superpowers. Kissinger brought his Ivy League credentials into an administration that at once despised and envied Ivy Leaguers; for Nixon, who measured his success against the standards of John F. Kennedy, attracting a Harvard mind to the administration was an end in itself. For his part, Kissinger cared little about who was in the White House, as long as he was invited in. He shared Nixon's temperament; both had a will to power that created an imperial style, a penchant for secrecy, and a distrust of everyone, including one another.

The Soviet Union and China Policy

In the face of changes in the international scene, Nixon and Kissinger sought to hold on to as much U.S. power as possible while recognizing that both the Soviets and Chinese would insist on maintaining predominant power in their respective spheres of influence. Beyond respecting this balance of power, they envisioned most of the Third World as a field of superpower competition. *Détente* never anticipated the elimination of conflict between the superpowers. Nixon and Kissinger hoped that agreements on the fundamental issues of security would allow both sides to live by certain restraints in the pursuit of lesser interests. Although Kissinger never spelled out what these restraints were and therefore when they could or could not be crossed, he and his boss intended to keep up pressure on the Soviets by building a new relationship with the Chinese. They also developed the concept of linkage by which, for instance, they would limit communist meddling in Africa by promising gains in other areas such as grain sales. *Détente* was not a thaw in the Cold War; rather, it was the Cold War fought on another level.

Playing the new diplomacy took a good deal of finesse—and, according to the main players, an enormous dedication to secrecy—for besides their mutual desire to prevent one another from developing close ties with Washington, the communist powers had different interests. Now that they had achieved rough parity in nuclear arms with the United States, the Soviets wanted an official recognition of the doctrine of mutual destruction. Mutual destruction did not recommend arms reduction so much as arms limitations and a slowdown in technological improvement, an area in which the United States had a confident advantage. Beginning in April 1970, the Strategic Arms Limitation Talks (SALT I) bogged down over the U.S. demand to limit the number of Soviet Inter-Continental Ballistic Missiles (ICBMs) in exchange for limitations on the new American Anti-Ballistic Missile (ABMs) system. In an attempt to conclude an agreement and ensure that the president received all the credit, Kissinger skirted the negotiating bureaucracy and secretly made a deal with the Soviets that conceded some of the U.S. demands but ensured that Nixon would come to Moscow and conclude the agreement himself. On May 20, 1971, Nixon announced to the nation that an agreement had been reached, and for once even the liberal press praised him.

Dealing with the Chinese was simpler and more dramatic. The United States never had established relations with Communist China, and the Chinese saw recognition as a symbol of their legitimacy as a world power. Although he wanted Chinese help to fence in the Soviets, Nixon knew that they were losing influence over the North Vietnamese and consequently were no longer the main power behind the Vietnam War. Beyond diplomatic considerations, Nixon relished the chance to confound his liberal enemies by opening relations with the Chinese.

Improved relations with the United States doubtlessly promised more advantages for the Chinese, who were feeling a bit embattled by 1969. They had suffered a series of political setbacks after many prominent nonaligned nations, especially India, had denounced China's Third World leadership. China had to wonder who its allies were, and those whose support it was sure of, such as North Korea, were not exactly illustrious nations. The Chinese view of the U.S. war in Vietnam was shaped within this diplomatic isolation; the more isolated they were, the more ambivalent they were about the U.S. presence in Asia. They could never see it as a good thing, but they were increasingly inclined to see it as a counterweight to the growing Soviet influence in the region.

Although the interests of the two nations dovetailed, the opening to China was a surprise and thus provided a moment of public theater that even cultural radicals might appreciate. In late May 1971, coinciding with the SALT successes, the Chinese agreed to a visit from Nixon. "This was the most important communication that has come to an American President since the end of World War II," Kissinger told Nixon. The Chinese, in Nixon's words, "agreed to almost everything we proposed regarding the arrangements and schedule for my trip." On July 15, Nixon stunned the nation with his announcement of "a major development in our efforts to build a lasting peace": he intended to go to China.

So momentous was the very idea of going that the trip itself, which took place in February 1972, was anticlimactic. In spite of a round of intense talks, sightseeing, and toasts, the two sides failed to secure consequential agreements. Nixon claimed that the most important accomplishment was simply the effort itself, which bridged "16,000 miles and twenty-two years of hostility." Nixon, for once, may not have been exaggerating. As far as he was concerned, he realized immediate ends. The opening spurred the Soviets to take a more cooperative stance in the ongoing SALT talks and led them to seek a similar summit. Then there was the domestic payoff: the liberals could only praise him, and he prepared to employ his new image as a great diplomat for the upcoming reelection effort.

The Arab-Israeli Conflict

Of all the conflicts that ran their course under the umbrella of *détente*, the most important was the Arab-Israeli struggle. The United States was committed to Israel; This in turn presented the Soviets with an opportunity to expand their influence among the Arab nations. In the aftermath of the Israelis' striking triumph in the 1967 Six-Day War, Egypt and Syria turned to the Soviet Union for military aid, which the Soviets provided in abundance. In the first Nixon term, the region was accorded such a lowly status by the administration that it was put under the supervision of Secretary of State Rogers, the quiet, unassuming, gracious presidential friend who had been thoroughly displaced and routinely abused by both the president and Kissinger. Left mostly to his own devices, Rogers managed to hold together a rough truce. From 1970 to 1972, the main antagonists, the Egyptians and the Israelis, bided their time, during which nothing much was accomplished but nothing much was damaged. Then in mid-1973, the Egyptians, led by Anwar

Sadat, abruptly turned on the Rogers plan, allied with Syria, and launched the October Yom Kippur War.

An area that had been of no more than secondary concern in the first term instantly became the foremost area of superpower competition, with each side strutting to the stage to protect its clients. At this point, Rogers was gone, Kissinger held both the National Security Council and secretary of state positions, and Nixon was embroiled in the Watergate scandal. Kissinger was in complete command.

The Egyptian surprise attack gave them the initial momentum, but with a huge influx of U.S. aid, the Israelis launched a counteroffensive that brought them to the brink of destroying Egypt's crack Third Army. Fearing not only the defeat of their ally but also the loss of influence in the region, the Soviets insisted on a joint U.S.-Soviet peacekeeping intervention. When Kissinger refused to participate, the Soviets warned that they might be forced to intervene unilaterally, and Kissinger trumped that threat by putting U.S. global forces on alert. Having done so, he throttled the crisis by pressuring the Israelis to recognize a cease-fire short of victory and began a dizzying round of diplomacy that had him flying from capital to capital for more than a year. In the end, he brought a firmer basis of peace to the region, extended U.S. power and influence, and spurred the Egyptians to expel the Soviets. For the same reason, however, Kissinger's Middle East triumph undid some of the goodwill he had built with the Soviets. He also incurred the opposition of the oil-producing nations, which initiated an oil boycott that hamstrung Western economic growth and heightened inflation.

The Domestic Agenda

Just as he wavered between moderation and aggressiveness in foreign policy, so did Nixon befuddle those who expected him to toe a conservative line in domestic affairs. In domestic economic policy, Nixon typically had been a moderate. He sought a balanced federal budget and, if possible, a reduction in taxes, but neither of these goals was urgent to him. They were not irrelevant to the economic problems that he faced—continued inflation or increasingly expensive entitlement programs for instance—but achieving a balanced budget and lowered taxes would not have had the sort of dramatic and clear effect that politicians hope for. In any case, neither would have been easy to achieve as long as the Vietnam War continued.

Nixon focused on two programs that were both innovative and safely moderate. Almost as an afterthought during the election, he proposed to reorganize the federal bureaucracy, a proposal with which no one could argue. He was never completely clear about what the reorganization was. He spoke partly of a "new federalism" that would restore power to the states; the mechanism for doing so was "revenue-sharing"—returning tax money to the states for use in social programs. Nixon probably never took governmental reorganization seriously, but the net result of reorganization that did take place during his administration was to consolidate more power in the hands of a centralized administrative unit than liberals were ever able to achieve.

In contrast, Nixon's welfare policy would have made a sharp break with liberal policies of the past but not in the direction that conservatives expected. In part because of his own intellectual and cultural insecurities, Nixon brought into his administration the maverick liberal Daniel Moynihan, whose pet scheme by the late sixties was the guaranteed annual income, a sort of negative income tax that provided cash grants to citizens on the basis of income.

As we have seen, there was ample good cause to revolutionize welfare policy, and Moynihan's scheme, drawn from his bitter experiences with community action, was designed to get directly to the heart of poverty and move away from the cultural emphasis of the Great Society. Nixon liked the idea partly because it would help the working poor; he also believed that the plan would provide strong incentives to work. But he toyed with the guaranteed-income plan for less noble reasons. Moynihan promised that, in the long run, the Family Assistance Plan (FAP) would reduce the welfare rolls significantly, even though it would have immediately expanded the rolls by adding intact families and the working poor. Carried out on a national basis, it would have required no commitment to the messy business of racial integration. Unlike the Great Society, FAP was not intended primarily for nonwhites; Nixon consistently stressed the importance of selling it as a program for all the poor. He also saw it as another way of reducing the scope of the federal government, and he relished the idea of destroying the social-work bureaucracy. Nixon asked whether the plan would "get rid of social workers." Moynihan responded: "It will wipe them out!"

Driven by personal grudges and political considerations, Nixon was never sufficiently committed to FAP to lay the necessary groundwork for its passage. It was not a program likely to appeal to conservatives; for them it was even more obviously a "handout" than Great Society programs. Liberals, meanwhile, were apt to think it was a repackaged attempt to destroy social programs and at worst a tricky form of race-baiting. Beyond partisan considerations, FAP was expensive (Nixon's chief economic advisor Arthur Burns argued against it on these grounds) and had the potential of adding to inflationary pressures. No one knew how it would affect the economic behavior of those on the margins of plan; it was possible, as Moynihan admitted, that those who earned slightly above any cutoff point would have less incentive to continue working or working as hard as they might otherwise. These considerations, added to the sheer inventiveness of the plan, guaranteed it a difficult reception in Congress. Nixon touted the plan as the centerpiece of his domestic policy, but he did precious little arm-twisting to see it passed. Instead, he presented it suddenly and sprang it on Congress as a surprise, a strategy that suggests he was more interested in its public relations value than in its substance. Not surprisingly, it failed twice.

At moments in his first term, Nixon could be as aglow with goodwill as any liberal. Assessing himself at midterm, he told reporters that he sought a "driving dream" of a nation living well with "clean air, clean water, open spaces . . . , a welfare reform program that will provide a floor under the income of every family with children." If they wanted proof that he was accomplishing more good than the liberals, he could point out that federal spending on social programs under his administration was higher than it had been under Johnson. By mid-1971, he was able to make the even bigger boast that his economic policies were traveling well beyond the boundaries of liberal Keynesianism. In an effort to check inflation, which had become an otherwise intractable problem, Nixon announced the imposition of a ninety-day wage-and-price freeze, an unprecedented rejection of the free market. Although in this case both congressional Democrats and his own economic advisors put strong pressure behind the policy, the wage-price freeze, like FAP, was presented with great fanfare as another example of Nixon's firm leadership. Probably more than FAP, it worked to Nixon's satisfaction. It astonished both conservatives and liberals, for obviously different reasons, and it encouraged a Wall Street rally. In the long run, it did very little to affect the economy one way or the other, which is to say that inflation was stopped for ninety days and then resumed its historic, decade-long march.

The Congressional Elections of 1970

Still, Nixon's political position was not an easy one. He had been the first twentieth-century president elected without carrying either the House or the Senate. The weakness of his domestic policies, the ongoing demonstrations against the war, the episodes of political violence, and most important, the war, made his long-term prospects less than certain. In addition to these obstacles, which a career politician like Nixon recognized instinctively, the president's difficulties with the media continued. All of his moderation seemed to go for naught; nothing he did convinced the media that the new Nixon was in the White House.

As the Republicans began to gear up for the elections, both Kevin Phillips's *The Emerging Republican Majority* (1969) and another book, *The Real Majority* (by Richard Scammon and Ben Wattenberg, 1969), which reaffirmed Phillips's thesis that a majority coalition was waiting to be fused together, dominated the administration's political perceptions. A quirky book, *The Real Majority* came to the administration's attention not only because it reaffirmed Phillips but because its authors were Democrats writing in hopes of generating some common sense within their own party. To Scammon and Wattenberg, the 1968 election showed that, in addition to the "bread-and-butter issues" that still drove people to the polls, a majority of voters were being moved by the "Social Issue," a catch-all term for attitudes about "law and order, antiyouth, malaise, change, or alienation." Future success would come to whichever party understood that "the great majority of the voters in America are unyoung, unpoor, and unblack; they are middle-aged, middle-class, and middle-minded." The average voter, they hypothesized, was a 47-year-old housewife from the outskirts of Dayton, Ohio, whose husband was a machinist, who was afraid of crime, ambivalent about having black neighbors, worried about her children slipping into the drug culture, and pressed for money. From Nixon's point of view, the obvious strategy was "to preempt the Social Issue in order to get the Democrats on the defensive. We should aim our strategy primarily at disaffected Democrats, at blue-collar workers, and at working-class white ethnics. We should set out to capture the vote of the forty-seven-year-old Dayton housewife." This strategy demanded that the Republicans focus on law-and-order, forced busing, and antiradicalism in hopes of helping the Dayton housewife forget that her sons were being drafted and that her husband's job at Frigidaire was being moved to Taiwan.

They initially hoped to employ Vice President Spiro Agnew as the "brass-knuckles" of the administration. Agnew was the son of a Greek immigrant, Theofrastos Anagnostopoulos, who ran a restaurant in Baltimore. There was a healthy Greek community in that city when Spiro was growing up, but his family remained on the edges of it, preferring assimilation, upward mobility, and, symbolically, the suburbs. A self-made man and a one-time county politician, Agnew became governor of Maryland in 1966, an unlikely victory in a race for a job that Republicans seldom win. Not a particularly distinguished man, he was not a particularly distinguished governor, neither notably conservative nor liberal. That his Democratic critics called him the "Ronald Reagan of the East" was less a commentary on Agnew's conservatism than an indication that he hardly cut a figure of his own. He had been a Rockefeller man, but, as the 1968 election approached, he warmed toward Nixon and began to take up the law-and-order theme.

Agnew was given his chance to step into the spotlight as the administration's leading liberal-basher well before the 1970 election. When the president's "silent majority speech" in November 1969, during which he announced the policy of Vietnamization, generated a favorable public response but less enthusiasm from the media, the White House decided to strike back with Agnew. Speaking before Republicans in Des Moines on November 13, Agnew lambasted the national media with a barrage that stunned many observers. The news anchors and their peers in the national press were a "small and unelected elite," Agnew charged, dictating opinion to the rest of the nation, even though that opinion was not at all shared on Main Street.

The fight was on. Agnew lumped together the protesters, the professors, the media, and the hippies as the nation's main enemy. Together they were "an effete corps of intellectual snobs," "hard-core dissidents and anarchists," and a "glib, activist element" given to "a spirit of masochism." By spring 1970, the White House had the atmosphere of an encircled armed camp. "You were either for us or against us," one White House aide recalled. "It was real confrontational politics." White House strategy called for Nixon himself to remain "presidential" and stay out of the campaign, but often in off-the-cuff remarks or speeches he contributed to the polarization. On May 1, just after the Cambodian invasion was announced, for example, while on an impromptu visit to the Pentagon, a woman whose husband was in Vietnam thanked him for his hawkish policy. Nixon responded by comparing the "average" kid with "these bums" who were "blowing up the campuses." That fall, Nixon launched a national speaking tour with the zeal of someone whose own election was on the line. At a stop in San Jose, he met a large antiwar demonstration, and, as he writes in his memoirs, "I could not resist showing them how little respect I had for their juvenile and mindless ranting." He jumped on the hood of his car and flashed his trademark "V for victory" sign and was pelted with a barrage of rocks, eggs, and vegetables. It was an ugly moment. It was not exactly "presidential" for Nixon to goad protesters, and his explanation—he couldn't resist it—suggests that self-restraint was a rare commodity all around.

The attempt to turn the backlash to the administration's political benefit failed. In the 1970 elections, the Democrats retained control of both houses of Congress and increased their overall vote. Ultimately, most people probably voted their pocketbooks, on which inflation was feasting. In attacking intellectuals and students, the administration was probably doing itself no harm. But Nixon's behavior turned off many in the silent majority, who, as Scammon and Wattenberg put it, were dedicated middle-of-the-roaders and as dismayed over polarization from the right as from the left.

The administration's handling of the Kent State shootings is a case in point. Nixon's response to the tragedy, which took place just after the Pentagon visit, offered nothing in the way of conciliation but instead warned that unrest often ended in bloodshed. He offered no calming words, no empathy for the families of the innocent victims. Many people felt for the father of one of the slain students when he bitterly remarked: "My child was not a bum." The 1970 off-year elections demonstrated that Scammon and Wattenberg were only half right; the average voter might have been a 47-year-old housewife from Dayton who probably was dismayed over the cultural politics of the left, but that did not mean that she approved of the backlash politics of the right.

Nixon had sensed as much in 1968 and now in 1970 seemed to have lost his bearings. He had campaigned, as Attorney General John Mitchell said, as if he were running for county sheriff rather than standing as president, and the election results favored Mitchell's interpretation. Nixon learned from the off-year mistakes, but as was his habit, the lesson cut two ways. Henceforth, he would behave in public as befit his dignified office. In private, however, the administration resolved to go to any lengths, legal or illegal, to discredit opponents, undermine enemies, and avenge itself against critics.

Watergate and the End
of an Era

Richard Nixon recovered his political bearings in time to win a landslide victory in 1972. Everything was going his way. He had embarked on *détente*, he could report that "peace was at hand in Vietnam," and he was at least working on the problem of inflation. The Democrats, meanwhile, had helped him by turning away from their most formidable candidates and nominating a very weak one in George McGovern. Nixon took 60 percent of the popular vote, won in every state but Massachusetts and Washington, D.C., tore whole blocs of traditionally Democratic voters away from McGovern, and ate into the Wallace vote. The magnitude of the victory convinced him that the silent majority shared the intensity of his hatreds and would approve of dealing with protesters, radicals, and establishment opponents by any means necessary.

At the time of the election, the public did not have even the dimmest idea of how far Nixon already had gone. Neither, for that matter, did the Democrats, some of whom charged that the Committee to Re-Elect the President (CREEP) was involved in a bizarre burglary attempt at the offices of the Democratic National Committee in Washington's Watergate office complex on June 17. Common sense suggested that no matter how devious they were, the president's men would not have done something so stupid. Why risk being caught when the Democrats were busy destroying themselves?

The answer to this question gets to the heart of the Watergate scandal. The immediate answer was that reelection was not the sure bet in June 1972 that it was in October. The president did not develop his enormous lead in the polls until after McGovern's nomination in July, and Nixon knew better than to consider early polling data a reliable indicator of how people would vote in November. The longer answer was that the Watergate burglary was only one episode in a systematic program of domestic spying, political dirty tricks, and governmental harassment, some barely legal and some clearly illegal. The Watergate scandal must be understood as the consequence of Nixon's relentless drive for power coupled with his contempt for opponents.

Nixon's self-defense has always rested on two points: that his administration was forced to engage in domestic surveillance in order to protect national security against violence-prone radicals; and that bugging political opponents was a standard procedure begun in Washington by the Democrats. He was right on this last point, although that hardly exonerates him. The first point, however, is questionable to say the least.

The Huston Plan

The domestic harassment and surveillance schemes dated back to the beginning of the administration, when an ambitious ex-Marine and White House aide Charles Colson drew up an "enemies list" that eventually included some 200 Democratic politicians, political radicals, foundation heads, reporters, and professors. It was essentially a declaration of war against what the White House considered "the establishment." Over the next year and a half, the White House discovered that neither the CIA, which by law was prohibited from domestic operations, nor the FBI, which J. Edgar Hoover was reluctant to employ for partisan purposes, would hound its enemies. So Nixon and his aides enacted a plan formulated by Tom Huston, a young loyalist, for controlling radical groups such as Weatherman and the Black Panthers with wiretaps and, if necessary, burglary. To Nixon, the threats justified extreme measures. "I was satisfied that none of the special techniques would be used indiscriminately, and that none of them represented any special threat to legitimate dissent."

Quite the opposite happened, and Nixon knew it. The Huston plan provided the basis for an array of escapades over the next two years perpetrated by various individuals working in different capacities for the White House for reasons that ranged from sophomoric political harassment to personal vendetta.

The Plumbers Unit and Dirty Tricks

In June 1971 Daniel Ellsberg, a defense analyst who had worked on Kissinger's National Security staff, leaked the documents that became the Pentagon Papers to the *New York Times*, and the White House, including the president himself, moved to discredit Ellsberg and clamp down on all potential leaks. Convinced that the intelligence agencies were incapable and unwilling to take the necessary steps to stem the information flow, Nixon ordered his presidential assistant, John Ehrlichman, to set up an independent unit. Ehrlichman then turned the task over to the gung-ho Colson, who recruited ex-CIA agents G. Gordon Liddy and E. Howard Hunt and put together the "Plumbers" unit. Because Ellsberg himself was not the most balanced of people, the administration believed he could be embarrassed, and in an effort to dig up damaging material, the "Plumbers" broke into the Los Angeles office of Ellsberg's psychiatrist, Dr. Lewis Fielding.

Nixon may have ordered the Fielding break-in, but no hard evidence exists on this point. Whether or not he did is less important than that the harassment of Ellsberg showed a group of powerful men gone mad. Nixon had no pressing reason to destroy Ellsberg; the Pentagon Papers, after all, dealt only with the early and liberal years of Vietnam and did not touch him. If anything, one would think the Papers might give Nixon more ammunition to use in blaming the liberals for the mess in Southeast Asia. But the escape of information signaled a loss of control to Nixon, a team failure, and it was all the more insulting that the information wound up in the hands of the *Times*, a paper he particularly hated.

The White House domestic operations continued to grow and resulted in any number of barely coordinated schemes. Only the president was in a position to know about all of them. Nixon chose his favorite targets—Edward Kennedy, Edmund Muskie, George McGovern, George Wallace, Ellsberg, and Democratic National Chairman Lawrence O' Brien—and his subordinates attacked.

The clearly partisan attacks began when H. R. "Bob" Haldeman, a longtime Nixon associate, and Ehrlichman, one of Nixon's top aides, sent hundreds of thousands of dollars to the campaign of Wallace's rival in the Alabama gubernatorial election and then goaded the IRS to harass Wallace. Because he was the Democrat to beat in the early 1972 presidential primaries, Edmund Muskie became the special target of five different White House groups and was plagued by dirty tricks: stink bombs, phony campaign literature, disrupted fund-raisers, infiltrators in campaign headquarters, and phony claims of private comments insulting various groups, all of which took their toll on Muskie's performance and gradually wore him down, forcing him from the race.

With Muskie's exit, the White House began to focus on McGovern. The South Dakotan was less impressive than Muskie, and Nixon assumed he could be beaten through an aggressive political campaign. Not people to waste the chance, the Plumbers, now at work for CREEP, cooked up what White House lawyer John

Dean called "a million dollar plan that was the most incredible thing I have ever laid eyes on: all in codes, and involved black bag operations, kidnapping, providing prostitutes to weaken the opposition, bugging, mugging teams. It was just an incredible thing." The actual Watergate bugging was a scaled-down version of this "million-dollar plan."

As soon as Liddy's men were arrested following the June 17 break-in, CREEP and the White House began trying to cover up any trail that might lead to them. Nixon's inner circle arranged to funnel money to the burglars, ostensibly to defray legal and personal costs but in fact as hush money. Temporarily purchased silence gave them room to maneuver. The White House received important breaks when both the civil suit brought by the Democrats against CREEP and the trial of the burglars were postponed until after the 1972 election.

The Unraveling

That comfort zone began to contract soon after the new year. The burglars' trial opened in January 1973 in the courtroom of independent-minded Judge John J. Sirica. Meanwhile, Senate Democrats voted to convene a special investigating committee to be headed by Senator Sam Ervin, a North Carolinian who would soon become famous for his folksy common sense. As the legal process got underway and the many individuals caught up in the sordid White House business began to consider their own positions, the potential for disaster grew. Too many people were involved, and too many people had bits of knowledge that could implicate the White House. The main Plumbers, Hunt and Liddy, had been connected to the White House for some time. Liddy was not a great concern: he was thought to be crazy. "Liddy is in jail right now," Dean told Nixon in their most famous meeting, "serving his time and having a good time. . . . I think Liddy in his own bizarre way the strongest of all of them." Hunt was not so reliable. He was distraught after his wife had been killed the prior December in an airplane crash while carrying a large sum of cash for payments to the burglars into Chicago.

On March 21, Dean met with Nixon to warn him that there was a "cancer" spreading around the presidency as people began scurrying to protect themselves. At this time, Ervin's Senate committee was gearing up; the burglars' trial was ending, and Sirica was preparing the sort of stiff sentences that might provoke wholesale confessions; a federal grand jury was convened to investigate Watergate; and new allegations that Attorney General Mitchell and Vice President Agnew had engaged in unrelated crimes surfaced. "What really troubles me," Dean explained to Nixon, is what could happen if "they do find a criminal case against a Haldeman, a Dean, a Mitchell, an Ehrlichman." It was getting to the point where the insiders were going to have to find a way that "this can be carved away from you, so that it does not damage you or the Presidency. It just can't. You are not involved in it." "That is true!" Nixon responded.

Nixon settled on a strategy that combined a determination to fight back with a readiness to see what was revealed. But that strategy left Nixon's aides to fall one by one. Dean, concluding that he was as vulnerable as anyone, hired a criminal attorney in the aftermath of the late-March meetings. Privately, Mitchell refused to be the scapegoat, and in public his rambunctious wife, Martha, complained to the press that her husband was being set up. In mid-April, Dean and White House aide Jeb Magruder implicated Haldeman and Ehrlichman in the payment of hush money. Nixon then fired Dean and forced Haldeman and Ehrlichman, his two closest aides and two of his oldest associates, to resign, leaving both men embittered. At one point even Ehrlichman contemplated "throwing myself against the controls" of the presidential plane during a trip to Mississippi with Nixon and Haldeman; "We'd all be gone in about a minute and a half."

The Tapes

Nixon hoped that a change of staff would help distance the Oval Office from the scandal. Unfortunately for the president, at least one of his new appointees had principles, and in May, his new Attorney General Eliot Richardson appointed Archibald Cox, a Kennedy Democrat, as special prosecutor and gave him wide powers of investigation under the protection of the Justice Department. Stalwart Republicans, including Barry Goldwater, began to worry that Nixon in his defiant fight would take the GOP down with him. John Dean proved the biggest threat when, in his June appearance before the Senate committee, he claimed that Nixon knew of the coverup before the March 21 meeting, which was when the president claimed he was first informed. Finally, a Haldeman assistant, Alexander Butterfield, let slip in the Ervin hearings that there was a recording system in the White House that routinely taped presidential meetings, which ultimately secured the case against the president.

In and of themselves, the tapes were ambiguous evidence. There is no question that Nixon held meetings in order to create the appearance of innocence. The most audaciously contrived meetings were held in spring 1973, however, and tapes made earlier, particularly during the summer of the break-in, revealed the extent of Nixon's early participation in a coverup effort. Most damaging was the tape of a June 23, 1972, meeting with Haldeman in which the two decided to pressure the FBI and CIA to drop their investigations of the break-in. The mere act of secretly recording friends, foe, and family confirmed the public's impression that the president was obsessed with secrecy control and was downright paranoid. The old Nixon seemed to return in tapes where he was routinely vulgar, insulting, and obscene.

Butterfield's revelations led to the last stage of the Watergate crisis, which threatened to upset the traditional separation of power and create a far-reaching constitutional crisis. Both the courts and the Congress demanded copies of the taped material, but, claiming "executive privilege," Nixon agreed only to provide the Ervin committee with edited transcripts of selected material. The president, Nixon claimed, was under no constitutional obligation to share the inner workings of his office with any other branch of government. It was a shaky position, laughably incriminating, distressingly evasive, and totally self-serving. Both the Senate and the special prosecutor were outraged by Nixon's stonewalling. Forced to reveal more, Nixon proposed to have the White House staff compose transcripts of seven tapes that Cox wanted and to have Senator John Stennis, a conservative Democrat, verify their accuracy. Cox refused this arrangement, as Nixon evidently expected he would, and the president believed that he had grounds to fire the special prosecutor. On October 20, Nixon asked Attorney General Richardson to fire Cox. But Richardson refused and resigned. When the president then ordered Deputy Attorney General William Ruckelshaus to fire Cox, Ruckelshaus tried to resign, but the president fired him first. Solicitor General Robert Bork ascended to acting attorney general, and he fired Cox. The "Saturday Night Massacre" ran its course.

More charges poured forth: Nixon had cheated on his taxes while president (he did); he had used federal money to make improvements on his Florida and California homes (the improvements were of an official nature); and he had engaged in shady financial dealings in real estate with the help of friends (he had, but he had done nothing technically illegal). Several weeks after the Massacre, one of the White House tapes turned up with an 18-and-a-half-minute gap of silence on it. Nixon's private secretary, Rose Mary Woods, testified that she had erased the tape while trying to talk on the phone and transcribe the tapes at the same time. Her testimony was immediately subjected to national ridicule. When asked to demonstrate how exactly she could have committed the blunder, she showed reporters a pose that almost required a contortionist. *Newsweek* put her on the cover of its next issue doing the "Rose Mary stretch." So few people believed her that other members of the administration offered their own theories. New Chief of Staff Alexander Haig blamed a "sinister force," which was even more ludicrous than Woods's excuse. H. R. Haldeman later theorized that Nixon took the tapes with the intention of expunging damaging parts, but he was so inept with anything mechanical that he left one huge gap and then gave up trying.

Resignation

Beginning in October 1973, impeachment grew as a very real prospect. Pressure on Nixon to resign mounted steadily from all directions—the press, his political opponents, and even members of his own party. The pressure merely reinforced his instincts to fight and to rely on himself. The House Judiciary Committee then began the impeachment process, which eventually resulted in four general charges: obstruction of justice; abuse of presidential powers; contempt of Congress; and fraud. Nixon continued to enjoy some support; trips through the South remained friendly; New York rabbi Baruch Korff organized a Committee for Fairness to the President; and some loyalists stood by him—Haig, press secretary Ron Ziegler, speechwriter Ray Price, and, of course, the Nixon family. Just as the number of his friends narrowed, so did the grounds of his defense, which had to rest on a continued denial of the Dean charges and therefore on a tenacious hold on the most incriminating tapes, especially the June 23, 1972, tape. Haig and Ziegler did not see the transcripts of that meeting until late July 1974, and when they did they knew that Nixon's position was hopeless. On August 1, Nixon decided to resign, and while doing so spared him impeachment, nonetheless he left under the greatest cloud of suspicion, acrimony, and public disillusionment in U.S. history.

After his resignation as president in August 1974, Richard M. Nixon bids an emotional farewell to members of his staff on the White House lawn.
[UPI/Bettmann Newsphotos]

Nixon never acknowledged any wrongdoing in the Watergate affair. He subsequently defended himself by claiming that he was misunderstood or that he misunderstood what was going on around him. His defense is no more believable in memoir form than it was in 1973 and 1974. What stands out is quite the opposite: not only did he know what his people were doing, but also throughout the affair he worked to prevent the consequences of criminal activity from destroying him. Nixon has coupled this plea of misunderstanding with assertions that he did nothing wrong. He believed he was playing the dirty game of politics, where spying on enemies, harassment, and wiretapping were all standard procedures invented by the Democrats. For that reason, Nixon believed that the Watergate scandal was political in nature: it was part of his own partisan efforts aimed at political opponents, and the scandal was the result of vengeful political enemies hoping to tarnish the momentous success of 1972. He never believed that Watergate betrayed a lack of ethics or a shabby morality because he never believed those virtues had anything to do with politics.

Throughout the debacle Nixon remained convinced that he was fighting his traditional enemies and needed to fight them as he always had. In his mind, he had succeeded against "them"—the liberals, the press, the professors, the establishment—only because of his toughness. Again and again, Nixon complained of the partisan nature of his persecution. As he told Admiral Elmo Zumwalt in a rambling conversation in December 1973, his whole predicament showed how the "eastern liberal establishment was out to do us all in." According to Zumwalt, Nixon thought Watergate was "part of a vast plot by intellectual snobs to destroy a president who was representative of the man in the street." He battled constantly with the White House press corps, particularly CBS's Dan Rather. In response to a set of Rather's questions, he lashed out at the media for "frantic, hysterical reporting." A Rather colleague then asked what exactly it was about television coverage that made him so angry. "Don't get the impression that you arouse my anger," Nixon retorted. "You see, one can only be angry with those he respects." He made his purely political interpretation of Watergate most clear in an interview with Rabbi Korff. "I am the press's favorite pin-up boy," he complained. "If it hadn't been for Watergate there would probably have been something else. . . . If I were a liberal Watergate would be a blip." Having become the establishment's greatest foe, having dealt it telling blows by achieving peace in Vietnam and realizing *détente*, he had become its most important target. Watergate was "the last gasp of our hardest opponents," he told John Dean. "The establishment is dying" and was using the scandal to overturn "the successes we have had in foreign policy and in the election."

Understanding Watergate as a political fight allowed Nixon to factor out moral and ethical considerations and also obliged him to turn it into a fight for the silent majority. To give up was a betrayal of the people. This curious reading also gave him confidence, for if the scandal was the creation of the liberal establishment, then few people outside Washington would care. He was convinced that Watergate did not scandalize the average American, who would understand the entire business as the usual stuff of politics. Nixon was so deeply certain that he represented the common American that he could not distinguish his unethical actions from the average voter's view of U.S. politics. He made many political errors after 1972, but perhaps the most glaring was his assumption that the American public was as cynical as he was. Many of his constituents had looked to him because he seemed a ballast in an era of political insanity. But Watergate exposed Nixon as just another politician, no different from the Democrats who had misled the nation about Vietnam and had reneged on their liberal promises. It did Nixon no good to claim that Kennedy and Johnson had done essentially the same things he was being attacked for; that was precisely the problem to the silent majority. By the time he resigned, he was the most despised man in the United States.

In June 1974, less than two months before he relinquished power, Richard Nixon went to Moscow to push the SALT agreements to Soviet Premier Leonid Brezhnev. He failed to secure an accord, but he and Brezhnev had several thoughtful personal conversations. During a yacht trip on the Black Sea, the two men, leaders of the greatest military powers on earth, meeting to discuss the possibilities of limiting one another's capacity to destroy the earth, turned instead to the possibility that both nations might collapse from within. Nixon mused that the advanced nations faced the danger of having their very success and power result in "the weakening of character." No doubt thinking of his fellow citizens, Nixon pondered the possibility that, "as people got more material goods, they became less 'hungry,' lost their drive, and [became] almost totally obsessed with self, selfishness, and every kind of abstract idea."

No one could have foreseen in 1974 how close the Soviet Union was to complete collapse. But Nixon sensed that his United States was closing out an era. Since the beginning of the American Century, Americans had done great things. They had changed the world. They had risen from an upstart nation to the greatest power in history. They were primarily responsible for vanquishing fascism. If they had not shared their tremendous wealth with the rest of the world, they had produced the measure of what a good society could be and created the powerful impression that material abundance and political freedom were inherently connected.

Richard Nixon was a product of and a staunch believer in this historic America, and yet here he was in June 1974, on the verge of becoming the first president ever thrown out of office, contemplating the possibility that the United States' historic greatness had become a curse. Americans had created fabulous cities but could not now govern them. They had begun to make good on providing justice to their most oppressed fellow citizens, only to back away when it became clear that achieving lasting justice might require altering the economic system that provided the nation's abundance. They had turned their anticolonial heritage into a vicious mockery by engaging in a systematic campaign to destroy people seeking independence. They had begun to rethink their prudery and intolerance, only to forsake the task of rebuilding the cultural will and judgment necessary to replace Wasp puritanism with democratic culture; instead, they settled on a new culture given to avarice and tastelessness. They had begun to appreciate the diversity inherent in their society, only to demand a subtle submission to homogeneity and to pit ethnic groups against one another.

What Nixon told Brezhnev was not very profound, but in the context of the waning of the American Century, it had substance. The trouble with Nixon's musings was that he failed to see how much he had helped bring on the end. Nor did he appreciate that he was a symbolic figure for doing so: that in his own rootlessness, in his own striving—not after wealth but after acceptance, acclaim, and a self remade to meet external circumstances—he demonstrated the deeper rootlessness of his society. It is fitting that Nixon was a Californian, a product of the most rootless, most mobile, least stable of all U.S. regions, home to both John Birchers and bohemia. Had he been born forty years later, Nixon, the chaser after respectability, may well have wandered past Joan Didion in the Haight, a lost soul among other lost souls.

Essay on Sources

Neither Todd Gitlin, *The Sixties: Years of Hope, Days of Rage* (New York: 1987), nor Allan Matusow, *The Unraveling of America* (New York: 1984), are comprehensive accounts of the United States in the sixties, but they are the two works that have influenced me most. Because I believe that the sixties must be seen within a web of developments that reaches well beyond the decade itself, however, I also have found a number of broader treatments of the post–World War II United States helpful: William Chafe, *Unfinished Journey*, 2nd ed. (New York: 1991); Frederick Siegel, *Troubled Journey* (New York: 1984); and Richard Polenberg, *One Nation Divisible* (New York: 1980). Narrower accounts of the period include William O'Neill, *Coming Apart* (Chicago: 1971); and Kim McQuaid, *The Anxious Years* (New York: 1989). Gerald Howard, ed., *The Sixties* (New York: 1982, 1991), collects a useful array of writings on culture, art, and politics from the period. Manning Marable, *Race, Reform, and Rebellion*, 2nd ed. (Jackson, Miss.: 1991), is a general account of African-American politics after World War II, which I have found particularly helpful on the politics of black nationalism. One can see the persistent political stalemate by comparing Sohnya Sayres, et al., eds., *The Sixties without Apology* (Minneapolis: 1984), and Peter Collier and David Horowitz, *Destructive Generation* (New York: 1989).

Chapter 1   The End of Liberalism

One consequence of the tendency to see a sharp break between the fifties and sixties is the absence of solid studies linking Stephenson liberalism with the New Frontier. To date, the connections are most clearly seen through John Kenneth Galbraith's autobiographical writings, *Annals of an Abiding Liberal*, Andrea D. Williams, ed. (Boston: 1979), and *A Life in Our Times* (Boston: 1981). The continuity of liberalism is plain enough when the influence of Galbraith's *American Capitalism* (Boston: 1951) and *The Affluent Society* (Boston: 1958) is traced ahead into the Kennedy era. Arthur Schlesinger, Jr., meanwhile, spelled out the direction of the New Frontier in "The New Mood in Politics," *Esquire* (January 1960). His lament about the nation's "primal curse" of violence appeared in "America 1968: The Politics of Violence," *Harper's* (June 1968).

Between his early optimism and later pessimism, Schlesinger authored one of the most complete insider histories of the Kennedy Administration, *1,000 Days*

301

(Boston: 1964). Other insider accounts focus more narrowly on internal politics: Lawrence O'Brien, *No Final Victories* (Garden City, N.Y.: 1974), and Theodore Sorensen, *Kennedy* (New York: 1965). The journalist Theodore White said much that was perceptive about Kennedy and televised politics in *The Making of the President, 1960* (New York: 1961). Two other studies concerning Kennedy and television are Mary Ann Watson, *The Expanding Vista* (New York: 1990), and Joseph P. Berry, *John F. Kennedy and the Media* (Lanham, Md.: 1987).

Kennedy has never lacked for biographers, although the family continues to restrict information about his personal life, and other official information about his administration remains classified, especially in regard to Vietnam. See David Burner, *JFK and a New Generation* (Glenview, Ill.: 1988), as well as Burner's study of liberal politics, *The Torch Is Passed* (New York: 1984), and Thomas Reeves, *President Kennedy: Profile of Power* (New York: 1993). The revisionist criticism of Kennedy as aggressive and reliant upon media image is most succinctly posed in Thomas G. Paterson, "Bearing the Burden: A Critical Look at JFK's Foreign Policy," *Virginia Quarterly Review* (Spring 1978). David Halberstam, however, was the first to set down a thorough-going criticism of the administration's obsession with technique and intelligence in *The Best and the Brightest* (New York: 1972). Norman Mailer's celebration of Kennedy as the new hero appears as "Superman Comes to the Supermarket," in *Presidential Papers* (New York: 1964). Herbert Parmet, *JFK* (New York: 1984) is a conventional biography; William Manchester, *One Brief Shining Moment* (Boston: 1983), is biographical adulation.

Kennedy's foreign policy was probably the least unique aspect of his presidency, not least because, rather than taking Stephenson's advice about improving U.S. relations with the developing world, Kennedy merely applied Cold War thinking more aggressively to those regions. Thus his policy should be understood as an outgrowth of American containment policy, which is how John Lewis Gaddis sees "flexible response" in *Strategies of Containment* (New York: 1982). Thomas Paterson, ed., *Kennedy's Quest for Victory* (New York: 1989), is useful. Specific studies include Jerome Levinson and Juan De Onis, *The Alliance that Lost Its Way* (Chicago: 1970), which remains the most complete study of the effort to secure Latin America in the aftermath of the Bay of Pigs invasion; Trumbull Higgins, *The Perfect Failure* (New York: 1987), on the Bay of Pigs; and Michael R. Beschloss, *The Crisis Years* (New York: 1991), on U.S.–Soviet relations. Walt W. Rostow, *The Stages of Economic Growth* (New York: 1960), meanwhile, presents the ideological basis for Kennedy's developing world policy.

The administration's relationship to the civil rights and women's rights movements ought to be understood against Galbraith's justification of interest-group liberalism in *American Capitalism*. In both cases, the administration sought to attach these movements to the Democratic party while paring them down into interest groups that, as distinguished from grass-roots movements, were easier to tame. My understanding of interest-group liberalism is shaped by Theodore Lowi's important *The End of Liberalism* (New York: 1967), which, while written in the sixties, was entirely out of step with practically all contemporary thinking about public life. Harris Wofford's personal account of his time as an aide on civil rights,

Of Kennedys and Kings (New York: 1982), provides ample testimony to how political considerations prevented the Kennedys from acting on their better instincts by putting federal power forthrightly into civil rights. Carl N. Brauer, *John F. Kennedy and the Second Reconstruction* (New York: 1977), ably covers the administration's civil rights program. Burke Marshall, the Justice Department official in charge of civil rights, explained the ultimate limitations on federal policy in *Federalism and Civil Rights* (New York: 1964). For the origins and history of the National Committee on the Status of Women, see Judith Hole and Ellen Levine, *The Rebirth of Feminism* (New York: 1971), and Leila Rupp and Verta Taylor, *Survival in the Doldrums* (New York: 1987). Ethel Klein, *Gender Politics* (Cambridge: 1984), links the feminist revival to postwar demographic change. Susan M. Hartmann, *From Margin to Mainstream* (New York: 1989), serves as a general account of the movement in the sixties. Among NOW's original participants, Betty Friedan has been the most articulate. Her collection, *It Changed My Life* (New York: 1976), distinguishes the feminist movement's mainstream from its radicals and yet puts the movement squarely in the context of the New Politics. Robert and Jane Hollowell Coles record their long conversations with the Cambridge maid in *Women of Crisis* (New York: 1978).

There are three recent scholarly biographies of Lyndon Johnson, of which the shortest, least controversial, and, to date, only complete one is Paul Conkin, *Big Daddy from the Perdenales* (Boston: 1986). The first two volumes of Robert Caro's projected three-volume work, *The Path to Power* (New York: 1982), and *The Means of Ascent* (New York: 1989), are thorough but hostile, and should be balanced by Robert Dallek's equally impressive, *Lone Star Rising* (New York: 1991). Of the older biographies, Doris Kearns, *Lyndon Johnson and the American Dream* (New York: 1976), is the most important because of the personal participation of Johnson himself in the book. Harry McPherson, one of Johnson's more liberal aides, depicts LBJ as a tragic figure—well intentioned though prone to mistakes—in *A Political Education* (Boston: 1971).

The internal politics and thinking behind the Great Society is best covered in Nicholas Lemann, *The Promised Land* (New York: 1992). Peter Marris and Marty Rein, *Dilemmas of Social Reform* (Chicago: 1967), emphasizes the good intentions behind sixties reformism. John Donovan, *The Politics of Poverty* (New York: 1967), is mostly drawn from published sources as opposed to insider knowledge but holds up well. For an able defense of the effort, if not of the particulars, of Great Society reforms see Sar Levitan, *The Great Society's Poor Law* (Baltimore: 1969). Other works include Frances Fox Piven and Richard Cloward, *Regulating the Poor* (New York: 1971), and Daniel Knapp and Kenneth Polk, *Scouting the War on Poverty* (New York: 1971).

Norman Mailer, *Miami and the Siege of Chicago* (New York: 1969), is a characteristically lively account of both national party conventions. William Chafe, *Never Stop Running* (New York: 1994), exaggerates the importance of its subject, the left-liberal Allard Lowenstein, but is an insightful work on the renegade who, among other things, pushed the "dump Johnson" campaign. Eugene McCarthy recounts his candidacy in *The Year of the People* (New York: 1969). Arthur Schlesinger, Jr., was more convinced of Robert Kennedy's goodwill than of JFK's, and it shows in *Robert Kennedy and His Times* (Boston: 1978), which is particularly good on RFK from his stint as attorney general through the assassination. Jack Newfield paints RFK as a "hip" candidate in *Robert Kennedy* (New York: 1969). Kennedy explains the purpose of his candidacy in *To Seek a Newer World* (Garden City, N.Y.: 1967). Hubert Humphrey's account of his political career in the sixties, *The Education of a Public Man* (New York: 1976), includes his dismay over his treatment at the hands of the Kennedy machine in the 1960 primaries as well as an attempt to describe the bind he found himself in during the 1968 nomination process. Lewis Chester, Godfrey Hodgson, and Bruce Page give a thorough journalistic account of 1968 in *An American Melodrama* (New York: 1969), that is most perceptive about the Democrats, who were, admittedly, a good deal more interesting than their Republican opponents.

Gary Hart, McGovern's campaign manager and later Democratic presidential hopeful in his own right, gives the optimist's account of the 1972 election in *Right from the Start* (New York: 1973). See also McGovern's *Grassroots* (New York: 1978).

Chapter 2   The Civil Rights Movement

Today, one must begin a study of the civil rights movement with Taylor Branch's magisterial *Parting the Waters* (New York: 1989). Whereas Branch places the movement within a broad context of social history and in so doing sees Martin Luther King, Jr.'s influences as similarly broad and varied, Stephan Oates, *Let the Trumpet Sound* (New York: 1982), believes King's family and religious background was the source of his direction in public life. Both books have their faults: Branch probably exaggerates the influence of the liberal theologian Reinhold Niebuhr on King; Oates fails to appreciate how deeply embedded King was in the unique culture of southern black religious communities. I have relied on Henry Hampton, Steve Fayer, and Sarah Flynn, eds., *Voices of Freedom* (New York: 1990), for many of the personal observations quoted in Chapter 2. Other important books on the movement as a whole are Harvard Sitkoff, *The Struggle for Black Equality* (New York: 1983), from which I draw much of the general discussion of the sit-in movements; Steven Lawson, *In Pursuit of Power* (New York: 1985), which contains an excellent discussion of the Voting Rights Act and its benefits; and William Chafe, *Civilities and Civil Rights* (New York: 1980), which demonstrates just how important the local community of Greensboro, North Carolina was to the sit-ins—a story about local resistance to white supremacy that was repeated in more obscure ways across the South. CORE director James Farmer's memoir, *Freedom—When?* (New York: 1965), provides a good account of the Freedom Rides, including both organizational strategy and life in Mississippi jails. King's "Letter from Birmingham Jail" appears in *Why We Can't Wait* (New York: 1964).

It is perhaps fitting that the best historical accounts of SNCC, Howard Zinn, *SNCC* (Westport, Conn.: 1964); Doug McAdams, *Freedom Summer* (1984); and

Emily Stoper, *The Student Non-Violent Coordinating Committee* (Brooklyn: 1989), pale before the personal accounts of the dangerous and heady days of Mississippi Summer and the Voters' Education Project. For a vivid picture of what VEP was up against see James Silver, *Mississippi: The Closed Society* (New York: 1964). In *The Making of Black Revolutionaries* (Washington, D.C.: 1985), James Forman argues that SNCC should have undertaken nothing less than guerrilla war against white supremacy, and although written from the safety of distance and time, the argument is surprisingly plausible. Forman also includes a number of SNCC documents in his memoir, including Bobby Moses's analysis of the intractable situation of 1963, which served as the point of departure for the Freedom Summer plan. Elizabeth Sutherland, ed., *Letters from Mississippi* (New York: 1965), collects letters from white volunteers to their parents and friends in the North, among which are the incredulous comments about the routine danger blacks faced. Mary King's autobiography, *Freedom Song* (New York: 1988), contains many important observations of SNCC and Freedom Summer, but it is also one of the great autobiographies of the sixties, maybe, indeed, the very best. King testifies to the sincere idealism that drove many people into public life but also demonstrates—with even judgment and without self-righteousness—how aimless much of that idealism turned out to be. For other testimony, see Howell Raines, *My Soul Is Rested* (New York: 1977).

The shift from civil rights to black power emerged just as the mainstream movement began to recognize how large the gulf was between the southern revolution and the northern ghetto. Bayard Rustin's important essay on the gulf, "From Protest to Politics: The Future of the Civil Rights Movement," appeared in *Commentary* (1964) but is reprinted in his collection of essays, *Down the Line* (Chicago: 1971). Stokely Carmichael and Charles Hamilton, in *Black Power* (Nashville: 1967), present a cogent defense of black power that never quite evolved into practice, at least not in the short term. It was precisely its impracticality that King took issue with in his chapter on black power in *Where Do We Go From Here?* (New York: 1967). For the Black Panthers see Bobby Seale, *Seize the Time* (New York: 1970), and Eldridge Cleaver, *Soul on Ice* (New York: 1967). Two fine recent autobiographies, Elaine Brown, *A Taste of Power* (New York: 1993), and David Hilliard, *This Side of Glory* (Boston: 1993), should have ignited a revival of interest in the Panthers. That they have not perhaps can be accounted for by the light they both shed on the Panthers' animosity toward cultural nationalism, which remains so strong in our own time and, in its longevity, indicates that Huey Newton's suspicions about its tepid radicalism were substantially correct.

Chapter 3   The Vietnam War
and U.S. Foreign Policy

The Vietnam War is the one part of sixties history about which the "last word" has been said—at least for now. While it is true that much documentary evidence remains classified and unexamined, it is hard to see how any new material would decisively alter the harsh realities of a war fought for no good reason. At this point, then, George Herring, *The Longest War*, 2nd ed. (New York: 1986), stands as the most judicious and complete work.

William Appleman Williams anticipated the moderate New Left critique of American policy in Vietnam in his prescient book, *The Tragedy of American Diplomacy* (New York: 1959). On the Eisenhower administration and the Geneva Accords, see Lloyd Gardner, *Approaching Vietnam* (New York: 1988). Ronald Specter, *The United States Army in Vietnam: Advice and Support* (Washington, D.C.: 1984), covers the early relationship with Diem and includes General Collins's skeptical assessments of the regime. Edward Lansdale, the CIA chief in South Vietnam, was as close to Diem as any American, but he too doubted Diem could establish himself as a popular political figure: see Lansdale's *In the Midst of Wars* (New York: 1972). Robert Scigliano, *South Vietnam: Nation Under Stress* (Boston: 1963), is an excellent contemporary examination of South Vietnam under Diem. David Halberstam comments on Madame Nhu in *The Making of a Quagmire*, rev. ed. (New York: 1987). William Duiker, *The Communist Road to Power* (Boulder, Colo.: 1981), is the best Western study of the Communist side of the war, and on it I base much of my understanding of Ho Chi Minh's strategy. I quote the comments of villagers on Diem from James Trullinger, *Village at War* (New York: 1980). The rural and traditionalist nature of South Vietnam is ably detailed in Frances Fitzgerald, *Fire in the Lake* (New York: 1966).

In *Promises to Keep* (New York: 1971), Chester Bowles describes the 1961 debates within the Kennedy administration over the ultimate direction of policy. Kennedy's quandary over finding the "non-essential areas" is noted in Parmet, *JFK*. Roger Hilsman, *To Move a Nation* (New York: 1967), includes a good deal on the strategic-hamlet program, as well as the author's account of the Diem coup. King C. Chen, "Hanoi's Three Decisions and the Escalation of the Vietnam War," *Political Science Quarterly* (Summer 1990), contains details about the Saigon-Hanoi talks of 1963 as well as an assessment of Hanoi's thinking.

William Westmoreland provides his explanation of search-and-destroy strategy in *A Soldier Reports* (New York: 1976). A well-known critique of Westmoreland's strategy is Harry G. Summers, *On Strategy* (New York: 1982). The bureaucratic nature of policy making is covered in Douglas Kinnard, *The War Managers* (Hanover, N.H.: 1977). On Rolling Thunder see James Clay Thompson, *Rolling Thunder* (Chapel Hill: 1980). James William Gibson, *The Perfect War* (Boston: 1986), is a broader account of the air war, especially as it was directed against the North. The bewildering tunnel network of the Iron Triangle and the U.S. military's various attempts at destroying it are the subject of Tom Mangold and John Penycate, *The Tunnels of Cu Chi* (New York: 1986).

Lyndon Johnson's long, self-pitying analysis of his wartime policy appears in the Kearns biography, cited above. Also see Herbert Schandler, *Unmaking of the President* (Princeton: 1977). There are a number of oral histories on the Vietnam War. Richard Ford III's comments about Nha Trang appear in Wallace Terry, *Bloods* (New York: 1984). Bernard Edelman, ed., *Dear America* (New York: 1985), contains a number of letters from REMFs; see also Al Santoli, *Everything We Had* (New

York: 1981). The journalist Seymour Hersh covered the My Lai massacre in *Cover-Up* (New York: 1972). Clark Clifford recounts his long study session with the Joint Chiefs and his conversion from hawk to dove, in "A Vietnam Reappraisal," *Foreign Affairs* (July 1969).

Since its publication, William Shawcross, *Sideshow* (New York: 1979), has generated debate over the extent to which the United States must shoulder blame for unleashing the chain of events that led to the Cambodian genocide under Pol Pot. Truong Nhu Tang was the NLF official who read the Cambodian invasion as a blunder in Truong Nhu Tang and David Chanoff, *A Vietcong Memoir* (San Diego: 1985). I also take from Tang the view of internal NLF politics; if his account is correct, the worst policy the United States could have followed if it wanted an independent, noncommunist regime in the South was the policy of war. Studies of the peace process and the dismal end of the war include Allen E. Goodman, *The Lost Peace* (Stanford: 1977); Gareth Porter, *A Peace Denied* (Bloomington, Ind.: 1975); and Frank Snepp, *Decent Interval* (New York: 1977).

Chapter 4   The Social History of the War

McGeorge Bundy's advice about fighting the quiet war appears in *The Pentagon Papers*, Gravel edition (Boston: 1972). Two very good books on the media, the war, and the antiwar movement are Daniel C. Hallin, *The "Uncensored War"* (New York: 1986), and Todd Gitlin, *The Whole World Is Watching* (Berkeley: 1980). Both of these works stress how the media employs its institutional impulse toward "objectivity" as a means of claiming a voice in public affairs. An earlier study is Michael J. Arlin, *The Living Room War* (New York: 1969). Harrison Salisbury's report on the bombing around Hanoi was *Behind the Lines—Hanoi* (New York: 1967). Kathleen Turner, *Lyndon Johnson's Dual War* (Chicago: 1985), is not unsympathetic to Johnson. On Tet and the media, see Peter Braestrup, *Big Story*, 2 vols. (Boulder, Colo.: 1977), and Don Oberdorfer, *Tet! The Turning Point in the Vietnam War* (Garden City, N.Y.: 1971).

In *The Past Has Another Pattern* (New York: 1982), George Ball recounts Kennedy's assertion that he was "crazier than hell" for suggesting that Vietnam might turn into a long-term engagement. See also Ball, "Top Secret: The Prophecy the President Rejected," *Atlantic* (June 1972). Walter Lippmann's clash with Johnson is covered in Ronald Steel, *Walter Lippmann and the American Century* (New York: 1981). On J. William Fulbright there is William C. Berman, *William Fulbright and the Vietnam War* (Kent, Ohio: 1988). Fulbright's *The Arrogance of Power* (New York: 1967), is a minor classic.

The most complete study of the antiwar movement to date is Charles DeBenedetti, *An American Ordeal* (Syracuse: 1990). The strength of DeBenedetti's work is its ecumenical spirit; it leaves much room, meanwhile, for further interpretations. Nancy Zaroulis and Gerald Sullivan, *Who Spoke Up* (New York: 1984), focuses on the New Left in the peace movement. Thomas Powers, *The War at Home* (Boston: 1984), is less comprehensive than either of these accounts but ably demonstrates that the movement was forced into the streets in response to the administration's refusal to engage in reasoned debate.

Both sides of the teach-in movement are covered in Louis Menashe and Ronald Radosh, eds., *Teach-Ins: U.S.A.* (New York: 1967). Jack Newfield describes the Progressive Labor party as a "hereditary left" in *A Prophetic Minority* (New York: 1966). A. J. Muste voiced his concerns with the movement's fragmentation in "Crisis in the World and in the Peace Movement," *Liberation* (June/July 1965). Dave Dellinger defended SDS's decision to include communists in "The March on Washington and Its Critics," *Liberation* (May 1965). Dellinger's autobiography, *From Yale to Jail* (New York: 1993) is one of the less effective personal accounts of life in the sixties but is still informative. Norman Mailer, *Armies of the Night* (New York: 1968), is the classic account of the Pentagon siege—seen, of course, from Mailer's peculiar perspective. Dellinger's ambiguous description of the siege as "hard to concretize" appears in "Resistance: Vietnam and America," *Liberation* (November 1967). For accounts of the attempted seduction of the troops and the charge of the federal marshals: George Dennison, "Talking With the Troops," and Martin Jezer, "Pentagon Confrontation," both in *Liberation* (November 1967).

Michael Ferber and Staughton Lynd, *The Resistance* (Boston: 1971), provides a justification for and an account of draft resistance. Lawrence Baskir and William Strauss, *Chance and Circumstance* (New York: 1978), remains the essential book on the Vietnam-era draft, which the authors describe as a "social Darwinist" policy. See also David S. Surrey, *Choice of Conscience* (South Hadley, Mass.: 1982), for a thorough discussion of the varied and bizarre exemptions available to young men, as well as information about the extent of noncompliance. Renee G. Kasinsky, *Refugees from Militarism* (New Brunswick, N.J.: 1976), is also helpful. Melvin Small, *Johnson, Nixon, and the Doves* (New Brunswick, N.J.: 1988), meanwhile, provides a helpful account of the government's response to the antiwar protests.

For public opinion concerning the war see Lou Harris, *The Anguish of Change* (New York: 1973). Two excellent efforts at getting the grass-roots view offer quite different readings of public opinion. Where Gloria Emerson is consistently critical of prowar opinion in *Winners and Losers* (New York: 1976), Myra McPherson, *Long Time Passing* (Garden City, N.Y.: 1984), is sympathetic to working-class supporters of the war, particularly those from South Boston. Brenden and Patricia Sexton, *Blue Collars and Hard Hats* (New York: 1971) includes poignant interviews with common folk who express their sense of betrayal over the war and the antiwar movement alike. For the sensibilities of Vietnam soldiers, see Philip Caputo, *A Rumor of War* (New York: 1977), and Mark Baker, *Nam!* (New York: 1981), which contains the story of the Johns Hopkins student who blundered his way into the military. Baker's collection also shows rather forcefully how the nation's expectations of young men carried many into the war. Michael Anderegg, ed., *Inventing Vietnam* (Philadelphia: 1991); William J. Searle, ed., *Search and Clear* (Bowling Green, Ohio: 1988); and John Hellmann, *American Myth and the Legacy of Vietnam* (New York: 1986) are attempts to consider the wider cultural issues of the war.

Chapter 5   The Reddish Decade

James Miller, *Democracy Is in the Streets* (New York: 1987), quite rightly finds the early New Left a more honorable subject for study than the post-1968 movement and is the one necessary work on the New Left. Among other things, Miller includes the entire Port Huron statement as an appendix—a service in its own right. The much older Kirkpatrick Sale, *SDS* (New York: 1973), is still good, Miller notwithstanding. Richard King, *The Party of Eros* (Chapel Hill, N.C.: 1972), is an excellent consideration of the intellectual history of sixties radicalism. The vast majority of essential New Left writings and speeches, from Paul Potter's "name-the-system" speech at the 1965 Easter March to Hayden and Wittman's essay "An Inter-Racial Movement of the Poor," can be found within the following collections: Mitchell Cohen and Dennis Hale, eds., *The New Student Left* (Boston: 1966); Paul Jacobs and Saul Landau, eds., *The New Radicals* (New York: 1966); or Massimo Teodori, ed., *The New Left* (Indianapolis: 1969). Much of Gitlin's *The Sixties* is political memoir that includes the most self-critical writing on the New Left—a real feat among people not otherwise disposed to self-criticism. It is true that Tom Hayden is self-critical but also a bit too self-conscious in *Reunion* (New York: 1988); still the book is an excellent account of the New Left.

Maurice Isserman, *If I Had a Hammer* (New York: 1987), is the best study on the relationship of the leftist generations. But the memoirs of two radicals who sustained long and admirable careers, Irving Howe, *A Margin of Hope* (New York: 1982), and Michael Harrington, *Fragments of a Century* (New York: 1973), are quite useful. Harrington is apologetic about the treatment that the Port Huron group received at LID hands but remains rigorously skeptical about the whole project of sixties radicalism.

The theoretical shift from Port Huron to revolution for the hell of it can be traced in Paul Potter, *A Name for Ourselves* (Boston: 1970), an audaciously self-referential argument for revolution. Herbert Marcuse, *One-Dimensional Man* (Boston, 1964), finds its clearest imitation in Gregory Calvert, *A Disrupted History* (New York: 1971). See W. J. Rorabaugh, *Berkeley at War* (New York: 1989), for an overall account of Berkeley in the sixties, including the free-speech movement. The Columbia upris-ing, meanwhile, can be encountered in Mark Rudd, "Columbia—Notes on the Spring Rebellion," in Carl Ogelsby, ed., *The New Left Reader* (New York: 1969), and Jerry L. Avorn, *Up Against the Ivy Wall* (New York: 1968). On Yippies see Jerry Rubin, *Do It!* (New York: 1970), Marty Jezer, *Abbie Hoffman: American Rebel* (New Bruns-wick, N.J.: 1992), and Rubin's interview in Milton Viorst, *Fire in the Streets* (New York: 1979). Michael Rossman's criticism of Yippie plans for the Chicago siege appears in *Wedding Within the War* (New York: 1971). Requiems for sixties radicalism began as early as Carl Ogelsby, "Notes on a Decade Ready for the Dustbin," *Liberation* (August-September 1969). Tom Bates, *Rads* (New York: 1992), is an unnerving study of the radicals at the University of Wisconsin, Madison. The same forces at work in the allegedly tranquil midwest were also at work in Seattle, which was the scene of much of Susan Stern's unapologetic *With the Weathermen* (New York: 1975). Alice Echols, *Daring to Be Bad* (Minneapolis: 1989), is the finest study to date of radical feminism. Robin Morgan, *Sisterhood Is Powerful* (New York: 1970), is a famous collection of various writings of contemporary left-wing feminists, though Morgan's memoir, *Going Too Far* (New York: 1970), is in many ways a more helpful work on the late politics of the New Left. Martin Duberman's *Stonewall* (New York: 1993) is the first complete study of the event that sparked gay liberation.

Chapter 6 The End of Culture

Partly because of the coincidence of timing, partly because the political upheaval of the day coaxed the cultural shift from modernism to postmodernism to the surface, the counterculture and its advocates confused cultural rebelliousness with political radicalism from the very beginning of the postmodern period. This seems to me the fundamental mistake that ensnares the three defenders of sixties counterculture: Theodore Roszak, *The Making of the Counterculture* (Garden City, N.Y.: 1969), Philip Slater, *In Pursuit of Loneliness* (Boston: 1970), and Charles A. Reich, *The Greening of America* (New York: 1970). I am skeptical of the revolutionary claims of the counterculture, and by extension of the postmodern left, because I believe the contention that freedom is to be found in culture is at its very heart the creation of consumer capitalism, which has invaded the most intimate parts of our lives through its manipulation of psychology and sexuality, and in so doing has turned practically everything into a commodity for sale. I see no revolutionary potential in extending the free market to culture, anymore than I see the free market bringing economic justice. For the opposite view of both sixties culture and postmodernism, see Sally Banes, *Greenwich Village* (Durham, N.C.: 1993).

As I argue here, it was its hostility to consumerism and its accompanying commitment to serious art that distinguishes modernism from postmodernism. Harold Rosenberg's brilliant work helped convince me of this point: *The Tradition of the New* (New York: 1960), *The De-Definition of Art* (New York: 1972), and *Art on the Edge* (New York: 1975). Robert Motherwell's comment about the abstract expressionists' duty to the past is found in Irving Sandler, *The Triumph of American Painting* (New York: 1970). Mark Rothko's troubled life is recounted in James E. Breslin, *Mark Rothko* (Chicago: 1993). Paul Krassner's observation about how much had changed from 1960 to 1970 appears in his memoir, *How a Satirical Editor Became a Yippie Conspirator in Ten Easy Years* (New York: 1971). Krassner was one of the few countercultural figures who reached the discomforting conclusion that his side was winning. For the most part, cultural radicals conflated modernist art with middle-class sensibilities and repudiated "normal" living and aesthetic judgment as if they were one and the same. Susan Sontag, who should have known better, presents the repudiation of judgment as a new aesthetic in *Against Interpretation* (New York: 1964).

R. Kostelanetz, ed., *The New American Arts* (New York: 1965), includes a wide variety of essays examining the parallel developments in formal culture. John Cage speaks about the exhaustion of his music in *A Year from Monday* (Middletown, Conn.: 1967). On radical theater, see Robert Brustein, *Revolution in Theatre* (New

York: 1971). Stephan Schneck describes the Living Theatre as "paradise seekers" in "Le Living," *Ramparts*, November 30, 1968. On Andy Warhol, see Warhol and Pat Hackett, *POPism: The Warhol '60s* (New York: 1980). Warhol's friend Ondine witnessed the shooting of Marilyn Monroe and lived to tell about it: Jean Stein and George Plimpton, *Edie* (New York: 1982). On the Diggers, see Emmett Grogan, *Ringolevio* (New York: 1972). Sooner or later, the "new sensibility" was bound to end in R. D. Laing, *The Politics of Experience* (New York: 1967).

Literature enjoyed boom times in the sixties, even if fiction had to share the stage with the likes of Norman Mailer and Tom Wolfe. Morris Dickstein, *Gates of Eden* (New York: 1977), is still the best single work on sixties writing. Wolfe's books include *The Kandy-Colored Tangerine Flake Streamline Baby* (New York: 1964), *The Electric Kool-Aid Acid Test* (New York: 1967), and *Radical Chic and Mau-Mauing the Flak Catchers* (New York: 1970). Conrad Knickerbocker criticized Wolfe's hip affectations in a review of his 1964 work in *Life*, July 2, 1965. The following are the period's canonical works that I have taken as illustrative of wider cultural developments: Kurt Vonnegut, *God Bless You Mr. Rosewater* (New York: 1966), *Slaughterhouse Five* (New York: 1969), and *Breakfast of Champions* (New York: 1973). Thomas Pynchon, *V.* (Philadelphia: 1963), *Crying of Lot 49* (Philadelphia: 1966), and *Gravity's Rainbow* (New York: 1973). Ken Kesey, *One Flew Over the Cuckoo's Nest* (New York: 1961), and *Sometimes a Great Notion* (New York: 1964). John Barth, *The Sot-Weed Factor* (Garden City, N.Y.: 1960); and *Giles Goat-Boy* (Garden City, N.Y.: 1966). Philip Roth, *Portnoy's Complaint* (New York: 1970).

The rapid disappearance of the censor in the sixties was taken by most liberal commentators as a result of the determined struggle of selfless artists, when it is more accurately understood as the demise of a cultural ruling class and the indifference of the cultural marketplace to moral issues. For an overview see Eric Moon, ed., *Book Selection and Censorship in the Sixties* (New York: 1969). Charles Rembar recounts the legal battles over applying First Amendment rights to obscenity in *The End of Obscenity* (New York: 1968). Anthony Lewis trumpets the victory of the "sophisticated critic" in "Sex and the Supreme Court," *Esquire*, (June 1963). Albert Goldman understood that the greatest threat to the cultural radical was not the "Philistines," as dogmatic liberals such as Anthony Lewis believed, but the disappearance of the Philistines, whose absence destroyed the capacity to shock. See "The Trial of Lenny Bruce," *New Republic*, September 12, 1964. On film censorship, see Jack Vizzard's memoirs, *See No Evil* (New York: 1970). Actor Anthony Quinn is quoted in Nora Sayre, *60s Going on 70s* (New York: 1972). In *Slouching Towards Bethlehem* (New York: 1968), Joan Didion makes the same penetrating observations about the end of censorship that she renders about the counterculture as a whole. Pauline Kael understood that film violence had become as quickly gratuitous as had sex: *Kiss, Kiss, Bang, Bang* (Boston: 1968). For Monsignor Little's comment about nudity, see J. Stone, "The Legion of Decency: What's Nude," *Ramparts* (September 1965).

Norman Brown's work, *Life Against Death* (Middletown, Conn.: 1958); and *Love's Body* (New York: 1966), was never so widely acclaimed as that of Herbert Marcuse, but in the long run Brown has been more influential. Indeed his work has to be regarded as the original theoretical defense of the sexual revolution, on which arguments for gay and lesbian liberation have rested ever since. Shulamith Firestone combines Brown, Marcuse, and radical feminism in *The Dialectic of Sex* (New York: 1970). See also Kate Millett, *Sexual Politics* (New York: 1969). William Burroughs's comment about sexual repression appears in Daniel Odier, *The Job* (New York: 1974). On homosexuality and the sexual revolution see John D'Emilio, *Sexual Politics and Sexual Communities* (Chicago: 1983), as well as his *Making Trouble* (New York: 1992); and Estelle Freedman and John D'Emilio, *Intimate Matters* (New York: 1988). For Hugh Hefner as Doctor Feelgood, see his interview, "The Gospel According to Hugh Hefner," *Ramparts* (September 1965); and on the commercial value of sex, see Irving Mansfield's memoir, *Life with Jackie* (New York: 1983). On Eastern religion and hallucinogenic drugs, see Timothy Leary, *High Priest* (1968). Kesey's Palo Alto critics are quoted in Norman Melnick, "Ken 'Cuckoo Nest' Kesey: One Who Wigged Out," *Village Voice* (May 12, 1966). Alan Watts, meanwhile, made the appeal to eastern mysticism in *Beyond Theology* (New York: 1964).

On heroes and antiheroes, see Jules Feiffer *The Great Comic Book Heroes* (New York: 1965); Richard Kluger, "Sex and Superman," *Partisan Review*, (1966); Hunter S. Thompson, *Hell's Angels* (New York: 1967); Ross Wetzsteon, "Sleazy Cowboys Ride the Existential Range," *Village Voice* (February 23, 1967); and Jeff Greenfield, *No Peace, No Place* (New York: 1973). Jimmy Breslin is quoted on the New York Mets in "The Worst Baseball Team Ever," *Sports Illustrated* (August 13, 1962). On Muhammad Ali as theater, see Joe Flaherty "Sad Search for a King," *Village Voice* (August 10, 1967). On the impotence of cultural radicalism in the political sphere: Richard Goldstein, "The Theatre of Cruelty Comes to Second Avenue," *Village Voice* (October 31, 1968); and Donald Bartheleme, *City Lights* (New York: 1970).

Chapter 7 The Urban Crisis

Anyone who has read his work can readily see that William Julius Wilson fundamentally informs my understanding of the urban crisis. Although *The Declining Significance of Race* (Chicago: 1978), and *The Truly Disadvantaged* (Chicago: 1987), deal only secondarily with the sixties, it seems to me that the urban conditions of which Wilson writes matured in the sixties. The city's demise marked the exhaustion of the cosmopolitan ideal, of the hope that the city might constitute a site for the mutually beneficial mingling of a humane technology, art, work, folkways, and responsible governance. Lewis Mumford's *The Urban Condition* (New York: 1966), is so impressive because it measures the suburbanization of America against this earlier ideal and reminds us that the city so conceived was perhaps the last best hope for warding off the homogenizing force of contemporary capitalism.

Two general studies that reach beyond the sixties and thereby lay important groundwork for understanding the urban crisis are Kenneth Jackson, *Crabgrass Frontier* (New York: 1985), and Mark Gelfand, *A Nation of Cities* (New York: 1975). Richard Bernard and Bradley Rice, eds., *Sunbelt Cities* (Austin, Texas: 1983); and Richard Bernard, ed., *Snobelt Cities* (Bloomington, Ind.: 1990), both include wide-ranging essays pertaining to the sixties. Kenneth Kusmer, ed., *Black Communities and Urban Development in America, 1720–1990*, vol. 7 (New York: 1991), covers the sixties and includes a solid section on the riots.

For my discussion of the politics of housing and urban redevelopment, I relied generally on Leonard Duhl, ed., *The Urban Condition* (New York: 1963); Robert Weaver, *Dilemmas of Urban America* (New York: 1967); Alan Shank, *Political Power and the Urban Crisis* (Boston: 1969); Joseph Fried, *Housing USA* (New York: 1971); Nathaniel Keith, *Politics and the Housing Crisis Since 1930* (New York: 1973); and Bryan Downes, *Politics, Change, and the Urban Crisis* (North Scituate, Mass.: 1976). Martin Anderson, *The Federal Bulldozer* (New York: 1964), is an aggressive critique of the urban renewal programs. James Q. Wilson, ed., *Urban Renewal* (London: 1966), is a useful reader on the urban-renewal controversy. Robert Caro details the life and times of Robert Moses in *Power Broker* (New York: 1974). Though she hardly knew it at the time, Jane Jacobs in *The Life and Death of Great American Cities* (New York: 1961), was anticipating some of the postmodern architectural attacks on the modernist obsession with orderliness when she denounced all of New York's contemporary building schemes; the great flaw in the book was her strident criticism of Lewis Mumford, whom she erroneously chose to represent the urban planner. James Baldwin quips about Harlem's high rises in *Nobody Knows My Name* (New York: 1964). Besides Mumford, York Willbern, *The Withering Away of the City* (Tuscaloosa, Ala.: 1964); and Don Martindale in the introduction to Max Weber, *The City*, Don Martindale and Gertrud Neuwirth, eds. (New York: 1966), call attention to the qualitative transformation of the city.

For urban life, the starting point perhaps is Kenneth Clark, *Dark Ghetto* (New York: 1965), a classic rendering of Harlem. Elliot Liebow, *Tally's Corner* (Boston: 1967), subjects ghetto life to rather narrow sociological presumptions. Lee Rainwater's study of the Pruett-Igoe Homes in St. Louis, *Behind Ghetto Walls* (New York: 1973), is much less burdened with the assumptions of social scientists. Herbert Gans, *The Urban Villagers* (New York: 1962), is a splendid account of Boston's mostly Italian West End just before it was condemned as a slum and "renewed" through the construction of upper-income apartments. Besides a commentary on the blindness that urban planners were capable of, Gans's book demonstrates the integrity of an ethnic community as yet unmolested by consumer culture.

I gleaned most labor statistics cited here from the *Monthly Labor Review*. For somewhat easier reading on labor see Gus Tyler, *The Labor Revolution* (New York: 1967), and *Labor in the Metropolis* (Columbus, Ohio: 1972). On poverty, see S. M. Miller and Frank Riessman, *Social Class and Social Policy* (New York: 1968). Arthur M. Ross and Herbert Hill, *Employment, Race, and Poverty* (New York: 1967), includes many articles on urban labor and African Americans, as does Nathan Glazer, ed., *Cities in Trouble* (Chicago: 1970). Stanley Friedlander, *Unemployment in the Urban Core* (New York: 1972), is probably the most thorough book on the subject of urban unemployment. Daniel P. Moynihan, *Maximum Feasible Misunderstanding* (New York: 1969), is an insider's guide to liberal confusion. The Office of Juvenile Delinquency was inspired by Richard A. Cloward and Lloyd E. Ohlin, *Delinquency and Opportunity* (New York: 1960). Saul Alinsky, "War on Poverty—Political Pornography," in *Journal of Social Issues* (January 1969); Bayard Rustin, " 'Black Power' and Coalition Politics," in *Down the Line* (Chicago: 1971), and Sar Levitan, *The Great Society's Poor Law* (Baltimore: 1969). For a fair representation of the social-science literature on poverty that emerged in response to the poverty program see James L. Sundquist, *On Fighting Poverty* (New York: 1969). The conservative response is presented in Edward Banfield, *Unheavenly City* (Boston: 1970); Raymond L. Vernon, *The Myth and Reality of Our Urban Problems* (Cambridge: 1966); and Roger Starr, *The Living End* (New York: 1966). The clash between the mayors and the White House was detailed in Erwin Knoll and Jules Witcover, "Fighting Poverty—and City Hall," *The Reporter* (June 3, 1965).

Coming to terms with the urban riots should begin with the Kerner Report itself, which, whatever its ideological bias, contains a wealth of data. It appeared as the *Report of the National Advisory Commission on Civil Disorders* (New York: 1968). Sidney Fine, *Violence in the Model City* (Ann Arbor, Mich.: 1989), details the Detroit conflagration and is the most thorough study of any of the riots. Frank Besag and Philip Cook, *The Anatomy of a Riot: Buffalo, 1967* (Buffalo: 1970), also is a case study. Tom Hayden draws out the political and racial implications of the colonial analogy for the urban crisis in "Colonialism and Liberation as American Problems," in Roland L. Warren, ed., *Politics and the Ghettos* (New York: 1969). Richard Elman, *The Poorhouse State* (New York: 1966), presents a good treatment of the poor in New York City.

Chapter 8   Beyond the Melting Pot

Students of sixties social history are fortunate that Robert Coles was doing his best work at the time. Coles's voluminous writings—better described as recordings of obscure voices—were models of humanistic sociology that leave us with ample records of what common folks thought, with only minimal interruption from Coles himself. His most important works: *Children of Crisis* (New York: 1967); *Migrants, Sharecroppers, and Mountaineers* (Boston: 1971); and *The South Goes North* (Boston: 1971).

The legitimation of ethnic diversity begins with the discrediting of the Wasp ideal. And that an aspiring presidential hopeful such as John F. Kennedy could author *A Nation of Immigrants* (New York: 1960) for the B'nai B'rith Foundation suggests that the Wasps were already on the run at the beginning of the decade. Peter Schrag, *The Decline of the WASP* (New York: 1971), is the most thoughtful attempt to address the issue of the evaporation of a cultural ruling class. E. Digby Baltzell first employed the term *Wasp* in *The Protestant Establishment* (New York: 1964). The etymology of the term can be followed in Irving Lewis Allen, "WASP— From Sociological Concept to Epithet," in Andrew Greeley and Gregory Baum, eds., *Ethnicity* (New York: 1977). Charles H. Anderson, *White Protestant Americans* (Englewood Cliffs, N. J.: 1970), argues that the term *Wasp* is practically indefinable in simple ethnic terms. Robert S. Diamond, "A Self-Portrait of the Chief Executive," *Fortune* (May 1970), examines the ethnic background of American corporate executives, and G. William Domhoff, *Who Rules America?* (Englewood Cliffs, N.J.: 1967), also demonstrates that the economic ruling class survived without controlling culture.

For black nationalism and the Nation of Islam, the place to begin is C. Eric Lincoln, *The Black Muslims in America* (Boston: 1973); and Malcolm X and Alex Haley, *The Autobiography of Malcolm X* (New York: 1965). James H. Cone, *Martin and Malcolm and America* (Maryknoll, N.Y.: 1991), is more recent. In *And We Are Not Saved* (Garden City, N.Y.: 1970), Debbie Louis speaks about the value of cultural nationalism within black communities. Nikki Giovanni, *Black Feeling, Black Talk, Black Judgment* (New York: 1970), is a good collection of her various writings. Robert L. Allen, *Black Awakening in Capitalist America,* (Garden City, N.Y.: 1969), meanwhile, examines the compatibility between cultural nationalism and business. The most complete book on cultural nationalism, William L. Van Deburg, *A New Day in Babylon* (Chicago: 1992), similarly makes clear the entrepreneurial usefulness of the cultural message.

The insuperable dilemma for black nationalists has always been that cultural independence in America cannot be achieved without economic independence, which in turn means the embrace of capitalist values. In some of the finest writing on the issue, Harold Cruse concludes that an acceptance of capitalism cannot be separated out from black nationalism. See *The Crisis of the Negro Intellectual* (New York: 1967), and his more recent *Plural But Equal* (New York: 1987), in which, among other things, he questions the extent to which Martin Luther King, Jr., was committed to integration for its own sake. The battle of Cleveland is the focus of Louis H. Masotti and Jerome R. Corsi, *Shoot-Out in Cleveland* (New York: 1969). Julius Lester's analysis of the battle appears in *Revolutionary Notes* (New York: 1969). For the mayor's view of the clash, see Carl B. Stokes, *Promises of Power* (New York: 1973). The New York jazz critic Albert Murray registers his gentle criticism against cultural nationalism in *The Omni-Americans* (New York: 1970), partly on the grounds that it diminished the enormous achievements of African Americans in music.

For a general account of the emergence of ethnic consciousness, see John R. Howard, *Awakening Minorities* (New York: 1970). Cesar Chavez and the Farm Workers' movement are considered in Stan Steiner, *La Raza* (New York: 1970); John Gregory Dunne, *Delano* (New York: 1967); and Luis Valdez, "The Tale of La Raza," *Ramparts* (July 1966). Peter Nabokov, *Tijerina and the Court House Raid* (Berkeley: 1970), details the rise of the Hispanic version of Malcolm X. General accounts of the rise of Hispanic politics in the United States are F. Chris Garcia, ed., *La Causa Politica* (Notre Dame, Ind.: 1974); and L. H. Gann and Peter J. Duignan, *The Hispanics in the United States* (Boulder, Colo.: 1986). My skepticism about Hispanic politics, once it became a national movement, grows out of my reading of Peter Skerry, *Mexican Americans* (New York: 1993). For Native Americans, see Stan Steiner, *The New Indians* (New York: 1968); Vine Deloria, Jr., *Custer Died for Your Sins* (New York: 1969); and Rex Weyler, *Blood of the Land* (New York: 1982). Terri Schultz casts a dubious eye toward the famous siege at Wounded Knee in "Bamboozle Me Not at Wounded Knee," *Harper's* (June 1973).

The rise of the so-called white ethnics was manifested in the publication of Michael Novak, *Rise of the Unmeltable Ethnics* (New York: 1972). Sallie TeSelle, *The Rediscovery of Ethnicity* (New York: 1973), offers a critique of Novak. Richard Krickus, *Pursuing the American Dream* (Bloomington, Ind., 1976), presents a general analysis of the issue. See also Andrew Greeley and Gregory Baum, eds., *Ethnicity* (New York: 1977). Michael Lerner, "Respectable Bigotry," *American Scholar* (October 1969), remarks on the ethnic jokes making the rounds among the fashionably liberal in the late sixties. For ethnic politics, see Raymond E. Wolfinger, "The Development and Persistence of Ethnic Voting," in Lawrence H. Fuchs, ed., *American Ethnic Politics* (New York: 1968); and Nathan Glazer and Daniel P. Moynihan, *Beyond the Melting Pot*, 2nd ed. (New York: 1970). Michael Wenk, S. M. Tomasi, and Geno Baroni, eds., *Pieces of a Dream* (New York: 1972), is nostalgic to the same degree as Novak was defensive. Mikulski's bill of rights can be found in Thomas H. Clancy, "The Ethnic American—An Interview with Barbara Mikulski," *America* (December 26, 1970).

My understanding of "everyman" in the sixties begins with Robert Coles. Arthur B. Shostak, *Blue-Collar Life* (New York: 1969); Louise Howe, ed., *The White Minority* (New York: 1970); and Irving Howe, ed., *The World of the Blue-Collar Worker* (New York: 1972), are also helpful. The liberal estimate of Wallace is found in Pete Hamill, "Wallace," *Ramparts* October 26, 1968. The best study on George Wallace is Jody Carlson, *George C. Wallace and the Politics of Powerlessness* (New Brunswick, N.J.: 1981). For evidence on public opinion see Gary Marx, *Protest and Prejudice* (Westport, Conn.: 1967); Alan Altshuler, *Community Control* (New York: 1970); Peter Binzen, *Whitetown, U.S.A.* (New York: 1970); and Andrew Levinson, *The Working-Class Majority* (New York: 1974). Harry S. Caudill, *Night Comes to the Cumberlands* (Boston: 1963), sparked interest in the Appalachians. See also Todd Gitlin and Nanci Hollander, *Uptown* (New York: 1970); David S. Walls and John B. Stephenson, eds., *Appalachia in the Sixties* (Lexington, Ky.: 1972); and William W. Philliber, *Appalachian Migrants to Urban America* (New York: 1981).

Chapter 9   The Crisis of Authority

What more clearly could have signaled the arrival of the postmodern era than to have *Time* magazine trumpet the long-suppressed declaration of Friedreich Nietzsche, postmodernism's philosophical father, that God is dead, as it did in its April 8, 1966 issue? Although *Time*'s own survey showed that it was not God so much who had passed on as the commitment to organized religion, still American churches had long been struggling to remain relevant, and the theological developments of the sixties, particularly the radical theology of the God-is-dead movement, carried this process to its logical end. See Thomas Althizer and William Hamilton, *Radical Theology and the Death of God* (Indianapolis: 1966), and Thomas W. Ogletree, *The Death of God Controversy* (Nashville: 1966). Harvey Cox put radical theology in less extreme form in *The Secular City* (New York: 1966). Two surveys of school prayer are Robert S. Alley, *School Prayer* (Buffalo, N.Y.: 1994), and Edward Keynes, *The Court vs. Congress* (Durham, N.C.: 1989).

The generation gap became a growth industry for writers only toward the end of the sixties, a sign that a pervasive sense of generational schism was related to the wider public events of the period. True, Paul Goodman's *Growing Up Absurd* (New York: 1960), was important, but more because of Goodman's own sensitivity and skill than because he inaugurated a trend. The first major sociological study of the emerging adolescent world was James S. Coleman, *The Adolescent Society* (New York: 1961). Kenneth Keniston gained a deserved reputation as a sympathizer with the young because of his books, *The Uncommitted* (New York: 1965), and *Young Radicals* (New York: 1968). Robert R. Hansel, *Like Father, Like Son, Like Hell* (New York: 1969), attempts to mediate between the generations. Margaret Mead applauds the emergence of a distinct youth culture in *Culture and Commitment* (Garden City, N.Y.: 1970). See also James Digiacomo, *We Were Never Their Age* (New York: 1972), and William Self, *Bridging the Generation Gap* (Nashville: 1970). Malcolm Henry, *The Generation of Narcissus* (Boston: 1971), is an often skeptical look at the connections between the youth rebellion and the wider, consumer culture that young Americans were reveling in. If anything, however, Henry is not skeptical enough. Christine Chapman, *America's Runaways* (New York: 1975), is the best study of the growing problem of child runaways.

One very good general study of family life is Steven Mintz and Susan Kellogg, *Domestic Revolutions* (New York: 1988), particularly because the authors trace the transformation of sociological estimates of the family, as well as the institution itself. The most widely hailed treatise of the day was Robert O. Blood and Donald M. Wolfe, *Husbands and Wives* (New York: 1963). Betty Friedan, *The Feminine Mystique* (New York: 1963), is rightly regarded as the manifesto of the mainstream women's movement. But to do Friedan justice, the book ought to be read in addition as a sound consideration of family life and as an example of the period's increasing anxiety over alienation. On the pill and birth-control, in general see Linda Gordon, *Woman's Body, Woman's Right* (New York: 1976), and James Reed, *From Private Vice to Public Virtue* (New York: 1978). Ron E. Roberts, *The New Communes* (Englewood Cliffs, N.J.: 1971), is a general account of the commune movement. Nena and George O'Neill present their strident defense of relaxed family arrangements in *Open Marriage* (New York: 1972). Roderick Phillips, *Putting Asunder* (New York: 1988), meanwhile, is a good general account of divorce in America.

Mirra Komarovsky, *Blue-Collar Marriage* (New York: 1964), is a tremendous resource because it is at once so informative about working-class family life and so unabashedly biased against working-class culture that it reveals middle-class stereotypes as well. An earlier, less ambitious study of working-class families is Lee Rainwater, et al., *Workingman's Wife* (New York: 1959). The controversy over the Moynihan Report can be followed in Lee Rainwater and William L. Yancey, eds., *The Moynihan Report and the Politics of Controversy* (Cambridge: 1967), which includes the text of the report and a collection of the criticisms that appeared in response. Andrew Billingsley provided the best defense of the black family in *Black*

Families in White America (Englewood Cliffs, N.J.: 1968). Billingsley wrote this book amidst the radical climate of black nationalism and finds in the Moynihan Report ample reason why only black scholars should write about such issues. Yet compare this earlier work with his more recent one, *Climbing Jacob's Ladder* (New York: 1992), where Billingsley concludes that deindustrialization has been one of the prime culprits in the collapse of the black family—a conclusion, I suspect, that Moynihan would vigorously applaud.

Sixties humanists were never better than when writing about school children, and some of the most touching works came from writers committed to radicalizing the public-school system. Jonathon Kozol, *Death at an Early Age* (Boston: 1967), engaged the issue most passionately. But so too did John Holt, *How Children Fail* (New York: 1964); and *How Children Learn* (New York: 1969); George Dennison, *The Lives of Children* (Reading, Mass.: 1969); and Peter Schrag, *Village School Uptown* (Boston: 1967). The New York City school controversy had its origins in the over-bureaucratization of the system, which was the subject of David Livingston, *110 Livingston Street* (New York: 1968). Charles R. Morris describes the political background in his study of liberal ineptitude, *The Cost of Good Intentions* (New York: 1980). For the controversy itself, see Maurice R. Berube and Marilyn Gittell, eds., *Confrontation at Ocean Hill-Brownsville* (New York: 1969). Jonathan Kaufman, *Broken Alliance* (New York: 1988), lifts Rhody McCoy out of self-exile and is the best study of the ethnic clash embedded in the strike. J. Harvie Wilkinson, *From Brown to Bakke* (New York: 1979), covers the Supreme Court and school busing. Meanwhile, the text of the Coleman report is reprinted along with a number of critiques in James S. Coleman, *The Coleman Report on Public and Private Schools* (Arlington, Va.: 1981). Christopher Jencks mounted an attack on forced busing from what at that point was a radical perspective in *Inequality* (New York: 1972). Ronald P. Formisano, *Boston Against Busing* (Chapel Hill, N.C.: 1991), is a balanced study of the crisis there.

Chapter 10   Revenge of the Status Quo

The quintessential liberal interpretation of the Republican right is Richard Hofstadter, "The Pseudo-Conservative Revolt," in Daniel Bell, ed., *The Radical Right* (Garden City, N.Y.: 1964); and Richard Hofstadter, "Goldwater and His Party," *Encounter* (October 1967). For a general overview of the right wing see David W. Reinhard, *The Republican Right Since 1945* (Lexington, Ky., 1983), and John H. Kessel, *The Goldwater Coalition: Republican Strategies in 1964* (Indianapolis: 1968). The conservatives make their own case in Jack Bell, *Mr. Conservative: Barry Goldwater* (New York: 1962); Barry Goldwater, *Conscience of a Conservative* (New York: 1960), and *With No Apologies* (New York: 1979); F. Clifton White, *Suite 3505* (New Rochelle, N.Y.: 1967); and Russell Kirk, "New Direction in the U.S.: Right?" *New York Times Magazine* (August 7, 1966). The most acute observations of the New Right came from the Old Left: Irving Howe, "The Goldwater Movement," *Dissent* (Autumn 1964), and Michael Walzer, "Social Origins of Radical Politics," in *Radi-*

cal *Principles* (New York: 1980). Henry Nash, *Conservative Intellectual Movement in America* (New York: 1976), surveys the various strands of American right-wing thought. Murray Rothbard, "Confessions of a Right-Wing Liberal," *Ramparts* (June 15, 1968), confesses to bewilderment in a political age where he went from being considered a conservative to being lumped with the radicals without ever changing his ideas. Richard J. Whalen, *Catch the Falling Flag* (Boston: 1972), is the work of a party loyalist disillusioned with Richard Nixon.

For Nixon, see Stephen E. Ambrose's three-volume work: *Education of a Politician* (New York: 1987), *Triumph of a Politician* (New York: 1989), and *Ruin and Recovery* (New York: 1991). Richard Nixon, *RN: The Memoirs of Richard Nixon* (New York: 1978), is characteristically self-exculpating. Fawn Brodie, *Richard Nixon* (New York: 1981), is one of the several attempts at psychobiography.

On the 1968 election see Joe McGinniss, *The Selling of the President, 1968* (New York: 1969), which covers the media campaign. Kevin Phillips, *The Emerging Republican Majority* (New Rochelle, N.Y.: 1969), and Richard M. Scammon and Ben J. Wattenberg, *The Real Majority* (New York: 1970) are the two famous analyses of voting patterns that revealed the shift to the homogenized electorate. William Safire, *Before the Fall: An Inside View of the Pre-Watergate White House* (New York: 1975), and Jules Witcover, *The Resurrection of Richard Nixon* (New York: 1970), are two treatments of Nixon's political career at this point. The attempt to ride the white backlash through Spiro Agnew is clear from Theo Lippmann, *Spiro Agnew's America* (New York: 1972); and the sympathetic John R. Coyne, Jr., *The Impudent Snobs* (New Rochelle, N.Y.: 1972).

For Nixon's foreign policy, one might start with Henry Kissinger's account of his years with Nixon, *The White House Years* (Boston: 1979). Tad Szulc, *The Illusion of Peace* (New York: 1978), is a good overview. Otherwise, see Roger Morris, *Uncertain Greatness* (New York: 1977), and Robert D. Schulzinger, *Henry Kissinger* (New York: 1989).

The best general study of the events leading up to Watergate and the temperament in the White House is J. Anthony Lukas, *Nightmare* (New York: 1976). As if to prove how much they learned from Nixon, the main White House actors during Watergate wrote books to deflect blame away from themselves: John Dean, *Blind Ambition* (New York: 1976); H. R. Haldeman, *The Ends of Power* (New York: 1978); and John Ehrlichman, *Witness to Power* (New York: 1982). The transcripts of the infamous White House tapes appeared as *The Submission of Recorded Presidential Conversations to the Committee on the Judiciary of the House of Representatives* (Washington, D.C.: 1974). Carl Bernstein and Bob Woodward, the two *Washington Post* reporters who dogged the story until they broke it, tell of the adventure in *All the President's Men* (New York: 1974).

Index